YOUNG GIFTED And BLACK

THE STORY OF TROJAN RECORDS

LIVERPOOL JOHN MOORES UNIVERSITY
Aldham Robarts L.R.C.
TEL. 051 231 3701/3634

Liverpool John Moores University LEARNING & INFO SERVICES			
Accession Number	CT45837W		
Class Number	781.646 DEK		
Site	A ✓	M	V

D0308989

Printed in the United Kingdom by MPG Books Ltd, Bodmin

Published by Sanctuary Publishing Limited, Sanctuary House, 45-53 Sinclair Road, London W14 0NS, United Kingdom

www.sanctuarypublishing.com

Distributed in the US by Publishers Group West

Copyright: Michael de Koningh and Laurence Cane-Honeysett 2003. CD ℗ and © Sanctuary Records Group Ltd

Original cover illustration courtesy of Mystery Design – mystery.co.uk

All rights reserved. No part of this book may be reproduced in any form or by any electronic or mechanical means, including information storage or retrieval systems, without permission in writing from the publisher, except by a reviewer, who may quote brief passages.

While the publishers have made every reasonable effort to trace the copyright owners for any or all of the photographs in this book, there may be some omissions of credits, for which we apologise.

ISBN: 1-86074-464-8

YOUNG GIFTED And BLACK

THE STORY OF TROJAN RECORDS

LIVERPOOL JOHN MOORES UNIVERSITY
Aldham Roberts L.R.C.
TEL. 051 231 3701/3634

Michael de Koningh & Laurence Cane-Honeysett

Sanctuary

Contents

CD Notes

1   THE ETHIOPIANS: 'EVERYTHING CRASH' (2:31)
     Original UK issue: JJ Records DB1169 (1968)
     Over a heartbeat rhythm produced by Sir JJ Johnson, lead singer Leonard
     Dillon recounts the strife caused by industrial strikes throughout Kingston in
     1968. Everything did indeed crash back then, as he observes, 'Firemen strike,
     watermen strike, telephone company too...'

2   THE MAYTALS: 'PRESSURE DROP' (2:58)
     Original UK issue: Trojan TR7709 (1969)
     The Leslie Kong-produced powerhouse rhythm aided by Frederick 'Toots'
     Hibbert's country-gospel vocals and his vamping cohorts made this song one
     of the dancehall staples on both sides of the Atlantic. It is a simple song of the
     pressures of ghetto suffering. The group can be seen in the studio performing
     'Pressure Drop' in the feature film *The Harder They Come*.

3   THE PIONEERS: 'POOR RAMESES' (2:34)
     Original UK issue: Trojan TR698 (1969)
     Vocal trio The Pioneers offer another paean to a racehorse that gives its all in
     the race. 'Poor Rameses' never captured the national charts like 'Longshot
     Kick The Bucket' but is an equally fine example of their group sound.

4   CLANCY ECCLES & THE DYNAMITES 'MR MIDNIGHT (SKOKIAAN)'
     (2:37)
     Original UK issue: Clandisc CLAN200 (1969)
     A skinhead favourite with a lazy Clancy Eccles And The Dynamites' rhythm
     interpreting an age-old simple melody.

5   DAVE BARKER & THE UPSETTERS 'SHOCKS OF MIGHTY' (2:53)
     Original UK issue: Upsetter US331 (1970)
     On a rhythm Lee Perry obtained from producer Bunny Lee, originally used for

the obscure 'Bhutto Girl' by The Inspirations, Dave Barker struts his 'Yankee DJ' style, just warming up for the UK chart topper 'Double Barrel' in 1971.

6   Joe The Boss: 'Skinhead Revolt' (2:32)
Original UK issue: Joe JRS9 (1970)
A heavy UK production from Joe Mansano with DJ Dice The Boss and trombone player Rico Rodriguez combining to great effect. Not a well-known record at the time, but since has become highly sought after and is certainly one of the best 'made for skinheads' records.

7   Freddie Notes & The Rudies: 'Shanghai' (2:37)
Original UK issue: Trojan TR7713 (1970)
With an insistent rhythm and catchy tinkling piano, this UK production style of reggae was eagerly collected by the white skinheads at the time. It mirrored much of the output of notable Jamaican producers such as Lloyd Charmers and Derrick Harriott, whose records were also sought after.

8   Bob Andy: 'You Don't Know' (3:19)
Original UK issue: Green Door GD4060 (recorded 1970, released UK 1973)
A chilling observation of the effects of cocaine, incisively written and sung by Bob Andy, who is undoubtedly one of the foremost singer/songwriters ever to emerge from Jamaica. The rhythm track was recorded at Dynamic Studios in Kingston and the song was voiced at London's Chalk Farm on one of Bob Andy's post 'Young, Gifted And Black' visits to London.

9   Keith Hudson: 'Melody Maker' (2:09)
Original UK issue: Summit SUM8541 (1972)
Cracking wah-wah guitars and gut-wrenching bass lines are producer Keith Hudson's standards as he, above all his contemporaries, looked to the influence of the funk of the nearby USA. With work ranging from straight reggae to funk-rock, Hudson never failed to experiment, and when he got it right as with the heavily versioned 'Melody Maker' there were few to touch his genius.

10   Ken Boothe: '(That's The Way) Nature Planned It' (2:44)
Original UK issue: Trojan TR7910 (1974)
If anyone can take a soul tune and make it his own, it is Ken Boothe. Combined with the lush, but not cloying, production genius of Lloyd Charmers, it is no surprise that Ken hit the top spot with 'Everything I Own' just a few months after this recording of the Four Tops' hit.

11 I-ROY: 'RED, GOLD AND GREEN' (3:10)

Original UK issue: Trojan TRLS63 (1973)

Over a suitably reverent rhythm pre-dating the socially conscious roots reggae era by some three years, master wordsmith Roy 'I-Roy' Reid succinctly preaches peace and love, and offers a praise to His Imperial Majesty Haile Selassie. The rhythm used is Ken Boothe's majestic self composition 'Black, Gold And Green', another outstanding pre-roots record issued on Trojan TR7893.

12 SUSAN CADOGAN: 'NICE AND EASY' (3:18)

Original UK issue: Trojan TR9028 (recorded 1974, released UK 1977)

Sexy, sultry Susan Cadogan breathes her way through a typical mid-1970s Lee Perry production. This was recorded prior to her hitting the UK national Number Four in April 1975 with another Lee Perry production, 'Hurt So Good'.

Acknowledgements And Thanks

This book was very much a team effort and I have to offer my great thanks to the following people:

First and foremost Laurence Cane-Honeysett, who provided interviews and discographical information and acted as a contact with Trojan Records.

Mike Atherton for his endless pertinent snippets of information and enlightening tables of '25 Soul Covers/R&B Covers' etc. He also attempted to edit my rather peculiar style of English into literate sentences, something for which all readers will no doubt thank him as they progress through the book.

Marc Griffiths for the mass of various label discographies, an unenviable task, but now we all have the information in print. He also contributed to the whole with odds and ends which I for one certainly wasn't aware existed.

Very special thanks to my wife Kathy, who, to her great surprise, became chief researcher and added structure to the whole project. She selflessly devoted many hours of the limited time with which a very busy job left her to wring facts and figures from all manner of sources. Her brother (my brother-in-law) Neil Davies also has to be thanked for his out-of-hours research material.

All the people who gave interviews and put up with my endless questions have my heartfelt gratitude. This, after all, is their story and I hope I've got it right. In particular I would like to thank Bob Andy, Rob Bell, Joe Sinclair, Bruce White, Janis at I-Anka, Sid Bucknor, Dandy, Vic Keary, Clive Crawley, Colin Newman, Graeme Goodall, John Reed, David Betteridge, Dave Hendley, Nick Bourne and the Trojan Museum Trust. I've no doubt missed somebody out and offer my profound apologies as it wasn't intentional.

I also want to thank the 'old timers' who offered memories and sparked my ageing brain into action: Danny Hatcher, Reg Stanley, Trevor and Denny Ball, Dave Sandford, Pete Fontana, Rob Faulconbridge and Mike Pealing.

Acknowledgement must also be paid to three seminal archivists of Jamaican music: Steve Barrow, Roger Dalke and Chris Prete. Without these guys, we wouldn't know half what we do today.

Michael de Koningh
April 2003

Preface

So the Trojan story will be told. This I learned from Michael, who has taken on the project. How pleasantly surprised I was that he asked me to involve myself by contributing a preface.

Trojan and I go back over 30 years – in fact, as far back as when Marcia Griffiths and yours truly discovered that we had a single running up the UK charts. 'Young, Gifted And Black' was on its way to becoming a memorable hit and would eventually place itself firmly in the history of the birth, development and growth – in a word, the evolution – of Jamaican music in all its genres.

Marcia and I were completely taken by surprise when we were told to get our passports and pack our bags hurriedly. This was like a dream – until then, we'd never even remembered that we had recorded this particular work together!

Nina Simone, who originally sung the song, had always been a favourite performer; I appreciated the melodic and lyric content and the message that the song was sending out. But the cover of the song was not done expressly because we related to those sentiments; it was just one of those things.

The title has endured the test of time, made the transition from vinyl to the CD format, and now also to this book.

Writing this piece reminded me of how shocked I was to see throngs of young white people chorusing to the tune of 'Young, Gifted And Black'. I am still amazed!

The financial rewards from the record were not great. However, it opened up a brand new world to me. I had the privilege of getting a glance into the different culture and lifestyles of Europe. The United Kingdom also became a second home for me. Some of my favourite people who are currently active in my life reside in the UK. I have also done a great deal of work at various times in my career in British recording studios and live venues. My record label, I-Anka (Annville Ltd), and my publishing company, Andisongs, to this day are still registered in the United Kingdom.

This book tells the story of how a famous record label contributed to the marketing, promotion and selling of the early Jamaican music. It should give fans of Jamaican music everywhere an insight into the workings, the behind-the-scenes machinations and the development of a truly unique music.

Bob Andy
April 2003

Foreword

The name of Trojan Records is synonymous with Jamaican music the world over. *Between its formation in 1968 and the demise of reggae music in the public consciousness in 1975, prior to Bob Marley's assault on the bastions of white rock, Trojan led the way. *

It had competitors, such as the Pama group of labels and Melodisc Records' Fab imprint, but no one moved units and created a brand identity in the marketplace like Trojan Records. Trojan had the knowhow, or maybe just the luck, to be in the right place at the right time and, with the right staff and the right musicians behind it, to capture the musical moment.

It rose on the crest of the skinhead youth culture wave of the late 1960s and maintained a presence after the demise of that culture, with a swansong of major pop hits from Ken Boothe and John Holt in 1974.

It championed a minority music initially imported for the swelling West Indian population of London, Birmingham, Bristol and many other cities across the UK and carried it far from home and into the bedroom of many a teenage record buyer.

But, just as importantly, Trojan Records created a fertile ground for UK-based Jamaicans to grow their own brand of reggae music. The Shrowder/Bryan/Sinclair partnership, later known as both Bush and Swan Productions, produced some of the most satisfying club sounds of the early 1970s. Their collective work with powerhouse groups such as The Rudies vied with Jamaican productions week after week as the most sought-after tunes of the moment. London-based Joe Mansano's heavyweight work with DJ Dice The Boss shook up the dancehalls with the same force as any Kingston sound by King Stitt. And let's not forget the most prolific artist and producer of all, Dandy, whose chuckling 'Reggae In Your Jeggae' must have filled every dancefloor in every club across the British Isles as the new sound of reggae broke.

That's not to discount the input of Jamaica, from one of whose top producers, Duke Reid The Trojan, the company took its very name. The demand for his swinging, jazzy and mellow rocksteady inspired Island Records to move further into the UK market, and they accordingly dedicated a label to his work. Initially

12

little more than an overspill from the parent Island label, 35 years later the name Trojan is as strongly associated with reggae as Biro with ballpoint pens, Hoover with vacuum cleaners and Motown with soul.''

Lee Perry, the madcap 'Scratch The Upsetter', established his own label within the Trojan confines and poured out his patented idiosyncratic music, helped no end by the studio band that Bob Marley would filch as his own after their collaboration on the *Soul Rebel* sessions. 'Return Of Django' by that studio band The Upsetters, with its catchy heavyweight rhythm topped with Val Bennett's raucous saxophone, helped put reggae on the popular-music map. It also put Trojan on the financial map as it shot into the hallowed Top Ten in October 1969.

Trojan picked up Bob Marley And The Wailers long before anyone outside the reggae community had heard of them and released some of their finest compositions, major songs that Bob would revisit many times during his tragically short career. Sadly for the Trojan coffers, Mr Marley had moved on before superstardom struck, but few would deny that the Marley/Perry/Trojan work has a sullen brilliance which Bob would never recapture.

Trojan Records championed the new 'toasting' (DJing or rapping) phenomenon, from the formative work of U Roy over sublime Duke Reid rocksteady rhythms to the harsh and prophetic warnings of Big Youth and I-Roy as the Rastafarian '70s moved on. Artists like these felt the pulse of the Kingston dancehall and ran with the flow of new lyrics, keeping ever abreast of the changes that influenced the US rap, which it pre-dated by some ten years.

There is no doubt that luck played a big part in the rise of Trojan Records, but there's no doubt either that the company guided the UK reggae market rather than being guided by it. Even when Trojan was losing ground to the roots-and-culture brigade and floundering in the string-laden swamp in which it would finally drown, the label still managed to pull musical rabbits out of the hat – not once but twice, as Ken Boothe and John Holt both tickled the Top Ten and gave the media image of reggae one last flash.

Even at the very end of the '70s, Trojan surfaced for air, releasing a handful of superb contemporary albums and 12" singles, their last thrash at issuing the 'now' sounds of Jamaica before apparently slipping from view for good, only to break the surface once again as a 'revive' label.

The last 20 years have seen the rise and rise of what's commonly called 'revive music', a retrospective scene playing the reggae of yesteryear. Maybe this burgeoning scene arose as a backlash against the current brash ragga and dancehall, engendering a desire to return to the mellower styles of former times. Maybe it was fostered by the numerous 30-somethings who yearned for their misspent youth and found solace in their old friends of sound.

Whatever the reason, thanks to employing some of the most knowledgeable connoisseurs of the music as compilers and annotators, Trojan Records have gained an enormous market share in this growth area. Under the guidance of their new owners, they are finally mining the cavernous depths of their massive back catalogue.

So this book is the story of a record company. It does not attempt to be the story of Jamaican music, though of course the two are tightly intertwined. It is the story of a name that has passed through various hands, with each new owner looking for that magic ingredient for his acquisition: money!

Trojan Records was set up to release Jamaican music in Britain. But let us not think for a moment that this was an altruistic venture; it has always been a business, and as with all businesses the bottom line is to make hard cash, in this instance from the sale of vinyl records and, latterly, compact discs. This was true for Island Records in 1967, and it holds equally true for the Sanctuary Group, who now own the mighty name and its equally mighty back catalogue. Bear this in mind as you voyage through the book: artistic creativity is a wonderful gift, but unless it is properly channelled and marketed, it does not put food on the table.

Lee Gopthal, the first owner of Trojan after its split from Island in 1968, was a professional accountant who sought to organise a company that would feed him and his employees. He was a shrewd man, and much criticism has been levelled at him and his successors regarding artists' rights, royalties and general financial workings. Thirty-odd years on, Mr Gopthal is no longer with us to present his side of the story; all we have are scant paperwork and the fallible memories of staff, singers and players. Any commentary in this area is either from government and press sources, to which anyone can freely gain access, or a direct quotation from a protagonist.

In putting out records at such a rapid rate in the late '60s and early '70s, Lee Gopthal and his Trojan staff unwittingly created an important musical legacy. They were selling records to make a living and could not have imagined the extensive monument of sound which they were building. It is only now, with the benefit of hindsight, that we see the contents of Sanctuary's vast vaults as history – history which was often laughed at and reviled at the time but which is now revered and enjoyed by music fans the world over.

Whatever they may think of Trojan's working practices, no one can deny that the company created one of the richest and most varied collections of the art form that is Jamaican music, utilising both the guys across the Atlantic and those trying to make their mark on this side of the ocean. I doubt that, beyond Clement Dodd, Duke Reid and Prince Buster, any producer or label can offer as much variety and supreme quality as the Trojan catalogue.

This book is a testament to all those artists and their endeavours, but it is also dedicated to a veritable host of backroom boys, from producers to chart compilers. They were part of one great whole, a creative process that came under the banner of Trojan Records and whose spark of ignition sent reggae music on a fast path to *Top Of The Pops* and into the hearts of millions of listeners across the globe.

Michael de Koningh
April 2003

1 Early Years

The long and winding story of Trojan Records did not start, as you would expect, in a hot and dusty recording studio in downtown Kingston, but much nearer to home in suburban Croydon.

The building boom of the 1930s had turned this pleasant town on London's southern outskirts into a sprawling mass of overspill centred around Britain's first commercial airport. Industry grabbed greenfield sites to cater for the ever-increasing demands of the consumer.

Into this climate came a small but well-established and successful motor-vehicle manufacturer which sited its engineering works in Purley Way, just beside Croydon Airport. The company, Trojan Ltd, had been producing cars and light commercial vehicles since Leslie Hounsfield had founded it in the 1920s. The 1950s were particularly good years for the firm as they built not only vans but that icon of the age, the bubble car.

Trojan specialised in fitting their basic and sturdy chassis with all manner of back bodies, from flatbed to security boxed, while their customers ranged from one-off buyers to fleet purchasers such as the Royal Mail, the RAF and, most famously, Brooke Bond Tea. With the post-World War II export boom, they started exporting vehicles to many overseas countries, particularly the then still-numerous British colonies, including the small Caribbean island of Jamaica. These exports would consist of chassis, engine and cab only, and the lucky new owner would then fit his truck out to his own specification.

One such Jamaican owner was Arthur 'Duke' Reid.

Reid was born in 1915 and, after leaving school, spent ten years serving as a police officer in the island's capital, Kingston. Of necessity, he developed an aggressive and hard-faced approach in dealing with the dangerous situations that a hot Saturday night in the city's poorer areas could produce. Of necessity too, he became a crack pistol shot. His dexterity with firearms stood him in good stead during his time as a policemen, and a gun would never be far from his side for the rest of his life.

In the early '50s, Reid's wife, Lucille, won a substantial lottery prize, which she invested in their future by buying a business, an off-licence called the Treasure Isle

Liquor Store, which was located in the same run-down ghetto area that the Duke had patrolled for a decade. The store was such a success that, in 1958, they relocated to larger premises at 33 Bond Street.

It was normal practice around Kingston for shopkeepers and bar owners to play recorded music as a tactic to attract customers. Not to be outdone, Reid rigged up a 78rpm record player in the shop, with a speaker outside the front door, and discovered a formula for increasing his turnover. Nothing drew in the music-hungry local people like a Wynonie Harris record rocking out through the speaker and carrying right across the street.

But Reid went a step further than most of his rivals. On 9 July 1950, Jamaica's first radio station, RJR (Radio Jamaica Rediffusion), had commenced broadcasting. So that as many of the population as possible could hear its programmes, even though most of them couldn't afford their own radios at that time, the station installed wirelesses in local gathering points like schools and shops.

On this fledgling network, Reid took his first steps into showbusiness by sponsoring and presenting a programme called *Treasure Isle Time.* Using alto saxophonist Tab Smith's 'My Mothers Eyes' as his theme tune, he would catch the listeners' ears with the driving R&B of Amos Milburn and Rosco Gordon or the tear-stained ballads of Johnny Ace, then regale them with news of the latest booze bargains available in his off-licence. He had an excellent knowledge of and taste in American R&B, which was all the rage in '50s Jamaica, and soon found himself presiding over a highly successful show. Still, Reid was ambitious, and he decided to launch a sound system.

Sound systems the Jamaican equivalent of the mobile disco – had risen with the demise of live big bands as the 1940s had turned into the 1950s. These live bands, such as Eric Dean's and River Cook's, had played a mixture of mento (the Jamaican equivalent of calypso) and replicated US swing in the Count Basie mould. However, there was one problem with such bands: their predilection to break for half an hour for refreshments, leaving the dance patrons in silence. Dance promoters therefore favoured recorded music because of its ability to keep their patrons entertained all evening, making them less likely to wander off to a rival dance and more likely to stay and consume rum and beer, which was where the profits were made. So the sound system was born.

Enterprising dance organisers favoured sound systems also because to hire one cost much less than paying the musicians of a big band. Although primitive, with only one record deck, a 'sound' could keep the music flowing and the revellers dancing all night. The inevitable gaps between records were bridged by slick DJ patter copied directly from the New Orleans jocks whose radio shows beamed across the Caribbean to eager Jamaican listeners. A sound system had to be powerful, as most dances took place outdoors with the dance arena, or 'lawn', bounded by temporary, rough corrugated-iron fencing.

The sound system also became important in the structure of working-class Jamaica, particularly for the city dwellers of Kingston, as it provided much-needed escape and relaxation from the trials of everyday living: for them, it was as much a meeting place as any bar or liquor store. The audience at any dance consisted mainly of poorly-paid working people and the even poorer ghetto underclass.

The mainly white ruling and upper echelons of society had always swung to a different beat; they liked a more refined sound and didn't like voyaging to the seedier parts of town. The arrival of US R&B – with the powerhouse sounds of BB King, the great blues shouter Big Joe Turner and raucous instrumentalists like Big Jay McNeely – polarised the social groups still further.

Swiftly, Duke Reid moved forward by constructing his first 'set' (so called because the first sound systems were little more than radiogram sets with extra speakers) and took his music and his money-spinning liquor out to the evening dancers. That slow but hardy van which he had purchased to carry the bulky equipment to locations around his area gave the set its name. As it approached, fans would shout 'Here comes the Trojan!', and so he became known as Duke Reid The Trojan, playing out around his territory in the Bond Street and Pink Lane area of Kingston.

The slot on RJR was providing a great advertising place for both Reid's store and his sound system, and it also created a demand for those tough R&B records which he played. By the mid '50s the Duke was unstoppable, with the might of radio and his exclusive R&B records – dredged from dusty locations in the nearby continent – rocking him to the top, supplanting rival sound owner Thomas 'Tom The Great Sebastian' Wong.

Prince Buster credits Thomas Wong as the original sound-system champion and the man responsible for pioneering the modern Jamaican dancehall. With Count Machuki, his DJ, playing the latest R&B sent over from the USA by his brother, Tom moved from playing out of the front of his hardware store to building the formative sound system and taking it to the dancehall. Known as a gentleman, as competition grew fiercer he resigned from the race and later opened the Silver Slipper club further uptown. Eventually, he mysteriously committed suicide by gassing himself in his car.

Seasonal cane-cutting in the USA was a major source of employment for lower-class Jamaicans throughout the post-war years, and whilst away working they would be introduced to the smoky inner-city R&B music via bars and the radio. Many of them supplemented their meagre cane-cutting wages by returning with a pile of the latest R&B 78s, which they would then sell to various sound-system operators, sometimes for a substantial profit. One such cane-cutter was a young man by the name of Clement Seymour Dodd.

As a youth, Dodd had been a promising cricketer, so much so that he was nicknamed 'Coxson' after Bill Copson, a Derbyshire fast bowler who had greatly impressed cricket-loving Jamaicans by taking five wickets against the West Indies in a test match at Lord's. Coxson picked up the hottest R&B and jazz discs and initially sold them on his return to Jamaica. Apparently Duke Reid purchased some of his latest finds to use on his newly founded Trojan sound system.

In 1954, Clement Dodd launched his own sound, named Sir Coxson The Downbeat (*Down Beat* was America's leading jazz and swing magazine), and put his vast knowledge and collection of R&B and jazz to good use. He rose rapidly to become a direct challenger to Duke Reid, and alongside Vincent Edwards – with his mammoth 'King Edwards The Giant' – he became the third member of the ruling elite of operators.

So by the late 1950s there were three major sounds vying for premiership, with other fast-rising systems like Count Smith and V Rocket snapping at their heels. Competition was fierce and each new sound system would try to outclass its rivals with incredibly obscure American records and increasingly powerful amplifiers. Proven hit makers like Fats Domino or Louis Jordan no longer impressed the punters; a hip DJ had to spin a Clifton Chenier, Big Mike Gordon or Zu Zu Bollin platter if he wanted to be at the cutting edge.

Despite the competition, Duke Reid proved how enduringly popular his Trojan sound was. He was crowned King Of Sounds And Blues in 1956 at the Success Club, in 1957 at the Foresters' Hall, and in 1958, again at the Success Club, by his appreciative and ever-growing army of followers.

Without doubt, it wasn't just his musical ear that gave him this meteoric success; equally it was his muscular arm, backed up by a crew of henchmen recruited from the underworld of the Back o' Wall ghetto, which he had patrolled a few years earlier. The Duke's vicious way of literally beating down other sounds is legendary, with tactics including cutting speaker cables, throwing stones into the midst of the dancers and flashing knives in their faces. He would use every method he could to subdue and overrun the opposition so that many smaller operators simply relocated to more hospitable areas outside the ghetto territories in order to escape injury and destruction.

Although Reid's henchmen were the most feared and notorious, all the sound-system operators had to be seen to be tough. Doctor Bird label owner and sound engineer Graeme Goodall recalls that they could all be violent if they had to be: 'You had to be tough, albeit in those days, remember, no firearms *per se* – firearms hadn't permeated society – and so the smashing up was bottles, bricks, pieces of iron pipe, two-by-fours, maybe an occasional knife. But it was the old bar-room-brawl type of violence.'

Singer, producer and former sound-system DJ Lee Perry agrees: 'In those days you had to be a toughie, and to make it you had to be monster tough. In those days Duke Reid and all those people were the toughest guys. It was like those guys…all the time they wanted power.'

Due to Reid's fearsome ways of (sometimes literally) flattening a rival sound, the other rigs had to employ tough roadies to counteract his henchmen. Among Coxson's muscle was a certain Cecil Bustamente Campbell (aka Prince Buster), an ex-boxer and a well known figure in the rough ghetto quarter where he had been born in 1938. In 1960, Buster left Coxson's employ to set up his own sound system, Voice Of The People, whose title reflected his position absolutely, as his roots were in the ghetto and he was now playing especially for his downtrodden brothers. No one was ever to be more 'from the people and for the people' than Prince Buster, who was justly proud of his impoverished pedigree.

But the Duke, Coxson and King Edwards were at the top of the music pile when it came to exclusive, driving R&B discs, for which they had scoured out-of-the-way record shops on their many trips throughout the southern United States. These discs would be used against all comers in sometimes violent sound clashes (competitions between two rival sound systems).

The object was to play records which would get the crowd moving, thereby ensuring their support and 'killing' or 'flopping' the other sound. The more exclusive the sound – usually via the use of one-off special recordings – the more likely it was to gain the support of the crowd, who would declare the winner as the purveyor of the best tunes, and also the one who managed to deafen his patrons with the loudest set-up. What did a little loss of hearing matter when Dodd was playing tunes like 'Coxson's Hop' and 'Coxson's Shuffle'?

These were actually US R&B discs whose labels had been blanked, by Willis Jackson ('Later For Gator') and Harold Land ('San Diego Bounce') respectively. These Downbeat 'exclusives' kept the rivals at bay. With no indication of the real title of the dance-buster visible, even if you could get close enough to see it (which the roadies made sure you couldn't), the others would have to find even more underground sounds to fight back.

This practice of scratching all the details from a record's label was necessary to keep tunes exclusive to the one sound system, as the minute a rival held the same piece of shellac, its drawing power was over. In that climate of intense rivalry, the instant that you lost the best sounds, you lost everything. Crowds were as fanatical as any football supporter, but far less loyal: they would switch their fickle allegiance to another player in a flash.

By the mid '50s, Bill Haley and Elvis Presley were unwittingly creating a major problem in Kingston as, much to Mom and Pop's displeasure, blue-jeaned, white middle-class America found out how to rock 'n' roll. The Kingstonian's staple diet for a rousing night out at his favoured sound system dance was a chilled bottle of Red Stripe and an earful of driving R&B. However, new R&B records were in short supply as American studios rushed to record every clean-cut, clean-shaven white singer they could find. The old hands found themselves out of a job, and the sound systems found themselves running out of music.

Rock 'n' roll was fine for the children of the Land of the Free, with their newly slicked-back hair, but in Kingston it was a disaster. Dancers simply did not like the new hillbilly bop purveyed by Carl Perkins *et al* and thirsted for the greasier shuffle of Bill Doggett or Nappy Brown. Suddenly, the pickings became slim: sound men returned almost empty-handed from their record-buying trips to North America. There wasn't enough old stock to go round, and little new music that fitted the bill was being recorded.

So Coxson and Duke Reid, in particular, had an acute need to replenish their steadily dwindling stocks of new records if they were to stay top dogs in the sound-system stakes. In the late '50s, these two – along with lesser lights such as Simeon L Smith of Little Wonder Sound – found a simple answer: try out some local talent.

Kingston was full of aspiring Little Richards and Nat 'King' Coles eager to wow crowds as their idols did on a Saturday night via the pumping sound systems. Foundation singers like Owen Gray, Wilfred 'Jackie' Edwards, Derrick Morgan and Laurel Aitken all ran the gauntlet of the crowd at Vere Johns Junior or Victor Sampson's volatile talent contests, where the patrons would launch anything to hand at the stage should the performer displease.

'My first recording,' recalls Derrick Morgan, 'was in 1959, but the first time I sang in public was 1957 in the Vere Johns contest, and I came first that night. I was imitating Little Richard at the time, singing "Long Tall Sally" and "Jenny Jenny Jenny", and I came ahead of Monty Morris, Owen Gray, Wilfred Edwards and Hortense Ellis.'

So it was that, among the puppet shows, comedians, contortionists and jugglers, the sound men sought out singers with enough ability to convince an audience, via records, that they were gritty Kansas City blues shouters or dreamy balladeers. King Edwards, Coxson Dodd, Prince Buster and Duke Reid became talent scouts and formative producers who, almost by chance, kick-started the whole Jamaican recording industry.

Prior to their involvement, only one recording studio existed on the island. Motta's Recording Studio was run by radio and electrical dealer Stanley Motta. The studio was behind his shop and was primitive in the extreme, with only two microphones and with the walls draped with old carpets and sacking to deaden the sound – the spitting image of Joe Von Battle's Hastings Street studio, in which a young John Lee Hooker had kicked off the Detroit recording industry a few years earlier.

The enterprising Motta had started to record traditional mento folk singers in around 1951 or 1952. As there were no mastering and pressing facilities on the island, he had to send his recordings to England, where major label Decca manufactured the discs, via Emil Shallit's Melodisc company. The fragile 78s were then exported back to Jamaica.

But it was Coxson, Duke Reid, Buster and King Edwards – alongside Australian-born sound engineer Graeme Goodall, aided by future Island Records boss Chris Blackwell – who would really found the island's recording industry proper. The four sound-system men needed a plentiful supply of new, exciting R&B sounds to keep their demanding dancers happy. Their records would be especially for use on their sounds and were not initially issued for public consumption.

The Blackwell–Goodall partnership, on the other hand, started to make records after Blackwell gained six juke boxes in a business deal. In typical Jamaican fashion, he decided to make his own records to stock his juke boxes, rather than buying them from elsewhere. When he first met Goodall (who was then working for RJR) at a wedding reception, they mooted this plan, and in 1958 the pair were sneaking into RJR's studio afterhours to record local musicians. At about the same time, future Jamaican Prime Minister Edward Seaga formed WIRL (West Indies Records Limited) to record local talent approximating that authentic R&B music.

The band on these pioneering RJR sessions was built around four Australians who had come to Jamaica to work at Tilly Blackman's Glass Bucket Club: guitarist Denis Sindrey, pianist Pearce Doddard, drummer Lol Morris and a clarinettist whose name no one can remember but who soon left anyway, according to Graeme Goodall. Local nightclub musicians like double bassist Lloyd Brevett (who would find fame a few years later as a member of The Skatalites) and guitarist Ernest Ranglin would augment the Aussies. They needed to be night owls, for sessions would run from late evening, after RJR had closed down, until five in the morning.

'It went from there,' remembers Graeme Goodall. 'My term was up at Radio Jamaica, and after putting in at JBC – Jamaican Broadcasting Corporation – we built their transmitters for them, shared facilities, shared transmitter sites. So I was involved in that, establishing the FM links through the island, but the music was the love, while the engineering was paying the bills. Mind you, I loved the engineering side of it too. However, I was not an RF [Radio Frequency] man. Deep down, I was an audio man.

'But during this time I met Ken Khouri. Ken had gone up to Miami to buy a car, evidently, and he was wandering around and I think next to the car dealership he wandered into a pawnshop. A guy – a musician – had just come in and pawned a Presto portable disc recorder, with a supply of 20 blank discs, and so Ken asked me, "What's this?" And I explained it to him, and I think he had, like, a half an hour with this musician who had pawned this thing, and he packed it all up in the back of this Ford Fairlane which he'd bought and brought it back to Jamaica, the idea being that he was going to record people and teach Stanley Motta a thing or two.

'But of course he'd forgotten – or at least nobody bothered to tell him – that in the meantime disc recording had been bypassed and there was tape recording. So Ken and I were talking and we became firm friends – Papa Khouri, as we called him; Papa Kool. And so he went back up and bought a Magnecord recorder and a box of tapes, and he said, "Well, when can we do this?" By this time, he was pressing 78 records from stampers for Mercury Records that were sent down from America.

'We went out the back of his record-pressing plant which was in Upper King Street, and we found an old building. It was like a ramshackle sort of outhouse, with termites running up and down the wall and everything, but I got the bright idea that I'd strengthen the walls by pouring sand down them to give me some sort of isolation.

'We poured sand in there and it went well until I got about six feet up the wall and the whole wall collapsed. So I thought I'd better go back and re-examine the engineering of this thing. We filled it up with fibreglass and anything else we could find – carpets, dead dogs, you know – and so we had this Magna with a three-channel mixer. Ken went on recording calypsos and things like that. But it was an attempt. It was a start.

'When I decided to leave Radio Jamaica, I went to see Ken, 'cos he really wanted to get into it, and he'd already started building Federal Records. So he said, "Let's build a studio," and I went in there. He had an Ampex, I believe, and a four-channel mixer, and we worked out of two rooms. We had air conditioners, wall units that we used to switch off during recordings. Then we'd record for 2 minutes 45 seconds, switch the recorder off and switch the air conditioning back on!

'I modified the mixer and got another two channels out of it, plus three feeds for echo. Ken and I built an echo chamber, a physical echo chamber out of cement blocks. We begged an old RCA amplifier and speaker from Alec Durie, who was one of the original investors in Federal Records. We installed those and a Neumann microphone, and then I tried to get some Jamaican masons to build a room without any parallel surfaces.

'They couldn't understand this crazy white guy who spoke funny telling them to build a room like they'd never built before, where nothing was parallel, everything was angled. Anyway, it worked quite good.

'But there was one occasion when I heard a noise in the mixer and I couldn't figure out what it was. This was night time and I was recording Byron Lee, I think. There was this terrible chirping noise. It took me about an hour to track it down, and eventually I found that a cricket had got up inside the speaker and he was singing along with the music.

'Of course, when I went in to check it, he thought, "Oh-oh, human being approaching, I've got to keep quiet now," and he'd keep quiet till we started recording again, and then he'd start chirping again.

'So we had one tape recorder and a Neumann microphone. We'd record from Monday through Thursday, then Friday was dub day.'

At those early sessions, the real job of producing was down to the bandleader and the studio engineer, who would take the basic song and shape it to fit. Dodd, Reid and others certainly financed the formative sessions, but they offered minimal input into the actual recording process. This was to change as they gained experience, discovering what the people wanted to hear and which records moved the most copies. Consequently they took a greater interest in their investments as time rolled on.

The sound system would play a new recording on a dub plate (a soft wax one-off pressing) for as long as it drew the crowds. Sometimes a year would pass before the dancers' passion for it cooled. Then it was a quick trip down to the Federal Records pressing plant with the master tape to gain maximum benefit from the recording as it was made commercially available to an eager public.

The success of his home-grown recordings gave Duke Reid the impetus to build his own recording studio of wood in 1962, above his Treasure Isle off-licence. Now, with his new resident engineer Byron Smith, he could achieve a high quality of production and experiment with new sounds and rhythms, as Graeme Goodall remembers: 'Smithy eventually went to work for Duke Reid when Duke built his own studio above the liquor store. It was incredible: it was right up on the roof of his place, built of wood, with pigeons and God knows what up there.'

Coxson Dodd followed suit soon afterwards, in late 1962, and opened his Studio One recording set-up in a former nightclub at 13 Brentford Road, Kingston, where one of his first employees was the future Upsetter Lee Perry, along with esteemed engineer and producer Sid Bucknor.

Derrick Morgan witnessed Duke Reid's tough tactics in the studio: 'He was all right, but he always went around with his two guns. It's true that, if you were singing in a session and he didn't like it, he would shoot his gun and the musicians would get timid. That's why the music was so good!' It does sound like a powerful incentive to do your best.

'Yes, he used his gun during recording sessions,' agrees Graeme Goodall, 'but he was one of the nicest men in the world. But remember, niceness you could not show:

too much niceness, to a lot of people there in the music business, would be seen as a sign of weakness!' Engineer and producer Sid Bucknor agrees with Goodall and also recalls that, although Reid was fond of guns, he was a perfectly reasonable employer.

Before you climbed the starry ladder of success as a recording artist, you had to pass the audition. These were crowded affairs, with flocks of aspiring young singers hoping to grab the dream and launch themselves out of the ghetto and into the nation's hearts. One of those young hopefuls in 1959 was a 19-year old Derrick Morgan: 'I went to Duke Reid and sang four songs for him and he picked two which we then recorded. The first song was "Lover Boy", which got the alias of "South Corner Rock", and then "Oh My". The first song I heard on the radio was "Oh My" on *Treasure Isle Time*, Duke Reid's radio programme. I recorded the song Wednesday, and Saturday I heard it on the radio. You can imagine the first time on radio – I was so excited, I started jumping around all over the place. It was so nice, you know? Well, Duke used to keep those songs for his sound system and he never wanted to release them for the public.' Both tunes saw release the following year.

Earl Morgan of vocal trio The Heptones remembers auditioning for the Duke some seven years later: 'We checked Duke Reid and sang "Fatty Fatty" and "Only Sixteen" and all them tunes. There'd be lots of people in a line to do recording. We'd probably be about number 59 or 60 in the line, and by the time you reached him, you'd be a little bit shocked, 'cos the man was an old police officer and he had a big gun over his shoulder.' The Duke turned them down that time and they moved to Ken Lack and then Coxson, where they finally waxed 'Fatty Fatty' and 'Only Sixteen', along with some of their most endearing and enduring love songs.

The very first Jamaican records – those pressed by Decca for Stanley Motta – were 10" 78rpm shellac discs, but by the time of the birth of Jamaican R&B at the end of the '50s they were the new and (comparatively) unbreakable 7" platters, spinning at 45rpm, resplendent with labels bearing the names of the producer and/or his sound system. There could be little doubt as to who produced these early 45s, as label names like Coxsone, Duke Reid's, Prince Buster – Voice Of The People and Smith's proudly announced their provenance.

In keeping with the other players in the island's new recording industry, Duke Reid founded his own imprints. He first issued a handful of 78s bearing the Trojan imprint after his powerhouse sound system, calypsos by Lord Power And The Calypso Quintet, but founded his Duke Reid's label for his productions from 1959 onwards. Later he added Dutchess (*sic*), named after his beloved wife Lucille, and the renowned Treasure Isle, named obviously after his studio. The last-named, along with a revived Trojan, would establish his name in the UK.

While Reid and Coxson concentrated on making records which sounded right on their sound systems, other non-system-owning producers were also gaining footholds in the music business in 1959. In reality, Chris Blackwell and Edward Seaga (more of a financier than a producer), were chiefly responsible for taking recorded sound into people's homes. Although both men supplied the occasional special (exclusive recording) for sounds, their releases were made for juke boxes and home record players.

In 1959, Blackwell hit big with Cuban-born Laurel Aitken's 'Boogie In My Bones' on his R&B label and Seaga matched him with (Joe) Higgs And (Roy) Wilson's 'Manny Oh' on WIRL. These records were very much instilled with the sound of mid-'50s black America, with walking bass lines and raucous brass, as on Owen Gray's paean to the Downbeat sound 'On The Beach' or singer/pianist Theophilus Beckford's easy-rocking boogie 'Easy Snapping', with piano chords that pre-dated the ska pattern by a couple of years.

Other strands of black American music influenced those pioneering Jamaican recording artists. Some essayed doo-wop, one as sublimely as Derrick Harriott & His Jiving Juniors on intricately harmonised finger-snappers such as 'Over The River' and 'Sugar Dandy', and sentimental R&B ballads as purveyed by Keith & Enid on their hit 'Worried Over You' and the honey-coated tones of Wilfred 'Jackie' Edwards, who scored with 'Your Eyes Are Dreaming', 'Tell Me Darling' and other seductive late-night sides before becoming an in-demand songwriter in the 1960s.

As the '60s dawned, the sound of R&B was being reinvented by Jamaican musicians such as Coxson's studio crew Clue J And The Blues Blasters, with a less harsh edge and a more shuffling beat. The shuffle was the direct precursor of the rousing ska rhythms that would shake the island for the next five years. Inspired largely by Rosco Gordon, the Memphis-based singer/pianist who played in a 'back-to-front' style – stressing the second and fourth beats of each bar – and who played live shows in Kingston about this time, the music began its long journey away from its American origins and towards a uniquely Jamaican identity.

2 Windrush To 1974

Lee Gopthal And The Growth Of British Trojan

Among the numerous passengers alighting from the SS *Empire Windrush* at Tilbury Docks on 21 June 1948 was 28-year-old Indian-Jamaican Sikarum Gopthal. Giving his address as 'the International Club, East Croydon', and his occupation as 'mechanic', he started a new life in post-war Great Britain. According to his son Leichman (or Lee for short), he made the move 'to escape the consequences of a life of heavy spending'.

A few years later, Sikarum, by now a tailor, set himself up in commercial premises at an address which would later become familiar to the first generation of British R&B and blue-beat fans: 108 Cambridge Road, London NW6. Lee followed him over from Jamaica in November 1952, stayed with his father in the flat above the shop and entered into the employ of a firm of certified accountants. An ambitious young man, he further studied the profession in the evenings.

Sometime in the early '60s, Sikarum decided to return to the Isle of Springs, leaving his son as the sole occupant of number 108, which, as a fast-rising accountant, he was soon able to buy. To help him with the mortgage payments, he advertised the empty basement to let and promptly found a prospective lessee in fellow West Indian immigrant Sonny Roberts, who wished to turn it into a nightclub.

It was probably Lee's desire to sleep at nights that led him to refuse this suggestion. Undaunted, Sonny came back with a plan that would put the humble building on the music map. Still with music in mind, he now wanted to turn the basement into a recording studio. Lee agreed, doubtless thinking that sessions would take place during the day and thus not disturb his sleep, and so in 1962 Sonny Roberts constructed Britain's first black-owned recording studio, a primitive affair with old egg-trays lining the walls to dampen the sound. In this basement, he recorded early UK ska and operated his Planetone and Sway labels. One of his most notable visitors was trombonist Rico Rodriguez, who cut some formative R&B sides at the studio.

At this time, the ground-floor shop was empty, as it had been since Gopthal Sr decamped back to Jamaica, although a group of men who hoped to get a betting shop licence for it were paying the rent. In the autumn of 1962, as the unsuccessful turf accountants pulled out, opportunity literally rang as a young man named

David Betteridge called to say that his boss, Chris Blackwell, would like to come and see the place.

Blackwell had been licensing work to jazz label Esquire's Starlite offshoot, run by Carlo Krahmer, but had recently moved to London to pioneer the West Indian market. He had arrived after being shown unlicensed UK pressings of his productions and decided to stay in the city as there appeared to be a ready market for his recordings of Owen Gray, Jackie Edwards and others. He formed the UK version of his Island Records label with his girlfriend Esther Anderson, his future sister-in-law Francine Winman and Australian sound engineer Graeme Goodall.

The original idea was for Jamaican producer Leslie Kong of Beverley's Records to supply the material, and for Island to market it in the UK. Sadly, this idea did not work; as David Betteridge says of Kong, 'He was a talented man, but *so* laid back!' With Blackwell as the driving force, this lack of material forced a change of plan. More recordings were urgently needed to satisfy the growing market. Luckily, Chris Blackwell, a white Jamaican, could deal with the island's producers with ease, as he could slip into the patois at will when the time came to cut a deal. Among the producers who provided sounds for Island was Duke Reid.

David Betteridge, Blackwell's right-hand man in the fast-growing company, had started his career working for Lugton's, an old-established record distributor which had commenced business in 1910. His father had worked there for 50 years, gaining a good reputation as a sales manager. David recalls those early years: 'I was a buyer for a company called Lugton's, which in around 1962 – along with Thompson, Diamond and Butcher, Selecta and EMI – were mainstream distributors of all sorts of things. EMI didn't just distribute EMI; it distributed Decca, and Decca distributed EMI. Everybody distributed everyone else. Lugton's was independent, and two of the lines I dealt with were Melodisc and Esquire, which was basically a jazz label, but it had also developed West Indian music on its Starlite label.

'So one day I got this phone call, and later Chris Blackwell came in. He was charming, tall, and he was with a Chinese-Jamaican called Leslie Kong. So Chris played me "Hurricane Hattie" [by Jimmy Cliff] and "Independent Jamaica" [by Lord Creator]. So I went up to see my director, the head of the record department, and he said, "Well, we don't really want any more lines. We've got a lot." It was a time when there was a lot of uncertainty around.

'So I rang Chris and said, "Look, I'm sorry, I can't help," and he asked me what I could suggest. I gave him the names of one or two people to get in touch with. He rang me two or three weeks later and said, "You know, every time I go and talk to someone, you seem to be the guy who knows about distributing and selling these things. Would you be interested in coming to talk to us?"'

So David Betteridge went from a steady, safe position to selling records from the back of his mini-van and Blackwell's Mini Cooper, operating from their base at Chris's flat at 4 Rutland Gate Mews, off Connaught Square. To begin with, resources were slim.

'It was one of those circle things,' explains David. 'When you've got some cash, go to the plant and buy the records, sell the records to the retailer and come back with the cash and start again, so the circle gets bigger and bigger as you take on more records.'

By late 1962, Island was outgrowing Chris's flat and was looking for larger premises. Enter Lee Gopthal and his roomy shop to let. So Blackwell and Betteridge set up an office in the rented shop and began to distribute West Indian music from there. Blackwell was keen to get his landlord involved, but in those early days Gopthal could see no incentive that would tempt him to give up accountancy. 'Eventually, however,' he recalled years later, 'he started having a lot of trouble selling his records and he asked me if I'd be interested in setting up a mail-order business. I told him that I thought the only way we could get to the potential buyers was to go to their homes, because a lot of West Indians were too google-eyed by the television to go out much.'

Lee Gopthal and his new partners advertised for agents to go around the West Indian areas of London, selling records from door to door. 'The biggest problem we had,' he recalled, 'was to persuade customers to pay for their records before they got them, since we didn't have the finance to risk losing money.'

Eventually, Lee and four old school friends – Jim Flynn, Barry Creasy, Alan Firth and Fred Parsons – controlled a squad of 16 salesmen from his bedroom at 108 Cambridge Road. (All the remaining rooms were either occupied by Island or let out to others from necessity, as cash was short.) By early 1963, the enterprising Lee, along with future Charisma label owner Tony Stratton-Smith, formalised this *ad hoc* selling operation into a proper record-distribution company, which they called Beat & Commercial Records ('because records had a beat and somebody talked about being commercial'). B&C became a limited company – Beat & Commercial Records Limited – on 19 April 1963.

This was just before Island, via a licensing deal with major label Fontana, cracked the national pop consciousness with 'My Boy Lollipop', by diminutive ska singer Millie Small. As soon as 'Lollipop' was recorded, Blackwell realised that it was not only a catchy pop record but a sure-fire chart hit. As Island were still basically operating out of the back of a van, he placed the record with a major label who had the financial and marketing push which he, as yet, didn't.

His hunch was right, and 'My Boy Lollipop' rocketed up the charts, coming to rest at the Number Two spot in March 1964. It was the first record based on a Jamaican rhythm to crack the magic Top 20. It also convinced Lee Gopthal that this was the time to quit his accountancy career to focus fully on the music business. Along with Blackwell and Betteridge, he went out looking for a retail shop in a suitable location.

Thus was the Musicland chain born. The first shop was in Willesden Lane, off Kilburn High Road, where Lee himself stood behind the counter, serving the music-hungry buyers. From this point, he concentrated on the retail side of the business, leaving Blackwell and Island to license and press the product. So successful was he that within two years he had four shops, plus a stall in Shepherd's Bush Market. He bought this with some trepidation (the asking price of £60 was a considerable sum at the time) and installed one of his former salesmen, Webster Shrowder, behind the counter. Nearly 40 years on, Webster's Record Shack is still trading.

Another former salesman, Desmond Bryan, stepped off the street to run another of the shops, and a young man named Joe Sinclair was hired as manager of another. Future producer and skinhead hero Joe Mansano also learned his shopcraft under Sinclair's wing before opening his own Joe's Records in Brixton, south London. Of Gopthal's original partners, Barry Creasy and Alan Firth moved over to Musicland while Jim Flynn and Fred Parsons threw in their lot with B&C.

So many of the key players who would shape British reggae over the next decade were learning their trade at Musicland, a chain that sold all types of modern popular music. Sister chain Muzik City, which started in around 1970, grew as some of the Musicland shops were converted to Muzik City outlets and catered more specifically for the West Indian community by purveying the latest in soul, reggae and calypso. Although basically owned by Trojan, Muzik City stocked a veritable host of other labels' product too. The Muzik City Record Shops chain became a limited company on 21 August 1972.

A certificate of change of name (no 758078) is lodged with Companies House showing that Beat & Commercial Records Limited changed their name to Musicland Record Stores Limited on 29 July 1970. Musicland Record Stores Limited, meanwhile, is recorded as being dissolved on 14 February 1977. (Beat & Commercial Records Limited is not to be confused with B&C Recordings Limited, which has continued to exist up until today.)

Lee Gopthal would carry on running Musicland until late in 1972, when he sold out to rival dealership Scene & Heard, giving the new owners some 20 branches in total.

(The April 1972 Companies Act return for Musicland Record Stores lists the directors as Lee Gopthal, with 352 shares; James Sydney Flynn, with 154; Fredrick William Parsons, with 100; Barry Creasy, with 124; Alan Fredrick Frith, with 100; David Joseph Charles Betteridge, with 70; and Christopher Gordon Blackwell, with 100, giving a total of 1,000 shares.)

By the mid '60s, Island Records was well established at 108 Cambridge Road, which was now listed as the registered address of the 'gramophone record wholesalers' business. Every time someone moved out, Blackwell would commandeer the vacant room until his empire had engulfed almost the entire premises. Even the rat-infested cellar-*cum*-recording studio that had been vacated by Sonny Roberts was in use as a storeroom for the ever-expanding business.

Official documents from 1975 reveal the Muzik City Record Shops directors to be Lee Gopthal, Webster Shrowder, Joe Sinclair and Desmond Bryan, with Gopthal holding 60 per cent of the share capital, Shrowder 14 per cent and Sinclair and Bryan 13 per cent each. Muzik City Record Shops went into voluntary winding-up on 22 January 1976 (Desmond Bryan signed the notice of 'Extraordinary Resolution' in his capacity as director), with a final winding-up meeting of members and creditors on 1 December 1978.

A devout blues fan, Rob Bell joined Island in 1966 and recounts his years there: 'I called Island in September of 1965 to see if they had any openings. I was 18 and in London for the day with my father, who had set me up with an interview earlier that day with Leslie Perrin, publicist to The Rolling Stones and many others. I left that interview with some time to spare before catching up with my father for the journey back to Winchester, my hometown. Thus I called Island, thinking I might get to work for Sue Records, Island's R&B label, run by Guy Stevens. Little did I know that Sue was a small money-losing division of Island!

'I went to their offices at Kilburn and met with David Betteridge, who was looking for a van salesman. Realising I wouldn't get the job if I told him I didn't have a driving licence, I fudged the issue by saying I was taking lessons and expected to pass any day. Actually, I had never driven a car in my life. David, who I am proud to say is still a very good friend, told me to report for work the following Monday. So I had a job; I just had to learn to drive! After a few days I had to confess to David that my driving career wasn't quite as advanced as I had intimated, but he, taken I imagine with my youthful *chutzpah*, laughed and said he had by now guessed as much, and that I could carry on doing telephone sales and working in the stores with Tim Clark, who had started a few weeks before me. Tim and I are still great buddies. He now manages Robbie Williams.

'Those days were wild. Ska permeated London and the clubs. Nights we'd go to Count Suckle's Cue Club in Paddington, or the Scotch of St James. Soul music was hot, too; Island imported albums from the US – Otis Redding, Garnett Mimms, Joe Tex, Don Covay. Down in the stores, which were in the basement below Island's offices, Tim and I pulled orders for the two London van reps, Tom Hayes and Bob Glynn, and the Midlands rep, whose name I now forget.

He was later replaced by Dave Bloxham. Island then had the Island label (WI 209 "Go Whey"/"Shelter the Storm" by Jackie Opel was released the week I joined); Black Swan, which was by then pretty much discontinued; and Aladdin, Island's pop label.

'Albums were the Island series. Then of course there was the Sue series, and Surprise, which were risqué LPs of the Rusty Warren/Belle Barth variety. The two biggest sellers were *Rugby Songs Volumes 1 & 2* by the Jock Strapp Ensemble. In fact, those two albums probably provided a very decent chunk of Island's total income back then.

'Around May of 1966, David called Tim and myself into the office and tearfully told us we would have to go, that Island was in a bad state and that the company had to cut back on its employees. I think at that point there were seven or eight people employed there: Tim, myself, David, Tom, Bob, the midlands rep, Neville the accountant, Charles someone or other, who was a phone sales guy, and Deidre Meehan, the receptionist. I believe Neville had a part-time assistant. So Tim and I split. I went to Transatlantic Records and Tim went to Saga.'

The company weathered the storm and continued to grow. Then, one day in 1968, a different kind of panic set in. Out of the blue, Lee Gopthal received a letter from the local council informing him that the house was to be demolished to make way for a new roundabout.

Lee, along with David Betteridge (now marketing manager of Island), had little option but to set out to find new premises for their expanding businesses. One of their discoveries was the former premises of mail-order traders New Fairway House Ltd, a large and now deserted warehouse at 12 Neasden Lane in the north London suburb of Harlesden. As Gopthal and Betteridge considered the possibility of the place as their new premises, a discarded pair of pink bloomers flapped gently and ominously high up in the draughty interior.

One thing was clear: it was too big for Island and too big for B&C. But as a shared site, it was just right. After Chris Blackwell agreed to the move, the new joint occupancy was cemented and the lease signed. The rather ramshackle building was promptly and somewhat grandiosely named Music House, the address that would be synonymous with Trojan Records during its glory years,

Inspired by Island's example, Lee Gopthal began to strike deals with Jamaican producers, and he aimed high. Indeed, his initial agreements were with the island's top two. The mighty Clement Dodd saw his myriad productions issued in Britain on the Studio One, Coxsone and Tabernacle labels. Duke Reid's primary releases were on the label named after his off-licence, Treasure Isle, but its overspill label, Trojan, was part of the expanding Gopthal empire. Its first release, on 28 July 1967, was titled 'Judge Sympathy' b/w 'Never To Be Mine' (TR001) and credited to Duke

Reid, although the top side was actually by The Freedom Singers And The Duke Reid All Stars, and saxman Roland Alphonso took care of the flip. However, Trojan was not established as a household name until later that year.

Gopthal also established a new label for the London-grown product of artist/producer Robert 'Dandy Livingstone' Thompson. When they first met, in early 1967, Dandy was working for R&B Discs, helming their Giant label, but in the following year he established a lucrative partnership with Lee, working as a freelance producer and recording artist. He was given his own Downtown label, the original imprint being deep red with black text, although this was quickly revised to a more striking two-colour design. The prolific Dandy would later have a second Trojan label, J-Dan, dedicated to his productions.

Lee also saw the lucrative opportunity of radio advertising. As there weren't any legal commercial stations in Britain at that time, he decided to advertise on Radio Caroline and Radio London, the infamous offshore pirate stations. This was evidently a very lucrative decision. 'People thought I was mad to advertise on London and Caroline,' he later said, 'but I was selling a hell of a lot of records and making a lot of money over a couple of years.' It obviously paid off as Desmond Dekker reached Number 14 in the UK charts on 12 July 1967 with '007' (his song about Jamaican rude boys) on the Pyramid label, in which Gopthal had an interest.

All the early Trojan-related single releases had TMX matrices stamped into the vinyl, irrespective of the label on which they were issued. 'Tunes would sometimes get mastered before a label was decided upon or, more accurately, a catalogue number was assigned,' explains Rob Bell. 'That actually is the real purpose behind the whole concept of having matrix numbers in the first place. Matrix is Latin for master. Assigning a master number and then recording the master numbers in a book means that one is able to keep track of masters at the plant. A master is a metal plate used to grow stampers from. Having a number on it keeps everything organised – or so we always hoped!

'Vic [Keary] at Chalk Farm did all our UK sessions, overdubs, all that kind of stuff. Tony down at Pye, at Marble Arch, did all our mastering – all those dubs from discs! Many is the time I'd take something to Pye, waiting for the lacquers to be cut, and then take them to Orlake, in Dagenham, filling up all the space in my car, or sometimes my old 1943 jeep with boxes of whatever was hot off the press for the return journey to Music House.'

In such a fast-moving market, the need to turn a record around rapidly was paramount – and Trojan were equal to the task: 'Oh man, we could be fast! If a tune was really hot, and the clamour for its release deafening, we could, and would, get the thing mastered at 9am – or whenever we could persuade Tony to open up

Pye in the morning – have it at Orlake by 11am, and they would then start processing the lacquers. I think they called it "silvering".

'A lacquer is a wax master – an acetate, if you like, a record cut by the cutting lathe. It is the final master. Upon arrival at the pressing plant, it is suspended in a tank of chemicals and electroplated. After a certain period of time – an hour or several, I can't remember exactly how long – a metal father is formed, or grown. A reverse record, if you like. From that father, mothers are then grown, and from the mothers, stampers are made. Stampers are, like the fathers, reverse records. It is these stampers that are put upon the press and that are used to press the records.

'It is possible that Orlake could be pressing records by mid-afternoon, and a few hundred could be back at Music House by the end of the day. If a record was really hot, we'd have it up on several presses, and if it was charting, we'd have it being pressed at perhaps Phillips' Croydon plant and/or at one of the EMI plants. Thus then I would have to deal with three separate stocks of labels, product and pressing plants.

'This was exactly what was happening when I first started production at Trojan, when we had four Top Ten records. I was dealing with three plants and potential stock problems on four catalogue numbers – times the three plants! Plus the regular dozen or so new releases each week.

'John Rooks was the general manager at Orlake – great guy, fantastic manager. Of course, we were the big customer, so we had some very real clout. There would be times we would take over Orlake's entire capacity, 24 presses. I'd call John, get a pressing figure on a particular number, tell him that would get me through the next two days, have him take that one off the press and put up in its place such-and-such a number and so on. This would go on all day long, week after week, month after month. The pressure we put on him was tremendous, but he always came through. Very exciting days.

'We had constant hassles with Lee Gopthal about the amount of money we'd spend on having cabs bringing over product at the end of the day. Orlake would deliver by truck every day, of course, but that truck would basically bring what had been pressed the day and evening before. Lee would grumble about the amount we spent on cabs, but at the same time he would rant and rave if such-and-such a title wasn't in stock for his Musicland stores to sell. So we cabbed 'em over and to hell with the expense.

'So we could turn stuff around really fast. It was a strange business – a tune could be hot one week and dead if you released it a week later. So there was always this pressure to get things out quickly if they were being asked for. And if we got wind that Producer X or one of the more, shall we say, free-wheeling producers might have given one of "our" titles to Pama, then of course we rushed things.'

★

Mainstream DJs working for that bastion of British broadcasting, the BBC, refused to programme Jamaican singles in their shows and only reluctantly gave them airplay once they had finally broken through to the general consciousness (except, that is, the ribald Judge Dread, whose early-'70s discs would be forever banned from BBC radio). Accusations of being boring and monotonous, with incomprehensible lyrics – even though many records were to all intents and purposes instrumentals – and the skinhead/bovver connection were all levelled at reggae music as reasons for its dismissal by the nation's hit-pickers.

So it was left to the pirates – who, on the other hand, had picked up on the new youth culture way back in the swinging '60s – to slip into their playlists exotic gems such as bandleader Baba Brooks's rolling 'Girls Town Ska' and The Skatalites' rousing 'Guns Of Navarone', which both gained very healthy sales outside the West Indian market. The trendy, hip pirate-radio listeners, the club DJs and the skinheads were much more in touch with the grass-roots sounds that set the reggae ball rolling.

John Peel, an influential ex-pirate-ship DJ now working for the BBC and specialising in non-mainstream music, declared that he quite liked reggae, and later in the '70s he would champion notable roots-reggae groups such as Misty In Roots and Culture, but he was still too hungover from the psychedelic '60s to get really involved. Tony Blackburn, the breakfast-time DJ of BBC's new pop station Radio 1 and the man people loved to hate, was against it right from the start and sided with the 'boring and monotonous' lobby, so it was left to champions like Mike Raven and the grandly named Emperor Rosko to drop the new music in the public's lap.

Raven started out on Pirate Radio 390 before becoming the first presenter to have an R&B show on the newly inaugurated Radio 1. On his pioneering hour-long Sunday evening show, Raven would always slip in two or three 'blue beat' records alongside the rousing US rhythm-and-blues and soul releases.

The high-profile Emperor Rosko, meanwhile, was born Michael Pasternak in Los Angeles, California, on 26 December 1942, and his first radio experience was on the aircraft carrier USS *Coral Sea*'s station, KCWA. He then moved to France and, later, to England, where he arrived in 1965. A stint on Radio Caroline followed before he went to Radio Luxembourg's French-language station, where, as Le President Rosko, he started a successful pirate-style show called *Minimax* ('Minimum de bla-bla, maximum de musique'). In late 1967, BBC Radio 1 beckoned, and Rosko was to take the hot seat there for some ten years.

Rosko produced his own shows and thus was not bound by the conventions to which the BBC held. Consequently he was not confined to playing the hits of the day and featured a much broader width of music. His patronage of an unknown record could turn it into a hit, so strong was his following. He programmed a whole lot of soul and, alongside it, the bright new sound of reggae.

Reggae artists saw Rosko as such a champion of their music that not only did he have a record dedicated to him – Dice The Boss's eerie 'Tea House From Emperor Rosko', released on Trojan's Joe subsidiary – but he even got to enter the hallowed Chalk Farm Studios to recut Prince Buster's 'Al Capone' to a reggae beat. (It was issued on Trojan with a limited-edition picture sleeve, but it didn't manage to set the charts alight.) He also graced the sleeve of the Trojan compilation LP *Club Reggae Volume 4* and, aside from Judge Dread, is one of the few white males to make it onto a reggae album's cover shot.

Almost as soon as Island and B&C moved into Music House, David Betteridge and Lee Gopthal started to discover the advantages of working so close together. As at this time the two companies were in fact rivals, the Jamaican producers started to play one off against the other. The hopeful producer would phone and offer the self-same 'exclusive' new recordings to both companies, little knowing that they were sitting almost face to face in the roomy London warehouse.

David and Lee compared notes and soon realised what was going on. They turned the tables on the wily producers by each offering less for a new recording than the other had done. In the end, the pair decided to fly out to Jamaica to regain control of the situation, and they also cut a few new deals while they were there.

Chris Blackwell, meanwhile, had discovered the financial advantages of rock music after signing The Spencer Davis Group, who became a significant force within the pages of the *NME* and *Melody Maker* and chalked up a string of pop hits between 1964 and '67. Blackwell had signed them to Island's great advantage and was determined to lead Island along the golden path of white rock. The cash injection to the small company from just one successful pop group was already showing its significance, compared with their numerous Jamaican releases. At the same time, Blackwell was losing faith in Jamaican music, apparently due to difficulties with the producers and their 'soon come' attitude, so in 1968 he decided to sell his subsidiary labels to Lee Gopthal.

In conjunction with Island, B&C then formed Trojan Records Ltd, which was in fact a partnership between Lee Gopthal, Alan Firth and Graham Walker, but unfortunately no official records survive to give an exact date for the formation, although the first singles issued by the company officially saw issue in July of that year. The previous Trojan, the Duke Reid subsidiary label from a year earlier, had been quickly deleted, and it was with this new company that the brand known to reggae lovers throughout the UK was formed. After all, the situation had become silly, as Gopthal recalled in a 1973 interview: 'Both Island and ourselves were chasing around Jamaica after the same producers, so, as we were already operating from the same premises, we decided to form Trojan as a joint label.'

Dandy Livingstone remembers the original Trojan staff as Lee Gopthal, Graham

Walker, Alan Firth, Fred Parsons, Jim Flynn, Tilly the secretary and a familiar face who had returned to the fold: Rob Bell, who came back in 1968 to run the distribution side of the business. 'I joined Trojan – you will recall Island owned 50 per cent of Trojan and worked out of the same building – in 1969, as production manager. I became general manager when Graham Walker left to start the US end of the operation in 1970.'

Returning to Trojan was a definite shock for Rob: 'I can't remember the date but most definitely recall that we had four 45s on the charts, all in the Top Ten: "Elizabethan Reggae", "Liquidator" and probably a Desmond [Dekker] and a [Jimmy] Cliff... It was the only time Trojan had such a concentrated chart showing.

'It was baptism by fire! I am proud to say that we never went out of stock of any of those titles... I do recall waking up in the middle of the night many times wondering if I was going to run out of labels on a particular number, of having nightmares of endless catalogue numbers, a mad dreamscape of numbers and prefixes.'

Rob goes on to give an outline to the Trojan US operation: 'Graham left for the US around the end of 1970, or possibly early in 1971. The idea was to set up Trojan in the US. I really can't recall that much, but I do remember he was there for about six months, mainly in New York City. Brooklyn, as you probably know, had – as it still does – a sizeable Jamaican population. I don't know if he actually released anything, or what happened, except that Trojan USA never got off the ground. It is possible that Jamaican producers already had outlets there, or that they shipped finished product and that was more profitable.

'I do remember much ribald laughter over the fact that Trojan in the US is the leading condom manufacturer, and that *Trojan* was then synonymous with *rubber*. I believe this came as a surprise to Graham.'

A small series of 7" singles was in fact pressed in the USA with the familiar Trojan label design turned to black and white and the catalogue prefix CATTR. These were the product of Graham Walker's unsuccessful mission to convert the USA to Trojan reggae. It was normal practice for the record-pressing plant to print single-colour labels for their smaller releases, as opposed to paying a high price to a printer for a full colour version.

Rob Bell was left in charge of the British end of Trojan: 'Until Graham's departure, I had been production manager, scheduling and organising the releases, which meant getting 45s and albums mastered, labels printed, sleeves printed and records pressed. When Graham left, I became general manager, assuming many of the duties he obviously couldn't handle from New York City. When he returned, he wanted his old job back. Also, there was talk of the company being sold to Marcel Rodd, of Saga. Under the circumstances, I split and returned to work for Island.

'Shortly thereafter, I moved to Island's other offices, the Basing Street/Lancaster

Road complex just off the Portobello Road. There I worked with international director Tom Hayes and spent a lot of time working in Europe, especially Scandinavia.'

Rob also recalls the 7" pre-release singles, which would be pressed with blank white labels and bearing the matrix GPW (signifying Graham P Walker) plus a numbering system in the vinyl: 'They were pre-release. Graham and Lee [Gopthal] would press between 50 and 200 white labels and Lee would sell them through his Musicland stores at a hefty price.' These were very desirable items for the top-flight DJs as the music was fresh and unavailable elsewhere, hence the high premium that could be charged for the discs. Other labels, such as Pama, put out similar pre-release singles at the same time. Some of the GPWs would find general release later, after the input from the Musicland stores and DJs was taken in to account, while others would disappear in to obscurity.

Rob recounts a story to make all of today's record collectors weep: 'I hadn't been back at Island for long in 1968 before I realised that no one there really had an eye for the company's Jamaican history. Everyone there worked in the here and now, with no thought for the likes of folks like you and I, in the year 2003, trying to reconstruct things... Often we dubbed from disc in the absence of having master tapes, so there was not much of a tape archive to begin with. Thus, around 1969, I instituted a policy whereby three or four of every new release was put aside in a corner of the stores. (You will recall that Trojan released anywhere from 6 to 16 singles every week). Every now and then, I would box these up into a large box and store them at home, in order to avoid pilferage.

'When I left Island at the end of 1972, I very conscientiously returned these boxes – which probably numbered seven or eight two-by-two-by-two-foot boxes full of 45s – to the then store manager for safe keeping. I remember my words: "Look after these. These boxes are the company's archives, and thus the company heritage. Put 'em in a safe place!" I think they were stolen within a month.'

There are many factors which contribute to the rarity of certain Trojan releases on the collectors' market: 'Maybe once a year we'd dump – literally – tens of thousands of records. This is an amazing story...but first a little background. This was in the days before VAT. Items sold at retail then were liable to what was known as Purchase Tax. On a 45, it was I think about 1/9d, nearly ten pence in decimal money. As wholesale price to a store was about four shillings and sixpence, this tax represented a fairly large sum of money. And it was charged upon all the inventory.

'Thus one could not sell the records for less, because the Purchase tax remained the same. One couldn't get it reduced. It was calculated from the factory delivery notes/invoices. The only way not to pay this tax was to have the records certified as being destroyed.

'We first achieved this by hiring a large box van and filling it with dead stock.

Once a record stopped selling, it was dead. If it had been a strong seller at time of release, it might have a decent life for a few years, but given the sheer amount of product we put out, there were inevitably those that were dead on arrival. They took up valuable warehouse space, which was obviously finite. So we'd clean out the warehouse, take all the dead stuff and load it into the hired truck and then drive it to the municipal dump in St Albans. We'd meet the tax man there – I think it would be a guy from Customs and Excise – and give him the list of what we were dumping. He'd watch as my cohort and I slung box after box out of the back of the van, until we had an empty van and a mountain of 45 boxes. Then a bulldozer would bury the lot, the tax guy would be satisfied they were destroyed and the tax liability was lifted.

'After a couple of these adventures, 45s started showing up in stores around St Albans – word was obviously getting out, and the stuff was getting unearthed and offered for sale. Big problem, as far as the tax men were concerned. So from there on, we had to physically destroy the records before taking them to the dump. This entailed filling up the parking lot of Music House with boxes of 45s and then smashing the boxes with axes, drilling with electric drills, wielding sledge hammers and generally going berserk, much to the astonishment of passersby, who would chance upon this scene of mayhem and linger, gazing with glassy-eyed amazement as these long-haired lunatics went about their work with grim and sweaty countenances.

'There were, of course, the inevitable puns about a "smashing time" and "breaking all records". However, the taxman was satisfied and money was saved. And this is the reason why so many of the records we put out are now very rare indeed!'

Record collectors who are not actually in tears by this stage may read on...

'Every now and then,' recalls Rob, 'we would receive these huge orders from Lagos, Nigeria and Freetown, in Sierra Leone, accompanied by the most delightfully malapropactic letters...written in a kind of bureaucratic Sunday School English. Sadly, they usually never included any money for payment but proposed amazingly convoluted propositions for future payment. Of course, on some occasions money was forthcoming and we'd ship an order of early ska stuff – Keith And Enid, Jackie Edwards, that kind of thing.

'During much of the 1960s, dreadful things were happening in Nigeria – the Ibos and Hutus were at each other's throats, spurred on, no doubt, by the charming Mr Idi Amin. I recall having to clean out the apartment above Island's old Cambridge Road offices sometime in 1968 or '69. A Nigerian guy was squatting there, in horrible squalor. He ultimately left, and we got into the place. There were many letters from his family lying around the floor, and we read them – sad, awful tales of people going missing, being killed, tortured...written in halting English but wrenchingly potent, starkly evocative. The entire upstairs apartment was littered with ska records... We filled a truck with them and sold them at about three pence each to a guy in Portobello Road, probably around 50,000 45s. He was selling them for years, a villainous looking guy with a patch over one eye that completed the look.

'I don't recall us exporting much finished product to other countries. Obviously, if we had a hit in the UK, we could exert strong pressure for a European licensee, such as Ariola, to release the record there. Holland, Spain and Germany were the three markets in which we had the better successes.'

Rob also comments on the aspect of any racism that may have arisen within the multiracial company. The majority of the management were white (Lee Gopthal was Indian-Jamaican), while most of the artists and producers were of West Indian origin: 'It's interesting how strong is the desire to impose charges of racism on a situation that, from our perspective here in 2003, would seem to just *have* to be rife with it! In fact, I really don't recall any instances of racism, but then I was a middle-class white guy who considered himself to be free of any and all prejudices. The aim of the company was to make money, plain and simple.

'I'm sure that Trojan, like any company inside and outside of the music business, sought to achieve the very best advantage it could. The fact that most, if not all of the producers and artists were black, and many of the Trojan staff were white, most obviously gives the producer/artist faction cause, in their eyes, to cry, "Racism!" I'd basically disagree and cry, "Capitalism!" Nevertheless, there were many folks that I am sure will disagree with me simply because, in my eyes, they confuse capitalism with racism, or equate one with the other. And just for the record, I am not really a capitalist; an anarchist is more accurate. Of course, it can be argued that capitalism is anarchistic at base. In fact, I left the music industry at the end of 1972 because, one, I disliked the music I was then promoting at Island – Cat Stevens, King Crimson *et al* – and two, I wanted out of the waste and greed of the record industry. I spent the rest of the '70s working on a farm on the edge of Exmoor, digging the air, the views and enjoying country life.

'To return to the racist thing, it is interesting to note the following facts. Trojan was the progeny of B&C and Island. The management of both were, in the main, white. I don't think either company ever hired white over black as a matter of policy. White was the colour of the folks who started up the companies, and most folks who applied for work there were white. I went back to Island in 1968, in the summer, to run their stores and distribution. I was the only guy in the warehouse. Island was starting to build up a head of steam, and after just one week in the job I had to hire another guy. Six months later, I had 20 guys working for me. I think I probably hired all of them myself, certainly 90 per cent of them. As far as I can recall, they were all white. I really don't recall any black guys coming for interviews. And here is the kicker: this was at the height of the hippie era. The majority of the hires were university dropouts, smart guys.

'So the workforce that came to us was by and large very intelligent, and thus formed a wonderful pool of talent that ultimately rose up through the ranks of Island. It was from this pool that we promoted guys to other jobs within the company. They were proven and had some expertise by then. On the B&C side, there were more West Indian guys, mainly through the Musicland stores…but really, there was no percentage in being discriminatory. Making money was the name of the game, not keeping people down. To be sure, I can recall small store owners coming in to buy product. Those that were on a cash basis would sometimes call us, or even me, racist, because they didn't have credit. They didn't have credit because, if we gave it to them, we simply wouldn't get paid – because they had no money, not because they were black. All of them had track records of having had credit in the past that they had fucked up. Basic capitalistic theory put into practice.'

By 1970, it was all go for reggae. Major labels entered the market: MCA UK, with Count Prince Miller guiding them through the murky waters, and an EMI production deal with an R&B Production Co (apparently unconnected with the R&B Discs record label in existence at the time) and Pye, and later Decca, to distribute Charles Ross's hopeful Sugar label. However, Sugar would dissolve after a handful of singles and albums failed to entice the cash from buyers' pockets, and R&B Production Co appear to have produced no records.

Trojan was growing fast, and so was its label roster. David Betteridge explains: 'If you had six releases, you couldn't put them all out on the same label. The culture in Jamaica is such that a shop in Orange Street will have its own label, rather like Our Price having its own label. Because we had an inflow, we needed to have different channels for different products, especially when we merged Island and B&C/Trojan, and before that Rio and Doctor Bird, which Graeme Goodall had. If we had six or eight records, we couldn't put them all on the same label.'

Each new label needed its own design, as David recalls: 'I remember Alan Smith, who in those days had CCS Advertising Associates Ltd, which was our design company, coming up every other week with new designs for labels, some of which were quite nice when I look back, primitive but quite fun. They had to be bright and simple.'

Most producers in Jamaica had their own labels, such as Joel 'Joe Gibbs' Gibson's Amalgamated and, obviously, Duke Reid's Treasure Isle. To enter the burgeoning UK market, Trojan Records decided to duplicate these labels, feeling that a familiar label would quicken the sales of records, so Harry J (for Harry Johnson's productions), Song Bird (for the work of Derrick Harriott) and Upsetter (for Lee Perry) all came into being early in 1969.

'In the UK, we had labels printed by Harrisons, in High Wycombe,' says Rob Bell. 'Harrisons also printed postage stamps and other high-quality work. They would print, say, 100,000 backgrounds and then would overprint the label copy for each individual release. The labels would be shipped to the pressing plant, or, if the title was selling very fast, I would leave my house in Hemel Hempstead at 5am, go to Harrisons and collect the labels, and then drive to Dagenham, to Orlake, our principal pressing plant, drop off the labels and pick up whatever product they might have ready for us, and then be at Music House at perhaps 9am. A mad frenzied time.'

Another significant move in that year was the appointment of St Kitts-born Joe Sinclair. Joe had been with the Musicland shop at 23 Ridley Road since 1965 (no official documentation can be found to substantiate that this branch was trading as early as that, but much paperwork of this age has now been destroyed by Companies House) and had elevated the premises to be the number-one retail outlet of the chain. He was rewarded with an appointment as the manager of Trojan Records.

Joe was an accomplished keyboard player and, as well as being responsible for the day-to-day running of the office, moved into playing on and producing records. He founded the Grape label in late 1969 as 'a take on Apple' and started to record UK-based group The Rudies on crunching skinhead-friendly numbers like the revamped 'Guns Of Navarone'. Some of their records were covers of other artists' tunes, such as 'Shanghai', which was similar to the Lloyd Charmers original, already released by Pama. 'That was just to make some money,' chuckled Joe in a recent interview, adding that it was standard practice in Kingston, if someone had a hit, to version it to oblivion, with many people avidly pulling together every variation on the theme. Trojan did the same, as did all the reggae labels vying for hits as the new decade dawned.

The other problem that confronted Sinclair, and that had caused headaches far back for Chris Blackwell, was the producers' philosophy of getting as much mileage out of a record as possible. Sometimes Trojan were offered a brand-new recording from Jamaica; they would buy the master tape from the producer and issue it on one of their labels. Pama would have gone through a mirror-image situation with the same producer, who would have two or even three copies of his 'exclusive', which he would proceed to sell to rival companies before jetting back to the sunshine with a maximum profit.

Sometimes two rival companies' labels would release a record almost simultaneously – such as Marley's 'Lively Up Yourself', which appeared on Trojan's Green Door imprint and Pama's Punch label – or, if one unfortunate owner saw it already out on the street, they would just shelve their release. Trojan Records own a considerable number of recordings that they have never released due to this problem, and one can conjecture that the other labels active at the time also had a box of unuseable master tapes. Rob Bell and Joe Sinclair were astute and tried to be alert to competitors' releases so that Trojan would not fall into this trap, but alas some did slip through his net.

'Big problem,' recalls Rob of the double-selling practice. 'Folks like Producer X would fly over, come see us and sell us a bunch of tunes, and then drive up to Neasden High Road, to Pama's place, and sell them the same songs. And then fly back to Jamaica. The next week, the new releases would come out and the phone would start ringing, either Harry Palmer calling us or us calling him: "What the *fuck?*" And Producer X would be back in Jamaica. It was a good game, and several producers played it. A short-term advantage was gained, in that the producer got a quick bit of extra cash but rapidly gained a shocking reputation. We liaised with Pama fairly closely with some guys in order to stop the confusion... Advances were constantly being adjusted and contracts rewritten to reflect duplicity by these guys.'

Bell and Sinclair were also very much aware of the musical needs of the new crop-headed public. Joe, aside from producing some exemplary sides himself, hired skinhead favourite Laurel Aitken to record and produce some tracks. Aitken had his finger on the youth-market pulse and, under the guise of King Horror, cut some classic talk-over or DJ sides such as 'Loch Ness Monster' and the ribald 'The Hole'.

Although not directly under Sinclair's control in the studio, south London record-shop owner turned producer Joe Mansano recorded some crunching numbers aimed directly at the skinhead market, moonstompers such as his own 'Skinhead Revolt' and Laurel Aitken's (in his King Horror guise) 'Dracula, Prince Of Darkness', which were received very well by the new audience. Mansano was rewarded early on with his own Trojan offshoot label, Joe, and proceeded to entice money from both West Indians and white skinheads, so popular were his records.

Joe Mansano had come to the UK in 1963 to study in a London college. In May 1965 he found a job with two Jamaicans setting up a new cosmetics shop, Len Dyke and Dudley Dryden. Alongside their cosmetic wares Dyke & Dryden became one of the only places to buy the latest imported records from Kingston.

Mansano was soon treading the streets with the records as he sold them door to door and enticed many buyers in clubs and house parties. This was aside from the booming trade in vinyl at Dyke & Dryden's store. News of his aptitude as a record salesman reached back to Jamaica and Graeme Goodall came over to launch his UK Doctor Bird label at the Dyke & Dryden shop in 1966. Late in 1967, Island

MD David Betteridge visited Joe Mansano and offered him his own record shop, which was to be called Joe's Records and would fall under the control of the new Trojan Records company that was just being formed.

Joe soon progressed from selling records to producing them, and one of his first, 'The Bullet' from trombone player Rico, was a strong seller. 'Brixton Cat' came a little later and encouraged Trojan to issue an album of the same name featuring Mansano productions and then set up his own imprint.

Two main bands carried out the session work for the majority of Trojan's UK-related recordings. Joe Sinclair favoured The Rudies, with Freddie Notes as lead vocalist (Joe Sinclair says that no one can remember what Freddie's real surname was to this day), Earl Dunn on lead guitar, Trevor Ardley White on bass, Danny Bowen Smith on drums and with Sonny 'SS' Binns normally ensconced behind the Hammond organ. Formed in the mid '60s, this London-based five-piece band soon gained a formidable reputation on the local West Indian scene with their powerful live performances. They were soon in the studio, recording under a number of different guises as well as Freddie Notes & The Rudies, and scored a major chart hit in 1970 with a reworking of the Barry Bloom pop hit 'Montego Bay'.

The other Joe, Mansano, looked to The Cimarons as his main players. The band comprised Maurice Ellis (drums and percussion), Locksley Gichie (guitar/vocals), Franklyn Dunn (bass guitar/guitar/percussion), Carl Levy (keyboards/harmonies/percussion) and Winston Reid (lead vocals/percussion). The first four members noted here formed the band in 1967 without any finance or knowledge of the music business. Initially the Cimarons backed visiting Jamaican artists, with Reid joining a little later, but after a considerable number of years serving with the group he took a solo career move which hit paydirt with 'Dim The Lights', a particularly smooth reggae love song which took the renamed Winston Reedy to the top of the reggae charts in 1983. The Rudies' keyboard player, Sonny Binns, was also a member of The Cimarons early on in their career.

Like The Rudies, The Cimarons can be heard on a considerable number of UK-recorded discs from the late 1960s through to the early 1970s, under many spelling variations of the band name. They also found fame as The Hot Shots, with producer Clive Crawley on lead vocals, and their 'Snoopy Vs The Red Baron' single – released on the B&C-owned Mooncrest label – hit Number Four in the national charts in June 1973. An album was soon issued, named after the hit single, along with further singles, such as 'Yesterday Man', but the band failed to follow up on their run of good fortune.

Brixton-based Hot Rod sound-system operator Lambert Briscoe also made use of The Cimarons' tight sound when he formed the Torpedo label, with the aid of The Equals' Eddie Grant, in 1970. Renaming the group after his sound as The Hot

Rod All Stars he proceeded to record and release some choppy, fast, semi-instrumental sides aimed squarely at the white skinhead contingent, such as 'Skinheads Don't Fear' and 'Moon Hop In London'.

Trojan also rewarded Briscoe with his own brand, Hot Rod, where the majority of the recordings were by The Cimarons, under their alias, where they recorded some straight-to-the-jugular skinhead sides like 'Skinhead Speaks His Mind'.

Neither the Torpedo nor the Hot Rod singles sold particularly well. Very few enthusiasts of the time recall any of the titles beyond Winston Groovy's 'Please Don't Make Me Cry', which was Torpedo's only real hit with the reggae public and also found release (as a slightly different recording) on Trojan's Explosion label.

In its early days, the way in which Trojan was run was vital to its success, as Rob Bell explains: 'First of all, nearly all the sales came from product that originated in Jamaica. UK-produced things usually died a death. If a record was a success in Jamaica, it was just about certain to be a success in the UK. The degree of that success was, of course, unknown. A good seller sold 2,500 to 5,000 in the West Indian market. Perhaps it might go pop, and then it could do 40,000 to 200,000 or more. The two things that made Trojan a happening label were the facts that its two owners, Island and B&C, had the following going for them: Island had the distribution and the clout in Jamaica (ie contacts with the producers) and B&C had the retail outlets.

'Island's van reps called on all the West Indian stores in the UK. B&C owned several stores in the lucrative London market. Record buyers would ask the stores if such-and-such record was available yet, a record they knew about from reading the *Jamaica Gleaner* [a newspaper published in London for ex-pat West Indians], or from a visiting relative, or because they heard it at a sound system on an import from Jamaica.

'The stores in turn asked the van reps about this record or, if they were Musicland stores, phoned Music House. One way or another, we – Island, B&C, Trojan – knew very quickly indeed which records had the potential to be hot or not. The demand for some tunes would be at a fever point; we'd get the tape, if it was a quality producer like Leslie Kong, or dub from a 45 if it was Bunny Lee or one of those guys, who only occasionally sent us tapes. The trick was to get the record out ASAP, while the demand was there. A delay of a week or so could often kill a record.

'We rarely got test pressings on a record. If it was a potential pop thing, then of course we did, but a regular shot at the West Indian market didn't usually require a test. However, we did occasionally press up pre-release – the GPW matrices. This killed two birds with one stone. Firstly, a few copies – a very few – were circulated to a few key sound systems. This was to either gauge reaction, or more likely to build demand. The sound systems in Jamaica had a long tradition of scratching off the labels of US releases to confuse the opposition. This morphed into the white-label system of pre-release, whereby only the initiated knew the identity of the disc. However, while some white labels did indeed help promote a future official release; the majority were pressed for very simple capitalistic reasons. Graham and Lee sold them to stores and sound-system operators at a high price – say 7/6 to 15/-.'

At the start of the '70s, two other successful shop managers, Webster Shrowder and Desmond Bryan, joined Joe Sinclair to form one of the best-known UK production teams, Shrowder/Bryan/Sinclair, with Joe describing himself as the driving force. The team recorded under different name groupings, depending on who was in the studio with the artists. Records can be found with just plain 'Sinclair', and also 'Shrowder/Bryan', as well as 'Shrowder/Bryan/Sinclair' as the producers.

The group also used Bush Productions and Swan Productions as their joint production-house name, the latter of which was taken from the revived Black Swan label (originally an Island subsidiary), which carried their production work, such as the hit Steel Pan version of Montego Bay, 'Mo' Bay', by Selwyn Baptiste in 1970. According to Joe Sinclair, the label's revival was due to a desire to have a brand that was already familiar with record buyers.

Along with Joe Mansano and Dandy, Shrowder/Bryan/Sinclair were responsible for nearly all of the London reggae released on Trojan labels, including Judge Dread's big pop hits 'Big Six' and 'Big Seven', major breakthroughs for the company's Big Shot label. 'I bought the two Judge Dread rhythms in from GG's – Alvin Ranglin – and Bunny Lee for £500 each,' recalls Joe. 'I also played keyboards on "Big Seven" and recorded the rhythm track for Ken Boothe's "(That's The Way) Nature Planned It" in London, which I later sold on to Lloyd Charmers.'

Joe paid £7,000 for Ken Boothe's recording of 'Everything I Own' to producer Lloyd Charmers in 1974. The money was well spent, as it was a major chart success for all concerned, becoming a Number One pop hit. Aside from these major hits, Sinclair played with The Deltones and the London version of The Uniques. 'It would be me on piano and Sonny Binns on organ, or the other way round,' he explains.

Early in the '70s, Trojan had a plethora of labels catering for a prolific number of artists and producers. The sheer amount of vinyl released was summed up by a former Trojan employee: 'Throw enough records at the wall and some of them will stick. Those that did stick, we'd press up a few more.' It was said – somewhat facetiously – that anyone with sufficient prestige and with a record soon to be released by Trojan could demand a label of their own and the company would oblige.

The figures are startling. In 1970, the year of its heyday, the company issued 500 singles across its many labels, with sales of over 1.5 million discs to West Indians (and skinheads) and with pop-market sales (ie discs that made the national charts) of roughly half a million. In the same year, major rival Pama Records managed 300 single releases, with sales in excess of two million, mainly selling to the West Indian market and the skinheads.

'Pama was Trojan's main rival, really the only rival,' says Rob Bell, 'so we did our best to stay on top, keep producers happy and coming to us. On a day-to-day basis, we were friendly. No reason not to be. I'm sure their presence in the market kept us on our toes, made us more competitive and probably helped lead to the policy that Trojan adopted of attempting to monopolise the market, and thus ultimately led to its demise. Of course, I do have to interject here that I was never privy to the company's finances, so the preceding is simply an assumption based on rational observations.'

The quality control of the releases has always been something of a mystery, as some discs were obviously losers and yet still gained issue. Rob explains how these rogues appeared: 'There was no quality control at all, really. I don't think either Graham [Walker] or Lee [Gopthal] had a huge amount of artistic appreciation. The majority of the folks involved saw the whole thing merely as a business, which of course it was.

'Here is the core explanation. Trojan was the major UK – read international – player. In order to maintain that position, the label tried to corner the market and sign up every producer. They had already been giving Kong, Reid, Coxson Dodd, Mrs Pottinger, Joel Gibson etc their own labels. Each new signee wanted his own label *and* a guaranteed amount of releases a year. Thus Trojan was obliged to put out a certain amount of records on each producer, and sometimes that meant we put out shit just to keep the quotas current. Stupid, of course, but it is what happened. I know that, when I was production manager, I never put out less than eight 45s in a week, and I remember putting out 16 releases one week.'

Dandy recalls that Lee Gopthal often called him into the office to listen to some new Jamaican music that Gopthal was interested in purchasing. On one occasion in 1971, when The Pioneers were actually staying around the corner from Dandy's house in Leyton, east London, Lee asked him to pop round and chat to Sidney Crooks. The pair hit it off, and a week later the group were in Chalk Farm Studios recording the song 'Let Your Yeah Be Yeah', although it took Dandy to persuade them to record it, as they did not like the number. History shows their dislike was wrong, and the song gave them a Number Five hit in the pop chats.

Each Trojan release was afforded little marketing, and the ones which succeeded did so on merit or just plain luck, such as getting on the playlist at Count Suckle's Cue Club in Paddington, which could literally make a reggae hit in a weekend. By this time, Chris Blackwell at Island had discovered, via its progressive rock acts, the art of promotion and the rewards that could be reaped from the correct marketing of an artist. Island were to follow this path with Bob Marley in 1973, pushing him to the white music press and to great long-term success.

A constant problem for the administration of Trojan was the matter of artists' royalty payments. David Betteridge on payment and royalties: 'The interesting thing about the ownership of a lot of the material from the late '50s and certainly the '60s and early '70s is, in many cases, people just don't know who owns them. Because it really wasn't catalogues; it was somebody who just came along that had some tracks of songs – it might be a retailer in Jamaica – who would do some productions on the side.

'Apart from Duke Reid and Coxson Dodd, there were about 20–30 people, perhaps ten of which were regular, and the difficulty is [the way in which] a lot of those deals were done. I mean, we've all heard the famous stories about a T-shirt and bottle of coke [for payment for material]. Well, that's not dissimilar to what happened, because there were certainly times I can remember in the early days where proof of contract was the returned cheque, signed by the person who cashed it.

'A lot of the time there wasn't royalties; it was an outright purchase, which is of course absolutely unknown today, really. There was no copyrighting ownership, who owned what, in Jamaica for many years, so it wasn't ratified. There wasn't a contract, we didn't have renewals, options. You bought the music not off the artist but straight from the producer.'

With the company paying the Jamaican producer for the recording, the onus was on him to pay the singer – that is, if the performance hadn't been bought for a flat one-off fee. Another means of forming a deal with an artist would be to mail out a contract along with cheque made out to the performer, and if the cheque was cashed then the contract would be deemed in force.

In an interview between Dave Barker and Rob Randall in the 15 January 1972 edition of the *NME*, where Barker is complaining of being paid only £1,000 for his contribution to the smash hit 'Double Barrel', Lee Gopthal is quoted as saying: 'In fact, Barker and Collins aren't legally entitled to any share at all of the proceeds of the record's sales… You see, Ansel Collins had sold the backing tapes to Winston Riley [the producer] outright and Dave Barker was simply brought in as a session singer and paid a straight session fee.

'This is one of those deals, common in the record business, when the producer takes the gamble of laying out cash on an untried product. If, as is the frequent case, the disc fails to sell enough to cover production costs, the producer bears the loss and doesn't ask the artists or technicians to return their fees. So if, on the other hand, the gamble pays off and the record makes a lot of money, those same artists and technicians can hardly reasonably expect a share of the profits. In this case, Riley has given the boys £1,000 each out of the goodness of his heart.'

Rob Bell remembers Dave and Ansel and their Jamaican-style relaxed attitude: 'Dave and Ansel...two great guys who didn't have a clue [about promoting themselves]. Our promo guy, Dave Bloxham, set up a *Top Of The Pops* for them. Getting an act on *TOTP* meant a hit record, meant selling probably 10,000–40,000 copies after the show. Dave and Ansel never bothered to show. "Soon come, mon." Of course, they should have had someone to busy them along, but it didn't happen. Lost opportunity.'

But Trojan could not believe their luck as the minority music of reggae sidled up the glittering Top 20 and filled the coffers of a company that, not long before, had been peddling its wares out of the back of a minivan. Every record label owned a van or car that would travel around the record shops selling their particular brand of reggae. This small-man-and-a-van syndrome had originated in Kingston, where it had sometimes been taken to extremes with a guy on a pushbike hawking half a dozen singles from shop to shop.

The surprising buying power of the skinheads had taken Trojan and, marginally, its rivals Pama and the Melodisc offshoot Fab Records into the big time. This was no longer a little company just ticking over – it was big business, and so was reggae. Even the hallowed pages of the *NME* and *Melody Maker* were forced to pay respect, with exotically named experts like Henderson Dalrymple and the amalgam Brutus Crombie pronouncing judgement on the latest sounds from Music House. The end of the '60s and the beginning of the new decade were indeed Trojan's halcyon days.

The problem of publicity was always high on the agenda with little or no help from the Jamaican producers whose work Trojan were anxious to promote as their main interest was in the song not the singer. Rob Bell again: 'One of the problems was that reggae was pigeonholed, just like blues is today... One paper – *NME*, I think – had a reggae columnist for a while, Rob Randall. Thus a photo [of an artist] might get published there. Also, we only got what was sent us from JA, and it was hard enough to get master tapes, let alone publicity stuff! So it was an uphill struggle from every aspect. And of course, the producer situation being what it was, there was often great confusion as to even who the artists were sometimes. Indeed, I myself was responsible for one cock-up, and that was calling toaster U Roy on his early UK releases Hugh Roy. As you know, Jamaicans tend to drop Hs, and to add them sometimes, *viz* Marley's line in "Trench Town Rock" "an 'ungry man is a hangry man".

'So little old middle-class Rob Bell, one of whose tasks it was to prepare label copy, very carefully typed Hugh Roy on the copy for those releases... As I did all

49

the label copy for at least two years, I am sure I am responsible for many cock-ups! However, in my defence, I took the details from the Jamaican label, or got the info from the producer – both sources being, of course, absolutely infallible!

(If it's any consolation to Rob, the toaster's debut LP, *Version Galore*, was issued by Duke Reid in Jamaica in a sleeve proclaiming the artist to be I-Roy!)

'Sometimes I would correct spellings – Hugh Roy again! – or insert better composer info. But by and large I used the information I was given. To return to a by now well-worn theme, the producers just weren't too bothered about the artists – and to be fair, it was the sound that sold records, not really the name.'

Rob then goes on to give an overview of the pitfalls of the artist riding on the crest of a hit to the UK and then being stranded: 'In JA, it was the producer, rather than the artist, that really called the shots. Thus when something went pop in the UK, there was pressure to come up with a follow-up that was equally commercial. Often by that time the artist was living in the UK, and his producer was in JA.

'His producer obviously wanted to capitalise on the UK success, but at that point Trojan UK was also in the mix, and there were, to some extent, conflicting points of view as to just what the follow up was to be, and also how it was to sound. The focus was on a follow-up single, rather than really developing the artist long term. And by that I mean developing the artist with material which brings out his or her creativity.

'The most obvious example of the right way to do this was Blackwell's involvement with Marley and The Wailers. The freedom to be creative without record company meddling is just one aspect. A degree of financial autonomy is another... But it was that second factor that Blackwell supplied to The Wailers...letting them spend time in the studio and paying them, too. (I know that all those monies would be treated as advances against royalties, but that is the record business – the fact is that he made it happen.) Thus one had the scenario of a JA artist moving to the UK upon achieving UK chart success, thus kind of divorcing themselves from their original source of creativity – their JA producer – being promoted as a pop act and concentrating on 45s rather than a rock act and concentrating on more profitable albums. I dig that this was in many ways a kind of self-fulfilling situation in that these acts came to success via a 45, and also that 45s were proven in the reggae/pop market and that albums were not. Nevertheless, with hindsight, had Trojan been able to spend more on developing these artists, perhaps they would have lasted longer. It is a subject that one can speculate upon endlessly.'

In interviews of the time (1969–71), many visiting artists commented on their versatility and ability to sing and play a far wider scope of music than just the reggae. They regarded the UK pop industry as a far more attractive proposition than the limited reggae market and were anxious, through the interviews, to make the point that they were happy with the commercial angle taken on their work with string arrangements being added. They would be very happy, they said, to sing pure pop songs or reggae-tinged chart music.

With the relocation to London, many did branch out, while resident London performers who had always incorporated soul and blues numbers within their repertoire continued to expand on that base. Due to a number of these artists now, in recent interviews, reversing their views of wanting and liking the commercial wash added to their work, few names can be mentioned. However, in the 28 August 1971 issue of *Disc*, Jackie Robinson of The Pioneers commented, 'We'd like people to stop calling us reggae singers. That makes it sound like we can only sing reggae… We can sing a lot of other things, styles, besides. We do a lot of soul in our act. Music is just music.'

This quote highlights the fact that many artists were very keen to be seen as just singers and were prepared to drop reggae and retune to pop and supper-club work in the expectation of making a far better living.

Rob Bell on the way Trojan marketed its product to the new skinhead audience: 'Trojan had its "Hot Shot" series. This was a marketing ploy to differentiate records that had pop potential as opposed to strictly ethnic appeal.

'The skinheads were seen as the pop end of the market. If they bought it, we loved them. At that point, the skinhead movement hadn't been co-opted by the National Front and the racist right. It was just another British teenage fad fuelled by Britain's mass-circulation papers. For some strange reason…the British music fans have always seemed to form clubs or movements, *viz* the Teds, Mods, etc.'

The 'Hot Shot' sleeve, with a bright orange target design, was overprinted in black with the record title, artist and catalogue number. Rob Bell: 'Thus we'd sleeve the first, say, 5,000 of a new Pioneers release, with the idea that the retailers and the public at large would get the idea that this particular release was "special."' Jimmy Cliff was even given the prestige of a full-colour picture sleeve for the 'Wonderful World, Beautiful People' chart single.

On the 'Maxi single' series, Rob says, 'The Maxi singles were, as I remember, a little gimmick to make them stand out from the clutter. The retail price was the same as for a regular single. An evolution from the "Hot Shot" concept, if you like.'

Trojan also instigated the 'Trojan Target' logo on album sleeves at this point, and produced T-shirts and other odd advertising merchandise. 'Trojan Target' was the album version of the 'Hot Shot' single sleeves, aiming for higher awareness of certain releases in the pop/skinhead market.

Thanks to Rob, we can at last answer the age-old question as to why a producer dedicated label such as Harry J or Song Bird would suddenly release work from other sources: 'The obvious answer would be that Trojan and the producer went

LIVERPOOL JOHN MOORES UNIVERSITY
LEARNING SERVICES

their separate ways, and Trojan was left with a useable quantity of label backgrounds sitting at Harrisons, the printers. Or that sales were so low on that producer's product that a decision was made to make that label a general-release type of label, handling product from various producers who didn't have their own designated label.'

One quite out-of-the-ordinary singer arrived at Trojan's door one day in 1970. Rob: 'Here's one artist probably no one in the world knows had a Trojan connection – Clyde McPhatter, lead singer of The Drifters in the early '50s, who then branched out to a solo career by around 1955 or '56. Huge influence on R&B – you can listen to thousands of R&B or doo-wop recordings from the '50s and hear Clyde's influence. Enormous.

'He was in London for a while around 1971 [the master index shows that Clyde recorded in 1970 for Trojan], down on his luck. I don't know how he showed up at Trojan, but he did. We cut a session with him and The Rudies, with ex-Pioneer Sydney Crooks as producer. Four tunes, assigned Song Bird matrices. Somewhere around SB 1027 to 1032 A and B, as far as I can recall... For some reason, Graham [Walker] and Lee [Gopthal] hated him, and I remember having to tell Clyde that we had no bread for him on the one occasion that I met him.

'It is not a moment that I recall with relish. He seemed like a nice man and was certainly a singer for whom I had a very high regard. As far as I know, these titles have never been issued.' In fact, one single, 'Denver', was released on the pop-slanted B&C label, and was one of the great vocalist's last records before alcoholism killed him prematurely in 1972.

In November 1969, Lee Perry and a small group of his Upsetters comprising Aston 'Family Man' Barrett on bass, his brother Carlton on drums, Alva 'Reggie' Lewis on guitar and Glen Adams on keyboards arrived at Heathrow Airport for a six-week string of dates set up on the success of 'Return Of Django'. A pre-recorded appearance on *Top Of The Pops* was also scheduled and recorded while the band were in Europe. The tour was organised by Commercial Entertainments, run by Bruce White and Tony Cousins. Bruce White gives some background to the company: 'Commercial Entertainments was started by myself and Tony Cousins in the mid '60s, and our first office was at 4 Denmark Street, aka Tin Pan Alley. We started booking artists to clubs and ballrooms throughout the UK and most of Europe. It was not too long before 50 per cent of our artists were of Jamaican origin when Delroy Williams – a nine-piece band at the time, with dancers [The Soul Explosion] – became one of our most in-demand bands.

'Not long after this, we met Graeme Goodall, who owned the Doctor Bird label. He had just released 'Israelites' by Desmond Dekker, on the Pyramid Label, and asked for our assistance on the promotion side. We agreed to help and decided we would service Radio 1 and other stations throughout England in the hopes of getting radio play.

'We contacted Leslie Kong of Beverley Records, JA, and arranged to bring Desmond Dekker & The Aces over to England for a promo tour. Our hard work on the radio stations paid off, and when we collected Desmond from the airport his record had reached Number One. We had approximately five bookings per week for Desmond, and he played Mecca Clubs such as Hammersmith Palais and the Orchid Ballroom, Purley, and also the Bailey's Clubs up north. He consistently broke box-office attendances. Desmond was an immediate success, and we'd often have to sneak him into the venue as there were queues of screaming fans encircling the building.

'We negotiated with Desmond and Leslie Kong to become his managers, which continued for approximately ten years. After this initial success we arranged promotional tours for many JA artists and we also became their managers.'

The Upsetters' tour took in a number of dates all around the UK but was subject to Lee Perry's erratic behaviour, although the tour was considered a success. Further Trojan/Upsetter singles – 'Night Doctor', 'The Vampire' and the suggestive 'Live Injection' – all did well, thanks, no doubt in part, to the tour.

Trojan Records assembled an Upsetters album titled *Return Of Django*, complete with a quality art-board gatefold sleeve. The album was issued in January 1970 and comprised the skinhead sound of tight rhythms and pumping organ. Three of the tracks, 'Night Doctor', Soulful I', and 'Man From MI5', had actually been issued on Trojan's debut Lee Perry album, *The Upsetter*, in November the previous year, although the company marketed *Django* as Perry's first album.

As the tour finished, Lee Perry's profile as a hitmaker had expanded and he had deals going with both Trojan Records and their main rival, Pama Records, and he spent much of his time jetting back and forth across the Atlantic. The four UK Upsetter band members – the two Barrett brothers, Reggie Lewis and Glen Adams – were left somewhat stranded in London, and Bruce White and Tony Cousins under the alias of Bruce Anthony (Bruce-and-Tony) offered to finance and produce an album with them. As Bruce White recounts, 'We liked the group and their music. Also, we were their managers and wanted to progress their career and felt they needed an album release.' He continues, regarding the recording sessions, 'Both myself and Tony were joint producers, involved musically, and we paid for the sessions. This was all recorded at Chalk Farm Studios with engineer Vic Keary.'

The resulting album, *The Good, The Bad And The Upsetters* saw issue on Trojan Records, resplendent with a sleeve shot of a group of West Indians in cowboy outfits and toting pistols, while a single from the album, 'Family Man' b/w 'Mellow Mood', found issue on Trojan's main label early in May 1970.

Rumour had it that some of the tracks were not by The Upsetters but instead by UK-based session players. This was not the case, however, and the album really did feature the four Kingston players, with the confusion possibly coming from the fact that the recording took place in London.

The end of the swinging '60s and the beginning of the new decade were to be the halcyon days for Trojan, with artists like Lee Perry's Upsetters hitting Number Five in October 1969 and Bob & Marcia making number five in March 1970 with Nina Simone's black pride anthem 'Young, Gifted And Black'. Although sung and made famous by Simone, she wrote only the music; the lyrics were penned by J Irvine Jr. Producer Harry Johnson already had the backing track recorded at Byron Lee's Dynamic Studio when he invited Bob Andy to voice the Nina Simone song over the top. Bob then invited his childhood sweetheart, Marcia Griffiths, to duet with him.

Although a gifted songwriter, as a creature of vibe and impulse Bob just felt like doing a recording at the time Harry J happened to approach him and was happy to cover such an outstanding piece of work. 'I didn't have any above-average expectations for the record's performance before it was released, and as far as I know neither did Harry J,' said Bob of the recording in a recent interview.

When asked about the overdubbed string arrangement, Bob said, 'I didn't know about the strings until we got to England, but I liked them; I always wanted to see greater attention paid to arrangements in reggae.' The first Bob and Marcia knew of the success of 'Young, Gifted And Black' was when producer Harry J asked them to ensure their passports were in order and to have their bags packed. The song was a smash hit in the UK and they were booked to appear on the hallowed *Top Of The Pops*.

In the recent interview, Bob was asked if he was surprised that 'Young, Gifted And Black' sold into the white market and that reggae music in general was supported massively by the skinhead youth culture over here. 'It was overwhelming' he replied. 'I didn't know anything about this angle [the skinheads] before I came. Bob Marley must have felt the same when he came. We knew that the majority of the country was white but couldn't have anticipated the avalanche of interest from the white fans. It was a head-spinner. It was a perfect example of how music can transcend all barriers and cultural differences.'

When asked of his first visit to the UK and how Trojan treated him in comparison to Coxson or Harry J back in Kingston, Bob replied, 'It was exciting. [Trojan] were excited to have another set of artists in the charts, and prospects looked good. But

I soon discovered they were excited about records rather than artists – they didn't think in terms of artist development.'

In the 17 July 1971 edition of *Record Mirror*, Simon Burnett interviewed Bob and Marcia and asked the pair how they saw their music. Bob's thoughtful reply underlined the power struggle in all aspects of Jamaican life and culture: 'I don't think that there is a real classification to put our music into. I suppose it could be called sunshine music. Jamaican music is crying out for social and economic freedom and for justice and it all involves politics. That's not because music is involved with politics but because politics is involved with everything.'

The follow up to 'Young, Gifted And Black', 'Pied Piper', and an album of the same name, were recorded at London's Chalk Farm Studio as Bob started to divide his time between the UK and Jamaica.

The engineer at Harry Johnson's session at Dynamic Studios on the day that 'Young, Gifted And Black' was recorded was Sid Bucknor. A first cousin to Clement 'Coxson' Dodd, Bucknor started his recording career at Studio One in around 1963. He was with Lee Perry when the youthful Wailers first auditioned for the studio and was impressed by their sound. History vindicates his opinion.

Sid estimates that, by the end of the decade, his hand was present in around 70 per cent of all the recordings coming from the small island, so great was the demand for his talents as a freelance producer and engineer. He estimates that the average number of recordings he would undertake in a normal day was a staggering 12. He never had to look for work as his reputation preceded him and most producers looked to him to turn a song into a hit.

As a professional engineer and producer at Dynamic Studios (after leaving Studio One and his freelance career), he recorded work for, among others, Bunny Lee, Harry Mudie, Alvin GG Ranglin and Leslie Kong. He was the engineer on Johnny Nash's smash 'I Can See Clearly Now', engineered the formative DJ work of producer Keith Hudson with Big Youth on 'Ace 90 Skank' and worked on the first three Marley Island albums. He has also remixed both Duke Reid's and Coxson's work at various times to give 'a more up-to-date sound'.

Sadly, much of Sid's work has been unrecognised, and it is only now that account has been taken of his vast input to Jamaican music. He recalls that, in the reggae heyday of the start of the '70s, 'I would be asked to do two mixes of a tune, one for Jamaica and a lighter one for the UK,' which is indicative of the increasing awareness of the producers of the UK as a new burgeoning market for their products and their need to retune the sound accordingly.

With the reggae boom in full swing, Sid was enticed to relocate to London, where he worked freelance at Chalk Farm Studio from 1974 until its closure. As a

YOUNG, GIFTED AND BLACK: THE STORY OF TROJAN RECORDS

freelance, the more work you did, the more you were paid, and he recalls working from 8:30am right through to starting a session at 3:30am the next morning with 'just a little sleep on the studio carpet'. He recorded 16 sessions a day as normal, so in-demand was he and the studio, with all the minor and major UK reggae players booking time either to voice-over pre-recorded Jamaican rhythms, overdub strings or lay down fresh home-grown reggae.

The technology was 'like from a different planet' Sid says with regard to the primitive Jamaican studios in comparison to Chalk Farm's more up-to-date controls. It says much for his skill that he was able to coax such marvellous sound from Studio One and Dynamic, despite the basic nature of their equipment.

One visitor to Chalk Farm, rock artist Wild Willie Barrett (quite often paired with John Otway), commented to Sid that the studio looked like an upturned dustbin, but the sound they got was great, and of course that was what counted. Of Chalk Farm, Sid recalls, 'I enjoyed my days there,' and of Trojan, for whom he cut many later sessions, 'They deserve credit for getting reggae music out there which no other reggae company could do.'

The man responsible for the string arrangement on 'Young, Gifted And Black was Clive Crawley, in conjunction with Chalk Farm Studio owner and engineer, Vic Keary. Clive recounts how the inspiration came about: 'We used to get the masters over from Jamaica and I decided to put brass and strings on them, and the first one I did was "Young, Gifted And Black". That was in 1970. The reason why I did it was that reggae was considered dance music at the time – the radio stations wouldn't play the music because they felt it was more for discos and parties – so I was just trying to make the records radio-friendly. I was wearing my record-plugger's hat and wanted to get the records aired. Anyway, I remember after that we did "Love Of The Common People", by Nicky Thomas, and The Pioneers' ["Let Your Yeah Be Yeah"]. I arranged for the overdubs to go on those all those.

'Johnny Arthey did that arrangement. [Arthey was an experienced bandleader and arranger but was more used to working in mainstream pop. His other claims to fame included producing hits for Vince Hill and acting as musical director for the 1970 and 1971 British entries in the Eurovision Song Contest.] It was the funniest thing, actually. I phoned up Johnny and I said, "I'm gonna send you down a tape of a song called 'Young, Gifted And Black'," 'cos Johnny was at the height of his fame in those days. He'd just done "Eloise" with Paul And Barry Ryan, which was an enormous hit. It was a wonderful arrangement, a fantastic arrangement.

'And so I sent him this record down and I said, "Now, what I want you to imagine Johnny is, listen to this record and imagine the strings on it. They don't have to be technically brilliant, but they must be fantastically rhythmic." He said,

"I understand." So he got tape and he made the arrangement and that was that. So that was an enormous hit, as you know.'

Many of the Trojan master tapes bear Crawley's name as producer, but the finished record often has a different name on the label. 'That's life,' says Clive. 'But if you just look at the realities…if the rhythm track and the vocals for a record were laid down by a guy in Jamaica – ie 'Young, Gifted And Black' – and I've picked up the tape over here and added to it [with overdubs], you don't really know the reason the record was aired on radio.' In other words, who should be given credit for the record's success at getting radio play – the Jamaican originator or Clive Crawley, who created a different soundscape with the overdubs?

Clive continues, 'But I was quite happy. They gave me the money for doing it, and all I was interested in was pound notes in those days. But what I didn't realise, what I should have realised, was the credit was worth more than the money. But at that time, I was a novice – I didn't understand – so I was enjoying myself so much, I didn't give a monkey's, really.'

Crawley's background had been originally in sales, and then record promotion for B&C and Trojan Records. 'I got into the music business as a result of a £10 bet, funnily enough,' he recalls. 'I was in a pub one night having a drink with Lee Gopthal and I asked him how business was. He had some [Musicland] retail shops as well as the record company, and he said the record shops were doing great but the record company was a bit slow. So I asked him, "Why is that?" and he said, "Well, we're not getting exposure on the records."

'"What do you mean?" I asked.

'"Well," he said, "we send them to the BBC but they never play them."

'"What do you mean, 'send them'?"

'"We post them."

'"No, that's not the way to do it. I don't know anything about it, but would imagine they call that 'plugging'."

'"Yeah, I suppose they do," said Lee, "but I couldn't do that." So I said, "Well, I bloody well could!" So I had a bet with him. I bet £10 I could get his record played on the radio.

'The next one he had coming out which was a song called "Kansas City", sung by Joya Landis. I went down and played the record, but I thought, "This is going to be tricky," 'cos, although it was a good record, it wasn't really a radio record, more a dancing record. But I went home and got a copy of the *Radio Times* – I've a £10 bet on this, this was half a week's wages, you know? So I go off down to the BBC, having looked up the names of these record shows, and the very first play I got was by guy called Ian Fenner, who produced a show called *Late Night Extra*, which was hosted by Terry Wogan.

'This was in 1968, and it went on every night of the week, Monday to Friday, from ten o'clock till midnight. And he's the first guy I go and see, this guy Fenner, and I gave him a lot of nonsense, you know, told him a few stories, a few dirty jokes, whatever, and eventually he said, "Are you going to play me something else?" I said yeah, and he said, "What have you got?"

'"Well, it's a new kind of music from the West Indies called reggae, and if you put it between a Frank Sinatra and an Ella Fitzgerald, it might sound half tidy."

'He quite liked that. "I'll play it Wednesday night, just before the 10:30 news," he said. I thought, "Christ, this is easy!"

So anyway, Wednesday night comes along and I'm sitting indoors with News at Ten on, transistor down one side of the armchair, and sure enough at about 10:25 Wogan comes on and says, "Now we got a new kind of music from the West Indies called reggae, and here to sing 'Kansas City' is Joya Landis."

'Well, you can imagine! I leaped out the chair and the following day I was down there [at Trojan], collecting my tenner. And then [Lee Gopthal] said, "Clive, why don't you carry on doing this? I'll give you a fiver for every play you get." And that was the start of my career. That led to 30 years in the record business.'

Crawley and the other UK-based producers would make use of the afore-mentioned Chalk Farm Studio, located in north London, as the normal place to lay down tracks and overdub string sections onto imported Jamaican rhythms with the assistance of engineer Sid Bucknor. The studio was owned and run by south Londoner Vic Keary, who gives an insight to his career up to opening Chalk Farm: 'The [first] studio was just an amateur thing. It must have been about 1957, but it was in a cow shed and the cows were still downstairs, so we were in the upstairs bit – it was quite a tall barn. We were recording local rock bands – it was the days of Cliff Richard And The Shadows. Having got my certificate from the college, first of all I went to Lansdowne [Studios], which is still one of the biggest three studios on London. It's in Lansdowne Road, in Notting Hill Gate.

'I got involved, oddly enough, with Adam Faith, because I also used to run a club in Farnborough, just a little thing while I was studying, and [Faith] used to come down to the club. He got involved with Larry Parnes [a leading pop impresario] and he said, "So why don't you go down to Lansdowne and see if they have anything going?" So I did, and they didn't.

'I then went on to do some work in television and didn't like it, and then I got a call from Lansdowne, and they said they had a place available and would I like to come down for an interview? I did and I got the job. That was 1960, when Joe Meek left, 'cos he was the chief engineer there and he went on to produce his own things.'

The shift in to Jamaican music happened almost by chance: 'I got a bit fed up with Lansdowne because I wasn't getting paid enough – as usually happens in studios in this country – and managed to start my own place. I managed to borrow some money and I worked in the old Radio Atlanta studios that then had become Radio Caroline. That was the top floor of 47 Dean Street, in the West End, and in fact we had a pirate flag on the roof because of the pirate-radio connection. We were on the top floor and there were nine flights of stairs and it was a bit of a job carrying a Hammond organ up nine flights of stairs and no lift. And having bands coming in and out was a bit hairy. That was '64 and '65. So we had Sugar And Dandy coming in...'

The recordings were issued on the small independent label Carnival: 'The one that really did well at this time was the Mel Turner single "White Christmas", on Carnival. That was brilliant. I got some television on that. Of course, the thing was, the distribution of Carnival was absolutely rubbish. There was a great demand for the thing, but nobody could buy it.'

The Carnival label was run by Alan Crawford, an Australian, recalls Vic: 'He also had a label called Cannon Records, and they did a sort of *Top Of the Pops* thing: they had a six-track EP with cover versions of all the hits. And that was pretty good practice for a sound engineer, to be frank, as you had to copy all the hits of the day. Old Ross McManus, who's Elvis Costello's father, used to come in and do a lot of the vocals – he just changed his voice on different records.

'Anyway, then I got involved with Dandy Livingstone, who sort of stuck with me for a long time, because we left the West End because Alan Crawford's company went bust, and we were kicked out so we started another studio in the Old Kent Road, in what is now the Workhouse. [This was the famous Maximum Sound.] We had Prince Buster and Rico, the trombone player, in there. These things came out on Blue Beat. In fact, I used to work for both Blue Beat/Melodisc and R&B/Ska Beat. I used to sell records for them around 1967/68... I decided to take a break from making music and went on the road, selling. I used to drive a van up and do the north of England – Leeds, Birmingham Manchester, Liverpool and about as far as Leicester.'

Vic remembers the main nucleus of the studio band and an embarrassing moment for The Cimarons: 'It used to be The Cimarons plus Trevor Starr. Trevor is now the boss at Theorum Music – he was a bloody good guitarist. The other band was of course Greyhound, aka The Rudies. They used to do quite a few backing tracks.

'The Cimarons once said to me, "You'll never get a Jamaican sound here. You have to be in Jamaica to get the right sound." They used to get annoyed, as they felt it was my fault that they could never get the right sound at Chalk Farm.

'Then Sly and Robbie came over and Trevor was also on the session, and they used The Cimarons' drum kit, but Robbie had his own bass and he said, "Just plug the bass in, man. Don't do anything to it. It'll sound perfect." So I did that, and it did. And Sly just sort of retuned the drums a bit, and it was the way he played them. He played them much quieter than The Cimarons did, and it sounded just like it came out of Kingston – exactly the Jamaican sound. Of course, The Cimarons were really brought down by that.'

Chalk Farm Studio, although not tied to Trojan, suffered badly with the latter's downfall in 1975, having been in operation since 1968, and found it a struggle after their departure. About 70 per cent of the studio's work in the early '70s was for Trojan.

'We used to do a lot of work for Bunny Lee,' remembers Vic. 'Bunny would come over with a lot of tapes, and he had a guy called Ken Elliott, who played synthesiser, and we had this band that recorded as The Vulcans. Bunny did an awful lot with Ken. But about every six months, Bunny would turn up totally unannounced and say, "Hey man, I just want a couple of hours in the studio to do some voicing." And he'd turn up with all these guys – Scratch Perry would go around with him as well. I got used to this, as he'd ask for a couple of hours and spend about 12 hours – that was his usual average. So he'd ring around, either Trojan or Pama or Creole, and say he was at the studio and ask them if they'd pay for studio time, and almost always they'd say yes. So that was it. He'd ask for a couple of hours and stay all night.'

Sadly, the Chalk Farm Studio is now an off-licence. Vic describes the final days of the studio: 'It wasn't just the money that Trojan owed us when they went in to liquidation, which was quite a lot in those days; it was also the fact that the whole reggae thing died. The studio was mainly geared to reggae and we really put most of our eggs in one basket – Trojan was our biggest client by far, although we did quite bit with Creole and Pama. So after Trojan went down, the studio was a struggle until about 1982, and then the rent went up to about triple what it was before, as Chalk Farm became a very desirable area and we were sort of forced out. We just couldn't afford it, so we packed up.'

The first major Reggae Festival, held at the Empire Pool, Wembley, on Sunday 26 April 1970, found Bob & Marcia performing their hit, with Desmond Dekker, The Pioneers, The Maytals and John Holt in the line-up and with backing from Byron Lee's band and The Pyramids. The show was compered by Count Prince Miller, who also belted out a lively rendition of his current smash, 'Mule Train'. 'What a guy!' enthuses Rob Bell. 'A big, big man with an equally big sense of humour.' The appreciative audience was a mixed bag of West Indians, hippies, the curious and, of course, those new appreciators of the sound, the skinheads.

The event was captured on film by director Horace Ove in a documentary called simply *Reggae*, which cut the concert performances in between interviews with leading figures in the music of the day. DJ Mike Raven provided a very succinct and insightful progression of the music and the trials of getting mainstream airplay. He also commented that the newer UK sound wasn't to his taste and he preferred the 'real Jamaican stuff'.

Trojan Records' Lee Gopthal and Graham Walker concurred on the difficulties of getting daytime radio play, providing illustrations of the vast numbers of units sold with still no help from the BBC. Gopthal went on to say that general record buyers did not classify music; they just bought what they liked.

Meanwhile, UK producer Dave Hadfield, along with Doctor Bird Group owner Graeme Goodall, confirmed just how hard it was for non-Jamaicans to pick up the beat. They predicted that they saw reggae as the next big thing, albeit in a more commercialised style.

Reggae saw a very limited release into specialist cinemas at the time. Sadly, it has now not been aired for over 30 years and is unavailable on any video or DVD format. This is a great pity, as it is one of the only professional films covering the UK side of reggae development as the '60s turned to the '70s and has some sparkling concert footage.

Rob Bell recounts a story regarding The Maytals which may well have taken place at the time they were performing at the Reggae Festival in Wembley: 'I remember a buddy of mine being asked to find some grass for The Maytals for a very early UK tour of theirs. He managed to find a pound, which back then – even in those euphoric days – was a heck of a lot of marijuana. The story went that The Maytals smoked it all in two days and returned to JA on the third day complaining about the dire English winter weather and the absolute dearth of smokeable pot. Whether this is really true, I don't know, but it is a fine story.'

By 1971, Bruce White and Tony Cousins' Commercial Entertainments agency had made significant inroads into the Jamaican music business. 'We managed, or were agency for, most major Jamaican artists,' affirms Bruce. 'It was at this stage that we were approached by Graham Walker of Trojan Records to see if we were interested in them buying 50 per cent of Commercial Entertainments. Meetings were subsequently set up with Lee Gopthal and Dave Betteridge, directors of Trojan Records. We negotiated a deal between us for £7,000 and formed Trojan Artistes Management Ltd between us. The directors were myself, Tony Cousins, Lee Gopthal and Dave Betteridge.

'Myself and Tony Cousins moved the company into Music House, Neasden Lane – Trojan's base – so that we could work closer together with the record company. More hits followed, and Tony and I handled the booking and management of the artists. By now, Tony and I had become very interested in the record side of the business and sold our 50 per cent of Trojan Artistes Management Ltd to the other directors and moved on to pursue our record career.

'About six months later, we were asked to attend a meeting with Lee Gopthal and Graham Walker where they asked us if we would consider managing Desmond Dekker again. This we did, and not long after many other artists followed. Commercial Entertainments became active again! It was total coincidence that Lee's company was called Beat & Commercial, and it was in no way connected to Commercial Entertainments.'

In March 1971, a new sound captured the coveted Number One spot: the sound of 'Double Barrel' by Dave And Ansel Collins. Dave Barker's enthusiastic DJ work over a rolling rhythm was the first many people had heard of the new craze sweeping the Kingston dancehalls. The track's producer Winston Riley, in an interview published in *NME*, said of the track, 'The approach to "Double Barrel" was a conscious attempt to create something different, an unusual song with an unusual treatment in a bid to knock down a great deal of the competition back home.'

'Double Barrel' appeared on a UK version of Riley's Techniques label, which Trojan had formed to carry his production work in the UK. The backing rhythm track had been recorded by keyboard player Ansel Collins, who then sold it on to Riley, as he was unable to finance its progression on to vinyl. This was standard practice, as Collins had previously recorded and sold the 'Night Doctor' recording to Lee Perry, who achieved considerable success with it under his alias as The Upsetters.

Riley decided to spice up the organ-based sound of 'Double Barrel' and employed vocalist Dave Barker to strut his DJ stuff over the top (in every sense) prior to its release. So Dave and Ansel were not a duo in the accepted sense of the term. 'When "Double Barrel" was already a best selling single, Ansel Collins and I hadn't even met,' revealed Dave in an *NME* interview of 15 January 1972. By this time, Ansel Collins and Winston Riley had returned to the Kingston studios to cut more rhythm tracks and Dave had opted to stay on in London and 'make it on my own as Dave Barker'.

Lee Gopthal was justifiably proud of the success of 'Double Barrel', as he recounts in an interview for *Melody Maker* conducted by Rob Randall: 'I spent months trying to encourage our pluggers to push it for me, but they said, "Look, we'll be laughed out of the Beeb." Our promotions man was a DJ before he joined us. [I said], "We've got a very good plugger in Clive Crawley. I feel we've got fantastic promotion and that, once we see a little bit of action, we can make a record. All we need is the right response from, say, the airplay situation."'

The airplay was at first grudgingly given until the mainstream retailers reported a growing demand, and Radio 1 then started programming it into their prime-time shows. The fact that 'Double Barrel' made it out of the reggae clubs at all says a lot for Gopthal's faith in his staff and product.

While on the Double Barrel tour, Dave Barker spoke to *Record Mirror*'s Lon Goddard about the music scene back home: 'Reggae is the big thing back in Jamaica. Reggae is the big monster beat – it swings with a down-to-earth soul feeling. There aren't any heavy blues bands there; most people like a lot of reggae and most of the Tamla records.

'I would love to see some of the other bands back home have some success. People like Delroy Wilson and John Holt make reggae records that could do very well here. Sometimes the English reggae records are a little more like rock 'n' roll to be the real thing.'

As reggae gained a firm hold in the charts and minds of Mr Average Record Buyer, the stars of rock took notice, including The Rolling Stones, who had championed black music since their early days. Under the headline 'Rudies Play At Mick Jagger's Wedding', the 10 June 1971 issue of US music magazine *Rolling Stone* reported, 'At the slightly seedy Cafe des Arts, where the reception was held, a local band opened the show and flopped. Next came The Rudies, a thumping reggae group big in their own scene in Britain. They lifted up plenty of souls ready for a set by Terry Reid and his band.'

The traditional way a Jamaican bought his music was on a seven-inch single. This accepted norm was the result of the original sound-system culture of the late '50s, after the passing of the fragile shellac 78rpm records. DJs would play seven-inch singles or one-off soft wax dub plates. Also, the major producers' first forays into record retailing to the general public were mainly singles, with only the odd LP, which usually collected the producer's work with a variety of artists. In general, the album format was restricted to more traditional folk songs or mento recordings of local groups, which big-spending tourists could buy and take home. For Kingston residents, a quick fix of The Skatalites or Jackie Opel, running in sometimes at little over two minutes, was the desired way to hear the music.

In Britain, Island had tried out the long-playing format as early as 1963, with albums by their top signings such as Derrick Morgan's *Forward March* and the uplifting two-part harmonies of *The Blues Busters*, while R&B Discs issued collections of The Maytals and Delroy Wilson, but none had succeeded in selling in appreciable quantities. Island had also issued, in 1967, the *Duke Reid Rock's Steady* LP, with the Island ILP prefix, but on a deep-orange 'Trojan' label specifically designed for Reid's UK releases. It too had sold poorly, even though the music contained in its bands was some of the finest of the age and many of the tracks had been good sellers as single releases.

In 1968, Trojan tried their hand at the album market and issued their first three long-players. Two were at full price and marked with the TRL (Trojan Records Long-player) prefix: 'single-artist collections *Follow That Donkey* from The Brother Dan All Stars' (alias the ubiquitous Dandy) and *Dandy Returns* (also from Mr Thompson, *sans* pseudonym). The third was a budget various-artists album of Dandy productions, with the TBL (Trojan Budget Long-player) prefix, entitled *Let's Catch The Beat*. None of these titles made any appreciable impact on the scene and instead merely served to emulate what Island and R&B had already discovered.

Undeterred by this, Lee Gopthal commissioned a market-research survey to find out what the problem with albums was and why so few were purchased, at a time when the LP was overtaking the single in the pop and rock markets. The results threw up two facts. Firstly, they were considered too expensive. Secondly, the overall sound of a single-artist album made for uninteresting listening. Buyers wanted a variety of sounds: different tempos, different rhythms and, above all, different voices, just as they would hear at a sound-system dance.

With this in mind, the astute Gopthal decided to launch a series of budget albums, but at such a low price that sacrifices had to be made. To cut costs, he decided to use existing material that had already seen the light of day on singles (and which had therefore amortised its original costs). The first LP to roll of the presses was *Tighten Up*, which consisted mainly of previous Trojan singles and was identified as a budget release by its TTL prefix (although no one can now recall what these initials stood for).

Rob Bell remembers, 'Full-price ska/reggae albums sold in minute quantities. The *Tighten Up* series did sell well, but that was because they consisted of compilations of singles that had already sold very well indeed. Trojan wanted to piggyback other titles...hence the ambitious TTL reissue project.'

Priced at just 14/6d – the cost of two singles – this album moved units, and its first pressing on the original all-orange Trojan label sold out quickly. It was repressed with a slightly altered sleeve design using the new orange-and-white label design, which was introduced in 1969.

The other side of the rock-bottom-priced TTL series was to be a lavish reissue programme of previous Island albums from notable artists like Derrick Harriott and Derrick Morgan, alongside early collections of singles like 'Club Ska 67'.

Rob Bell again: 'You will recall Island owned half of Trojan, with B&C owning the other half. Island formed Trojan in order that Island focus on pop. Island still wanted to market its Jamaican masters, and old product was reissued through Trojan. The entire Island Jamaican LP catalogue was scheduled to be reissued on the TTL series. I think everything got mastered, but possibly not everything got released.

'There was always a market for oldies. Singles, for instance, had a fairly long life – providing, of course, they had been good sellers to begin with. So the reissuing of old product made some sense. It may perhaps have been a way for Trojan to physically get its hands on catalogue that was previously owned by Island. Also, we exported a modest amount of stuff to Africa, especially older stuff. Also, it may well be that, when the expansion of the TTL series – using the old Island albums – was planned, it was also the time of the anticipated Trojan invasion of the USA. There is always good money to be made from exporting finished product. I recently came across a Beverley's Jamaican pressing of *Forward March* in a TTL jacket with "Copy For Trojan" handwritten across the front.' No doubt this was the master copy to be dubbed from to create the Trojan issue. In actual fact, a considerable number of ex-Island TTL album titles were advertised but never found their way to the high street.

By this time, the skinheads had got involved in reggae and, as many of them were too short of cash to buy all the singles as they were released, a budget-price collection suited them just right. They didn't mind the time lapse between the various tracks' issue on seven-inch and the arrival of the album, and pushed high street retailers into opening new 'Reggae' sections in their racks. Even so, that time lapse could be quite considerable, with a record sometimes gaining a release in London six months behind Kingston, with the *Tighten Up* album series collecting the tracks together a few months after that.

Tighten Up Volume 2 appeared quickly afterwards and was not only much more up to date in its tracks; it was also a sizzling selection of recordings. It really hit the spot with both West Indians and the skinheads, who flocked to every record store to grab a copy. Gone was the Caribbean BOAC picture of a happy West Indian girl and in came a bare female midriff with the album title written in what looked like lipstick on her stomach. *Tighten Up Volume 2* was Trojan's all-time best-selling album and would remain available for many years, such was its enduring popularity. It even scored in the pop-album charts, the entry rules for which were promptly revised to exclude budget records!

Tighten Up Volume 3, issued in 1970, took the pretty girl off the sleeve and on to the bedroom wall with a splendid double-album-sized poster nestled in a die-cut sleeve. The young lady peeped through the central hole and, when the poster was opened out, revealed the titles of all the album's tracks painted on her finely toned body. It may have been a gimmick, but because of the poster *Tighten Up Volume 3* became legendary in every school classroom and extremely popular on the skinheads' walls.

The *Club Reggae* and *Reggae Chartbusters* series of albums followed the *Tighten Up* lead in the budget-album racks. Trojan, in their desire to enlighten the music world to the delights of reggae, duplicated many tracks across the three series of LPs, although a cynic might say that this was done to derive maximum profit from their recordings.

Single-artist sets, like The Ethiopians' superb *Reggae Power*, which was a favourite with West Indians and skinheads alike, and single-producer sets like *Hot Shots Of Reggae*, showcasing Leslie Kong's bouncing board work, soon appeared, still at budget prices.

Many of these compilations were nothing more than a collection of singles placed together by Trojan. Joe Sinclair remembers pulling together The Maytals' *From The Roots* LP from some of their currently popular singles, alongside working out which titles would go on the *Tighten Up* series from Volume 5 onwards. (The previous four had been compiled by Rob Bell.) Joe and Rob also compiled the superb 1972 triple-album set *The Trojan Story*, the first retrospective collection of Jamaican music (the *History Of Ska* album had been issued by Bamboo Records but covered only the R&B to the ska-beat periods), most of whose vintage tracks were dubbed directly from Jamaican vinyl copies in Joe's collection.

Trojan's album sleeves were a mix of re-using Jamaican graphics, the 'pretty girl' image (some of the early *Tighten Up* series were graced by professional models) and contrived shots taken around the area of the Trojan offices. Rob Bell recalls the *Liquidator* album cover: 'My secretary, whom I inherited from Graham [Walker], was Bertilia someone or other. Everyone called her Tilly. She was on the *Liquidator* cover, together with Henry Glasgow, who was a contractor – he did odd jobs around Music House sometimes. She may be on other covers.' In fact, she also appeared on the front cover of the *Soul Rebels* LP.

The sleeve of the debut TRL album, *Follow That Donkey*, shows Musicland shop managers Webster Shrowder and Desmond Bryan along with Desmond's brother, 'Lenky'. Anyone available was drafted in to form a picture, whether it be relevant or not, should there be no available graphics from the Jamaican counterpart.

Shortly after compiling *The Trojan Story*, Rob Bell, tired of the London rat-race, left Trojan and moved to Wales, where he spent some years as a shepherd. He returned to the music business in around 1980 to manage a hot new US band called Roomful Of Blues, a post he held until 2002.

Many high-street retailers disliked stocking reggae singles due to their poor sound quality. Joe Sinclair explains the reason: 'Apart from the big producers like Leslie Kong and Byron Lee, who provided us with master tapes, we always had to dub off a record for our releases.' In other words, a normal Jamaican-pressed record would be used as the master copy for the Trojan release. All the inherent faults of the none-too-special JA pressing would thereby be transferred to the UK issue, along with a second step away from master-tape sound quality.

As the expansion of the reggae market took hold, individual producers were allotted their own singles labels by Trojan, as we have already seen. In addition, a few albums were issued with distinctive producer branding. Sonia Pottinger's production on The Hippy Boys, *Reggae With The Hippy Boys*, appeared on her High Note label in 1969, the same year that Clancy Eccles' *Fire Corner* set – featuring King Stitt And The Dynamites – appeared on Clan Disc. Lee Perry had a whole host of long-players issued on his Upsetter brand, including The Wailers' moody *Soul Rebels* set, which reappeared a few months later on the main Trojan label. 'That was probably because it made the distribution set-up easier,' opines Rob. 'Phillips distributed Trojan – at least the "Hot Shot" series – but not all the other labels. Thus having all the albums on Trojan, rather than Amalgamated, Big Shot or what have you, meant we could sell more product.

'Trojan really got under way in 1969. The first Trojan 45 series [issued in 1967] was an Island label, 100 per cent. Then Island and B&C formed the joint venture called Trojan. The new Trojan 45 series then started at TR601. After a few weeks or months, product that was previously Island now was switched to Trojan, and then it became gradually apparent that it made sense to have more LP titles on Trojan in order to get them distributed through Phillips.'

Despite Trojan's efforts to make buyers aware of the benefits of the LP format, albums accounted for only one-ninth of the total sales for 1970, and the majority of those were various-artists compilations. The single was, and would always remain, the dominant force in Jamaican music, a situation which today's club culture carries forward, even after heavy pressure by the major labels to relocate all music to CD and, latterly, the new darlings of the age, SACD and DVD.

By the early 1970s, local radio had at last arrived in the UK. Even the BBC had to take notice of the number of chart placings afforded to reggae records and, as the trend appeared to be continuing, Auntie Beeb looked to set up minority music shows on those local stations thought to cover the inner-city areas where the music had its core audience. Unfortunately, by the time the behind-the-scenes machinations of the BBC got the shows in place, the skinhead cult was waning, and basically the corporation missed the boat, as far as peak audiences for reggae were concerned.

Nevertheless, tight one-hour slots were allocated to 'ethnic' broadcasting. One such programme was *Reggae Time*, hosted by Steve Barnard and transmitted every Sunday lunchtime from 1 pm to 2pm on BBC Radio London. Steve, in his inimitable, slightly haphazard manner, would play some of the latest releases, and the oddly named Tony Fish would scale the list of notable London-area dances at lightning speed.

It was an all-too-brief show. Radio London latterly elongated *Reggae Time* to two hours at the tail end of the '70s and installed Tony Williams as presenter, soon to be joined in 1978 by one David Rodigan, a white actor-turned-presenter who quickly gained his own show, alternating week by week with Williams.

Capital Radio, London's new independent station, latched onto the black music scene much more quickly than the grand old BBC and, from its inception, quickly filled its time slots with the best club music around. Its *TV On Reggae* was aired on Saturday nights, with ex-pirate DJ and hard rocker Tommy Vance somewhat out of his league in attempting to present a reggae show. Luckily, he had a sidekick by the name of Cliff St Lewis, who knew his stuff and was an occasional Trojan recording artist. And as the hard roots era moved across from Jamaica, London was lucky enough to have two legal reggae radio shows.

The stumbling *TV On Reggae* did not last too long, and in 1979 David Rodigan was installed at Capital Towers with his own Saturday late-night show *Roots Rockers*, which initially went out from 11pm to 1am and then moved to an earlier slot, while Tony Williams was left with the BBC show.

Rodigan was to host the show for 11 years before moving across to the newly legalised Kiss FM, where Joey Jay was already running a roots reggae show on Sunday evenings. Rodigan was to concentrate more on the modern dancehall business while Jay took the listeners through new and old roots classics. London sound system Menassah also ran a show on Kiss FM, running through Saturday night to early Sunday morning, playing the latest in UK dub alongside exemplary roots-reggae sides.

The music press of the mid '70s continued to report frustration that chart success was not an easy thing for a reggae artist to achieve, due to the vicious circle of 'no hit, no airplay; no airplay, no hit'. The problem remained the same – the specialist soul and reggae shops were not included in the sales-charting process. 'These early sales are important,' noted Lee Gopthal. 'Once a record shows at the bottom of the chart, most shops will stock it, Radio 1 will start to play it and the pop fans will pick up on it.'

A reggae record could sell a staggering 35,000 copies and still not reach the national Top 50. Many artists felt disillusioned about trying to change their musical style to get commercial success. In 1972, when 'Have A Little Faith' by Nicky Thomas had shot to the Number One position in the Jamaican charts and sold a massive 50,000 copies out there, its UK Trojan pressing was given no airplay on the BBC. By this stage, Trojan was exploiting every possible promotional outlet. Clubs and discos received promo releases, as did a network of over 100 reggae and soul shops and even hospital and factory radio stations.

In 1972, Island and B&C ended their joint ownership of the Trojan group due to what they described at the time as 'policy differences', and B&C took full control. Island, utilising their newly inaugurated Blue Mountain label, decided to concentrate on developing specific artists, such as The Wailers and Toots & The Maytals, as opposed to tying in with particular producers. Lee Gopthal recognised the wisdom of this move.

The palatable, easy-listening sound of strings dubbed over reggae rhythms proved to make a narrow pathway to the Top 20 and the odd spot on *Top Of The Pops* in the early '70s, although these were still almost token appearances to appease the many underground-reggae fans. In 1973, Trojan, under the guidance of Joe Sinclair, issued two volumes of *Reggae Strings*, with top rhythms of the day awash with sweeping and diving string arrangements by Johnny Arthey. 'This was my pet project,' observed Joe Sinclair, 'a kind of driving music, as I had a Jensen at the time with an eight-track stereo, and I thought it would sound good.'

In that same year, also through Joe's inspiration, the Shrowder/Bryan/Sinclair set-up instigated the first album of reggae tracks overdubbed with synthesiser, courtesy of Ken Elliott, masquerading as 'The Vulcans'. Taking space and, more pointedly, the *Star Trek* TV series as its theme, the album of that name carried some well-loved rhythms from producers like Bunny Lee and redesigned them for the '70s easy-listening crowd. It was an inspired release and remains one of the highlights of Trojan's LP back catalogue.

By 1973, the sound of British reggae was well established and some record companies had decided to end their involvement with the Jamaican producers. The *NME* of 27 January that year carried an article by Danny Holloway catchily entitled 'Suddenly Reggae Is Up After Being Almost Booted To Death By The Skins'. In it, Jeffrey Palmer of Pama Records was quoted as saying, 'I have stopped dealing with the Jamaican scene because it is too hard to control. You never know what the producers are up to behind your back. They have been known to sell the same record both to me and to Lee Gopthal at Trojan. When that happens, neither one will sell because the record shops don't like it.' This reiterates the problem recounted earlier with Joe Sinclair and Trojan.

'We've had too many problems dealing with Jamaica,' continued Jeffrey Palmer, explaining Pama's new policy. 'Our future is now with reggae in England. We've got our own artists and facilities, and our reggae is different anyway.'

'I don't dislike the fact that the music has become anglicised,' said David Betteridge, by now the MD of Island. 'It needs to have strings and horns at times, like any music. I tend to lean towards pop reggae more than ethnic reggae. To me, a band like Greyhound are capable of playing good ethnic reggae, but a lot of people in Jamaica would disagree with me.'

The pop reggae produced in the UK was by now very different from its Jamaican counterpart, particularly as the JA style was evolving into the Rasta-roots sound. In a perceptive article in *The Times* on 19 March 1973, Richard Williams glimpsed the future: 'Sometime during the coming summer, reggae will become a vital force in pop music – perhaps, for a while at least, *the* force. For those who have not heard, reggae is the Jamaican version of rhythm and blues, black popular music based on a highly individual swaying, clip-clopping beat in which the musicians subtly imply as much as they actually play.

'Among British rock snobs, reggae has been a dirty word for the last couple of years. They have called it dull, crude and monotonous, entirely missing the point that this is functional dance music, still close to its people and a total stranger to sophistication. It is the story of the blues all over again. That attitude is changing, led by top white rock musicians. Paul Simon, The Rolling Stones, Cat Stevens and Elton John have all recorded in Jamaica, savouring its loose, relaxed atmosphere, while Paul McCartney's Wings and the J Geils Band have adapted the reggae beat to their own ends – with not entirely successful results.

'The next step is an album called *Catch A Fire* by a long-established Jamaican group called The Wailers. This record is the one which will snare rock fans, making them aware of reggae's inherent beauty and vast potential. Bob Marley, the group's leader and chief songwriter, has added slide guitar, electric piano and synthesiser to the basic rhythm section, thus spicing up the sound, but sparingly so that the funky essence remains.'

In actual fact, Marley had not instigated the overdubs to *Catch A Fire*, and The Wailers did not play the overdubbed instruments; these were provided by London-based session musicians hired by Chris Blackwell, who at that time had his eye firmly set to break Marley and co into the white rock arena. The Basing Street Studio overdubs had definitely done their job and caught the ear of the white-music press, as illustrated by Richard Williams' comments in same *Times* article: 'He is a marvellously flexible lead singer, stitching breathtaking little ornamental phrases on to memorable melodies – like the slow, sensual "Stir It Up", a magnificent love song – and his arrangements for the background vocals are quite the equal of, say, The Impressions. His bassist and drummer lie right back on the beat, keeping decoration to a minimum, and I defy you not to dance to it.'

Rob Bell had seen Marley's potential when his work was being issued by Trojan prior to the Island deal: 'I loved Lee Perry's Marley stuff: "Small Axe", "Duppy Conqueror" *et al*…really very different, very soulful. Riveting sounds. His singles on Upsetter sold very well, and it was no surprise to me when Blackwell got behind him.'

3 1975 To Date

Fall And Rise

By 1974, Joe Sinclair had left the employ of Trojan Records and his former producing partner, Webster Shrowder, had taken over the managing directorship of the mighty empire. By this time, Trojan were the UK market leaders by a country mile, controlling 75 per cent of the reggae market and with their records available across the counter in every high street store, something that their former rivals, Pama – who were taking a temporary break at this time – never managed.

Smaller, recently launched labels like Count Shelley, Lord Koos, Larry Lawrence's Ethnic and Ethnic Fight, Mr Coke's Magnet, Dennis Harris' DIP and the Creole/Cactus/ Rhino set-up, as well as a much-diminished Melodisc, competed for the other 25 per cent. As well as the reggae labels, Shrowder also controlled the People and Action soul labels at this stage, with hopes for a disco floor-filler like Don Downing's 'Lonely Days, Lonely Nights' always to the fore.

As MD of Trojan, Shrowder swung into action with a number of changes. He reduced the number of releases per week from ten to four, yet maintained the same level of sales as previously. He also streamlined the number of producers with whom Trojan had deals in Jamaica, ensuring too that new deals were made in conjunction with the artist as well as the producer. He explained his methods to *Black Music* magazine: 'Producers don't really look after the artists in Jamaica, so it's up to us to ensure that there's fair treatment, otherwise it will reflect on us. You see, there are only two companies in Jamaica, Dynamic and Federal. Most of the others are just little labels, one-man things. They hire an artist, produce a record, get it pressed and take it around on a scooter and flog it to the shops. Too much of it is amateurish, and that's why the artists get robbed. So we like to deal with producers who do their business properly. We do everything legally. We don't issue records unless a particular artist or product is contracted to us, and we only deal in royalties.'

With nationwide distribution through B&C, and as many records being sold through Muzik City shops, Trojan seemed to be at the top of the musical food chain with no natural predators. But an unfortunate remark from the aforementioned *Black Music* article gives an indication that Shrowder did not see the growing threat that was undermining Trojan's position. 'I don't know what these small labels are doing,' he said. 'I'd like them to be successful, but there's really no competition.' He was apparently oblivious to the threat that was creeping up on the giant.

By 1974, an underground reggae scene was thriving at clubs such as Bluesville in Wood Green, the Cobweb in Hornsey, the Crypt in Deptford, the Four Aces in Dalston and larger venues, such as the Pama-owned London Apollo in Willesden and the All Nations in Hackney. Even Ronnie Scott's, one of London's leading jazz clubs, ran specific reggae nights that attracted a different crowd from their usual bearded clientele.

The younger audiences at these clubs were dissatisfied with the pop reggae that Trojan was producing. They felt that the emotion that was the very soul of the music had been removed, and although the new music was popular with the older generation, their children couldn't relate to it. The youth market was struggling to find worthwhile Trojan releases to buy as the company's output focused tighter and tighter on desperate cover versions of happy pop songs. The smaller labels, however, had recognised that the so-called ethnic reggae was selling not only to the West Indian population of the UK but also to young white fans who wanted to hear of struggle and torment.

By late 1973, there were very few radio shows playing reggae music and music-magazine reviews had succinctly divided reggae into two opposing styles: in one corner nestled the chart-hopeful soft-and-cheery commercial product, while in the other stood bass-heavy, uncompromisingly raw reggae with firebrand lyrics of revolution and Rasta. This was ethnic reggae, which would evolve into the Roots-and-culture sound of a couple of years later, taking reggae from the ghetto to *Top Of The Pops*.

Speaking to *Black Music* magazine in February 1974, Dandy Livingstone explained the need to change his musical image to a new and deeper sound: 'I changed labels from Trojan to B&C/Mooncrest because I wanted to change my musical direction. I believe I wouldn't have been able to do that if I had stayed with Trojan.' Dandy did swing about, both in lyrics and in general sound, and made a handful of exemplary roots singles in the latter part of the '70s, but sadly his name was to be forever associated with the cheery 'Suzanne, Beware Of The Devil' and he found few listeners.

In a 1974 interview, Nicky Thomas reflected, 'I'm not interested whether the BBC want to play my songs or not. I lost £3,000 trying to make a song to please the BBC. I could have made down-to-earth ethnic reggae and the black people would have bought it. In future I'll make songs for the black market only.' Sadly, Nicky never regained his chart success, either in the pop mainstream or with ethnic West Indian buyers, and had faded from view by the end of the decade.

Old Trojan comrades like Lee Perry were enticed to sell their new, harder-sounding product to minor labels like Ethnic, who released some outstanding Upsetter material, such as 'Fist Of Fury', in the middle of the decade.

An indication of the mounting financial problems was the closure of various sub-labels like Upsetter, which ceased to exist in 1973. The use of cheap, plain, single-colour labels replaced the far more expensive multicolour designs in an effort to reduce costs. Harry J, Bread and Explosion, to name but three surviving labels, took to the monochromatic cover designs between 1973 and the sale of Trojan two years later.

White sound-system operator and independent producer Tony Ashfield recorded some one-off 'specials' with ex-Paragons vocalist John Holt in the early 1970s. The success of the records in the dancehall was spectacular and, based on that triumph, a Trojan employee suggested adding strings and orchestra to Holt's work in order to make it more smooth and palatable, in typical pursuit of the ever-sweetening reggae sound recorded in London.

The resulting *1,000 Volts Of Holt* album, released by Trojan Records in 1973 and awash with sweeping banks of strings and bittersweet melodies orchestrated by Ashfield, was a huge success. Based on this achievement, Trojan hired Ashfield as an in-house producer, with *carte blanche* to sign whomever he felt worthy, both in the UK and on trips to Jamaica.

Holt's 1974 chart smash 'Help Me Make It Through The Night' only furthered the Ashfield sound of sweetness. The collaboration between Holt and producer/arranger Keith Bonsoir continued the lush Ashfield tradition with the *2,000 Volts Of Holt* album, which was issued in 1976, just as the divide between JA roots-reality songs and London super-smooth supper-club reggae widened. Once again the nattily dressed Holt won new hearts with his exemplary crooning, aided by the full might of a horn-and-string section.

By the end of 1976, the suave John Holt orchestration had run its course, and when producer Bunny Lee delivered a no-frills Jamaican-recorded album of John singing reggae ballads Trojan decided to stay with the title, in keeping with the previous volumes. *3,000 Volts Of Holt* hit the streets early in 1977 and, although lacking the elaborate sophistication of its predecessors, still managed to become one of the label's all-time best-selling albums.

By this time, the new, harder-sounding product was starting to take hold both in the dancehalls and with the general reggae record buying public. At the same time, Trojan had complacently stocked the high street with sweet non-sellers and the little man was creeping into the market and moving his wares to the core audience that the crumbling giant courted.

At odds with their normal view of the current reggae sound, in March 1975 Trojan issued – somewhat surprisingly – the Dadawah album *Peace And Love*, featuring the unmistakable voice of Ras Michael Henry. *Peace And Love* was four long Nyahbinghi tracks spiced up with funky dub effects courtesy of the finest Kingston sessionmen. Producer Lloyd Charmers had captured the moving sound of the Rasta element in Jamaican music and combined it to perfect effect with the now sound of dub mixing.

The album charmed the reviewers (Carl Gayle gave it a four-star review in the April issue of *Black Music*) and the younger record-buying public, but Trojan failed to take the hint and continued to pursue the pop charts, although they did release some more 'roots'-orientated albums in May of the same year, such as Augustus Pablo's *Ital Dub* and the somewhat lacklustre Ras Michael album *Nyahbinghi*.

The particularly UK-based Lovers Rock scene was also just breaking out as 1975 moved along, with Louisa Mark's 'Caught You In A Lie' single on the tiny Safari Records imprint selling a staggering 10,000 copies in the first week of its release in June. Trojan almost missed the emerging sweet swinging new sound that was to sell an amazing amount of records as the decade moved on, with only the occasional record released, such as Matumbi's 'After Tonight', which was issued in 1977 after the Saga purchase. It was a style at odds with the harsh social commentary pouring from Kingston, with love and heartbreak the staples of the shrill-voiced teenage girl singers.

Black Music journalist Carl Gayle wrote a comprehensive piece on the fall of Trojan and the rise of the underdog small labels in the magazine's October 1975 issue. He also commented intriguingly on the success of Trojan sales to Europe, Australia and Japan, the latter of which had apparently had pressed and issued 30 Trojan albums just prior to the label's collapse and the Saga purchase. Sadly, no confirmation of these pressings has ever come to light.

So, despite releasing a couple of sizeable pop hits, the overall situation continued to worsen for Trojan as more strong-selling product was diverted from their door. The decline can be charted from the tail end of 1973 until 1975, when the company was taken over.

The details of this transfer are sketchy, but a report in the October 1976 issue of *Black Music* aimed to clarify the story. Trojan Records had made various allegations of professional misconduct against the magazine, and the article is summarised here in the absence of any other source of material facts.

Marcel Rodd, a Jewish businessman, had taken early retirement after a successful career in printing and publishing but had soon ended his self-imposed retirement to set up a pressing and distribution plant, specialising in children's records, in Kensal Rise, London W10. He had also licensed the Leisure Arts catalogue of classical albums from the USA. Frustrated by the monopolisation of high-street shops by HMV and Decca – the two leading classical-music labels in the 1950s – Rodd set up the mail-order company World Record Club. This flourished, and in 1960 he bought the Saga company, which specialised in budget-priced LPs of various types of music on its labels such as Saga and Fidelio.

By 1973, Rodd had built up a thriving and self-contained record company, complete with its own pressing plant, at the Kensal Rise premises and was seeking to expand his Saga empire. Indeed, he placed an advert in the trade paper *Music Week*, seeking to buy another record company as a going concern. Nothing came of this scheme at the time, but before long, and quite by chance, he became aware of Trojan Records.

In 1974, Trojan, frantically fulfilling orders for Ken Boothe's Number One hit 'Everything I Own', had used Saga's pressing capacity to manufacture £20,000 worth of records. They had difficulty paying for these, which of course brought them to the attention of Saga's chief accountant. This worthy, doubtless mindful of his boss's expansionist plans, duly told Mr Rodd about the company.

Wasting no time, Rodd attended a meeting with Trojan directors Lee Gopthal and the company's accountant, Brian Gibbon, to offer them a deal. According to *Black Music*, this deal would give Saga a ten-per-cent share of B&C/Trojan. In return, they would loan B&C/Trojan £150,000, which would be secured against the latter's audited assets of £600,000. However, the sagacious chief accountant then spent a week auditing the accounts himself and found that B&C/Trojan was grossly in deficit, with the result that Saga hurriedly pulled out of the deal.

Trojan then allegedly approached Saga and offered themselves for sale at a price of £25,000, valid for 48 hours only. The astute Rodd, not wishing to take on the company's liabilities, proposed that two new companies should be set up: B&C Recordings Ltd and Trojan Recordings Ltd. These firms would have the same directors as the previous companies and the same assets in terms of stock, record contracts, etc, but the financial liabilities of the previous companies would not be transferred to them. This 'what's in a name?' syndrome is a perfectly legal move for companies with cashflow problems, although for those workers involved whose jobs are on the line the procedure does not treat them particularly fairly.

So it was that these two 'new' companies that were immediately sold to Saga for £30,000. The article then reports that the funds received by the directors of B&C/Trojan should have been used to refloat the previous companies. Instead, the money was allegedly used to pay off overdrafts personally guaranteed by the B&C/Trojan directors. All the staff were dismissed and the companies went into voluntary liquidation. The latter part of this story seems to be somewhat supported by notices that appeared on 10 June 1975 in the *London Gazette*.

TROJAN RECORDS LIMITED

Notice is hereby given pursuant to Section 293 of the Companies Act, 1948, that a meeting of the Creditors of the above-named Company will be held at the Westbury Hotel, New Bond Street, Piccadilly, London W1, on Friday 20 June 1975 at 3:30 o'clock in the afternoon, for the purposes mentioned in Sections 294 and 295 of the said Act.

Dated this 4 June 1975. By order of the board (952).

L Gopthal, Director.

B&C RECORDS LIMITED

Notice is hereby given pursuant to Section 293 of the Companies Act, 1948, that a meeting of the Creditors of the above-named Company will be held at the Westbury Hotel, New Bond Street, Piccadilly, London W1, on Friday 20 June 1975 at 2 o'clock in the afternoon, for the purposes mentioned in Sections 294 and 296 of the said Act.

Dated this 4th June, 1975. By order of the board (954).

L Gopthal, Director.

These notices were followed in the same publication on 19 June, 1975 by this one:

In the High Court of Justice (Chancery Division).
Companies Court No 001980 of 1975.
In the matter of TROJAN RECORDS Limited and in the matter of the Companies Act, 1948.

Notice is hereby given that a petition for the winding-up of the above-named Company by the High Court of Justice was on the 10th day of June 1975 presented to the said Court by Mechanical Copyright Protection Society Limited, whose registered office is situated at Elgar House, 380 Streatham High Road, London SW16 3HR, and that the said petition is directed to be heard before the Court sitting at the Royal Courts of Justice, Strand, London WC2, on the 7th day of July 1975 and any Creditor or Contributary of the said Company desirous to support or oppose the making of an Order on the said petition may appear for that purpose and a copy of the petition will be furnished by the undersigned to any Creditor or Contributory of the said Company requiring such copy on payment of the regulated charge for the same.

Joynson-Hicks & Co, St Martins House, 140 Tottenham Court Road, London W1, Solicitors for the Petitioner.

NOTE: Any person who intends to appear on the hearing of the said Petition must serve on or send by post to the above-named notice in writing of his intention so to do. The notice must state the name and address of the person, or, if a firm, the name and address of the firm, and must be sent by post in sufficient time to reach the above named not later than 4 o'clock in the afternoon of the 4th day of July 1975.

An identical notice was also printed regarding B&C Records.

The later notices seem to imply some inability to pay royalties (the MCPS was, and is, the body responsible for their distribution), and this would certainly be supported by the negative feelings and reactions that have been encountered during the preparation of this book. The full details of the events that took place on these dates may never come to light; in researching this book, we have tried various official and unofficial sources of information and have come up with nothing but speculation. Even the MCPS are unable to assist, as their records have been destroyed after the passing of over a quarter of a century.

It appears that Saga thought that they were buying the rights to an extensive rock-music catalogue. However, by the date of the transaction, the B&C/Mooncrest (a B&C rock offshoot) contracts had expired and rock label Charisma had changed their distribution from B&C to Island. Marcel Rodd was therefore left with only an extensive catalogue of which he had no knowledge whatsoever. He recognised that Webster Shrowder would be a useful general manager, but soon this arrangement had to end as Shrowder had conflicting interests – he had formed his own reggae company, Vulcan, in association with former Bamboo label owner Junior Lincoln.

By the time of that *Black Music* article, the pressing plants were once again whirring into action, bringing Trojan back to life. As well as advertising on the full back cover of the magazine, Trojan was signing new acts and re-signing the popular acts from its former existence. Rodd was seen as a respectable and honest businessman with the initiative and professionalism to make reggae a money-spinner for those artists. But the circumstances surrounding that change of ownership have tarnished the name of Trojan to this day.

A number of artists had received little or no payment for their services when the original Trojan went into liquidation, and they turned to the new Rodd-owned company for reimbursement. As far as they were concerned, Trojan was Trojan, and Trojan owed them money, although of course all the outstanding debts were with the Official Receiver and Trojan Recordings Ltd was under no obligation to pay anyone for their previous efforts.

After the departure of Webster Shrowder, Bill Ross – previously the chief accountant of Saga – became a co-director of Trojan, along with Clive Stanhope, who was the ex-managing director of Dart Records. Stanhope knew very little about reggae music but had an extensive knowledge of record sales and distribution. Trojan hoped that his expertise would bring them back onto the marketplace.

Black-music journalist Tony Cummings filled the new company's A&R position, along with his assistant Floyd Lloyd Seivright, who also had an understanding of the reggae field. Floyd left after a short time, and noted reggae photographer and former Island Records A&R man Dave Hendley applied for the vacancy after a tip-off by distributor, DJ and label owner Mo Claridge. Dave recalls his lunchtime introductory interview with Marcel Rodd: 'We sat in his office – no windows, right down in the centre of the factory, with pipes all round the walls, nowhere near the Trojan offices on the top floor – and in comes this woman like a school dinner lady with a plate of dry ham sandwiches. That was the lunch!

'Marcel Rodd was a small wizened old man with a slightly sinister feel to him. He always wore a cream linen jacket, like out of *Casablanca*, and he had a slight air about him. The rumour that everyone in the reggae community knew was that he was supposed to have been Al Capone's driver and then a spy in the last war. I dunno why; I suppose just the way he acted and looked.'

With the departure of Tony Cummings, Dave Hendley was elevated to the A&R position, which was extremely well paid in comparison to similar jobs at other record companies. The good wages were strangely at odds with Marcel Rodd's 'penny pinching', as Dave called it, his determination not to pay the going rate for new work offered by various Jamaican producers.

So in the late '70s, Trojan was drifting, as the only product which producers would offer them was rejects from other deals or substandard work. Due to the company policy of not paying to the same level as their competitors, such as the rapidly expanding Greensleeves Records, Trojan's reputation in the marketplace had taken a dive. Marcel Rodd was determined to reverse this trend. And so February 1979 saw Dave Hendley, Mo Claridge and fast-rising reggae DJ David Rodigan heading out to Kingston. Dave's brief was to raise the Trojan flag in Kingston and sign up some acts – although the company had provided no contacts for him to visit.

Due to Dave's resourcefulness, the outcome was Sugar Minott's *Ghettology* album and The Morwells' 12" disco 45 'Kingston 12 Tuffie', with a stunning remix by courtesy of Prince Jammy. It wasn't much to show for the trip; the main problem was that Trojan, with their low money offers and poor contractual terms, just weren't competitive in the marketplace, as Dave explains: 'Trojan would pay £300 max for a disco 12" single, while the going rate was £400, and they would only pay up to £2,500 for an album, when up to £4,000 was the normal price. I badly wanted a Freddie McGregor album that Niney had and, give him his due, Rodd went to four grand, but Niney wouldn't let it go for that. Freddie was just so big back then. I tried for the 'Hard Time Pressure' 12" single from Sugar Minott but couldn't get it due to the money. In the end I put it out on my own Sufferers' Heights label. I offered Sugar a good deal and he took it.'

Neither were Trojan competitive contractually. They often offered low royalty rates and 'in perpetuity' contracts, which basically meant that they owned the rights to an artist's work for ever. Their rivals offered better royalty payments and a three-year contract, after which the artist's work was open to negotiation. Not surprisingly, Trojan found it hard to entice acts to sign on the dotted line.

Nevertheless, thanks mainly to Dave Hendley, Trojan did issue some excellent contemporary albums, such as a strong roots set by The Viceroys. In July 1979, Dave met Michael 'Mikey Dread' Campbell in New York and gained the rights to an LP that became one of Trojan's bestsellers of the late '70s, *Dread At The Controls*, which achieved significant sales in the white-student and new-wave markets. This was a rapidly-growing new area, leading on from the interest shown by the punks a couple of years earlier – when, for example, punk rebels The Clash had released a version of 'Police And Thieves – for the outspoken reggae with which they could identify, albeit only in spirit.

Island had been issuing LPs of Lee Perry productions such as the superb *Police And Thieves* set by Junior Murvin, which had been well received in the new-wave press, and they had put Marley well on the road to rebel-rock superstardom. Virgin's Front Line offshoot offered DJ Tapper Zukie, the supercool Gregory Isaacs and The Mighty Diamonds to the interested new listeners, while other names who drew large crowds at new-wave gigs included dub poet Linton Kwesi Johnson, Prince Hammer and the gruff-voiced Prince Far I.

These were established artists who had already tasted moderate success, but with the new white audience taking reggae and, more specifically, them to their hearts, major-label interest in reggae was rewarded, However, a couple of years into the 1980s, and after Marley's death, all the majors would drop their reggae rosters as the music swung into the dancehall era.

Before Dave Hendley's arrival at Trojan, Marcel Rodd had dropped the old orange-and-white album label and recoloured it to a pale blue or pale green, although the established brown Trojan shield design which had been in use since the early 1970s remained for the singles. The company then ran a series of reissues of what they thought to be popular albums of their time. In some cases, original album sleeves which had languished in the warehouse were restocked with new pressings of their accompanying vinyl albums.

Other old albums were wholly revamped, with new sleeves showing the new company address, such as the 1973 *Presenting I-Roy* LP, although in this case, according to Dave, 'There was absolutely no market for a five-year-old DJ album.' No one now remembers who was responsible for this reissue programme, but, judging by some of the albums which they chose to revive, whoever it might have been was aware of buyers' tastes of the time.

At the same time, music appeared on a completely redesigned version of the long-serving Attack offshoot. There was a series of 12" singles, a highlight being a reissue of Black Uhuru frontman Michael Rose's harsh 'Born Free', resplendent with a wild Prince Jammy's dub mix at the end. No more than 1,000 copies of each single were pressed, and while some fell by the wayside, others quickly sold out and are now sought-after collectors' items.

In August 1979, due to personal reasons, Dave Hendley left Trojan, although he was back by special request by the following spring. By this time, the Trojan offices were relocating from Saga HQ to Harlesden, an area of London that was a fertile breeding ground for reggae, with seemingly a small label operating out of every street.

The label slowly began to assemble a catalogue of new music, like the *Kamakazi Dub* LP. This actually came from Lloyd 'Prince Jammy' James, who sent it to the Trojan offices as an unnamed master tape with no track titles. Dave Hendley, who was in his kung-fu period at the time, proceeded to title the package and its tracks in martial-arts style and commissioned an appropriate sleeve design.

Dave also put together a definitive collection of earlier reggae entitled *Rebel Music*, which he described as 'purely self-indulgent – there was no market for this sort of collection and I just put together records that I really liked'. Much to Dave's surprise, the double album was a great success and moved many units for Trojan. That first tentative and surprisingly successful step took Trojan towards what would become their main profit area: the revival and repackaging of old ska and reggae recordings.

Based on the achievement of *Rebel Music*, Dave Hendley set to work once more and compiled the six-volume *Creation Rockers* series. This was a truly ground-breaking set; for the first time since the triple-LP *Trojan Story* in 1972, a series traced the progress of Jamaican music from the formative early ska days to the present. Unknowingly, but without doubt, Dave had sparked the whole retrospective scene within the reggae-music industry and had set Trojan on the lucrative course that it has pursued to this day. His stay at Trojan, however, was less lucrative for him, and in 1982 he became A&R man for another ex-Trojan employee, Clive Stanhope, at the latter's new CSA (Clive Stanhope Associates) label.

After the departure of Dave Hendley, Trojan began a period of comparative inactivity, seemingly reissuing the same few dozen golden oldies in as many permutations as possible, until it was sold to Sharesense Ltd in 1985.

Former chairman Colin Newman offers the background to his company's interest in the record label: 'As a business manager, I represented Chas Chandler, a former member of The Animals who was a very famous producer of artists such as Jimi Hendrix and Slade. He had a record label with Frank Lea – brother of Slade's Jim Lea – called Cheapskate Records, and when it started Frank worked out of our basement offices. And then Chas and Frank fell out and because Frank was actually working in our offices. We'd started to form some kind of friendship, and basically we started a new separate label, which was essentially a singles label, and then that progressed into an album-based compilation label.

'We spent about a year putting together about 15 compilation albums, for which we licensed product from different companies, which was in 1984/85. One of the albums that we licensed was a reggae album from Trojan...and we were quite pleased because we got a big order in from Woolworth's.

'About a week after the order went in, the distributor went bust, and we spent about a year extricating ourselves from the mess that we'd got ourselves into with that label. But it was a fantastic lesson of dealing with the majors and it set me and Frank Lea working together. And so at that point, I thought we needed to get a catalogue. Doing all this and going out doing compilation albums, licensing from the majors, was a complete nightmare. We'd have a rock album that had 15 tracks on it with 15 different licences, because it was a kind of 'rock best of', and I think we were a little bit ahead in terms of timing – the industry wasn't doing it; people weren't going around doing that kind of thing.

'So as I said we'd licensed one album almost completely from Trojan, which had in fact been the easiest of all of them, because it was one source. There was a chap who was loosely the managing director of Trojan, so we talked to him and then he introduced me to Marcel Rodd, the actual owner of Trojan and B&C.

'At our acquisition point, it was a label that was languishing. I mean, it had literally an accounting executive, who was loosely the MD. It had a pretty poor distribution agreement and it had a label manager. The label manager was in charge of putting together the first Lee Perry box set, and that was a work-in-progress item at the time of our acquisition. If you go back in history, there is one album within that box set which was an unreleased dub album. Essentially, it was two Lee Perry albums and an unreleased dub album. There was a lot of research went into that, and it was one of the first Trojan box-set releases.

'A lot of people initially actually thought we were fronting for Mr Rodd, but in fact that wasn't the case at all, and I found basically that he was a very tough businessman to deal with. Although at that time he was in his 70s, he didn't actually want to sell Trojan. It wasn't for sale.

'The reality was that I went to him and formed a good relationship with him, and I'd like to actually think that he liked me. He thought I was a man in business and knew what records were, old records in particular, and when it eventually came down to it I got the feeling he wanted me to buy it, and again it was interesting because obviously a lot of people come up with the question "How much did you pay?" Obviously, that's a piece of confidential information, but my final negotiating ploy with him was, "Well Mr Rodd, I really want to go ahead with this deal but can't afford it." It was a little ploy, really, on my part to try and get something off the purchase price. [And then he did] something I'll never forget: he put his arm around me and said, "Colin, I'll lend it to you!" And I knew at that point that I was snookered. It was over and done with, and we actually wrote all the contracts out ourselves, without the cost and expense of going to a major law firm, and completed the transaction in which we acquired Trojan.

'Obviously, we'd satisfied ourselves to an extent that it was a proper catalogue and there were tapes and so on and so forth. That was the beginning of it; that gave us what we saw as catalogue that we could package, and we could market and deal with the people. Then we went through the rather tortuous first 18 months of an onslaught of visitors and artists/producers who came in with the comment, "We never gave any rights, we've never been paid any money," etc.

'Basically, our policy has always been to be very artist-orientated. My whole career had been working for artists. We wanted to be helpful and sympathetic to people, and so we made a policy decision at that point that, if people came, we would do our best to research what their position was. We'd go try to find royalty statements, contracts, and we'd try and essentially make new deals with people so they weren't left with royalties in old pennies.

'We had a very early relationship with Lee Perry in 1986, and our policy then was also to try to talk to people and get them to make new records for Trojan. We had a vision at that point that Trojan should expand by making new recordings. We were probably hampered, looking back on it, by the fact that we had good knowledge of the record industry – good knowledge of the back catalogue, but not specifically at that time good knowledge of the reggae market.

'That's something that we acquired and built up over the years. My background to all this started with my hobby as a record collector. So I went out and basically trod the boards of the country, looking for – and finding – old records that were part of the Trojan catalogue so I could a) educate myself on it and b) build myself a library that would constitute the Trojan library of music.'

Colin goes on to describe the formative Newman–Trojan days: 'In that early time period, around '86, it started purely and simply as Frank Lea and myself and two other staff. Then we got a warehouse and a warehouse manager that we inherited from somebody else who had been distributing records, and we then had Enzo Hamilton, who was essentially an old-style record man but somebody who had an understanding of records and distribution and overseas sales.

'What really happened was that, when we took on Trojan, we found that they had deals in place with overseas distributors where they were really being exploited badly, and we would have situations whereby people would come on and say, "Well, we bought your records for £1 each from your distributor in Holland." And so over the first few years we embarked on a policy which just came about because of this problem, rather than being the result of any clever pre-planning, of actually terminating all licences and manufacturing agreements everywhere in world on the basis that, if you wanted Trojan, the only place in the world you could buy it was from one of our newly appointed distributors or from our warehouse in London. We would distribute directly from our warehouse in London to an overseas distributor, but you couldn't buy the Trojan label from so-called third parties, who were in fact people that we hadn't then started doing business with. I think that helped to control things and gave us sort of quality control and also price control. Our policy had always been to sell less copies at a proper price, rather than job out loads of copies at silly or cheap prices.

'At that time, Enzo Hamilton was our overseas sales person, basically being multilingual and able to communicate with overseas distributors. When we first took on the label, there was a label manager, Patrick Meads, who was employed by the old Trojan, and he was the one label employee who came on with us. There was a warehouse manager as well, but Patrick essentially came over and he was the compiler at that time, and eventually he left. He was so entrenched in calling himself "Patrick from Trojan" that he released a record on his new label, which was Big One Records, and he [stated that it was] "produced by Patrick T Rojan".

'Then, I don't recall exactly how, we came across Steve Barrow, because I was out meeting reggae experts and buying records. I built up a fantastic knowledge and collection of records across all the labels that had been owned and represented by Trojan and Steve Barrow came on board at that point. He had a deep and intimate knowledge of the music and the people.'

One of the first projects Steve instigated was the *Producer* series of albums, with each volume training the spotlight on one particular worthy creative Jamaican producer. They were a great success and solidified Trojan's position as a force to be reckoned with in revival reggae.

Steve Barrow stayed with Trojan for a comparatively short time before moving on to set up the Blood And Fire imprint. B&F continues Steve's meticulous dedication to detail in presenting fine collections of Jamaican music from the 1970s, both as single-artist albums and superb collections.

Chris Prete, another extremely knowledgeable Trojan and reggae enthusiast, was recruited on a freelance basis to replace Steve Barrow and began to assemble an excellent catalogue of compilations and reissues of past Trojan glories. Compilation albums put together by Chris such as *Babylon A Fall Down* once again took Trojan to the forefront of revival reggae by unearthing long-forgotten work and crisply presenting it to a new audience. Alongside Chris came long-time reggae scribe Penny Reel and Lionel Young, who both contributed excellent collections of work in a freelance capacity.

In 1990, Laurence Cane-Honeysett began freelancing for Trojan Records and brought his enthusiasm and expertise to bear on their vast catalogue.

Laurence gives an insight to his background and how he came to join Trojan: 'My first memory of hearing Jamaican music is back in the '60s, when my older brother, Tony, used to take me to Stamford Bridge to watch Chelsea play. We went to most home games from around 1968 onwards, standing at the infamous Shed end, although very much on the outskirts of the main area. At the time, Chelsea had one of, if not the largest skinhead followings in the country, and they used to play reggae and ska records over the tannoy before the game. Of course, "Liquidator" and all the other big Reggae hits of the day were played, but every now and then they also used to play less well-known records. I remember on one occasion "Sammy Dead" by Eric Morris blared out over the tannoy. It was fantastic and left an indelible impression on me.

'I grew up in Fulham, which was quite a working-class area in those days, and I remember at the local junior school all the boys of a certain age tried to emulate their elders and adopt a hard look. I had a pair of Tonik trousers and wore Ben Sherman shirts and the like, but of course we were just wannabes – too young to understand or appreciate the fashion. Of course, at the time everyone in the country was exposed to reggae – the hits were riding high in the charts and just about every home had at least a few reggae singles in their collections. My family was no different, and while my brother wasn't a great fan of reggae, my elder sister, Julia, had some of the records, which I played to death. Although my brother didn't much like the style, he did, however, introduce me to R&B and doo-wop, which eventually led me back to Jamaican music a few years later.

'As the '70s progressed, Jamaican music changed, and to be honest, it really put me off for a while – I was a young, white teenager growing up in London, and I just couldn't identify with all the roots and dub music that was coming out of Jamaica. So my musical tastes developed in other directions – I really got into '50s and '60s R&B and doo-wop in a big way, and by the late '70s I had a huge collection of the stuff, although most of the records I had were reissues. In fact, by this time my collection had grown to such an extent that I really ran out of things to buy, and I suppose it was this that made me look back to the Jamaican music I had loved as a kid, so I picked up a few old albums and soon began to realise the similarities of the styles. I remember one album that had a big influence was the *Wailing Wailers* LP on Studio One. Even the look of it was like an old Impressions album. I played it and thought, "This is fantastic." So it picked up from there and then, I suppose.

'Just a little after, there was the big Two-Tone thing, and suddenly ska was in the charts, although obviously a somewhat bastardised version. But nonetheless, I thought it was great. I loved 'Gangsters' and all the early Madness and Specials stuff, and it really spurred me on to dig deeper. Then, thanks to Dave Hendley, Trojan released *Rebel Music* and *Monkey Business*, and it all came flooding back – this was the real McCoy, really great music, great songs, great rhythms and great performances. Who could ask for more?

'I started to buy the records in earnest, and when the ska-revival bubble burst, I just carried on. I remember picking up a lot of great little collections from people who had briefly embraced ska as a fad, on the back of Two-Tone. I started hunting down records all over the place, and when record fairs started I began to go to all of those in the London area; in those days, you really could pick up reggae records for a song. It was at these fairs that I eventually became aware of Colin Newman, who, after acquiring Trojan in 1985, began to buy all the Trojan stuff. He became a major rival as a collector.

'Around this time, I also befriended a number of other serious reggae collectors, people like Bob Brooks and Dave Home, and we used to meet up at Bob's flat, off Ladbroke Grove, and exchange and play records. Bob was a good friend of Steve Barrow, who was working for Trojan at the time, and on a few occasions he asked if I'd help out with releases by lending some of my records, but I don't think I ever did, as, like most collectors, I wouldn't let my records out of my sight.

'But when Steve Barrow left Trojan, around 1990, I thought I wouldn't mind giving this compiling lark a go. At the time I was freelancing as an illustrator, after briefly trying my hand as a record dealer. Actually, I think by this time I'd already started doing the odd job for *Record Collector* magazine, after John Reed, who was one of the main editors there, had contacted me with a number of ideas about reggae articles and information. He'd got my name from a fellow collector, Jim Silles, who was, and still is, a very good friend. Of course, at this time I had no idea how important John would become in terms of Trojan and that, a decade or so later, we'd be working together, overseeing releases on the label.

'Anyway, back then, Chris Prete, Penny Reel [aka journalist Scotty Bennett] and Lionel Young had all begun to do stuff for Trojan following Steve Barrow's departure, and I was keen to give it a try – I was also trying to make a few bob, at the same time, of course. So I spoke to Colin Newman and convinced him to give me a go. The first releases I worked on were compilations of Desmond Dekker and Derrick Morgan's early recordings in around 1991.

'I can't remember who I mainly dealt with at the beginning, but I know Zep Gerson was there, doing sales. Arthur Sharp, a lovely bloke who had been the lead singer of The Nashville Teens in the '60s and had later gone on to work for Jet Records, dealt with the production side of things, and Dorothy Howe dealt with PR, although she left after a while and a very nice young woman called Hedge [Heather] filled her role.

'They all worked from the Camden office, while in Walthamstow the company had a warehouse run by Lars Gredal where, aside from the stock, there was a little studio and where the master tapes were kept. Of course, Colin was the head of the whole operation, but the MD was Frank Lea, the brother of Jimmy Lea from Slade.

'For the next few years, I carried on working for Trojan in a freelance capacity – I'd submit ideas for releases, with Frank and, to a lesser degree, Colin selecting what was issued. Once they gave the go-ahead, I'd get on with compiling the releases and writing the sleeve notes. This was all well and good, but after a while I began to get a little frustrated with the situation. To be honest, I wanted more control over what was issued, and since nobody had filled the void left by Steve Barrow, I thought that, if I began to work for the company in some capacity, my chance would eventually come.

'I knew that the master tapes had never been properly logged and was desperate to know what was available for release, and so I told Colin that I should do the job and he agreed. So from around the mid '90s I worked for the company full time, commuting to the warehouse every day. It was quite a trip, two hours each way, and to be honest it wore me out. Also, after a while I was given other duties and found I had less and less time to devote to the things I wanted to do, which was basically to manage the releases. In fact, I ended up getting involved with pretty much everything *but* that!

'My other roles at this time included dealing with certain licensing jobs, by liaising with Clive Wills, who had formerly worked for Island and who single-handedly ran Business Affairs; working with Patsy Kennedy, who oversaw the [songwriting] publishing side of things; listening to all new reggae product that was submitted by producers; compiling lists of recordings for any new contract schedules; seeking out tapes for new Trojan releases; liaising with the royalties department, run by Graeme Lamb; filling out the MCPS and PRS forms for new releases; and dealing with all the press and promo stuff following Hedge's departure. This was on top of trying to sort out the tapes and compiling and writing sleeve notes, as by now only myself and Chris Prete were doing all the Trojan releases.

'Anyway, after a few years, I found I hadn't really progressed in terms of managing the releases in the way I wanted to, and of course that had been my initial aim. In fact, many of the releases I worked on were someone else's concept – often Frank's – so I decided to go back to freelancing. Other than the press and promo side of things, I still did all the other stuff, but without having to do the horrible commute five days a week.

'By this time, Del Taylor had been brought in to be the label manager for Trojan. His initial position had been running Indigo label, which was a blues-oriented imprint Sharesense owned, but his role had widened since joining the company and he was made the general label manager for most of Trojan's releases, regardless of the genre.

'This situation carried on for the next few years. Although officially I was freelance, in effect I was pretty much full-time. And then, of course, in the summer of 2001, Sanctuary came in and bought Trojan from Colin Newman. By this time, I'd actually done a few jobs on the sly for Sanctuary, using pseudonyms – in truth, I'd done the same for a few other companies, most notably Westside, under Tony Rounce's management. Of course, by this time John Reed was at Sanctuary, after they'd bought the Sequel imprint in September 2000, and under the general management of Roger Semon and Joe Cokell he was given the job of overseeing the releases, exploiting all the new product that had come in from Trojan.'

Between Chris Prete and Laurence, a vast amount of music was unearthed and reissued for the first time, following on from Dave Hendley's groundbreaking collections and Steve Barrow's knowledgeable assemblies.

The new business had its humorous moments as well, as Colin Newman recalls: '[Once] we picked up an old file and found an old note of a meeting that Bill Ross, Mr Rodd's accountant, had with a particular artist, and it said that this particular artist thumped the desk and said, "You've got no contract with me, you've never had any contract with me and you've never paid me any money!" And so Mr Ross, who was a chartered accountant, pulled out a contract and some receipts, whereupon the artist leaped across the table and ripped the contract to pieces. And, in fact, in the file was an envelope with the pieces of this contract, and I always thought of that as a jigsaw. I'd try and piece this contract together again, but it got lost with the passage of time.

'But that summed it up, in a way. I think that many people don't understand the modern techniques of the music business, that we give advances, we sell records, the advance is against the royalty and that they would think that they're not being paid until recoupment. And I think it's an endemic view that the artist will always think that you've sold more records that you've actually sold and that you've used his creative process to feather your nest.

'Our whole policy with Trojan was, we had a lot of releases, we didn't sell in great quantity and we also had a lot of compilation releases – a producer series – which we developed. We produced these multi-artist compilations, and at the end of the day, if you know anything about royalty accounting, one track on a multi-artist compilation record that's likely to sell 3,000 to 5,000 units isn't going to attract a great royalty. But, understandably, artists think you owe them more than you do, and we understood that and tried to form new relationships with people. We tried to see them; we tried to bring in more people to be available to meet artists and producers.'

Colin also notes that some things never change in the reggae industry: 'We know on some occasions that we'd sign a contract with somebody for a worldwide right, and as soon as they could get out of our offices they'd be down to somewhere else and possibly deposit some of the same records elsewhere. On one occasion, we signed an album and we thought, "Oh, that's good, we'd better get it out quick," and a week later the actual released version of the album was out on import and available at Jet Star.

'No matter what some people want to say about the period in which we ran Trojan, we think we acted in manner that was fair and reasonable. We think we gave care and attention to the music, care and attention to the artwork, care and attention to the way the music was presented to the public. We enjoyed doing it and, as you know, we built up other labels which had other genres of music – again, all built up with direct artist relationships – with very few problems. We built up a big chart list of British singles charts, tracks that had individually been in the charts, and we mixed the benefit of those releases with Trojan's expertise, in terms of the ability of putting tracks on compilations and things like that. And we had some success with some TV ads, probably the most famous was 'Israelites' by Desmond Dekker for a TDK ad, with 'My Ears Are Alight', which we thought was great and very funny.

'We had Lord Tanamo with 'I'm In The Mood For Ska', again for a TV ad [for Paxo stuffing], we got one of the Toots tracks ['Broadway Jungle'] into the Adidas

TV ad over the Euro 2000 football tournament and we had one or two others. And again, we worked the label. We finished up doing well out of it, financially, but that's the reward for effort in life. We feel we had a great time with it.

'The point I'm making here is that the Trojan label was not 100 per cent of our business; it finished up being probably about half of our business. The other half was a complete mix of rock, pop, blues, jazz and other genres of music, which, with all respect to the Jamaican music, was in the main more commercially viable for European tastes. So a lot of the Trojan pop reggae we were able to do well with, because it went alongside a lot of our other pop and different genres of music activity. But when you look at our actual Trojan releases themselves, very few attained huge volumes.

'Obviously some of them were better than others. I think we can also take some credit for the *Trojan Histories* that were beautifully packaged in digipacks with very impressive artwork, and I think also the Trojan box-sets packages were brilliant – great value for money, three CDs in a box and well compiled. At the end of the day, I do genuinely believe we did something for the music, and we've still kept some relationships going with those who we felt were genuinely nice people.

'When Sanctuary came along, we felt that they were the right home, in that they understood the concept of a back-catalogue release and how to present music to the public. And we also thought that they would be able to achieve greater sales volumes than we could ever achieve – selling was not one of our strong points – and that if they achieved greater sales levels it would be beneficial all round, because it would increase the artist royalties, and so everyone would be happier.'

Aside from Trojan Records, Sharesense owned an array of other labels: Action Replay Records, which specialised in 'best of' collections; the old Mooncrest imprint (mainly folk); Morgan Blue Town (psychedelic); Clay (new wave); and Receiver Records (punk, pop and new wave). They also reactivated the old-style Yellow Attack label for a series of albums and formed the Trojan World label in order to offer South African township sounds to the world.

In 1987, the Burning Sounds imprint, which issued singles, 12" singles and albums in the mid to late 1970s and was owned by former Trojan employee Clive Stanhope, was up for sale and Trojan purchased it. Sharesense had noted its excellent releases, and it was thought that the albums would sell well in the mid-price arena.

Along with further establishing the brand of Trojan at the forefront of reissue reggae, Chris Prete also reformed the Trojan Appreciation Society. Originally, the TAS had appeared in 1970 as a newsletter informing members of forthcoming tours and releases by their favourite Trojan artists. Two enthusiasts named only as Helen and Rose, working from a private address in Kingsbury, north London, gave the low-down on all things Trojan and ran the society. By 1973, only Rose Barrie was still running the society and the address had changed to 8 Neasden Lane, very close to Music House at number 12. A little later in the year, Rose's name disappeared and the signature 'Titch' could be found on TAS letters.

After paying the vast sum of 72p, the new member would receive 'a full year's membership of the TAS, a bright shining Trojan medallion, a copy of the latest catalogue, a short history of reggae, postcard pics of your favourite Trojan artists and 12 monthly newsletters', according to the application form. 'Be the envy of all your friends – join the reggae people...' boasted the ad on the joining letter.

Initially, the monthly newsletter, although slightly erratic in its arrival, was full of interesting titbits, news and reviews of Trojan. It advertised posters of Trojan artists for sale and ran a 'Record Sales And Wants' page beside the pen-pal column. The last newsletter was dated May/June 1973.

In October of the same year, a new newsletter dropped through the letterboxes of all TAS members. The grandly named West Indian Music Appreciation Society, run by one E Denham from Berkhamsted, Hertfordshire, welcomed all to the newly formed society. The WIMAS newsletter proposed to cover not only Trojan releases but all reggae issued in the UK, as well as other West Indian styles like steel band and calypso. It was a jolly A4 stapled-together affair comprising a main feature, such as 'The Roots Of Reggae'; some reviews of (mainly Trojan-related) reggae records; a competition; a Trojan merchandise sales page; record sales and swaps; and a pen-pals correspondence page.

The seventh issue, dated September 1974, was accompanied by a photocopied letter announcing that this was to be the last newsletter. 'When I amalgamated my own society with the Trojan society, I was given to understand that help would be given with regard to the financial side,' ran the explanation. It went on to say that the subscription charge did not cover the actual production costs and postage stamps and that the majority of the costs had been borne by the writer. The letter continued, 'As no money has been received from Trojan Records, I will be sending the mailing lists and all correspondence back to them.' And that was the end of any form of Trojan newsletter for some quarter of a century.

Chris Prete revived the society in 1989 and proceeded to produce thick labour-intensive magazines bearing the new name of 'The Official Trojan Appreciation Society' (TOTAS). The magazine was named *Let's Catch The Beat*, after Dandy's debut album, and the A5-sized magazine became synonymous with superbly researched, in-depth articles, so much so that the magazines have become collectable in their own right and bear testament to Chris Prete's painstaking work.

In June 2001, the Sanctuary Group paid a massive £10.3 million for Trojan Records, thus becoming the curators of this renowned reggae label in the new millennium.

Sanctuary was founded in 1976 by Rod Smallwood and Andrew Taylor and was originally intended to be a music-management business. In 1979, Taylor discovered the heavy rockers Iron Maiden, whose gigantic international record sales (they chalked up five platinum-selling albums in a row in the USA) gave the company an ever-increasing income from mainstream rock throughout the '80s and into the '90s.

In December 1997, a company called Burlington paid £15 million for Sanctuary – good news for Smallwood and Taylor, who each had a 20 per cent stake in their company. Burlington, which had previously been known as Gold & Base Metal Mines, changed its name to the Sanctuary Group after the deal. Their empire has continued to expand, and as well as Trojan's massive repository of Jamaican music they now own the Castle label, which has issued many excellent oldies CDs and has a very enviable soul back catalogue. They also own the entire Pye label, a giant of '60s pop music.

Laurence Cane-Honeysett, Sanctuary's current Jamaican-music consultant, gives an overview of the purchase of Trojan and the plans for the future: 'After the sale went though, I was given the job as the Jamaican-music consultant. In fact, among the regular staff at the old owners of Trojan, I ended up being the only employee working for the company's new owners, but knowing and being a friend of John Reed's was obviously a great help, and he made sure I felt at home straight away. Soon I got to know everyone there, and I can say in all honesty, without exception, they're a genuinely lovely bunch of people.

'But back at the beginning of Sanctuary's ownership, it was all a little daunting and I wasn't sure how things would progress. Thankfully, we soon developed a workable system, which has worked well ever since. Now, John – who soon after the sale of Trojan to Sanctuary was made head of the whole Mid-Price division – and myself sort out the schedule together and deal with the day-to-day situations that need to be addressed, which can mean all manner of things, from the promotion of a certain release to working with a producer or artist.

'While John is in overall charge of everything that we release, he's obviously involved in all number of releases on the various Mid-Price – or Special Markets, as it's now termed – labels. So, in terms of getting new Trojan releases out, on a practical level it's up to me to manage things, from a creative perspective. I still do a large percentage of the compiling, although we're very keen to keep the appeal of the releases as broad as possible, so we do use freelancers to write liner notes and occasionally come up with new angles for releases, and of course I have to oversee their contributions.

'Among those who have recently undertaken work on Trojan releases are some really knowledgeable and respected people, including Dave Hendley, Noel Hawks, Stephen Nye, David Katz, Jeremy Collingwood, Mike Atherton and some bloke called Michael de Koningh. But of course, as you can imagine, after all these years, every obvious idea under the sun has been submitted to Trojan for release. I myself have put forward hundreds of ideas, of which a small percentage have seen release to date.

'Aside from compiling and working with contributors, there are other aspects of getting the releases together, and these include helping Richard Jaskeran and Mike Mastragelo in Archives find the best sources for the necessary recordings, coming up with all the information regarding label copy, sorting out the visual material for the booklets, briefing the designers and of course checking the final product, both in terms of the artwork and aurally.

'This is just to give you an idea of what's involved creatively from my point of view. There are, of course, other aspects, such as mastering and design, and the work of those who co-ordinate and oversee things in terms of the production – most notably Joe Smith and Nick Bourne – is essential in getting the releases together.

'Apart from the releases, there are other sides to my work, including liaising with Business Affairs, Contracts and Licensing and writing monthly sales sheets on all the Trojan releases. Other than that, I'm also there to assist, when necessary, [former Trojan employee] Dorothy Howe and Coalition, who handle all the PR for the releases, while I also check out and report on any new repertoire that's offered to us. So it's a pretty varied role, and while it's certainly hard work sorting out five CD releases and at least an additional three vinyl releases each month, it can be hugely rewarding. It's still early days, really, but I like to think that we can maintain the momentum and that, through our work, Trojan will continue to be arguably the world's greatest classic-reggae label.'

Nowadays, most of the production work for Trojan releases is done at external specialist studios, who are able to run the source through a Cedar unit, which can identify and remove the clicks and pops which are inherent in old vinyl records. The production process has come a long way since Joe Sinclair dubbed from Jamaican vinyl records to master Trojan's UK singles.

Laurence Cane-Honeysett, gives a quick run-through of the procedure: 'First, we decide on a release and compile a track listing, and that needs to be checked, in terms of the rights of usage. Then they are submitted to the MCPS for clearance. This ensures that the right people are paid royalties for their work. At this stage, each recording is given an individual code. In the meantime, the best sources are located, whether it's master tape, CD, exabyte, DAT [Digital Audio Tape] or vinyl.'

Sound engineer Nick Bourne explains the process for non-boffins: 'The new album will usually be recorded onto an exabyte. An exabyte is essentially a digital tape, bigger than a DAT and much better to use as a CD master than any other format. The reason is that you can encode it accurately, with PQ points and ISR codes, which is vital for CD masters. A DAT would only be able to hold less accurate ID points.

'PQs are literally pauses and cues, the times when the album has breaks in it and so on, and the ISR (Internatonal Standard Recording) codes are basically track identities. Each track, even different versions and variations, will have its own code to identify it. The code is on the label copy which gives the publisher, artist, composer and title, etc, so it is needed for royalties, in particular. If a track was played on the radio, for example, the code would be registered and royalties duly paid.

'The exabyte is sent up for a glass master to be made. A glass master is what a CD is made from, and this is in fact an extremely complicated process.'

'If we don't possess a clean digital copy of a recording,' adds Laurence, 'we either try to buy the original record or ask a collector if we can borrow his copy. Once all the sources are assembled, the release goes to mastering. It's at this stage that all the Cedaring – de-clicking, de-hissing and de-crackling – is done. We're then sent a CD-R of the mastered release for approval, which I will check along with the compiler.

'In the meantime, the sleeve notes need to be written, pictures sourced and the designer briefed. With Trojan, I sort out images and brief the designers. They then design a cover and, once it's approved by John and myself, it's used for the sales sheets, which also contain a blurb about the release (which I write for the Trojan releases), and this is then sent to the appropriate sales people at Sanctuary and subsequently on to all the retailers and distributors around the world who stock our releases.

'Once the liner notes and all the pictures are in, they're submitted to the designer, who sets about designing the rest of the package: booklet, liner tray and on-body label. He liaises with the product manager and consultant – in Trojan's case, Joe Smith and me respectively – and to a lesser extent with John Reed, the overall manager.'

A particular gripe that collectors have levelled at the past three owners of Trojan is their continual reissuing of the work of the most prominent artists, such as Bob Marley and Lee Perry. But the hard fact is that, whenever another collection of work by one of these seminal artists hits the streets, it promptly outsells every other Trojan release. Long-term collectors, of course, know these works inside out, but it must be remembered that reggae is one of the few musical styles that has a continuing influx of eager young, new appreciators, and it is to them that Trojan offer these compilations. For the die-hard specialist collector, expert compilers like David Katz, Dave Hendley, Noel 'Harry Hawk' Hawks and Trojan's own Laurence Cane-Honeysett offer their authoritative knowledge in bringing together outstanding releases. Thus the Sanctuary/Trojan label aims to cover all markets with their release programme, with something for all levels of Jamaican music collectors.

John Reed, head of specialist labels at Sanctuary, and ultimately the top of the pile as far as Trojan goes, appreciates the value of his company's newly acquired label: 'Trojan Records is a rare thing. Like Blue Note, Motown, Factory, Elektra and all the other great labels, it crystallises an era and is synonymous with a type of music from that era. In Trojan's case, they dominated the reggae explosion from 1968 to 1975 – a quick look at the reggae charts at the time reveals that they sometimes boasted 80 per cent of the best-sellers in any given week. Trojan, in short, was the Jamaican Motown.

'But unlike many other great labels, Trojan had never benefited from proper marketing. While many of their individual packages were strong and several initiatives over the years – like those cute three-CD box sets – were inspired, there was a feeling that the quality of the concepts and the packaging wasn't always as strong. And somehow, Trojan had failed to tap into that wider heartland of people who either grew up listening to it or belatedly discovered it. So our first priority was to prune the existing catalogue back, hence a major deletions programme in the first few months. Meanwhile, we worked on a schedule of releases which aimed at the various types of reggae fan. And finally, we searched high and low for a design house who could capture the rough-and-ready appeal of Trojan – and that company was Mystery Design, who have played a crucial part in rebranding the label.

John explains the various categories into which modern Trojan releases fall:

ARTIST ANTHOLOGIES
'Whether one- or two-CD sets, or more, these single out artists who are poorly represented or who needed a one-stop release for the casual buyer. So Bob Marley, Max Romeo, Horace Andy, Augustus Pablo and many others have been given this treatment.'

ARTIST 'BEST OFS'
'A quick look down the hit artists within Trojan revealed that they were poorly served with basic entrées – introductions – so all the hit artists are being treated to single-CD collections: Desmond Dekker, The Upsetters, Bob & Marcia, Toots & The Maytals, The Pioneers, etc.'

'GENRE COLLECTIONS'
'One of the backbones of the new Trojan thus far has been a series of mainly two-

CD various-artists collections that aim to define a given era or style within Jamaican music. So we did *Rough & Tough* (ska), *Let's Do Rocksteady*, *Punky Reggae Party* (late '70s), *A Place Called Africa* ('70s roots), *Flashing Echo* (dub), *Funky Kingston* (funky reggae), *Work Your Soul* ('60s soul), *Dancehall '69* (skinhead reggae), *High Explosion* (DJ) and so on.

'Part of the appeal here is the attractive and evocative artwork, with the generic slipcases featuring various Trojan labels across the top and the masking tape, which gives them a kind of DIY feel. Partly inspired by the superb artwork of companies like Soul Jazz and partly by the original Trojan look, this has managed to capture the appeal of the music, thereby introducing it to new audiences, as well as coming as a welcome surprise to older, perhaps more jaded fans.'

CLASSIC ALBUMS
'From the legendary *Tighten Up* series to landmark LPs by the likes of Jimmy Cliff, The Wailers, U Roy, Prince Buster, John Holt, The Maytals and Lee Perry, another facet of the new Trojan is to draw out classic LPs and re-present them as deluxe editions – often two-CD sets – with numerous bonus tracks. Part of the reason for this is that the Trojan catalogue was swamped with a plethora of various artist sets which, collectively, seemed to have no rhyme or reason – of course, they did individually, but not necessarily as a whole. Also, there was no sense of the "classics", so in a way, we're applying a rock-music approach to Trojan in a way which other record companies, post-Island, have done.'

THE TROJAN BOX SETS
'Despite all these initiatives, it was clear from the sales figures we inherited that we'd be insane not to continue the wonderfully simple three-CD box sets. Retail chains loved them, punters collected them – the only problem has been coming up with new concepts to keep the series alive! We've had some fun with projects like *Mod Reggae*, *X-Rated* and *Calypso* while also serving up real rarities on my favourite from 2002, *Reggae Revive*, and others. Long may this series continue! *Trojan Sisters* was given five stars in *Mojo*, so we still seem to be getting it right. But we can also dig deeper with something like the *Nyahbinghi* box set. Let's face it, outside hardcore reggae circles, no one's ever heard of Nyahbinghi!'

TV-ADVERTISED PROJECTS
'Aah, now we're talking. Part of Sanctuary's development in the last two years has been to enter the shark-infested waters of TV advertising, and so far, so successful. When Trojan was purchased, we knew we had a reggae hits package to rival anyone's, but none of us really expected *Young, Gifted And Black* to sell so well. A Top Five

compilation album that went gold within a couple of months, it wiped the floor with the competition to become the must-have classic reggae compilation.

'Comforted by this success, we lined up a companion follow-up, *Reggae Love Songs*, to try to crack the bearpit that is the Valentine's market. Every major record company hits this hard, and yet *Reggae Love Songs* got to Number Two – beaten only by the *8 Mile* soundtrack – outselling the competition, going silver week one, gold week two and significantly ruffling the feathers of those major record-company executives involved in back-catalogue TV-advertised projects. We have no doubt *Reggae Love Songs* will go platinum – it's already the fastest selling album that Sanctuary or Castle have ever released. And there'll be more to come, including *Young, Gifted And Black II* and possible joint ventures with other record companies.'

AND NOW FOR THE COLLECTORS...

'There has been much criticism of the new Trojan's willingness to revisit the tried and tested. First reason: the best-sellers are still the best-sellers. John Holt's *1,000 Volts* outsold pretty well everything else last year, other than the mighty three-CD box sets and the TV albums. Also, the initial feedback from UK retail was pessimistic – a lot of Trojan material had been licensed out to third parties, including many budget labels, and the feeling was that the racks were full. Oh, how wrong they were, in terms of sales potential of new product. But it's taken time to build retail's confidence, and that process started by revamping the titles they knew had a solid sales history.

'BUT! We have also tried to cater for collectors. If year zero for new Trojan was January 2002, then we kicked off with *Jamaican Memories*, the legendary Blue Cat collectable. *The Birth Of Trojan* included all the As and Bs from the original 1967 Trojan label. And Mark Lamarr's new collection, *Nuclear Weapon*, boasts rare or previously unissued Duke Reid productions from way back in 1962. Meanwhile, Dave Hendley re-presented his classic *Rebel Music* title, and many of the compilations boast rare tracks.

'As we roll through 2003, expect more albums aimed squarely at the reggae collector's market as other series kind of run their course. Albums might be devoted to individual producers, artists, labels and eras. It doesn't matter how it's compiled, Trojan has room for everything.'

4 Music History – Part 1

1950s To 1967 – R&B To Rocksteady

As the rockin' and rollin' US R&B sounds progressed into their Kingston equivalent at the tail end of the 1950s, other forces were afoot within the confines of music creation.

The Jamaican beat was loping forward into the first true sound of the West Kingston ghetto as shuffle beat took hold and became the staple diet of the dancehalls. Many dancefloor heroes' light twists across the floor gained them recognition in the social ranking of he ghetto. It was also a tentative step towards escape from the grinding tedium of the slum, with the hope of making their own music for the dance one day.

As those dancers shuffled their moves across the lawns, one day in 1959 Prince Buster was taking a revolutionary step himself. In Kingston's studio, he had ensconced three brothers with a song, plus a group of the blackheart men – those men who were shunned by all mothers, who berated their children to stay away lest the men's twisted locks should touch them and cause them to have chill dreams in the hot night.

These were the Rastamen, the outcasts of society whom no self-respecting citizen would be seen dead talking to, men who lived in the distant hills or in the dankest of ghetto townships. Chief Rasta Elder, Count Ossie, was laying down a drumbeat for Buster that was so different from the norm it could have been crafted in a different country – a beat closer to dusty Ethiopia than to colonial Britain, closer to Mother Africa than to Uncle Sam. Into this framework, the three Folkes Brothers – John, Meko and Junior – wove a simple, hauntingly sung song of love for a girl called Carolina.

In 1960, society was still trying to forget the black history which the Rastafarians spoke of with hot biblical references. This was the time when budding record producers still rejected the swelling mass feelings of the lower classes which the Rastas imbibed along with their communal chalice of herb. Yet here was a major player in the 'sound' stakes, not only accepting Count Ossie and his brethren but encouraging them to break new ground by committing the very sound of Rasta to vinyl.

Time has shown that the Rasta-percussive 'Oh Carolina' made headway both in Kingston and, more surprisingly, in London, where the newly formed Melodisc Records subsidiary Blue Beat took it up in early 1961. It was a song and sound way ahead of the times, and rarely would the Rasta Nyahbinghi (drumming and chanting) break through the wall of negative oppression that society had built around it until the red, gold and green 1970s. Buster himself would record many gospel-slanted gospel sides in the early '60s, but it would be a long time before he opened up the heartland of Rasta-Afrika in the studio again.

Jamaican independence, on 8 August 1962, was called from the very rooftops of Kingston as the city and the whole country celebrated their freedom from a distant motherland. A young Jimmy Cliff recorded an anthem of love for both his girl and his country, 'Miss Jamaica', for Leslie Kong, using the new ska sound to propel his cheery lyrics. The loping shuffle beat had moved up a notch by then and, with an input from the jazz masters of JA, such as guitarist Ernest Ranglin and trombonist Don Drummond, had snapped into place as ska.

A rough-and-ready rhythm from the poor quarter, dominated by former Alpha Boys' School musicians slotting jazz and blues riffs into the hypnotic framework, ska blew away all that had gone before it as it injected the dancehalls with an electric power to move you until you dropped.

In particular, the short-lived band The Skatalites had no rivals as they tore through mighty instrumentals for producers like Coxson, Buster and Justin Yap, to name but three lucky recipients of their combined talents. Yap's Top Deck, Tuneico and Sound Deck labels never made the big time, but with the likes of Jackie Opel on vocals and the mighty Skatalites blazing behind him, there was no better music to be heard in the hot city in 1965.

In 1963, Prince Buster released the loping ska of 'Madness', a title that would be remembered not just because of its compelling call to dance but as an echo of the future, when the best Two-Tone band of the late '70s adopted it as their name. Then, prophetically, in 1965 he issued the gangster-themed 'Al Capone', complete with tommy-gun fire and screeching car tyres. The record's theme was too close for comfort, however, and the ska era faded with the hot summer of 1966 as the angry ghetto youths known as Rude Boys took to the streets.

The 'Rudies' had grown from the impoverished rural folk who had moved to the city, hoping for work, as the new dawn of independence had risen. In reality, that dawn broke over hundreds of hapless people confused by the city and unable to find work or shelter. They gravitated to the poor areas and scratched out living there, seething with discontent as the promise of a brave new world was not fulfilled.

The complete antithesis of their impoverished background resulted in their sharply dressed, coolly shaded sons frequenting the dancehalls and bars, almost denying in their manner and clothes the very essence of where they lived. The Rudies were rough and tough, ruling their areas, running around town, causing disturbance and drawing comment from newspapers and singers alike.

That summer of 1966 was too hot to dance to ska, and a tryst between the musicians (who also came from the rough end of town) and the Rudies saw the musical pace dropping from a gallop to a walk. The Ethiopians' recording 'Train To Skaville' was ska in name only, with its insistent chugging beat and catchy peep-peep vocals. This was the new sound of rocksteady, the cool Rudies' music.

Violence was rife and ever-worsening at that time, as the Rudies ripped up the town. Desmond Dekker's '007 Shanty Town', resplendent with its shimmering rocksteady beat, commented on the situation and gave Dekker a taste of things to come as his record reached the UK charts in the summer of 1967.

Not to be outdone, Jamaican London saw the Rudies carving up their native city (and each other), and the fragile-voiced Dandy penned and sang 'Rudy A Message To You', a view from afar which was still pertinent in its comment. This gentle berating of the rude-boy culture was later recut in 1979 by The Specials, using the same trombonist from the original version, that stalwart of the London scene Rico Rodriguez.

But rocksteady wasn't all about the Rudies and their wayward habits; it could be the essence of beauty, with majestically sweeping horns gently driving the incomparable tight harmonies of groups such as The Paragons and The Techniques, who modelled themselves on wonderful US soul acts like Curtis Mayfield and his Impressions. The sound was all about sweet harmonies and haunting melodies, something Mayfield knew inside out. He became the musical icon of the age in Kingston, with every street-corner collective trying to capture that sweet bitterness. There were instrumentals, too, by sultry horn masters like Roland Alphonso and Lester Sterling which graced many a dance and echoed through the balmy nights on RJR.

Duke Reid was the past-master of rocksteady. He did little production work personally, but his funds lured the exemplary talents of Tommy McCook & The Supersonics to create such gentle dreams as 'The Tide Is High', written and sung by a pre-solo John Holt and The Paragons. A decade and a half later, the song became a hit for punk-poppers Blondie, and more recently it charted again with the pretty face of Atomic Kitten.

✳ Rocksteady had a brief but illustrious life, flitting across the dancehalls and airwaves for no more than a couple of summers before a new, brasher rhythm made Kingston's dancers sweat again. It was the new sound of the reggay. ✳

5 Music History – Part 2

1968 To 1972 – Reggay To Strings

The Maytals' blasting 'Do The Reggay' from 1968 kicked the dancers back to wild abandon after the shimmer of rocksteady. You just couldn't shimmer when Toots Hibbert started ripping out his lines. The song, such as it was, was interspersed with wild yelps of fervour from his cohorts and aided by a pounding rhythm so intense that it was literally a pulsating wall of sound.

Toots's gospel-drenched voice had long graced superior discs, from ska masterpieces like 'Hallelujah' and 'Mathew Mark' to crunching rocksteady gems such as the ganja-rap '54–46, That's My Number' and the howling call-and-response of 'Struggle'. Now he dropped like no other onto the new sound of the reggay, reggie or reggae.

'Bangarang', by singer Stranger Cole and alto-saxman supreme Lester Sterling, was another early reggie piece that made a big impression. In a recent TV interview, its producer, Bunny Lee, cited it as the very first record with the new beat, but many others also claim that coveted first, and we shall probably never know whose claim is true. A chugging non-entity of a song with a slightly ribald slant, 'Bangarang's rhythm did it all as it spun across the Atlantic to London and found eager new listeners keen to hear more of this new rhythmic structure.

By 1969, the musical iceberg was floating in, and this was reggae time in the truest sense, with the latest generation of producers finding new variations on the sound almost every day. London was basking in the freshest rhythms and, bolstered by the new white appreciation of the music, swiftly became a greedy market for reggae, whether flown in from Kingston or concocted by new local producers such as Dandy. Old-established labels like Doctor Bird, Studio One and Coxsone were given the boot by the new buyers, with only Blue Beat's resurgence as Fab really taking on the reggae and dropping into vacant slots in collectors' boxes. Discerning fans of more mellow tastes were going for Clement Dodd's new UK label, Bamboo, with its burbling Jackie Mittoo organ rhythms, but the big two who were squaring up for the marketplace battle in 1969 were Trojan and Pama.

Max Romeo's smutty 'Wet Dream' took London by storm in May 1969, slipping up to Number Ten and hanging in the charts for 24 weeks without a single play on national radio. Adopting the 1968 rhythm utilised by old hand Derrick Morgan for his 'Hold You Jack' and new, cheeky lyrics, it sold an astounding 250,000 non-chart return copies. This delighted its label owners, Pama, on whose Unity offshoot it appeared, along with the pirate radio stations that did play it and the kids who smirked at Max's near-the-knuckle lyrics. But it didn't delight the BBC or the music press, which derided its rude lyrics and repetitive rhythm.

Desmond Dekker was luckier with his (to some) lyrically incomprehensible 'Israelites'. 'Get up in the morning, baked beans for breakfast' was the playground chant of school kids. Little did they know of the painful reality: Dekker was actually singing, 'Get up in the morning, slaving for bread, Sir'! Nevertheless, the disc kicked Marvin Gaye's 'I Heard It Through The Grapevine' from the top spot in March 1969, only to be busted a week later by The Beatles' 'Get Back'.

Dekker's choppy follow-up, 'It Mek', grabbed a very respectable Number Seven position in June the same year, while 'Pickney Girl' only touched the 42nd slot during a brief chart run post-Christmas. All three records appeared on the familiar yet soon-to-disappear Pyramid label, which was resurrected by Trojan a few years later.

Trojan moved into the chart stakes with ace producer Lee Perry, whose spaghetti-western spoof 'Return Of Django', on his dedicated Upsetter label, rocked its way to Number Five in October, causing a spate of reggae records referring to Clint Eastwood and his outlaw Mexican buddies. Spaghetti was big in Jamaica – not the edible kind but master film director Sergio Leone's out-of-lip-sync flicks, which transfixed the small island with their reckless gunplay and dauntless heroes.

Trojan must have loved this offshoot label, for such was 'Scratch' Perry's prestige with the fervent new appreciators that any new Upsetter single would fly out of the shops unheard. One of Scratch's most loved records was called 'Live Injection', but Trojan saw it as a very healthy cash injection and a stab at Pama, who also juggled Perry's product on various imprints, notably their flashy Punch label.

A well-reggae-documented scientific wonder of the age was 1969's US moon landing. Almost as soon as Neil Armstrong's foot had pushed up the dust and made one small step, 'Moon Hop' landed. Recorded in London by old hand Derrick Morgan (who had relocated there to be closer to his new-found fan base) and premier UK band The Rudies, it was a dancer of sheer wanton enjoyment. A throbbing walking bass line aided by a yeah-yeah-yeah chorus and Derrick's exhortations added up to a skinhead delight, a moon-stomper *par excellence*. Indeed, it was so good that it scraped into the charts at Number 49 in January the following year, after selling by the cartload to all and sundry for months.

Such was the popularity of 'Moon Hop' that a replica recording entitled 'Skinhead Moonstomp' was hastily issued on the Doctor Bird subsidiary label Treasure Isle. The very capable outfit Symarip, who were the Pyramids more or less spelled backwards, had already made their mark in the soul and blue-beat field on the President label with their 'Train Tour To Rainbow City', which had reached a very respectable Number 35 in 1967. 'Skinhead Moonstomp' became a club anthem, with lead-singer/boss-skinhead Caleb announcing that he had the biggest boots and encouraging listeners to give it some of that 'old moonstompin'' across a mighty can't-keep-still rhythm.

Excited by its success, Trojan knocked together an album on the back of the single's popularity. The band shot was relegated to the back cover, while the front threatened any potential buyer with a full-cover photo of trying-to-look-tough skinheads, giving an obvious indication of the market at which the LP was aimed. Schoolkids everywhere pranced around with the LP – the ultimate status symbol of the moment if you could afford it – but very few actually played the thing, with its slightly hopeful sounds that didn't quite capture the spirit of reggae at its British best. The album's allure was similar to that of the trashy *Skinhead* novels written by Richard Allen: great cover, shame about the contents.

The sound of reggae – as it had become universally known, although the odd news piece still tried variants on the spelling, while some out-of-date scribes still called it by its old mod name of blue beat – now ruled London's dances. Every session was full of foot-moving gems of the new beat, alongside Tamla and Atlantic classics and some fresh soul nuggets. But it was the reggae, with its sweaty bass and pounding piano, that rocked the place. Some of the best records were now home-grown, like Dandy's cheerful 'Reggae In Your Jeggae'. No one had the faintest idea what a jeggae was, but they grooved along to this London-recorded sound anyhow. They grooved so hard, in fact, that many thought it would touch the national charts. As it turned out, due to heavy sales in shops that didn't file sales returns to the all-important BBC, it soared unnoticed.

Dandy did, however, nibble the nationals with his buddy Tony Tribe and a take on an old Neil Diamond song, 'Red Red Wine', on Trojan's new Downtown imprint. It hit the big five-oh for one week in July 1969, then resurfaced in August for one more week, this time finding its final resting place at Number 46. Tony was kitted out in the latest trendy gear of boots and braces for his debut (and only) *Top Of The Pops* appearance, paying homage to the new appreciators who eagerly snapped up the reggae.

As they had done with Mr Upsetter Perry, Trojan had inaugurated a label specially for Dandy's work, both as a singer and for his rhythmic London reggae productions. Kicking off in 1968, Downtown became synonymous with strong organ-led pumps aimed equally at the shaven-headed masses and West Indian buyers. After a run of productions that excelled in power, Dandy discovered sweet-voiced singer Audrey Hall and skipped off to MOR-reggae balladeering, much to the disgust of his many fans, who required a decent throb to their beat.

Jamaican vocal trio The Pioneers raced into the Top 40 with their paean to a racehorse that died in service. The wonderfully titled 'Long Shot Kick The Bucket' told the sorry tale of the horse that gave its all in a race at Caymanas Park, Kingston, and expired. The subject matter may have been sad, but Trojan Records were jumping up and down with joy as the tune cracked the national charts and stuck there for ten weeks, hitting Number 21 in October 1969.

At the same time that poor Long Shot's death was being musically exploited, 'Liquidator', a searing Hammond workout by the ubiquitous Harry J All Stars, clicked in at Number Nine during an amazing 20-week chart run through the tail end of 1969. It was a *tour de force* of instrumental reggae funded by Harry Johnson and played by crack sessioners led by Winston Wright, riding the mighty B3. It was held back from climbing higher by The Archies' prophetic-for-UK-reggae 'Sugar Sugar', which hovered at the Number One slot.

Another rhythmic rider into the charts was The Melodians' 'Sweet Sensation', recorded for ace producer Leslie Kong and grabbed by Trojan Records as a sure-fire club favourite. It managed Number 41 for just one week in January 1970. The Melodians also created the musical template for the disco-pop favourite 'Rivers Of Babylon', as used by Boney-M to infiltrate the nation in April 1978, when they grabbed Number One with the supposedly pious piece.

A talented young singer and songwriter, James Chambers, re-inventing himself as Jimmy Cliff, had made his mark way back as Independence and ska had boogied across Jamaica. By the time most of Great Britain came to hear of him, he had notched up minor hits with Trojan's then masters Island Records. Come 1969, his star rose far above the white-rock grooming that Island had planned for him as the bright and hopeful 'Wonderful World, Beautiful People' took him to Number Six in October, its cheery overtones belying a message of profound hope.

Jimmy's follow-up, 'Vietnam', cut straight to the jugular, although still retaining a smile in its sound, popping in at Number 47 in February 1970 and then popping out again before slipping back in the following week to better its placing by just one position. No doubt the climb of the single was hampered by the political message in its lyric content.

Returning to the Island label, Cliff then issued a Cat Stevens cover, 'Wild World', the backing on which was considerably slanted towards the white-rock world. He was rewarded with a pleasing Number Eight hit in August as 'Wild World' hung around in the charts for 12 weeks.

A month after the incisive 'Vietnam' came Bob [Andy] & Marcia [Griffiths]'s supercharged cover of the black-rights anthem 'Young, Gifted And Black'. Hit-making producer Harry J had scored again – the disc reached Number Five in March 1970. Nina Simone's epic cry had been overlaid with a string section and beefed up by The Harry J All Stars to create a swinging, harmonious joy, so reggae that many were surprised to find an American song hidden beneath the Caribbean sun. Pama Records issued the self-same recording untouched by the London-dubbed string arrangement, but it gained little ground as the Trojan version grappled the ladder of success.

Bob & Marcia's follow-up single release was 'Pied Piper', a jolly nonsense affair first recorded by US group Changin' Times in 1965 and later a British hit for Crispian St Peters. Jolly nonsense it may have been, but it was serious business for Trojan as it reached Number 11 and filled their coffers as it hovered around for 13 weeks. Gone but not forgotten by Bob was the angry social comment that hid in 'Young, Gifted And Black's grooves. Bob Andy was to emerge as one of Jamaica's finest songwriters as the soon-to-be-dread decade moved on, and his accomplished works and words still echo alongside Marley's as a prophetic judgement on those times.

Toots & The Maytals also courted the glittering chart in April 1970, first on the bottom rung at Number 50 and then again in May, when they re-entered and clambered up to Number 47 with the song 'Monkey Man', which had Toots regaling the world with the tale of a past girlfriend who had taken up with a man who was such an oaf that he must surely be part ape. Aided by producer Leslie Kong's finest bouncing rhythm, 'Monkey Man' scored well for the soulful Toots, and Trojan gathered together some Maytals/Kong gems on an album of the same name.

The Maytals never gained chart superstardom, but their uplifting belters like 'Pressure Drop', 'Sweet And Dandy' and the revamped '54–46 Was My Number' absolutely wrecked many a dancefloor with their impassioned power. To black and white alike, Frederick 'Toots' Hibbert was one of the finest voices ever to come out of Jamaica – or anywhere else, for that matter – and his records slid into the boxes of every DJ and collector.

As The Maytals were monkeying around, ex-Technique Bruce Ruffin was first tasting the big time with a moody version of Jose Feliciano's 'Rain' which took Trojan and him to Number 19 in May. His only other mainstream success would come on a different label, Rhino, with the lightweight sugar-reggae of 'Mad About You', which gave him a Number Nine.

As Mungo Jerry chugged 'In The Summertime' to Number One in June 1970, the distinctively voiced Cecil 'Nicky' Thomas called to mind the less fortunate people of the world with the melodic 'Love Of The Common People'. This gave Trojan a Number Nine and would give Paul Young a second hit over a decade later in 1983, after he had pinched a Marvin Gaye song for his first triumph.

Desmond 'Israelites' Dekker attacked the charts in a big way through August 1970 with the Jimmy Cliff-penned 'You Can Get It If You Really Want' and was kept from the crest only by Elvis, whose 'Wonder Of You' stayed at Number One for six weeks. Hovering in the second spot, 'You Can Get It' pushed hard during a 15-week chart run but couldn't quite crack the Presley barrier. Even now, the song is one of the all-time favourite reggae tracks at any oldies get-together.

Freddie Notes & The Rudies took singer Bobby Bloom's 'Montego Bay' – a song in praise of the paradise beach inhabited by the wealthy of Jamaica – to Number 45 in October 1970 with one of their customary reggae romps. The Rudies, being a highly versatile band, took rock, soul and reggae in their stride, but unfortunately for them their fans wanted only their best pulsing London-to-JA beat. Mr Notes would decamp a little while later to travel a more expressive path than that offered by a reggae session band. In keeping with many artists, Notes had no wish to be pigeonholed as 'just a reggae singer' and saw the glittering lights of rock, soul and pop as his street paved with gold.

Beneath the glittering sea of the national chart swam a multitude of supercharged reggae records as the new decade slid in to its second year. For those in the know and with full enough pockets, a voyage to Joe's Record Shack or Desmond's Hip City on a Saturday afternoon was the highlight of the week. It was then that the new and eminently desirable discs would be aired to the public.

You could hear the rhythmic thump way up along the pavement before your destination was in sight, and gaudy album sleeves would line the shop window, with smiling half-naked girls vying for space with the gospel according to country giant Jim Reeves. The West Indian love of ballads, country music and the odd sacred sound were almost at odds with the ribald chant to dance from such masters as Lee Perry, whose new record(s) of the week would get continual plays until all the copies were sold.

Most people had heard of Perry The Upsetter and his 'Django' hit, but it was his powerhouse rhythms, which the national-chart-lovers never heard, that really got the shop on its toes. Sticky, grinding sounds like the western-inspired 'Sipreano', who always shoots first were bought avidly. The Reggae Boys' chant-like 'Ba Ba' and its flipside organ version, 'Power Cut' (courtesy of the Upsetter's Hammond man, Glen Adams) rocked the very foundations of the shop on Pama's garish Gas label. ('Power Cut' was actually Perry's 'Cold Sweat' without the spoken introduction, which Pama rival Trojan had licensed from Mr Upsetter, but who cared? You bought them both anyway. That way you had both versions to confound your friends with that evening.)

Names like Lloyd Charmers and Derrick Harriott brought an instant grin when a new disc was brought forth over the shop counter and very rarely failed to gain approval. Both producers were old hands at the game and had retuned their output to the rocking reggae of the day. Charmers' '5 To 5' and 'In The

Spirit', with their fast-heartbeat bass lines and breathy exhortations, instantly hit the spot, while Harriott and his Crystalites band organned up The Kingstonians' mighty 'Sufferer' rhythm and retitled it 'Splash Down', to the immense approval of the dancers' feet. He also whipped out the intense Whitfield–Strong social conscience of 'Message From A Black Man', reggae-tuned to hypnotic effect and reggae-funked with John Shaft.

Not only was Kingston rocking the shop but the UK guys were having a ball as well. Organ-led instrumentals like The Rudies' 'The Split', which was hidden away on the flipside of a mediocre reggae cover of Clarence Carter's soul gem 'Patches', got the shop play and audience fever. 'The Split' was reused some two years later as 'Dread' and graced the flip to Judge Dread's 'Big Seven'.

London soundmen also had a go, such as Clancy 'Sir' Collins, who had already tried his hand at the rocksteady sound and who now went for the reggae. His few releases ranged between sentimental love songs aimed squarely at his West Indian clientele and fearsome, moody organ-fests directed at the new appreciators of the sound. His best, though, had to be the in-your-face 'Black Panther', with an unnamed DJ and eerie organ running over a bass to bust up the place.

Lambert Briscoe and his London-based Hot Rod Sound moved from speaker boxes to vinyl and zeroed in on the skinheads with sharp, bright instrumentals. Unfortunately, his records on the Trojan Hot Rod and Torpedo labels were so obscure that, even if you wanted one, the chances were that you would never find a copy to buy.

Laurel Aitken had climbed aboard the 'Skinhead Train' before most and knew just what buttons to push to gain a super-seller in the new market. Pama favoured him with the Nu Beat label, in return for which he favoured them with cash from such skinhead staples as 'Woppi King', 'Jesse James' and 'Pussy Price'. Even his commentary on politician Enoch Powell's chilling 'rivers of blood' speech on immigration control, 'Run Powell Run', received hefty sales and nightspot plays.

Trojan also enticed him, and he growled his way through some DJ work for them – like the ever-popular 'Dracula Prince of Darkness' title – under the name of his alter-ego, King Horror. By 1970, Laurel was in his James Brown soul phase and funked out 'Reggae Popcorn' and 'Sex Machine' alongside some reggae balladeering on the newly restyled Pama New Beat label.

As 1970 turned to winter, the chattering Kingston DJ work of such absurd names as Dennis Alcapone and U Roy were breaking new ground and giving the old-time singers plenty of trouble when it came to staying afloat in the charts. Everyone liked the DJs, or *toasters* – black, white or indifferent all rushed to grab hot tracks like Hugh 'U' Roy's 'Tom Drunk'. The new-style DJ records' popularity started to rise as the skinhead numbers peaked.

March 1971 saw one of Kingston's most distinctive voices making a break for the national charts. Dave (Barker) & Ansel Collins' 'Double Barrel' whipped up a storm as Dave rapped Yankee-style over keyboardist Ansel's running-bass-led track. The sound was deliberately different, the sound of now, then. The brash DJ had ridden in as he had in Jamaica, talking up rhymes and rocking the public. The song shot to Number One and stayed in the charts for 15 weeks, making a mint for Trojan, on whose Techniques subsidiary label it had appeared. The United States were also receptive to the new DJ sound and 'Double Barrel' hit Number 22 in the *Billboard* Hot 100.

In June, the two non-brothers came again with 'Monkey Spanner' and secured the Number Seven spot before Ansel Collins headed back home. Dave dropped anchor in London, using the stage name Dave Collins to get a little work. Meanwhile, Trojan whipped out the *Double Barrel* LP full of organ workouts and Dave's yelping vocals, and even managed to license it Stateside, where it appeared on the Big Tree label. However, US citizens weren't as broad-minded as London dwellers, and a mirror-image nude girl residing in the cartoon gun barrels on the sleeve front had to be sent home as American tastes obviously couldn't take such a beauty.

After Mr Notes' departure, London's premier moonstomp band, The Rudies, reconfigured as Greyhound and promptly nabbed a smash hit on Trojan with 'Black And White', which hit Number Six in June 1971. Then, in 1972, they raided the charts twice, first with a smooth version of Danny Williams' 1961 favourite 'Moon River', which pushed up to Number 12 in January, and then with the jaunty 'I Am What I Am', which reached the bottom rung of the Top 20 in March.

'Moon River' came in the three-track maxi Trojan format, with a different mix to the standard brown-shield-design label. The final track on the flip was 'The Pressure Is Coming On', which was a foretaste of the angry commentary that would follow in the harsh mid 1970s and was well ahead of its time for 1972 British reggae.

Meanwhile, The Pioneers, by now relocated to these shores, issued the ultimate pop-reggae singalong tune 'Let Your Yeah Be Yeah', a song which, once heard, stuck in the grey matter all day and moved enough units for Trojan to propel the tune to Number Five in July 1971. The hits were starting to come thick and fast for Trojan Records. But The Pioneers had by now begun to turn the corner into Stringsville, a path which the majority of London-based reggae performers would take over the next year. What was at first perceived as salvation would see the hits wither and desperation set in.

The last man who really flew the Trojan flag for a while was a nightclub bouncer from Snodland in Kent. Alex Hughes, or Judge Dread to his legion of fans, took his 'Big Six' to Number 11 in August 1972, and 'Big Seven' hit the Number Eight spot in December of the same year. But then, his next record – surprisingly titled 'Big Eight' – crept in unloved by the BBC to peak at Number 14 in April 1973 before the Judge changed court to the Cactus/Creole set-up and provided them with more Top 50 hits (although only one more Top Tenner, 'Je T'Aime', which reached Number Nine in July 1975) up until 1978.

As the hits switched off, the Rasta switched in across Jamaica, and although lacking in national hits, Trojan persisted in issuing some of the most accomplished Kingston recordings. These were so much at odds with their London sugar sounds that many either bought one style or the other.

The UK side, after The Gable Hall School Choir's 'Reggae Christmas' from late 1972, slipped increasingly towards the desperately happy face of string-orchestrated pop reggae. By 1973, you had on one hand The Pioneers chortling out 'At The Discothèque', a happy song of nothingness, and on the other Ken Boothe recalling Syl Johnson's epic 'Is It Because I'm Black', coupled with his own harsh 'Black, Gold And Green', two songs of majestic black pride and hope.

Meanwhile, in the same year, DJ I-Roy took the deep rhythm track of 'Black, Gold And Green', recoloured it to the Rasta 'Red, Gold And Green' and cut one of the most succinct raps of black awareness ever laid to wax for youthful producer Augustus 'Gussie' Clarke. I-Roy's *Presenting I-Roy* album, issued by Trojan in 1973, has become a benchmark for all aspiring social-commentary DJs to aspire to, and of his contemporaries only Big Youth could stand even close to his sharp, perceptive lyrics.

At this time, the divide between London and Kingston was ever widening, with new and not-so-new names offering views about the society in which they lived. Big Youth, I-Roy, Keith Hudson, Burning Spear, Bob Andy, The Abyssinians and the most well known, Robert Marley, all spoke of their observations. Marley's Upsetter-produced work from 1970 had been one of the few proto-Rasta-roots-type recordings which hit a chord on both sides of the Atlantic, but as 1973 rolled in it was definitely the sound of now.

Producer Perry was to go from strength to strength, his work culminating in the Black Ark sound by the turn of the decade. Trojan actively issued his work with tough new singers like Junior Byles and DJ providers like the stalwart Dennis Alcapone, along with some of his most beloved skanks in the shape of tunes like 'Jungle Lion' and the mad 'Cow Thief Skank'.

The final issue on the UK Upsetter label also took place in the spring of 1973. The top side was David Isaacs singing 'Stranger On The Shore', which was originally an instrumental Number Two hit for clarinet-playing Acker Bilk in 1961, while the flip was the side everyone wanted: 'John Devour' by a young fresh DJ named after US gangster Dillinger. Lester Bullocks was his real name and he was to progress through the 1970s to rise to the top of the DJ pile with seminal sets for Studio One and their near-namesake Channel One.

Album sleeves turned from showing pretty faces to depicting dreadlocked freedom fighters by the mid '70s as the grooves bore witness to the new roots sound, although quality singers would never be out of place and the likes of Delroy Wilson, Ken Boothe and John Holt released some exemplary work, such as Ken's album *Let's Get it On*, on which he performed new compositions and soul gems with equal ease. Indeed, 1974 found Ken riding to the top with the David Gates composition 'Everything I Own', solidly produced by veteran Lloyd Charmers, which hit the pop Number One spot in September and hung in the charts for 12 weeks. His follow-up, 'Crying Over You', gave Trojan another cash injection as it peaked at Number 11 in December of the same year.

Then, just before Christmas 1974, John Holt took Kris Kristofferson's 'Help Me Make It Through The Night' to the Number Six slot, just slipping above label-mate Ken Boothe. By then, however, running underneath the glitz of the national chart was a new-style roots rhythm courtesy of producer Bunny Lee and top youth singer Johnny Clarke. The 'flying cymbal' sound was exemplified by Johnny's stepping 'Move Out Of Babylon', issued in the UK on the Trojan Harry J imprint.

The charts might have been rocking to Ken Boothe, but the dancehalls on both side of the Atlantic were stepping to this latest bright rhythm structure, and a veritable host of variations were to follow in best Jamaican style.

The DJs were also doing the business in the better clubs for Trojan. One of the best tracks was Big Youth and youthful superstar Dennis Brown's 'Ride On, Ride On', using Dennis' own vocal hit 'Cassandra' as its basis. Issued on what was now a free-for-all sub-label, Harry J, the Winston 'Niney' Holness production carried the swing, as Jah Youth had been doing for a couple of years with rolling chants like 'Screaming Target', 'Cool Breeze' and his formative 'Ace 90 Skank'.

Trojan then had a long wait for their next chart attack, which wasn't until April 1976, when Pluto Shervington of 'Dat' fame carried the jolly 'Ram Goat Liver' to Number 43. Still, some exemplary records were slipping out from the Trojan warehouse almost unnoticed, such as 'African Dub' by vocal group The Silvertones. A revamp of the Lee Perry-produced 'Rejoice Jah Jah Children' from a couple of years earlier, complete with militant double drumming, this shot right into any roots collector's box. It was Maytals member Jerry McCarthy who, in one of his few excursions in the producers chair, really caught the dread sound of 1977.

Other reggae hits were still occasionally infiltrating the national charts through the latter part of the 1970s, but for Trojan there was no reward, despite some fine music being issued. Althea And Donna, Barry Biggs, Dennis Brown and, of course, Bob Marley And The Wailers all scored, but sadly not for Trojan.

The revamped Attack label, in 12" form, had some heavy gems hidden between the more average items, including joys such as Jimmy Riley's harsh 'Give Thanks And Praise' and Barry Brown's tough rocker 'Mr CID'. But beyond the reggae charts little was heard of these records, as there was such a plethora of 12" vinyl scattered across every record-shop counter come the end of the decade.

It was to be the Two-Tone and ska-revival scene, which sparked in 1979 and was up and running by 1980, that gave Trojan their next hit. The old Pioneers favourite 'Long Shot', backed with 'Liquidator' from Harry J and the boys, managed a Number 42 hit in March as Madness, The Specials and a host of others rediscovered not only Jamaican music but the whole skinhead style. With the style came the reggae music of a decade earlier, and from then on Trojan divided their resources between up-to-date 1980s dancehall business and retro-reggae compilations. They had already tested the retro-water in 1979 with a series of 14 maxi Trojan four-track EPs and found success with the new fans. Available for the roots fan was the garishly sleeved *Rebel Music* double album full of early-'70s sensations, with some tracks very few people actually knew.

As Two-Tone faded in the early '80s, so did Trojan's active involvement with new Jamaican product – the die was cast for delving back rather than looking forward. The last two decades have seen Trojan move from Rodd to Newman to Sanctuary, with each proud new owner rediscovering marvellous recordings, many thought lost forever or only to be found on scratch-ridden (and often very expensive) vinyl.

The techno-brilliance of digital cleaning has sometimes given a new lease of life to a much-played disc for both the die-hard vinyl lover who is happy to clutch a repress and the quick-stop CD-rack buyer. Through the long-play CD and the understanding of the needs of a vinyl lover, Trojan has brought much of the music to life again. It has made it available to the mass market buyer and reggae lover alike. Of course the real collector elements still crave the one and only original pressing, but at least even they can hear tracks they may never have known had it not been for a Trojan compilation CD.

Bob Marley's work, for example, has seen a multitude of CD covers, with each revamped issue selling well to eager new converts, while the marketplace for Jamaican – and, let's not forget, UK-based Jamaican – music compilations has never been stronger.

The British Trojan label has been with us for 36 years at the time of writing and has seldom been in better health. In that time, the company has issued literally thousands of ska, rocksteady and reggae performances on seven-inch single, 12" single, LP and CD. Who knows how the reggae fans of the future will buy their music? One thing's for sure, though: whether, as U Roy advised, they play the musical disc with a flick of their wrist or, as Freddie Notes once asserted, it comes from out of the sky, you can bet that a goodly proportion of it will be on Trojan and selling by the vanload.

Leslie Hounsfield would surely approve,

6 The Mods And The Skinheads

White Appreciators Of The Jamaican Sound

The youths known as the Mods were the first British appreciators of both American soul and Jamaican ska music, and they also sparked some of the most influential home-grown bands of the 20th century, such as The Who and The Small Faces.

The original Modernists appeared crisply dressed in Italian suits and clutching modern jazz albums in their manicured hands just as the '60s had dawned. Their group name was derived from their fondness for hip modern jazz, as purveyed by the likes of The Modern Jazz Quartet and Dave Brubeck, whose work they would endlessly discuss in steamy coffee bars around Soho.

This appreciation was a backlash against traditional – or 'trad' – jazz fever that was sweeping the country, with Kenny Ball and Acker Bilk heading up swinging New Orleans-style bands and drawing huge crowds in the pre-Beatles era. With the jazz came the cool image of the laid-back dude, suited in the finest continental fashion, with supple suede shoes gracing his feet.

There were few members at first, mainly because of their expensive tastes, but by 1962 the cult had grown from its small London beginnings. Shops such as His Clothes in Carnaby Street were discovered with their stocks of fine Italian and French fashions. The clothes were bold and statement-making, something that the emerging Mod desperately required. What's more, for the first time such clothes were cheap enough for those on middle incomes to afford.

Mod music, via the TV, was provided by Independent Television's trend-setting *Ready, Steady, Go!* show, hosted by Cathy McGowan, which supplied the Mod with not only the latest hip sounds but, by providing panning shots around the studio, the hippest fashions were displayed, as worn by the invited audience. Many of the audience were chosen because they were the top trend-setting 'faces' that hung around Soho and Carnaby Street and were instrumental in instigating the latest twist to the sharp fashion. With their faces on *Ready, Steady, Go!*, the programme was sure to be a winner, week in and week out.

On the day after each programme's transmission, record and clothing shops would be inundated with fashion-conscious Mods after the striped jacket 'that bloke wore on *Ready, Steady, Go!'* and the latest Motown pre-hit that had been aired for the first time.

Marc Bolan – or Mark Feld, as he was still known back then – was interviewed with a group of teenagers for *Town* magazine in 1962 and expounded about all things Mod in the first newspaper article on the growing cult, giving a new horizon for all teenagers reading his youthful words. As a 15-year-old fashion guru, he snobbishly recommended Bilgorri of Bishopsgate as a fine tailor – 'All the faces go to Bilgorri' – and moved on to comment on finding good clothes at Burton's and C&A.

The Mod preoccupation with clothes and looks was summed up in a colour feature in *The Sunday Times Magazine* of 2 August 1964. Denzil from Streatham, southwest London, comments, 'American styles are out, like madras cotton jackets… It's suits now and basket shoes… You need £15 a week to be a leader… Most Mods make between £8 and £10 a week and spend about £4 on clothes.'

'It's pure dress now,' said another face in the same interview.

The Mods had sprung up as the youth culture of the 1960s, much like the Teddy Boys of the previous decade, and like the Teds they adopted certain brands and a look as their own. Soon quality mohair suits, short neat hair, parkas (to keep the suits clean) and the all-important Lambretta scooters were pre-requisites for well-appointed clan members.

In the late 1950s, Lambretta Concessionaires Ltd, the sole distributors of Lambretta scooters in the UK, purchased commercial vehicle manufacturer Trojan Ltd as a going concern. At first, completed scooters were distributed through Trojan, but later, in order to reduce costs, they were imported in component form and assembled at the Trojan works.

Trojan Ltd continued to develop its own products, which included a Lambretta scooter sidecar. The agile Lambretta was an all-important Mod accessory for travelling around town, attracting the opposite sex and the infamous bank-holiday outings to coastal towns like Hastings and Brighton.

The difference between this time and the era of Teddy Boys was that rationing, spivs and the war were all way back in time for the Mods. While the Teds were the first generation not forced into National Service or to have ration-hungry bellies and inner-city bomb sites to wreck, the Mods had all-night cafés and the burgeoning concrete-jungle rebuilds of the same inner cities to roam around. And the Mods had new neighbours, the immigrants – mainly Jamaican West Indians – who had settled into all the major cities by the time the scooter ruled the road.

As the Modernists moved in, released from the constraints of being mini-grown-ups as their fathers had had to be, they embraced the growing club culture, both the existing London scene and the new Anglo-Jamaican sounds that were moving the feet of those in the know. It was just so trendy to mix into one of the new inner-city clubs with rocking R&B sounds shaking the grimy floor and snake-hipped Jamaicans wowing the patrons with their agile steps.

The Mods moved quickly from standing on the sidelines to picking up the young West Indian fashion epitomised by the rise of the wayward Rudie in Kingston and, more importantly, gaining a taste for the sounds of the Caribbean in the form of the new ska or blue-beat music that was shaking the Jamaican nation.

The Rude Boy problems had started in Jamaica after independence dawned in 1962, with promises of a new world of plenty for all. A multitude of rural youths and young men flocked to its capital, Kingston, searching for this promised work. The reality of the new dawn shone across hungry and homeless masses swirling round Kingston with no skill and no job. They gravitated to the only areas of the capital that could, or would accommodate them: the ghettos.

The heat was turned up in the swollen ghettos and flashpoints ignited, with violence, injury and death commonplace. This harsh living produced the dissatisfied ghetto youth who adopted his own stance against this forced way of life: the Rude Boy, whose image was that of being cool, deadly and sharply dressed – the complete antithesis of their grinding, poverty-stricken background. Every penny they could muster was spent on dense black shades and supple patent-leather shoes to enable them to strut their stuff in the dancehall.

Soon the young UK-based Jamaicans picked up on this cool style. Word was spread via relatives still in Kingston; via *The Gleaner*, which carried daily lurid stories of their vicious antics; and via the increasingly numerous records highlighting the problem that were being played by the sound systems.

The Rude Boys' white counterparts, the Mods, who were investigating these new and exciting inner-city clubs, soon took to the snappy new West Indian dress style and adapted some of the elements into their wardrobes. Almost as quickly, they started to fill their record boxes with the records they heard played in the clubs. The obligatory pork-pie hat was closely followed by the equally mandatory Prince Buster blue-beat record into the annals of Mod must-haves, along with a cut of Jimmy Smith's grooving Hammond B3 and a Small Faces album.

Prince Buster's blazing ska recording 'Al Capone' was somewhat belatedly hoisted to Number 18 in the UK national charts in February 1967 due to the demand created by none other than the Mods, who heard it in the clubs they frequented and on pirate radio. The power of the underground consumer was starting to have teeth, and further on the decade that same subterranean system would be the instrument that prompted the rise of reggae and Trojan Records.

But all was not well in the Mod camp early in 1967. The cult had continued to evolve into increasingly flowery thinkers and the whole thing was becoming impossibly elitist and imploding, with only the very best suits bought at Savile Row considered to be correct and supple patent-leather Italian shoes gracing the most immaculate pedicured feet. It was almost a return to the Modernist beginnings of the first years of the decade, with only the privileged few able to compete in the increasingly dandy stakes. This was fine for the well-heeled (or rich-parented) Modernist, but the ordinary guy or gal on the street didn't have much chance of joining the ranks. Many a hopeful would suffer derision for having had the misfortune to turn out in what the group perceived as the wrong shirt for an event.

Fragmentation soon appeared within the ranks. The working-class, lower-funded would-be Mods rejected the dandy paisley almost-hippy shirt-wearers and spent their limited cash in basic army-surplus and work-wear emporia, rebounding from the over-indulgence of their brothers. And so from curtained changing rooms across the country emerged the complete antithesis of the cultured highbrow, with tough weatherproof donkey jackets, army fatigues and solid work boots adopted as normal daywear. The beloved Levis hung on as the number-one jean and a quality shirt still graced the newly christened Hard Mod's back, but gone was the expensive soft, crisp and luxurious tailoring as hard denim took the brunt of the chill weather.

By the spring of 1967 the two contingents happily sat side by side, but it was obvious that a new thinking was moving the youth culture forward as more joined or changed sides, with workwear-clothed individuals infiltrating the traditional Mod groups more and more.

As the Hard Mods increased in presence, they gained the nickname of 'Peanuts' as their hair slowly became cropped even shorter. As if to mirror the tough, no-nonsense attitude to clothing, their outlook on life became very much more down to earth, no doubt a trait inherent in the very struggle of their working-class background.

By late 1968, old-school mods had retired to art colleges and hippy communes, leaving the streets of Britain's towns open to a new group of angry young men. At first they wore army fatigues, but, like all fashions, skinhead clothing evolved. By the end of the year, every skinhead wanted a Harrington jacket and a Crombie overcoat for Christmas. The old Mod way of thinking still ran through the cult, and quality clothing was always respected, particularly for eveningwear, for which the boots and braces were tucked away and sharp two-piece suits took the floor.

It was now easier on the pocket to achieve that quality look, as the rag trade zeroed in on the new youth money-maker, whipping out racks of Fred Perry T-shirts and crisp Levi's Sta-Prest trousers to every branch of John Collier's throughout the land. More dissatisfied working-class youths joined the new movement, more clothes hastened their way out of basement sweatshops and more eager ears listened to the equally underground sound of reggae.

Among the skinheads' inheritance from their Mod older brothers was a love of black music. They lapped up the soul sounds of Tamla-Motown, Atlantic and Stax eagerly enough, but the emergent reggae music was the real deal.

Quite why skinheads took reggae as their own music has been much debated over the years, learnedly but inconclusively, but it's a simple fact that the more kids listened to the music, the more they bought the records, which they then played to their friends, and so more and more people heard it. This ever-increasing circle would soon spiral out of the underground and make obscure Kingston artists into national stars, if only for a few short months, in some cases.

The Mods, although majoring on soul and The Small Faces, had always had time for ska – or 'blue beat', as it was commonly known to white Britons right up to the advent of the skinheads – so there was a background of appreciation of driving, exotic rhythms. However, quite why skinheads and reggae became so closely linked by the end of the '60s is pure conjecture. Some say that, just as white kids borrowed a few fashion ideas from their black friends whom they considered hip, such as the half-mast trousers and the shaved-in 'razor' parting, so they also appropriated their music. Another theory is that the skinheads' musical tastes were a reaction against the bloated, album-orientated progressive rock with which middle-class kids were currently boring the flares off each other; the raw spontaneity of reggae, perhaps heard at school discos or through friends' record collections, was more honest and immediate. It usually came on 45rpm singles, too, so you could afford to take more music home for your money.

Whatever the reason or reasons, by the time The Pioneers were climbing the glittering ladder of mainstream chart success with 'Long Shot Kick The Bucket' in October 1969, skinheads and reggae were inextricably intertwined.

The skinheads' passion for reggae music was invaluable in pushing the music out of the smoky clubs and independent record shops and into the mainstream of popular music. The buying power of the mods had moved Prince Buster and The Skatalites into the nation's consciousness for a few months, and Millie's throw-away ska bouncer 'My Boy Lollipop' had invaded British homes way back in March 1964, hitting Number Two in what was then called the Hit Parade. But it was the massive buying power of the boots-and-braces brigade at the tail end of the decade that really moved reggae units and elevated unknown Jamaican artists to transient stardom.

'The whole skinhead thing played a big role,' comments Robert 'Dandy' Thompson, a major player with Trojan during the late '60s. 'They were the ones who went out and bought "Red Red Wine" and "Reggae In Your Jeggae" when Trojan was on its face.'

Dandy produced one of the most collectable 45s of the era, 'Skinheads: A Message To You' by Desmond Riley, issued on Trojan's Downtown subsidiary in

1969, just as the skinhead cult was sweeping the country. But what were his friend Desmond's motives in making that record?

'I would say, to capitalise on the craze,' Dandy replies frankly, 'but also to quench the little violence that was around.'

In the public perception, skinheads and violence did indeed go hand in hand, as evidenced by this typical letter to *The Times* from a Mr DJ Chadwick of Keble College, Oxford, published on 22 November, 1969: 'At 9:30pm last Sunday, a graduate colleague of mine was assaulted by "skin-heads" whilst walking the few yards across Oriel Street from his college middle common room to the porter's lodge. Eight of these vicious teenagers used their hobnailed boots to such an extent that hospital treatment was required.

'Unfortunately, this is not an isolated incident, for, to my knowledge, one person has lost an eye and another has been injured about the face through being struck with a bicycle chain in the past weeks of this term.

'It is a sad reflection on the moral standards of some teenagers that it is no longer possible for members of the University to walk the streets in safety. I hope that your readers will join with me in a vigorous condemnation of such senseless violence and will encourage the police to do all in their power to bring young hooligans to justice.'

The very sight of a gang of booted youths entering a record shop would dissuade the proprietor from stocking their beloved moonstomping reggae records.

The 27 January 1973 issue of the *NME* carried an article by Danny Holloway entitled, 'Suddenly Reggae Is Up...After Being Almost Bottled To Death By The Skins'. In it, Harry Palmer of Trojan's main rivals Pama Records confirms the extent of the problem: 'When reggae began to establish itself in the charts, the skinheads came along and ruined it. We lost half our accounts because shops refused to stock reggae.'

'It just gave us another battle to fight,' confirms Trojan's Lee Gopthal in the same article.

Island Records' David Betteridge, meanwhile, wasn't so worried; he acknowledged that skinheads drew attention to reggae and recognised the good of a mix of skinheads and West Indian culture, although he didn't like the bad publicity that skinheads attracted.

The skinhead/reggae combination kicked off with Desmond Dekker's often lyrically misunderstood 'Israelites', released on the Pyramid label. This was Dekker's second UK chart climber, as his Rude Boy commentary '007' had managed to reach the respectable Number 14 position in 1967. Issued in 1968, 'Israelites' became an underground club smash before climbing the glittering ladder of success the following year.

While Pyramid wasn't owned by Trojan, being an offshoot of the Doctor Bird group of labels, owned by Graeme Goodall, the progress of 'Israelites' is a perfect example of the formative buying power of the skinheads and of their influence on a record's fortunes. Originally titled 'Poor Me Israelite' and issued in Jamaica on Leslie Kong's Beverley's Records, the track's catchy tune and Desmond's heavy patois-drenched lyrics won it instant dancehall success in Kingston. Jamaican-pressed copies hit the UK, impressing Goodall, who picked up the rights to the recording and issued it, retitling it simply 'Israelites', with an eye on selling a few thousand copies to the West Indian and club-going communities. But Goodall had reckoned without the skinheads' invasion of black nightspots and their appreciation of reggae music, which ensured a whole new audience for the record. As expected, West Indians asked for the record in their local independent record retailers', but meanwhile on the other side of town the skinheads were requesting their copies in the mainstream high-street shops – which filed chart returns.

Under this pressure from their shaven-headed clientele, the major stores stocked the record. The offshore pirate station Radio Caroline plugged it heavily, and was soon copied by BBC Radio 1. 'Israelites' was soon on the move and reaching far beyond its target audience, as one long-serving fan remembers: 'I was a student at Birmingham University at the time, certainly not a skinhead. One morning at breakfast I heard "Israelites" on Tony Blackburn's show and it just hit me like a missile. It was so damned catchy that it picked me up and carried me along with it. I reviewed my finances and calculated that I could afford either to eat lunch that day or go and buy the record. It was a no contest: I high-tailed it down to the Diskery in Hurst Street and returned to my digs clutching the record, hungry but happy. I must have driven my landlady mad by playing it six times in a row!'

Skinheads were very fashion conscious, and fashions extended beyond clothing. A copy of The Upsetters' 'Live Injection' clutched tightly to your Harrington jacket was as much a fashion statement as any pair of highly polished oxblood Dr Marten's boots. As the skinheads bought more and more reggae records, their appreciation grew, along with their collections.

Lists

25 COVERS OF US RHYTHM & BLUES HITS ON TROJAN LABELS (PLUS ORIGINAL ARTISTS AND LABELS)

Most of these originate from the days when sound systems played US tunes and show the enduring influence of R&B on musicians a decade or more later.

HUBERT LEE: Something On Your Mind (Downtown DT520) (Big Jay McNeely, Swingin', 1959)

THE RAVING RAVERS: Rock And Cry (Big Shot BI-507) (Clyde McPhatter, Atlantic, 1957)

THE SILVERTONES: Endlessly b/w Kiddyo (Upsetter US309) (Brook Benton, Mercury, 1959/1960)

LEE PERRY: Yakety Yak (Upsetter US328) (Coasters, Atlantic, 1958)

DERRICK MORGAN; Let Them Talk (Jackpot JP793) (Little Willie John, King, 1959)

JACKIE ROBINSON: Let The Little Girl Dance (Amalgamated AMG824) (Billy Bland, Old Town, 1960)

JOYA LANDIS: Kansas City (Trojan TR620) (Wilbert Harrison, Fury, 1959)

TOOTS & THE MAYTALS: Louie Louie (Trojan TR7865) (Richard Berry And The Pharaohs, Flip, 1957)

TOOTS & THE MAYTALS: Fever (Dragon DR1021) (Little Willie John, King, 1956)

TOOTS & THE MAYTALS: Daddy's Home (Dragon DRLS5002) (Shep And The Limelites, Hull, 1961)

AL T JOE: Prisoner's Song (Dynamic DYN429) (Warren Storm, Nasco, 1958, although originally a US pop hit in 1925 for Vernon Delhart)

MARVELS: CC Rider (Trojan TRLS67) (Chuck Willis, Atlantic, 1957, although originally recorded by Ma Rainey in the 1920s)

WINSTON WRIGHT: Silhouettes (Duke DU111)

DENNIS BROWN: Silhouettes (Song Bird SB1074) (The Rays, Cameo, 1957)

THE RUDIES: Night Train (Downtown DT424) (Jimmy Forrest, United, 1952)

NEVILLE GRANT: Sick And Tired (Downtown DT509) (Chris Kenner, Imperial, 1957)

VAL BENNETT: Baby Baby (Trojan TR640) (Ruth Brown, as '5–10–15 Hours', Atlantic, 1952)

DERRICK MORGAN: Hey Little Girl (Downtown DT520) (Dee Clark, Abner, 1959)

JIMMY LONDON: Shake A Hand (Randy's RAN514) (Faye Adams, Herald, 1953)

OWEN GRAY: Lovey Dovey (Trojan TR632) (Clyde McPhatter, Atlantic, 1959)

LASCELLES PERKINS: English Chicken (Big Shot BI618) (Louis Jordan, as 'Ain't Nobody Here But Us Chickens', Decca, 1946)

DERRICK MORGAN & PAULETTE: Lee's Dream (Harry J HJ6697) (Shirley And Lee, Aladdin, 1955)

JACKIE BROWN: One Night Of Sin (High Note HS057) (Smiley Lewis, Imperial, 1956)

JOHN HOLT: It May Sound Silly (Moodisc MU3513) (Ivory Joe Hunter, Atlantic, 1955)

25 TAMLA-MOTOWN COVER VERSIONS ON TROJAN LABELS

Not surprisingly, the sound of young America provided a fertile source of songs for Jamaican artists.

DELROY WILSON: Put Yourself In My Place (High Note HS011) (The Elgins, VIP, 1966)

DELROY WILSON: The Same Old Song (Jackpot JP795) (The Four Tops, Motown, 1965)

DELROY WILSON: Ain't That Peculiar (Green Door GD4060) (Marvin Gaye, Tamla, 1965)

DELROY WILSON: This Old Heart Of Mine (Jackpot JP800) (The Isley Brothers, Tamla, 1966)

DAVID ISAACS: Place In The Sun (Trojan TR616) (Stevie Wonder, Tamla, 1966)

THE PARAGONS: Left With A Broken Heart (Duke DU-7) (The Four Tops, Motown, 1965)

MAXINE: Everybody Needs Love (Smash SMA2301) (Gladys Knight And The Pips, Soul, 1967)

ALTON ELLIS: What Does It Take To Win Your Love (Duke Reid DR2501) (Jr Walker And The All Stars, Soul, 1969)

JOHN HOLT: The Further You Look (Horse, HOSS 22) (The Temptations, Gordy, 1963)

THE PIONEERS: Get Ready (Summit SUM 8517) (The Temptations, Gordy, 1965)

DERRICK HARRIOTT: Since I Lost My Baby(Song Bird SB1071) (The Temptations, Gordy, 1965)

DERRICK HARRIOTT: Let Me Down Easy (Explosion EX2071) (GC Cameron, Motown, 1973)

LLOYD CHARMERS: Come See About Me (Song Bird SB1002) (The Supremes, Motown, 1965)

ERIC DONALDSON: The Way You Do The Things You Do (Dragon DR1018) (The Temptations, Gordy, 1964)

THE TECHNIQUES: I Wish It Would Rain (Duke DU1) (The Temptations, Gordy, 1968)

KEN BOOTHE: You Keep Me Hanging On (Coxsone CS7043) (The Supremes, Motown, 1966)

ERNEST WILSON: If I Were A Carpenter (Studio One SO2057) (The Four Tops, Motown, 1968, although previously a pop hit for Bobby Darin, 1966)

FREDDIE NOTES & THE RUDIES: Yester-Me Yester-You (Grape GR3010) (Stevie Wonder, Tamla, 1969)

GLEN ADAMS: Never Had A Dream Come True (Upsetter US 367) (Stevie Wonder, Tamla, 1970)

THE GAYLADS: Stop Making Love (Trojan TTL 48) (The Four Tops, as 'It's The Same Old Song', Motown, 1965)

SIDNEY, GEORGE & JACKIE: Papa Was A Rolling Stone (Attack ATT8077) (The Temptations, Gordy, 1972)

DARKER SHADE OF BLACK: Ball Of Confusion (Jackpot JP758) (The Temptations, Gordy, 1970)

PAT RHODEN: Boogie On Reggae Woman (Horse HOSS59) (Stevie Wonder, Tamla, 1974)

RANDY'S ALL STARS: War (Randy's RAN505) (Edwin Starr, Gordy, 1970)

LLOYD PARKS: Stop The War Now (Trojan TRLS 109) (Edwin Starr, Gordy, 1970)

25 SERIOUSLY OBSCURE COVER VERSIONS ON TROJAN LABELS

All of these selections are either obscure in their own right or versions of obscure (and sometimes unlikely) American songs, demonstrating just how keenly Jamaicans followed US music in the 1950s and 1960s. In some cases, the cover version has become far better known than the original recording. Sometimes a change in song title increases the obscurity factor!

THE ETHIOPIANS: Good Ambition (Song Bird SB1047) (Roy C, as 'High School Dropout', Jameco, 1966)

JIMMY SHONDELL: Snake In The Grass (Horse HOSS35) (Paul Martin, Ascot, 1967)

WINSTON WRIGHT: Moon Invader (Trojan TR7715) (The Meters, as 'Look-ka-py-py', Josie, 1969)

ALTON ELLIS: Willow Tree (Treasure Isle TI7044) (Chuck Jackson, as 'My Willow Tree', Wand, 1962)

BORIS GARDINER: Elizabethan Reggae (Duke DU39) (Gunther Kallman Choir, as 'Elisabeth Serenade', German Polydor, 1964)

UNIQUES: Watch This Sound (Trojan TR619) (Buffalo Springfield, as 'For What It's Worth', Atco, 1967)

JOHN HOLT: I Had A Talk With My Woman (Smash SMA2303) (Mitty Collier, as 'I Had A Talk With My Man', Chess, 1964)

JOHN HOLT: Sometimes (Trojan TRLS 37) (Gene Thomas, as 'Sometime', Venus, 1961)

NICKY THOMAS: Doing The Moonwalk (Trojan TR7862) (Joe Simon, as 'Moon Walk', Sound Stage 7, 1970)

JUDY MOWATT: Way Over Yonder (Trojan TR7900) (Carole King, Ode LP track, 1971)

PAT KELLY: Just For A Day (Jackpot JP 764) (Chuck Jackson, as 'The Prophet', Wand, 1963)

JOHN HOLT: Stick By Me (Jackpot JP772) (Shep & The Limelites, as 'Stick By Me And I'll Stick By You', Hull, 1963)

THE TECHNIQUES: You Don't Care (Treasure Isle TI7001) (Major Lance, as 'You'll Want Me Back', OKeh, 1966)

JUSTIN HINDS: Here I Stand (Treasure Isle TI7002) (The Rip Chords [a surfing group!], Columbia, 1963)

TROPIC SHADOWS: Our Anniversary (Big Shot BI603) (Shep And The Limelites, Hull, 1962)

SIR LORD COMIC AND HIS COWBOYS: Ska-ing West (Trojan TTL48) (Billy Hope And The Badmen, as 'Riding West', Savoy, 1958)

THE TECHNIQUES: Queen Majesty (Treasure Isle TI7019) (The Impressions, as 'Minstrel And Queen', ABC-Paramount LP track, 1963)

LLOYD PARKS: Mighty Clouds Of Joy (Upsetter US395) (BJ Thomas, Scepter, 1971)

BOB MARLEY & THE WAILERS: African Herbsman (Upsetter US392) (Richie Havens, as 'Indian Ropeman', Verve-Forecast LP track, 1969)

DELROY WILSON: It Hurts (High Note HS011) (Ray Whitley & The Tams, as 'I've Been Hurt', ABC-Paramount, 1965)

THE BABA BROOKS BAND: King Size (Trojan TTL51) (Eddie Cantor, as 'Making Whoopee' in the film *Whoopee*, 1930)

ROLAND ALPHONSO: El Pussy Cat (Trojan TTL16) (Mongo Santamaria, Columbia, 1965)

THE MARVELS: Voice Your Choice (Trojan TRLS67) (The Radiants, Chess, 1965)
NICKY THOMAS: New Morning (Trojan TBL208) (Bob Dylan, Columbia LP track, 1970)
NICKY THOMAS: Love Of The Common People (Trojan TR7750) (The Everly Brothers, Warner Bros, 1967)

25 COVERS OF US POP HITS ON TROJAN LABELS

Of course, many soul records crossed over to hit the pop charts, but this list concentrates on records by pop acts (ie generally white bands or singers) that received the Jamaican treatment. Once again, in some cases the cover version has become better known than the original – who, for example, remembers The Joe Reisman Orchestra these days?

HONEYBOY MARTIN: Have You Ever Seen The Rain (Harry J HJ6643) (Creedence Clearwater Revival, Fantasy, 1971)
HOPETON LEWIS: Grooving Out On Life (Dragon DRA1011) (The Newbeats, Hickory, 1968)
THE SKATALITES: Guns Of Navarone (Trojan TTL16) (The Joe Reisman Orchestra, Landa, 1961)
SLIM SMITH: Just A Dream (Dynamic DYN428) (Jimmy Clanton, Ace, 1958)
JOHN HOLT: You Baby (Trojan TR) (The Turtles, White Whale, 1966)
JOHN HOLT: It May Sound Silly (Moodisc MU3513) (The McGuire Sisters, Coral, 1955)
BRENT DOWE & HORTENSE ELLIS: Put Your Hand In The Hand (Summit SUM8525) (Ocean, Kama Sutra, 1971)
BRUCE RUFFIN: Rain (Trojan TR7814) (Jose Feliciano, RCA, 1969)
BRUCE RUFFIN: Candida (Summit SUM8516) (Dawn, Bell, 1970)
BRENT DOWE: Knock Three Times (Summit SUM8521) (Dawn, Bell, 1971)
BOB & MARCIA: Pied Piper (Trojan TR7818) (Changin' Times, Phillips, 1965)
BARBARA JONES: Changing Partners (Attack ATT8077) (Kay Starr, RCA, 1954)
THE GAYTONES: Joy To The World (High Note HS054 (Three Dog Night, Dunhill, 1971)
THE GAYLADS: Love Me With All Your Heart (Studio One SO2017) (Steve Allen, as 'Cuando Caliente El Sol', Dot, 1963)
THE GAYLADS: Fire And Rain (Trojan) (Simon & Garfunkel, Columbia, 1965)
LLOYD CHARMERS: California Dreamin' (Explosion EX2041) (The Mamas & The Papas, Dunhill, 1966)
THE PIONEERS: Storybook Children (Summit SUM8535) (Billy Vera & Judy Clay, Atlantic, 1967)

DAVID ISAACS: He'll Have To Go (Upsetter US311) (Jim Reeves, RCA, 1959)

ALTON ELLIS: You Made Me So Very Happy (Duke Reid DR2512) (Blood, Sweat And Tears, Columbia, 1969)

JOE WHITE: If It Don't Work Out (Gayfeet GS203) (The Casinos, as 'Then You Can Tell Me Goodbye', Fraternity, 1967)

THE HEPTONES: I Shall Be Released (Studio One SO2083) (The Box Tops, Mama, 1969)

THE UPSETTERS: Na Na Hey Hey (Upsetter US332) (Steam, Fontana, 1969)

STRANGER COLE: Crying Every Night (Spinning Wheel SW 109) (The Guess Who, as 'These Eyes', RCA 1969)

WINSTON FRANCIS: The Games People Play (Studio One SO2086) (Joe South, Capitol, 1969)

NICKY THOMAS: If I Had A Hammer (Trojan TR7807) (Peter, Paul And Mary, Warner Bros, 1962)

25 COVERS OF UK POP HITS ON TROJAN LABELS.

You might expect this section to be crammed with London-recorded pop reggae of the kind which Trojan increasingly churned out in the mid '70s. In fact, more than half of the selections here are Jamaican recordings.

AL T JOE: Hitching A Ride (Dynamic DYN408) (Vanity Fare, Page One, 1969)

HOPETON LEWIS: Going Back To My Home Town (Dynamic DYN436) (Hal Paige And The Whalers, Melodisc, 1960 – recorded by Fury of New York, but a hit in Britain only)

DERRICK HARRIOTT: Eighteen With A Bullet (Trojan TR7973) (Pete Wingfield, Island, 1975)

WAYNE HOWARD: All Kinds Of Everything (Explosion EX2042) (Dana, Rex, 1970)

NORMA FRASER: The First Cut Is The Deepest (Coxsone CS7017) (PP Arnold, Immediate, 1967)

THE THREE TOPS: A Groovy Kind Of Love (Coxsone CS7033) (The Mindbenders, Fontana, 1966)

ROB WALKER: Puppet On A String (Jackpot JP761) (Sandie Shaw, Pye, 1967)

CYNTHIA RICHARDS: United We Stand (Pressure Beat PB5507) (Brotherhood Of Man, Deram, 1970)

ALTON ELLIS: A Whiter Shade Of Pale (Coxsone CSL8008) (Procol Harum, Deram, 1967)

VAL BENNETT: Stranger On The Shore (Upsetter US321)

DAVID ISAACS: Stranger On The Shore (Upsetter US400) (Mr Acker Bilk, Columbia, 1961)

JOHN HOLT: The Last Farewell (Trojan TRLS160) (Roger Whittaker, EMI, 1975)

JOYCE BOND: Ob-la-di Ob-la-da (Trojan TTL1) (Marmalade, CBS, 1968)

JACKIE MITTOO: Norwegian Wood (Coxsone CS7040) (The Beatles, Parlophone LP track, 1965)

NICKY THOMAS: Let It Be (Amalgamated AMG860, 1970) (The Beatles, Apple, 1970)

THE RUDIES: My Sweet Lord (Spinning Wheel SW106) (George Harrison, Apple, 1971)

BUSTY BROWN: To Love Somebody (Upsetter US308) (The Bee Gees, Polydor, 1967)

MARCIA & JEFF: Words (Studio One SO2047) (The Bee Gees, Polydor, 1968)

DAVE BARKER & THE WAILERS: Don't Let The Sun Catch You Crying (Upsetter US347) (Gerry And The Pacemakers, Columbia, 1964)

DANDY: What Do You Want To Make Those Eyes At Me For? (Trojan TR7854) (Emile Ford And The Checkmates, Pye, 1959)

THE MUSIC DOCTORS: In The Summertime (J-Dan JDN 4414) (Mungo Jerry, Dawn, 1970)

THE GAYLETS: Son Of A Preacher Man (Big Shot, BI516) (Dusty Springfield, Phillips, 1968)

THE PIONEERS: Blame It On The Pony Express (Trojan TRLS64) (Johnny Johnson & The Bandwagon, Bell, 1970)

DENNIS BROWN: Black Magic Woman (Explosion EX2068) (Fleetwood Mac, Blue Horizon, 1968)

PAT KELLY: He Ain't Heavy, He's My Brother (Jackpot 764) (The Hollies, Parlophone, 1969)

Musicland And Muzic City Chronology

1963

Beat and Commercial Records Ltd incorporated on 19 April, ref 758078

1966

Musicland outlets:
    13 High Road, Willesden Green

1967

Additional Musicland Outlets:
    13 High Road, Willesden Green (head office)
    42 Willesden Lane, NW6 (mail order)
    5a Extension Market, Shepherds Bush, W12
    230 Portobello Road
    20g Atlantic Road
    53 Watling Avenue, Burnt Oak
    256a North End Road

1968

Additional Musicland Outlets:
    44 Berwick Street (Mail Order)
    23 Ridley Road
(Note: 42 Willesden Lane no longer shown as Musicland mail-order outlet)

1969

Additional Musicland outlets:
    21 High Street, SE8
    153 Kilburn High Road
    96 High Street, Watford
    11a Church Street, Kingston
    153 High Road, Hounslow

1970

Notice in June issue of *The London Gazette* regarding the possible winding up of Musicland Ltd

Additional Musicland Outlets:
    12 Neasden Lane (head office)
    12a Extension Market, Shepherds Bush
    297 Portobello Road
    4 Soho Street, W1

Dropped Musicland outlets:
    20g Atlantic Road
(Note: 12 Neasden Lane becomes Musicland head office; directory records show Musicland as 'Proprieters: B&C' for the first time)

1971

Additional Musicland Outlets:
    135 High Street, Watford
    226 High Road, Hounslow
    44 Lewisham High Street

Dropped Musicland outlets:
    21 High Street, SE8
    96 High Street, Watford
    153 High Road, Hounslow

Musicland outlets converted to Muzik City outlets:
    5a Extension Market, Shepherds Bush
    12a Extension Market, Shepherds Bush
    23 Ridley Road, Dalston, E8
    42 Willesden Lane, NW6
    297 Portobello Road

New Muzik City outlets:
    21 High Street, Deptford
    30 Station Parade, Kensal Rise, NW10
    32 Goldhawk Road, W9
    72 Granville Arcade, Brixton, SW9
    94 Granville Arcade, Brixton, SW9

530 Harrow Road, W9
Balham Kiosk, Balham High Street, SW12

1972
Ref 1074876 – Music City Ltd set up
Ref 1066926 – Muzik City Records Shops Limited set up
Ref 1042071 – Trojanland Ltd set up
Reference to Companies House Certificate of Incorporation
Musicland (unknown which company) is sold

Additional Musicland outlets:
    66 The Broadway, Ealing
    Incredible Department Store, 94a Brompton Road
    Ravels, 44 Kings Road, SW3

Dropped Musicland outlets:
    256a North End Road
    4 Soho Street, W1

1973
Ref 43178 – Musicland Ltd dissolved
Musicland Head Office no longer shown as 12 Neasden Lane

Dropped Musicland outlets:
    53 Watling Avenue, Burnt Oak
    135 High Street, Watford
    11a Church Street, Kingston
    226 High Road, Hounslow
    Ravels, 44 Kings Road, SW3

Additional Muzik City outlets:
    Music House, 11 Neasden Lane
    11a Model Market, Lewisham, SE13
    96 Granville Arcade, Brixton, SW9
(Note: At this stage Music House is not shown as head office)

Dropped Muzik City outlets:
    32 Goldhawk Road
    94 Granville Arcade, Brixton, SW9

297 Portobello Road
(Note: Adverts also show 55 Atlantic Road – Desmond's Hip City – as an outlet, although this address is not noted in the Post Office Directory as Musicland or Muzik City)

1974

Dropped Musicland outlets:
   66 the Broadway, Ealing
   94a Brompton Road
   44 Lewisham High Street
(Note: Music House is shown as head office)

1975

Dropped Musicland outlets:
   230 Portobello Road
   44 Berwick Street
(Note: The only Musicland outlet remaining in this year is 153 Kilburn High Street, which did not survive into 1976)

Dropped Muzik City Outlets:
   21 High Street, Deptford
   530 Harrow Road
   Balham Kiosk
   42 Willesden Lane

Muzik City record shops went into voluntary winding-up on 22 January 1976, with a final winding-up meeting of members and creditors taking place on 1 December 1978. Musicland Record Stores Ltd was dissolved on 14 February 1977.

LIVERPOOL JOHN MOORES UNIVERSITY
LEARNING SERVICES

Suggested Listening

This section is intended as nothing more than a snapshot of some excellent albums that are available at the time of writing to give an idea of what is available. There are literally hundreds of other worthy releases out there, both reissues of old albums and modern compilations of earlier work.

BOB ANDY: SONG BOOK (COXSONE)

This album deserves to be in every music lover's collection with its heartfelt songs of hope, love and oppression, recorded at Studio One at the turn of the '60s into the '70s. Most of the rhythms, and the songs themselves, have become standards within the Jamaican music scene.

BOB ANDY: RETROSPECTIVE (I-ANKA RECORDS)

Following on from Bob Andy's stay at Studio One, this album collects together his work for a variety of producers between 1970 and 1975. As with *Song Book*, this collection further cements his reputation as one of the key figures of Jamaican music.

BOB MARLEY AND THE WAILERS: SOUL REBELS (TROJAN)

A pre-hit and, you could say, un-electrified Marley at his best from 1970. The songs are aided by Lee Perry's dense and mystical production, which only highlights the almost ethereal quality of tracks like the title cut and Peter Tosh's angry '400 Years'. To many connoisseurs, his later, over-orchestrated work for Island isn't a patch on the raw soul recorded here.

BOB MARLEY AND THE WAILERS: CATCH A FIRE (ISLAND)

The latest variant of this release is a double-CD set with disc one being the normal Island issue complete with London overdubs, as issued in 1973. It is the second disc which is of interest here, as it is the raw Jamaican mix of the album before Island got their heavy hands on it, and it is far superior. 'Concrete Jungle' is particularly chilling, with Marley bringing to the fore a sparse hopelessness completely lost in the Basing Street reworking.

I-ROY: PRESENTING/HELL AND SORROW (TROJAN)

Alongside Big Youth's *Screaming Target* set, this two-for-one CD epitomises the art of roots-reality DJ chat. Enhanced no end by the tough new rhythm structures produced by Gussie Clarke on *Presenting* (he also produced the Big Youth set) and by I-Roy on *Hell & Sorrow*, this is the new (1973), no-nonsense, tough-talking rapper at his best.

KEITH HUDSON: PICK A DUB (BLOOD AND FIRE)

Produced by Hudson and Wailers bass player Family Man Barrett, this album deconstructs some of Keith's finest rhythms. Released in 1974 alongside Augustus Pablo's *King Tubby's Meets The Rockers Uptown* and Perry's *Black Board Jungle Dub*, both of which were mixed by King Tubby, *Pick A Dub* offers some of dub's finest moments.

KEN BOOTHE: ANTHOLOGY (TROJAN)

A double-CD set of one of the most unmistakeable voices of Jamaica, covering the majority of his hits, both on the local scene and across the Atlantic.

THE SKATALITES: SKA BOO-DA-BA (WEST SIDE)

Producer Justin Yap's Top Deck and Tuneico labels issued some of the most satisfying ska sessions from The Skatalites. It is said that they gave some their best performances for him, as he paid them not only well but also on time.

U ROY: VERSION GALORE (TROJAN)

Version Galore is an album of such popularity that it is rarely unavailable in some form or another. The latest Trojan issue combines the original DJ album with all the respective original tracks that U Roy used as his base for the groundbreaking raps.

VARIOUS ARTISTS: DANCEHALL '69 (TROJAN)

A double-CD set of the rarer recordings enjoyed in the clubs at the time, not necessarily aimed at the skinhead audience by the artists but adopted by them all the same. One CD is of UK recordings while the other is all Jamaican.

VARIOUS ARTISTS: DARKER THAN BLUE – SOUL FROM JAMDOWN 1973-1980 (BLOOD AND FIRE)

Eighteen cuts of reggae with a funk or soul twist. A style derided at the time but which has now found its own market – very deservedly.

VARIOUS ARTISTS: FOUNDATION SKA (HEARTBEAT)

Sumptuous double LP/CD of the best ska band (The Skatalites) at the best studio (Brentford Road). Features rip-roaring instrumentals plus top ska vocals like Jackie Opel's 'Old Rocking Chair', with the unbelievable sound of Ernest Ranglin's guitar.

VARIOUS ARTISTS: SKINHEAD REGGAE (BOX SET) (TROJAN)

A bargain three-CD box set highlighting the more popular skinhead club tunes of the day.

VARIOUS ARTISTS: THE BIGGEST DANCEHALL ANTHEMS, 1979–82 (GREENSLEEVES)

When Trojan stumbled in the later part of the '70s, Greensleeves took the reins and proceeded to release a large proportion of the current new music being recorded in Kingston. This double CD collects all their major triumphs in an age when dancehall was just starting to usurp the Rasta-roots style and DJs like Yellowman were coming to prominence.

VARIOUS ARTISTS: THE COMPLETE UK UPSETTER SINGLES COLLECTION VOLS 1–4 (TROJAN)

Four double-CD sets with integral books chronologically charting Lee Perry's Trojan/Upsetter label with each A- and respective B-side from start to finish. All of the triumphs (and the few failures) are present and the series provides an excellent way to collect all of the Upsetter singles without paying an arm and a leg.

VARIOUS ARTISTS: THE FRONT LINE (VIRGIN)

Virgin, alongside Island, were grabbing all and sundry performers as reggae rose to prominence in the mid 1970s. This four-CD set with integral book collects many of the best moments from the label, with such roots artists as The Abyssinians, Culture and The Mighty Diamonds, while DJs like I-Roy, Big Youth and U Roy all get a look-in. A superb overview of 1970s roots reggae.

VARIOUS ARTISTS: THE HARDER THEY COME (ISLAND)

Perry Henzell's 1972 feature film captured the reggae moment in time, with Jimmy Cliff starring as a country boy who moves to Kingston and turns to crime via the record industry. The story may be a little well-worn now, but the sight of such luminaries filmed in the studio as The Maytals and DJ Scotty, plus the soundtrack itself, makes this essential for any reggae lover. Available on CD, vinyl, video and DVD.

VARIOUS ARTISTS: HISTORY OF TROJAN RECORDS 1968-1971 VOL 1 (TROJAN)/1972-1995 VOL 2 (TROJAN)

Two double CDs tracing not only Trojan's progression but also the ever-changing style of Jamaican music. *Volume One* is slightly misleading, as it starts off in the ska era of Island, prior to Trojan Records being formed, but both volumes combined provide an excellent musical ride through the years.

VARIOUS ARTISTS: REBEL MUSIC (TROJAN)

This album has recently been revamped by the original compiler, Dave Hendley, who replaced a couple of the more easily found tracks with some of equal quality but much higher scarcity. A definite must-have for anyone interested in where Kingston was at in the 1970s.

VARIOUS ARTISTS: STUDIO ONE DJs (SOUL JAZZ)

All of the Soul Jazz *Studio One* collections are well worth picking up, but the *DJs* set shows the roots of many of the US rap superstars of today, and the rhythm tracks are sublime as well.

VARIOUS ARTISTS: STUDIO ONE STORY (SOUL JAZZ)

An exemplary musical overview of the famous recording studio through the years, made even more desirable by a four-hour DVD featuring Mr Dodd in Kingston, plus live band/studio footage. The set comes with a 100-page book.

VARIOUS ARTISTS: THE BIRTH OF TROJAN - DUKE REID ROCKSTEADY 1967 (TROJAN)

Where it all began for Trojan Records, this album features the first 11 single releases on the then Island/B&C-owned Trojan label, mainly comprising sublime Tommy McCook-led rocksteady. It's easy to see why Duke Reid has always been regarded as the finest producer of the beat.

VARIOUS ARTISTS: TIGHTEN UP VOL 1/VOL 2/VOL 3/VOL 4/VOL 5 (TROJAN)

The highly successful *Tighten Up* series sold extremely well at the time, and the Trojan reissues with bonus tracks are even better value. As an overview and progression of what was happening on the reggae scene of the late '60s and early '70s they are invaluable, aside from being full of first-rate music.

VARIOUS ARTISTS: TOUGHER THAN TOUGH – THE STORY OF JAMAICAN MUSIC (ISLAND)

This four-CD set traces the progression of Jamaican music from its early beginnings to the dawn of the '90s. Steve Barrow compiled the set and wrote the text for the excellent integral book.

Suggested Reading

In the early '70s, books on Jamaican music just didn't exist. Thankfully, their number has been steadily growing, and now there are quite a few available. Below are some recommendations which are felt to be of particular use and interest to anyone requiring further reading.

BISHTON, DEREK: *Blackheart Man* (Chatto & Windus)
Subtitled 'A Journey Into Rasta', which is just what this is, with evocative pictures and an easily accessible text taking the reader from the beginnings of the religion to the present day.

GRIFFITHS, MARK: *Boss Sounds – Classic Skinhead Reggae* (STP Publishing)
The only book of its kind, as it focuses on just the 'skinhead' years of reggae music, checking out both UK and JA recordings. A detailed overview of the scene is complemented by a label-by-label description and record-buying recommendations.

REEL, PENNY: *Deep Down With Dennis Brown* (Drake Brothers)
A superbly presented book full of colour and black-and-white plates illustrating the (mainly London) reggae scene of the '70s and offering a snapshot of the then young (but now late) Dennis Emanuel Brown. Penny Reel writes evocatively and knowledgeably of his life and times.

KATZ, DAVID: *People Funny Boy – The Genius of Lee 'Scratch' Perry* (Payback Press)
Dave Katz offers an exhaustive (460-page) progression of the life and works of Lee Perry from his birth to the present day. Along the voyage, the reader is treated to biographies of a legion of other singers, players and producers, so the book far transcends its title as just a view of Perry's life and work.

DAVIS, STEPHEN and SIMON, PETER: *Reggae International* (Thames & Hudson)
Reggae International is a sumptuous large-format book and is now nearing 20-year anniversary since its first publication. As a guide to the genre, from the music's

African roots to the then-new sounds of dancehall, it is good, but when you add the superb colour and black-and-white plates, the book comes into its own. It is a volume well worth searching out.

BARROW, STEVE and DALTON, PETER: *The Rough Guide To Reggae* (Rough Guides/Penguin)
Without the slightest doubt, *The Rough Guide To Reggae* is the definitive book for any enthusiast. Alongside a very readable progression of the music and biographies of just about every individual involved from its formative R&B roots to ragga, the book offers commentary on over 1,000 LP/CD releases.

LARKIN, COLIN: *The Virgin Encyclopaedia Of Reggae* (Virgin)
A handy reference overview to reggae artists, but beware that there are occasional mistakes, such as Dave And Ansel Collins being cited as brothers in one entry.

Sources

CHAPTER 1: EARLY YEARS

Trojan Lorries website (with permission)
The Rough Guide To Reggae – Steve Barrow and Peter Dalton (Rough Guides/Penguin)
Derrick Morgan interview – LCH
Graeme Goodall interview – LCH
Earl Morgan interview – LCH
Mike Atherton

CHAPTER 2: WINDRUSH TO 1974

Public Records Office
Empire Windrush passenger list (PRO)
Companies House
The Guild Hall
Keep On Moving: The Windrush Legacy – Tony Sewell (Voice Enterprises Ltd)
The Rough Guide To Reggae – Steve Barrow and Peter Dalton (Rough Guides/Penguin)
David Betteridge interview – LCH
Lee Gopthal interview – Rob Randall (*Melody Maker*, 30 December 1972)
Joe Sinclair interview – MdK
Rob Bell interview – MdK
Robert Thompson interview – LCH
Greyhound CD sleeve notes – LCH (courtesy Trojan Records)
The Cimarons interview – Carl Gayle (*Black Music*, magazine July 1976)
'Reggae' – Mark Plummer (*Melody Maker*, 22 May 1971)
Dave Barker interview – Rob Randall (*NME*, 15 January 1972)
Jackie Robinson interview – unknown (*Disc*, 28 August 1971)
Bruce White interview – MdK
Bob Andy interview – MdK
Bob & Marcia interview – Simon Burnett (*Record Mirror*, 17 July 1971)
Clive Crawley interview – LCH
Vic Keary interview – LCH

Notes taken for the film *Reggae*, produced and directed by Horace Ove
Winston Riley interview – unknown (*NME*, March 1971)
Dave Barker interview – unknown (*NME*, 15 January 1972)
Dave Barker interview – Lon Goddard (*Record Mirror*)
'Rudies Play At Mick Jagger's Wedding' – unknown (*Rolling Stone*, 10 July 1971)
Jeffrey Palmer interview – Danny Holloway (*NME*, 27 January 1973)
Times article – Richard Williams (*The Times*, 19 March 1973)

CHAPTER 3: 1975 TO DATE
The Guild Hall
Companies House
Webster Shrowder interview – Carl Gayle (*Black Music* magazine, July 1974)
Club Scene – Carl Gayle (*Black Music* magazine, 'UK Reggae' feature, July 1974)
Dandy interview – Carl Gayle (*Black Music* magazine, February 1974)
Sid Bucknor interview – MdK
Nicky Thomas interview – Carl Gayle (*Black Music* magazine, February 1974)
Tony Ashfield/Keith Boviour – Trojan press release
Louisa Mark, Safari single sales – *Black Music* magazine, July 1975
Marcel Rodd interview – Carl Gayle (*Black Music* magazine, October 1976)
Notices – *The London Gazette*, 10 June 1975
Dave Hendley interview – MdK
Colin Newman interview – LCH
Laurence Cane Honeysett interview – MdK
Trojan Appreciation Society documents – MdK
Sanctuary financial information – various 'city' reports
John Reed interview – LCH/MdK

CHAPTERS 4 & 5: MUSIC HISTORY - PARTS 1 & 2
Trojan release sheets and charts – MdK
Black Music magazine charts – MdK
The Guinness Book of Hit Singles – Paul Gambaccini, Tim Rice, Jonathan Rice (Guinness)
The Complete Book of the British Charts Singles and Albums – Tony Brown, Jon Kutner and Neil Warwick (Omnibus Press)

CHAPTER 6: THE MODS AND THE SKINHEADS
Sunday Times Magazine feature 'Changing Faces' by Kathlene Halton (2 August 1964)
Mods – Richard Barnes (Plexus)
Marc Bolan interview – unknown (*Town* magazine, 1962)

Robert Thompson interview – LCH
Times letter – November 1969
Harry Palmer interview – Danny Holloway (*NME*, 27 January 1973)
Lee Gopthal interview – Danny Holloway (*NME*, 27 January 1973)
David Betteridge interview – Danny Holloway (*NME*, 27 January 1973)
Rob Bell interview – MdK
Mike Atherton

Label Profiles

AMALGAMATED

This label was set up by B&C in 1968 to issue the productions of Joel Gibson, otherwise known as Joe Gibbs. Unusually, there is absolutely nothing among its 72 issues that can be described as a bum cut, although the flipside of AMG 804, 'We Are Not Divided', was a Sacred effort and possibly originally destined for the short-lived Amalgamated Sacred series. The Pioneers crop up most on the label and their 'Jackpot', 'Catch The Beat' and 'Gimme Little Loving' are classics, also to be found on their *Greetings From The Pioneers* set. Other goodies are 'El Casino Royale' (Lyn Tait & The Jets), 'Good Time Rock' (Hugh Malcolm), 'On The Move (The Soul Mates) and 'Man Beware' (The Slickers). Another superb track is The Immortals' 'Red Red Wine' (flipside of AMG 869), which has nothing to do with its more famous namesake. Some of the best sides from 1968 and 1969 sides were collected on Amalgamated's *Jackpot Of Hits* compilation.

As is the case with a number of these producer-dedicated Trojan subsidiaries, it is now being discovered that not all of the issues were the work of the producer in question, and the sides by The Cobbs are believed to be Ken Jones's productions. The Victor Morris sides (AMG 813) are also from elsewhere and saw issue on the Double D label as well, where the production credits went to Bobby Aitken. All in all, though, Amalgamated really was a solid-gold Trojan subsidiary. The Pressure Beat label was created for Gibbs' productions in 1970 and Amalgamated was retained alongside it until the early part of 1971, when it was scrapped entirely.

ATTACK

Started in 1969 by Graeme Goodall's Doctor Bird Group, Attack was initially concerned with productions from Philip Chen's Philligree stable, which pretty much consisted of The Pyramids in their various guises (mainly as Family Circle) and the male vocalist Pat Sandy. With the exception of The Soul Directions' excellent 'Su Su Su', which was recorded in Jamaica and featured some, if not all, of The Pioneers, the label featured average-to-superior British reggae fare. The label folded at some point in 1970, when Doctor Bird went into liquidation.

Trojan then took up the reins, possibly around the time of ATT 8013, as for this release the label format and pressing type changed and a couple of Laurel Aitken releases were put out.

However, the label fared no better under Trojan's wing and the plug was pulled before the dawn of 1971. Things didn't stay that way, though, and the company later resurrected Attack – with original label design intact – in 1972 to deal with material of a variety of producers. It was to become a real survivor, lasting until 1979, when a 12" series was issued. Particularly strong titles include U Roy Junior's 'This A Pepper', Pat Satchmo's 'What's Going On' (and he doesn't do his customary Louis Armstrong impression, either), Gregory Isaacs' 'Love Is Overdue' and, from the later period, Michael Dyke's 'Saturday Night Special', although the pressings are absolutely diabolical on this one. During the 1974–5 period, the label changed to a plain black-and-white design, in common with other Trojan economy measures of the time, and there is relatively little of real quality from this era.

BIG

This subsidiary was initiated by Trojan for productions from Rupie Edwards, although it has come to light recently that the occasional non-Edwards track found its way in here and there. Without a doubt, the two strongest releases on the label are Dave Barker's 'Love Is What I Bring' and Errol Dunkley's 'Deep Meditation', although many fans find little to recommend on the label. The Gaylads' 'Can't Hide The Feeling' is an exception, however, as is the aforementioned Dave Barker track, itself a cut of The Uniques' classic 'Out Of Love'.

The label was wrapped up at the very end of 1972 with the release of the monstrous 'Christmas Parade', after which Rupie had product out on other Trojan subsidiaries like Harry J (particularly for The Ethiopians).

BIG SHOT

Launched by Trojan/B&C in the closing months of 1968, Big Shot lasted seven years and spanned a massive 120 issues. From the outset, there was some excellent early reggae from The Tennors ('Reggae Girl' and 'Another Scorcher'), Rudy Mills ('John Jones'), The Crystalites ('Biafra'), Ken Boothe ('The Old Fashioned Way'), Dennis Alcapone ('El Paso') and Niney ('Blood And Fire'). There are also three highly sought-after compilation albums on Big Shot, namely *Live It Up*, *Once More* and *Reggae Girl*. The 1968–71 era includes barely a duff release.

The label ran until 1975 and included almost all of Judge Dread's 'Big' series of records. With so many releases by so many artists and producers, it's difficult to form a definitive view of this long-running label. Worth seeking out, however, is the Shrowder/Bryan/Sinclair material from 1970 – much of which was collected together for the *Queen Of The World* compilation – and the Winston Riley productions from the same year. Album-wise, Big Shot bowed out with a handful of albums which either sold poorly or were of decidedly limited press, namely *Turntable Reggae* (various artists) and *Ready Or Not* (Johnny Osbourne and others).

BLACK SWAN (TROJAN SERIES)

Another old imprint revived briefly by Trojan/B&C, the second series of Black Swan issued productions in the main from Webster Shrowder, Des Bryan and Joe Sinclair, who were calling themselves Swan Productions at this time. The label's output is generally above-average British reggae for its time (1970) and worth a listen, particularly The Lowbites' 'I Got It' (featured on *Tighten Up Volume 4*), Selwyn Baptiste's steel-pan cut of 'Montego Bay' and Rad Bryan's super-smooth 'Girl You Rock My Soul'.

BLUE CAT

This label seems to have become a legend, largely through the *Jamaican Memories* album. It was launched by Island/B&C in around April 1968, and followed Trojan a few months later, when it became a separate company. The 1968 releases numbered around 50, which is something in the region of about six issues per month. The label was wrapped up in 1969, with the last eight or so releases having a different-coloured label design.

Without a doubt, the only tracks which turn up on anything like a regular basis are Dermott Lynch's 'I've Got Your Number', The Uniques' 'Girls Like Dirt', The Slickers' 'Nana', The Maytones' 'Billy Goat' and 'Loving Reggae', and Vernon Buckley's '2,000 Tons Of TNT'. There was a lot of very good Studio One music issued on Blue Cat during 1968 – titles such as The Hamlins' 'Sugar And Spice', The Thrillers' 'Last Dance' and The Righteous Flames' 'Seven Letters' – that seem to have been shunted away from the usual Studio One and Coxsone subsidiaries for some reason.

All of the most common releases mentioned earlier are worth hearing, as are Dennis Walks' 'Belly Lick', The Sparkers' 'Dig It Up' and 'Israel', and Ranfold (Ranny) Williams's 'Code It'. Probably 70 per cent of Blue Cat's output – but certainly not everything – is top notch.

BREAD

Launched by Trojan in 1970 as a subsidiary label for Jackie Edwards and his productions, Bread is perhaps one of the least known of the company's many labels. The music was pretty commercial, but not altogether bad, and was clearly aimed at the 30-something Jamaican market. The most popular sides were Danny Ray &

Jackie's 'Your Eyes Are Dreaming', Jackie's 'Johnny Gunman' (also on *Club Reggae Volume 3*) and 'I Do Love You'.

Almost exactly halfway through Bread's 20-issue existence, Jackie's output seemed to have been switched to Trojan and Horse, with other producers taking over. Of these, notable releases include Lee Perry's 'Station Underground News', The Maytones' Rasta-inspired 'All Over The World People Are Changing' and Dennis Alcapone's 'Musical Liquidator'. The label crumbled at the end of 1973.

Finally, there is a 'does it exist?' release, namely Bobby Foster's 'Tell Me Why You Said Goodbye', on either BR 1101 or BR 1102.

CLANDISC

Trojan established Clandisc in 1969 as the UK counterpart to Clancy Eccles' back-a-yard operation, and there is undoubtedly some truly superb music among the run of around 30 releases, including The Dynamites' moody 'Skokiaan (Mr Midnight)', Clancy's own 'The World Needs Loving', Andy Capp & King Stitt's 'Herbsman Shuffle' and The Silvertones' 'Teardrops Will Fall'. There's hardly a release that won't get your dancing feet on the move. Alongside the singles, there were albums by Clancy Eccles (*Freedom*) and three various-artists compilations: *Cynthia Richards And Friends*, *Herbsman Shuffle* and *Fire Corner*. Most of the compilations have a healthy proportion of instrumentals by Clancy's session band, The Dynamites.

Clandisc ground to a halt early in 1972 and Clancy seemed to disappear from the recording scene pretty much overnight. Trojan put out the *Top Of The Ladder* compilation on Big Shot late in 1973, but this seemed to include a bunch of discarded outtakes from a couple of years earlier, and while it featured the odd gem, it was a poor testament to Clancy's talents.

DOCTOR BIRD

Just three issues from this revived label. Of these, the most notable is Al Barry's 'Morning Sun', which is regarded as one of the best pieces of UK reggae from the time and, until its recent reissue on the Trojan *British Reggae* box set, remained for many years a forgotten classic.

DOWN TOWN

A label set up exclusively for Dandy (aka RL Thompson, RLT and Bobby Thompson, among other pseudonyms) soon after Trojan was formed, in the summer of 1968. As himself, Dandy really did have some wonderful music issued on it, such as 'Move Your Mule', 'Tell Me Darling', 'Pushwood' (appearing as by 'Mr Most'), 'Reggae In Your Jeggae' and 'I'm Your Puppet'. Dandy's session outfits included The Brother Dan All Stars, The Israelites and The Music Doctors, the line-ups of which were ever-changing, while featured vocalists were Desmond Riley, Lyndon Johns, Tony Tribe and Gene Rondo (also known as Winston Laro). All told, just over two-thirds of Downtown's 115 releases were produced by Dandy. The remainder were issued in the 1972–3 period, by which time Dandy had reinvented himself as Dandy Livingstone and was recording more commercially biased material on Horse and the main Trojan label.

Not everything on Downtown is worth checking out, however, as there are a few run-of-the-mill efforts by Audrey (some of which are admittedly good), Soul Explosion, The Megatons and Boy Friday. The albums, however – two volumes of *Red Red Wine*, The Music Doctors' *Reggae In The Summertime* and Dandy's own *Your Musical Doctor* – are all worth obtaining.

After around DT 491, Downtown dealt with all manner of producers and issued some very heavy-duty material from Big Youth ('S90 Skank' and 'Dock Of The Bay'), Hubert Lee ('There Is Something On Your Mind'), The Starlites ('You Are A Wanted Man'), Glen Brown ('Two Wedden Skank') and I-Roy ('Blackman Time' and 'Clapper's Tail'). Trojan finally scrapped the imprint late in 1973.

DUKE

Trojan originally initiated Duke in late 1968 to handle output from Duke Reid but, for reasons best known to the company, discarded this idea after only the second issue and gave it over to many different producers.

This really is a wonderful label with so much variety. The first release to make an impact was Herbie Carter's (actually Keble Drummond's) 'Happy Time', followed by Lloyd Charmers' excellent 'Cuyah', Clancy Eccles' 'Auntie Lulu' and The Beltones' 'Home Without You'. As outlined in the Joe label profile, there were around 11 issues from Brixton kingpin Joe Mansano with Duke numbers and Joe labels. Continuing with the London scene, Clancy Collins (aka Sir Collins) has seven of his productions on the label, including the thrilling 'Brother Moses' and 'Black Panther'. Freddie Notes & The Rudies, through ace Trojan producer Joe Sinclair, had a decent showing on Duke with 'The Bull' and 'Chicken Inn'.

The label hit paydirt with Boris Gardiner's 'Elizabethan Reggae', which reached the UK Top 20 early in 1970. Following this, there was a fair amount of material from Byron Lee, Duke Reid, Lloyd Charmers, JJ Johnson and – back to British again – Domino Johnson and Larry Lawrence. Unusually, The Ethiopians' 'My Girl' (DU 35) was soul, and there were two calypso sides by Emile Straker and Mighty Sparrow on 113 and 114 respectively.

Trojan wrapped up Duke late in 1973, when the label was top of the company's sales lists with 'Children Of The Night' by Norman Brown & Lloyd Charmers, masquerading as The Chosen Few – a brilliant marketing ploy. Presumably, with the scaling-down of operations in full swing, Trojan didn't need the label any longer.

DUKE REID

Twenty-four issues from the Mighty Duke, including all of U Roy's then-current (1970) hot favourites like 'Wake The Town', 'Rule The Nation', 'Wear You To The Ball' and 'You'll Never Get Away'. In fact, a third of the label's entire output came from Mr Beckford and it pretty much seemed to be a vehicle to raise his profile, with a few other current Duke Reid bits thrown in for good measure. Other notables include Hopeton Lewis's 1970 Song Festival success 'Boom Shacka Lacka', Justin Hinds' 'Say Me Say' and The Tennors' 'Hopeful Village', which is a truly wonderful sound. The label seemed to run out of steam four releases from the end, perhaps signalling Reid's diminishing status in the reggae-production world. There were no further issues after mid 1973.

DYNAMIC

This Trojan subsidiary dealt with releases from Byron Lee's Jamaican Dynamic Studio (formerly WIRL, or West Indies Records Limited) and spanned some 55 releases between 1970 and 1972. Aside from Lee's productions, Dynamic also put out material from a variety of other producers recording at Dynamic at the time, most notably Sid Bucknor, Lee Perry, Bunny Lee and Tommy Cowan. The Jamaican counterpart was a real one-stop recording organisation, with releases coming out on various Dynamic subsidiaries like Panther, Top Cat and Jaguar (a definite feline connection here!). As such, determining who was responsible for the various productions is often difficult, as almost everything was labelled as 'A Dynamic Sounds Production'. The bulk, however, did come from Byron Lee and was at the commercial end of Jamaican Reggae, although it really is worth checking out, as some of it is pretty good. Among the best cuts are Junior Byles' 'Pharaoh Hiding', Eric Donaldson's 1971 Festival song winner 'Cherry Oh Baby' (the biggest seller on the label), Barry Biggs's 'Got To Be Mellow' and Tesfa MacDonald's 'Life Is The Highest', which uses a strong rocksteady backing.

Quite a lot of Dynamic's output was conveniently spread across both volumes of Trojan's *Sixteen Dynamic Reggae Hits* compilation, with the second of these easily being the better. After Trojan scrapped the label late in 1972, Island's Dragon imprint continued as the main UK issuing outlet for Byron Lee until 1976, when Creole established a second series of Dynamic, with Barry Biggs's 'Sideshow' becoming a UK Top Three hit in that year.

EXPLOSION

Started in 1969, Explosion's first few releases were from Derrick Harriott, following which his output was moved over to Song Bird. The label was then given over to material from a multitude of producers. There are a few particularly good British productions from Laurel Aitken (Trevor Lloyd's 'Chinee Brush' and Dice The

145

Boss's 'Funky Duck') and Nat Cole (Billy Jack's cover of 'In The Summertime'). JA-wise, there was The Slickers' wonderful 'Gold On Your Dress' (flipside of 'Man From Carolina'), Lloyd Robinson's 'Death A Come' (Explosion's first release), The Hippy Boys' 'Vengeance' and Audley Rollen's 'Whisper A Little Prayer'.

There was a more commercial thread running through some of the 1971–2 releases with productions from Neville Willoughby and Federal Records. Before Trojan pulled the plug in 1974, the most notable releases were Carl Dawkins' 'I Feel Good', Dennis Brown's 'Black Magic Woman', Slim Smith's 'The Time Has Come' and The Tennors' 'Weather Report'. Interestingly, in the hardly memorable last gasp of Explosion's final 12 releases, eight were cover versions! This label certainly had its moments, but there was no real consistency of quality on it.

GAYFEET

The UK counterpart of Sonia Pottinger's JA imprint and a sister label to High Note, this imprint never really got off the ground. Only Junior Soul's 'Slipping' (by the artist later known as Junior Murvin) is really recommended.

GG

Trojan's main issuing outlet for Alvin Ranglin's productions, GG has a fair amount of very undervalued music, with The Maytones just about the most featured artists on it. Among the biggest and best releases are Cornel Campbell And The Eternals' 'Music Keep On Playing', Verne & Son's 'Little Boy Blue' (which provided the rhythm track for Judge Dread's 'Big Six'), Gerald McKleish's overlooked 'False Reaper', Cynthia Richards' 'Is There A Place In Your Heart For Me' and The Maytones' heavy cut of 'Black And White'.

Some of the best Ranglin music was released across a number of Trojan compilations, namely *Man From Carolina* (actually the only Trojan album pressed with a GG label), *Reggae Flight 404*, the second volume of *Reggae Reggae Reggae* and the scarce but less thrilling *Pipeline*. GG was wrapped up in 1973 as part of Trojan's rationalisation exercise, but Ranglin still had product released on some of the company's other outlets, notably Attack and Horse.

GPW

Not a formal issuing label but one which was used for blank pre-release discs containing sides that may or may not have been ultimately released by Trojan. (The GPW stands for Graham P Walker, who was Trojan's manager at the time.) These discs would be sold through the Musicland record stores at a hefty mark-up as the music was unavailable elsewhere and very valuable to sound systems and DJs.

GRAPE

This was started by Trojan in 1969 as an issuing outlet for Joe Sinclair's UK productions, although its first release was a Jamaican-recorded effort by little-known singer by Carlton Alphonso. There were some fine skinhead-reggae things on this part of the label from Freddie Notes & The Rudies, King Horror (actually Laurel Aitken, who produced for Grape) and Nyah Shuffle. Around the middle of 1970, Joe shelved his Grape productions set-up and formed Swan Productions with Webster Shrowder and Des Bryan, with whom he was increasingly working. This effectively resulted in the ending of the first phase of the Grape label.

In 1972, Trojan reactivated Grape as another ragbag label. Some of the output from this time was excellent, particularly Big Youth's 'Foreman Versus Frasier', Delroy Wilson's 'Can I Change My Mind' and Freddy McKay's 'Our Rendezvous'. The label was not a stand-out Trojan subsidiary by any means. The company discontinued it late in 1973 and the final issue had a very plain label design in appropriate purple, in contrast with the previous garish yellow and green one.

GREEN DOOR

Not a label to be overlooked as it featured some of the best of Trojan's early-'70s music, spanning as it did 1971 to early 1974, issuing some high-quality sounds from the likes of Bob Marley ('Lively Up Yourself' and 'Trench Town Rock'), The Charmers ('Rasta Never Fail'), The Wailing Souls ('Harbour Shark'), The Hoffner Brothers ('The King Man Is Back') and The God Sons ('Merry Up'). Trojan may have established Green Door to handle its more rootsy output from Jamaica, as a lot of what emanated from it is certainly in a pretty cultural vein. Particularly of note on the label are the aforementioned 'The King Man Is Back' and Shorty's 'President Mash Up The Resident' (on the 'My Conversation' rhythm). Sadly, the last dozen Green Door releases were a mixed bag of pleasant love songs, cover versions of a few current hits and a couple of Jimmy London's more mediocre efforts. Trojan seemed to have switched the heavy stuff somewhere else.

HARRY J

Most famous for its two chart hits 'Liquidator' and 'Young, Gifted And Black', Harry J was established by Trojan for Harry Johnson productions early in 1970, although a few sides pressed with a Harry J label were released on the Trojan 600 series. The bulk of the releases in the first year were given over to The Jay Boys, aka The Harry J All Stars, and collected together for the *Liquidator* compilation. The Cables, Bob Andy and Marcia Griffiths (either individually or collectively) were the other prominent artists on the label at this time. For reasons unknown, there were only four issues in 1971 and six in 1972.

The superior Harry Johnson-produced music resumed again in 1973 with The Ethiopians, Joe White and The Geoffrey Chung All Stars. Something clearly went awry just after this, however, as no more of his music was released on the imprint. It may have been that Johnson was giving his material to Island (for Blue Mountain) at this time.

So what of the rest of the music? It coincided with the 1974/5 struggling Trojan and could not be relied on for any real quality music. There was an abundance of covers of current pop hits – 'Walking Miracle', 'Rock Your Baby', 'Kung-Fu Fighting', 'Homely Girl', etc – and a few (literally) really decent offerings like Delroy Wilson's 'What Happen To The Youth Of Today', Bob Andy's 'Fire Burning' and The Ethiopians' 'Big Splish Splash'. There was also a plethora of relatively weak UK-recorded product from the likes of Sidney Crooks, Kush (The Cimarons) and Ellis Breary. When many early reggae fans are asked why they eventually went off reggae, they often point the finger at the Harry J label from specifically around this period. The label went out with a bang, however, with Johnny Clarke's superb 'Move Out A Babylon'.

HIGH NOTE

One of the formative Trojan/B&C subsidiaries, High Note was the company's main outlet for Sonia Pottinger productions and put out around 60 singles between 1968 and 1972. Most everything is worth picking up here, with the exception of the releases by The Creary Sisters and Otis Wright (which were Sacred) and Nora Dean (which was mento). There's plenty of really good music on here from the likes of Delroy Wilson (notably 'It Hurts' and 'Put Yourself In My Place'), Delano Stewart ('Dance With Me' and 'Got To Come Back') and The Hippy Boys ('Reggae Pressure' and 'Chicken Licken'). Perhaps the very best are Patsy's 'We Were Lovers' and the Victors' 'Reggae Buddy'. High Note was also responsible for three highly collectable LPs: Roland Alphonso's *ABC Rock Steady*, the various-artists compilation *Dancing Down Orange Street* and The Hippy Boys' *Reggae With The Hippy Boys*.

HORSE

Initiated by Trojan in 1971 as a pop/soul label, Horse was very much aimed at the middle-of-the-road punter. It was successful almost immediately, with white singer Scott English's 'Brandy' breaking into the UK charts. Then Dandy Livingstone hit the Top 20 with 'Suzanne Beware Of The Devil' and, later, the Top 30 with 'Big City'/'Think About That'. The label eventually stretched to over 150 releases, finishing in 1978.

There is little about Horse which is really commendable to the reggae connoisseur, although exceptions are Judy Mowatt's 'Mellow Mood', Marcia Griffiths' 'Sweet Bitter Love' and Carl Malcolm's 'No Jestering'. It tended to get tarred with the 'commercial' brush when some of the product issued on the label was, in retrospect, quite credible. Nicky Thomas was a Horse regular and his work is now highly regarded by some collectors. Similarly, Tito Simon's time will surely come; his 'Easy Come, Easy Go' is truly excellent. Add to these Jackie Robinson (one-third of The Pioneers), Lloyd Charmers, Barrington Spence and Owen Gray.

Bunny Lee productions seemed to dominate the label from 1975 through to 1976 and Johnny Clarke seems to proliferate. In truth, there were some pretty ropey items being released at this time, however, and the label really seemed to lose what little direction it had. Without doubt, an essential Horse release from 1975 was Joe White's 'Skank Indigo' (HOSS 85).

HOT ROD

Just 12 releases on this label, which Trojan established to showcase productions by Lambert Briscoe, who operated the Hot Rod sound system in the Brixton area of south London. The most highly prized record on the label is The Hot Rod All Stars' 'Skinhead Speaks His Mind'. Others include the very commercial 'I Wish You Well' (Delroy Dunkley) and 'Keep On Trying' (Tony Nash) and the much rougher 'Dog Your Woman' (Patsy & Peggy) and 'Remember Easter Monday' (Peggy & Jimmy). The latter was based on Alton Ellis's 'Remember That Sunday'.

Like the Joe label, almost everything on Hot Rod is collectable these days, in some cases undeservedly so, such as Josh's 'Leaving Everything', which is basically just an organ version of 'All Kinds Of Everything'. On the other hand, 'Prison Sentence' by Winston James is one of the most credible British-produced efforts from the period. Eddy Grant's Torpedo label also issued quite a lot of Briscoe's material but, given the absence of specific release dates, it is not known whether this appeared directly after Trojan had shut down Hot Rod. It should also be mentioned that a couple of Hot Rod productions appeared on the main Trojan 7700 series and on Duke. Again, it is never clear at all why they weren't issued on the producer-dedicated subsidiary.

JACKPOT

A UK version of Bunny Lee's Jamaican Jackpot label, but a huge wedge of the early releases contained a whole host of British material from producers Laurel Aitken, Clancy Collins, Nat Cole, Roy Smith and Larry Lawrence. Most people prefer the Lee offerings to the bulk of this, although Nat Cole's cover of 'Sugar Sugar' is a pretty credible reggae cover, if you can stand the song in the first place. Of the Lee material, The Twinkle Brothers' 'You Can Do It Too', Winston Williams's 'DJ Choice' and 'The People's Choice', Dave Barker's 'Girl Of My Dreams', and Delroy Wilson's 'Better Must Come' and 'Cool Operator' are very worthy releases. Some very solid rhythms, too. However, beware of some of the 1970-era pressings, which are woefully poor and seem not to have originated from the usual Trojan sources.

After Jackpot was concluded in 1973, Trojan switched Bunny Lee's output to other Trojan labels, including Horse and Attack. Never a person to put all his eggs in one basket, Bunny also had product being issued on Count Shelly's labels and Lord Koos during this time.

J-DAN

With some 17 releases, J-Dan lasted just over a year (early 1970 to around April 1971) and was intended to be a sister label to Downtown, which had been launched to highlight Dandy productions. Without a doubt, the biggest sellers were The Music Doctors' stepping 'Bush Doctor' and 'In The Summertime'. Apart from other Music Doctors titles, the rest is pretty run-of-the-mill stuff by the likes of Roy Gee and Boy Friday (another pseudonym for Dandy).

JOE

Joe catered exclusively for productions by Joe(l) Mansano, who owned and managed Joe's Record Shack in Brixton's Granville Arcade for some 15 years. Prior to Trojan giving him his own subsidiary, 11 of Mansano's productions had appeared on special Joe labels in amongst the main Duke catalogue numbers. Even before then, he had product out on Revolution (Clive Williams & The Heatwave's 'In Loving Memory Of Don Drummond') and Blue Cat ('Life On Reggae Planet' and 'The Bullet'). 'Brixton Cat' was one of those issued on the Duke numbering system with great success.

The main Joe label was very much directed at the burgeoning skinhead market, with the release of tracks like 'Trial Of Pama Dice' (Lloyd, Dice And Mum), 'Son Of Al Capone' and 'Skinhead Revolt' (Joe Mansano as Joe The Boss), 'Small Change' (Girlie) and 'The Informer' (Dice The Boss). One of the most popular releases on the label, and one with real lasting appeal, is the mournful 'She Caught The Train' by Ray Martell, who also recorded under the names Martel Robinson and Mike Robinson. After the 'Mansano sound' had run its course and skinheads had begun to decline, Trojan took no more product from Joe and pulled the plug on the label.

JJ

Only two known issues on this revived label. Originally a Doctor Bird Group offshoot with the records carrying the DB matrix numbering system – the Trojan version carries the JJ matrix.

JUMP-UP

Was calypso making a comeback in 1971? Trojan seemed to think so, putting out a few re-releases on Duke and just two on this revived Island subsidiary from the 1962–5 period. Actually, to be fair, they did select probably the two most topical issues for the time.

MOODISC

After producer Harry Mudie's sojourn with Pama, Trojan put out a first series of his Moodisc label during 1970/1. This short run of just 15 issues was notable for Cornel Campbell & The Eternals' 'Let's Start Again', Lloyd Charmers' organ workout 'Back Door' and The Eternals' soulful 'Push Me In The Corner', along with some worthy but unnoticed early sides from I-Roy. There were two albums put out on the imprint, namely Joe Joe Bennett's *Groovy Joe Joe* (issued on the back of his big-selling 'Leaving Rome' 45) and the first-rate *Mudie's Mood* compilation.

Curiously, however, by the close of 1971 Mudie had switched to Rita and Benny King's R&B Discs set-up, which issued another series of Moodisc (with a plain all-red label and HM prefix).

PRESSURE BEAT

Pressure Beat more or less carried on from where Joe Gibbs' Amalgamated label left off and put out just 15 releases between 1970 and 1973. (Gibbs also had a Pressure Beat label in JA.) Highlights include Lord Comic's 'Jack Of My Trade', Desi Young's cut-and-paste proto-dub 'News Flash', The Soul Brothers' 'Pussy Catch A Fire', Cat Campbell's punchy 'Hammering Version' and Peter Tosh's angry 'Them A Fi Get A Beatin''. Oddly, there were no releases on the label in 1971, suggesting perhaps that Gibbs was putting the bulk of his UK issued product with Pama at this time. Pressure Beat certainly wasn't a bad label, but neither was it a particularly memorable one. Quite a lot of Gibbs' 1971–3 output was usefully spread over two volumes of Trojan's *Heptones And Friends* albums, which were essentially various-artists sets containing a relative smattering of Heptones material.

PYRAMID (SECOND SERIES)

Amazing how Trojan resurrected these old labels without any apparent commitment to identity or longevity. Not a bad run of a dozen or so issues on this one during 1973–4, with highlights from I-Roy ('Tip From The Prince'), Gregory Isaacs ('Innocent People Cry') and Johnny Clarke ('My Desire'/'Lemon Tree'), but the quality didn't match the earlier Doctor Bird-administered imprint.

Q

Probably the Trojan label you're least likely to see, ever, and home to probably the worst record ever issued on a Trojan label, 'Tribute To Jimmy [sic] Hendrix'. Its four-issue output came courtesy of legendary soundman Count Suckle, and the label name came directly from his Q Club, in Paddington's Praed Street, which he ran for 20-odd years. There was one other Suckle production put out on the Duke label, namely 'Chicken Scratch' (apparently the Q Club's in-house dance), which also appeared on the *Funky Chicken* compilation.

RANDY'S

Trojan started this label in 1970 to issue productions from the late Vincent Chin's Jamaican Randy's and Impact labels. It's one that has few real goodies, although The Ethiopians' 'Mr Tom', Rocking Horse's 'Hard Time', Jimmy London's 'A Little Love' and Dennis Brown's 'Cheater' are all recommended. Probably the best-known release was Jimmy London's version of 'Bridge Over Troubled Water', which saw inclusion on the fifth volume of the *Tighten Up* series. There were a few superb Chin-less productions late in the series, with notable offerings from Lee Perry, Keith Hudson and Derrick Harriott.

In conclusion, there was a huge amount of wonderful music from the Randy's stable, but you'll have difficulty finding much of it on here.

SMASH

As Bunny Lee had a Smash label in JA, this was probably intended as its counterpart, although, like most other Trojan imprints, its focus drifted as time went on. From 1971, there are some noteworthy tunes from Clancy Collins, among which are Merlene Webber's heavyweight 'Hard Life' and Delroy Wilson's 'Satisfaction'. Otherwise, there is John Holt's best-ever cut of 'My Heart Is Gone' for Phil Pratt, which has a cracking bubbling bassline, and an early effort from Dennis Alcapone with 'Ball Of Confusion'. The label was eventually wound up by Trojan in 1973, after running for three years.

SONG BIRD

The first dozen or so issues on Song Bird (beginning in 1969) were given over to productions by Lloyd Charmers, Ken Jones, Stranger Cole and Trojan's own Joe Sinclair. Among these formative releases, Bruce Ruffin and The Techniques' 'Long About Now' was a solid-gold classic, while The Megatons' 'Memphis Reggae' is a belting organ instrumental in the Glen Adams style. Later in the year, however, Song Bird became dedicated to the productions of Derrick Harriott and his JA Crystal and Move & Groove outlets. For a reggae subsidiary, the label was consistent in its excellent-quality music and in having Harriott as the main man right through to 1973, when it was wrapped up. The bulk of Song Bird's output is by just a handful of acts, including The Crystalites (Harriott's house band), The Kingstonians, Scotty, The Ethiopians, The Chosen Few and Derrick's own super-smooth vocal talents.

Harriott was responsible for a quite staggering series of instrumentals, including the western-inspired 'The Undertaker', 'Undertaker's Burial', 'Ghost Rider', 'The Overtaker' and 'True Grit' (with Bongo Herman and Les Chen). Almost without a doubt, though, the biggest seller was The Chosen Few's cover of 'Shaft', which had some success in crossing over to the white market.

Song Bird was discontinued in 1973, after a few non-Harriott productions, with the man subsequently having some of his product out on Harry J (and of course he had nothing to do with Harry Johnson!).

SPINNING WHEEL

Named after a particular Lee Perry track (Melanie Jonas and Dave Barker's 'Spinning Wheel'), this subsidiary label issued half a dozen or so highly sought-after Perry productions. It is believed that Melanie Jonas, Perry's girlfriend at the time, peddled the tracks to Trojan as her own work during a visit to London, but they really emanate from Perry himself. Following these, the last handful were by Jimmy (Martin) Riley, The Cimarons, The Rudies and Stranger Cole. Stranger's 'Crying Every Night' is a most worthwhile issue, which also saw release on Pama's Camel subsidiary.

SUMMIT

Bar the last few issues, Summit focused on productions from Leslie Kong's Beverley's Records set-up in Jamaica. Kong's work with The Maytals, The Pioneers, Bruce Ruffin and The Melodians has never really been as eagerly collected in comparison with the likes of Perry, Dodd, Reid, *et al*, possibly because of its tendency towards the commercial end of Reggae and its generally 'international' appeal.

Of Summit's 43 issues between 1970 and 1973, 37 were provided by Kong, and some, like Tony Brevett's 'Staircase Of Time', Glen Brown's 'Collie And Wine' and Delroy Wilson's 'Got To Get Away' are really scarce. The biggest seller was undoubtedly The Melodians' 'Rivers Of Babylon', and the most neglected nugget is Brent Dowe's excellent 'Freedom Train'.

Following Kong's death in August '71, Summit continued to issue his productions posthumously, but after these had dried up Trojan put out a few oddities from other producers. Keep an eye out for some rogue issues with different B-sides, as these seemed to be pretty common the label.

TECHNIQUES

Started by Trojan in 1970, Techniques showcased the productions of Winston Riley, who had hitherto seen some of his material issued on Big Shot. It is best known for Dave (Barker) & Ansell Collins' 'Double Barrel' and 'Monkey Spanner', but generally the label doesn't seem to include really top-drawer Riley sides. Winston Wright's moody 'Top Secret' is probably the finest, barring the aforementioned.

The last ten releases were given over to producers other than Riley and highlights include Prince Jazzbo's 'Mr Harry Skank', The Silvertones' 'That's When It Hurts', The Eagles' 'Rub It Down' and KC White's elusive 'Anywhere But Nowhere'. In fact, one could go as far to say that the end of Techniques was an improvement on the beginning. The plug was pulled at the start of 1974.

TREASURE ISLE

The position on this one – at least, for part of it – is a bit unclear. Island issued the Treasure Isle label between 1967 and 1968, following which it was discontinued in around summer 1968. Almost exactly a year later, the label was revived by Graeme Goodall's Doctor Bird group for a handful of issues, including Andy Capp's 'Pop A Top', Symarip's 'Skinhead Moonstomp', a few other Symarip sides and an odd one from Boris Gardiner. It's not known, however, whether Trojan had a part to play in this relaunch, particularly since some pressings – such as 'Skinhead Moonstomp' – seemed to have been pressed by the same source used by Trojan. And then there was the *Skinhead Moonstomp* album, which appeared on Trojan. But whatever was going on, midway through 1970 Treasure Isle was scrapped yet again. Whether this coincided with the liquidation of the Doctor Bird group is also as yet unknown.

From issue TI7058 onwards, Treasure Isle was definitely in the hands of Trojan. The label reverted to dealing with Duke Reid product, just as it had during the period when it was administered by Island. As with the Duke Reid imprint, numerous U Roy recordings appear, with the DJ teamed with the likes of Hopeton Lewis and The Melodians, and with Phyllis Dillon for the wonderful 'Midnight Confession'.

One to look for is the great Justin Hinds' 'Botheration'. This run of 17 issues ended with Dennis Alcapone's 'Wake Up Jamaica'.

Trojan wound up Treasure Isle in 1973, since the Duke was by then producing very little in the way of new music.

TROJAN

Trojan issued product over four main series: the first short Duke Reid-oriented run during 1967 and 1968; the 600 run from 1968–9; the 7700s from 1969–76; and finally, from 1976 through to the mid '80s, the TRO series, which pretty much continued the 7700 series.

There is some nice rocksteady in the first series, but the 600s really came into their own with some excellent Dandy material (prior to the launch of Downtown), some early Lee Perry and Lynford Anderson offerings and a batch of top-notch Duke Reid sides. There is a smattering of more average fare from Owen Gray, Federal, The Merrymen and Byron Lee, but the rest can generally be relied on.

The 7700s led directly on from the 600s, with more top-quality music, notably from Leslie Kong and Duke Reid, but the label's commercial success with Desmond Dekker, Nicky Thomas, Bruce Ruffin *et al* in 1970 and 1971 had led to an overall sweetening of its output, with the addition of strings and an orchestra, courtesy of Johnny Arthey. The familiar orange-and-white label changed to a brown shield design.

The reasons behind the old Trojan's reversal of fortunes within a matter of years appear to be manifold. Sure, the hits had become few and far between, but there was more to it than that, and the core of the problem appears to have been a series of poor management decisions, as succinctly summarised recently by David Betteridge: 'Personally, I think that basically the company was under-funded. They had a big staff and when, in 1972, Island and Trojan went their separate ways, they just didn't have the revenue to maintain the company. To be honest, by the time we pulled out, Trojan was a bit of a pain. Island was having [pop] hits all over the place and a lot of the money earned from these went into to Trojan. So when Trojan and Island went their separate ways, the money just wasn't there any more. Lee [Gopthal] really should have brought in someone else to act in the same way that Island had done, but he decided to go it alone, which I think was a mistake. Also, the UK-[produced] reggae recordings were a bit of a mistake. When you look at Trojan's early success, it was with Jamaican product, and of course the overheads were much lower for those. We didn't have to pay for any production costs, and so we could budget much more effectively. And so the costs just spiralled and that of course had a big effect on the company's finances. I'm sure there's more to it than that, but I think that was basically the problem.'

Following Saga's takeover of Trojan, the TRO series never really established itself or the company. It appears that Saga thought that they were buying the rights to an extensive rock-music catalogue...

UPSETTER

As Trojan subsidiaries go, this must be the most extensively reissued. In fact, every known release from it has been reissued as part of Trojan's *Complete Upsetter Singles Collection*. The label was launched in 1969 to issue Lee Perry productions and issued a high proportion of Upsetters instrumentals such as 'Night Doctor', 'Man From MI5' and 'Soulful I', although the big one was, of course, 'Return Of Django'. Other regulars were Dave Barker and Bob Marley & The Wailers, while perennial connoisseurs' favourites are The Ravers' 'Badam Bam' (the vocal cut to 'Live Injection'), The Bleechers' 'Check Him Out' and The Upsetters' 'Cold Sweat'.

Trojan Singles Discography

1968–91

ACTION REGGAE SERIES (PREFIX ACT)

101	Knotty No Jester/Version – Big Youth (prod Clive Chin/Vincent Chin)	5.75
102	Natty Dread In A Greenwich Farm/Part 2 – Cornell Campbell (prod Edward 'Bunny' Lee)	6.75
103	Natty Dread Girl/Natty Dread Girl (Version) – Linval Thompson/ The Aggrovators (prod Edward 'Bunny' Lee)	1975

AMALGAMATED LABEL (PREFIX AMG)

800	Please Stop Your Lying/Feel So Fine – Errol Dunkley (B-side actually by Tommy McCook & The Supersonics)	2.68
801	Hope Someday/Just Like A River – The Leaders/Stranger [Cole] & Gladdy [Anderson]	2.68
802	Just Can't Win/Sometimes – The Versatiles/The Leaders	2.68
803	That's The Way You Like It/The Big Takeover – The Overtakers	3.68
804	Tit For Tat/You Take So Long To Know [Sacred] – The Marvetts (A-side actually by Neville Hinds & The Jets)	2.68
805	I'm Not Your Man/I'm Going Home – Errol Dunkley	3.68
806	Seeing Is Knowing/Music Is The Key – Stranger [Cole] & Gladdy [Anderson]/ Roy Shirley	3.68
807	The Scorcher/Do It Right Tonight – Errol Dunkley	3.68
808	The Upsetter/Thank You Baby – Lee Perry	4.68
809	Girl You Rough/Wooh Oh Oh – The Overtakers/Keith Blake	4.68
810	El Casino Royale/Dee's Special – Lyn Tait's Band (actually with Count Machuki)	5.68
811	Give Me Little Loving/This Is Soul – The Pioneers (B-side actually by Lynn Taitt's Band)	5.68
812	Fat Girl In Red/Trust The Book – The Melltones (actually by The Mellotones)/ The Versatiles	6.68
813	Now I'm All Alone/Fall & Rise – Victor Morris (prod Bobby Aitken)	6.68
814	Long Shot/Dip & Fall Back – The Pioneers	1968
815	The World Needs Love/Dance The A Una (actually 'Dance The Arena') – Roy Shirley	7.68

816   Having A Party/Day By Day – Dennis Walks/The Groovers   7.68

817   Feel Good/Soulful Mood – The Mellotones (actually by The Bleechers)/
      The Mellotones (actually by Tommy McCook & The Supersonics)   7.68

818   Holding Out/Get On Up – The Creations (A-side actually by Jackie Robinson) 7.68

819   Over & Over/Woman Of Samaria (actually titled 'If Woman Marry') –
      Jackie Robinson (B-side actually byThe Spanishites)   7.68

820   Love Brother/I Spy – Errol Dunkley/Errol Dunkley (actually by Lyn Tait & The Jets) 8.68

821   Jackpot/Kimble – The Pioneers/The Creators (B-side actually by Lee Perry) 8.68

822   People Grudgeful/Sharpen Ya Machete – Sir Gibbs (actually by The Pioneers) 8.68

823   No Dope Me Pony/Great Great In `68 – The Pioneers/Lord Salmons 8.68

824   Let The Little Girl Dance/I Want To Go Home – Jackie Robinson/Derrick Morgan 8.68

825   Train To Soulsville/Cinderella – The Check 'O' Mates (actually by Count Sticky)/
      Errol Dunkley   9.68

826   Tickle Me/The Time Has Come – The Pioneers/The Versatiles   9.68

827   Good Time Rock/Sleepy Ludy (actually titled 'Sleepy Lady') – Hugh Malcolm/
      Lyn Tait's Band   10.68

828   Catch The Beat/Janan (actually 'Jane Anne') – The Pioneers/Sir Gibbs All Stars
      (actually by The Immortals)   11.68

829   Man About Town/Mortgage – Cannonball Bryan [Karl Bryan] Trio/
      Hugh Malcolm   11.68

830   Sweet Dreams/Caterpillar Rock – The Pioneers/Don Drummond Junior
      (Vincent Gordon)   1968

831   Never See Come See/Jumping Jack – The Royals/Cannonball Bryan [Karl Bryan]
      Trio   1968

832   Secret Weapon/Jumpy Jumpy Girl – The Conquerors (actually by Ansel Collins)/
      The Conquerors (actually by The Viceroys) (A-side reissued on Pressure Beat PB
      5506B/B-side reissued on Amalgamated AMG 842B)   1.69

833   Don't You Know/Me Naw Go Believe You (actually titled 'Me Naw Go
      Bellevue') – The Pioneers   2.69

834   Hurry Come Up/Off Track – The Crashers (actually Winston Jarett & The Flames) 2.69

835   Mama Look Deh/Decimal Currency – The Pioneers/The Blenders   3.69

836   Them A Laugh & A Ki Ki/The Hippys Are Here – The Soulmates
      (B-side actually by The Hippy Boys   3.69

837   Private Number/She's So Fine – Ernest Wilson/Glen Adams (prod Derrick
      Morgan/Bunny Lee)   1969

838   What Moma No Want She Get/We To (actually 'We Two') – Stranger Cole
      (see also 'Amalgamated CSP Series')   3.69

839   Wreck A Buddy/Push It In – The Soul Sisters/The Versatiles   5.69

840   I'm Moving On/Who The Cap Fits – The Pioneers   6.69

841   Me No Born Ya/The Wicked Must Survive – The Reggae Boys (B-side reissued
      on Pressure Beat PB 5502B)   6.69

842   On The Move/Jump It Up (actually titled 'Jumpy Jumpy Girl') – The Soulmates
      (actually by Count Machuki & Joe Gibbs' All Stars)/The Soulmates
      (actually by The Viceroys) (B-side also issued on Amagamated Amg 832B) 6.69

843	The Reggae Train/Dolly House On Fire – The Reggae Boys	1969
844	Why Did You Leave?/Man A Wail – The Young Souls	1969
845	Hot Buttered Corn/It Is I – The Cobbs/Count Machuki (A-side prod Ken Jones)	1969
846	Apollo 11/Love Love Everyday – The Moon Boys/Errol Dunkley & The Pioneers	10.69
847	It's Alright/One Love – Ken Parker/The Cobbs (B-side produced by Ken Jones)	1969
848	Professor In Action/Reflections Of Don D – The Scientists/The Supersonics (actually by Johnny Moore)	1969
849	Space Doctor/Baby Reggae (actually 'Reggae Baby') – The Cobbs/Lloyd & Devon (prod Ken Jones)	1969
850	Alli Button/Death Rides – The Pioneers/The Hippy Boys	10.69
851	Bongo Jah/My Last Walk – The Immortals/Ansel Collins	1969
852	Man Beware/Mother Matty – The Slickers (A-side reissued on Amalgamated AMG 866B)	1969
853	Only Yesterday/Joe Gibbs Mood – Ken Parker/Ansel Collins	12.69
854	Lu Lu Bell/Long Long Time – The Versatiles	1.70
855	Nevada Joe/Straight To The Head – Joe Gibbs (A-side actually by Johnny Lover/ B-side actually by The Destroyers)	1.70
856	Niney Special/Danger Zone – The Destroyers (A-side actually by Niney & The Destroyers/B-side actually by Lloyd Willis & The Destroyers)	3.70
857	Take Back Your Duck/Nothing For Nothing – The Inspirations	1970
858	Franco Nero (Version 1)/Franco Nero (Version 2) – Joe Gibbs & The Destroyers (A-side actually by Count Machuki & The Destroyers)	3.70
859	Rock The Clock/Rock The Clock (Version) – Joe Gibbs (actually by The Destroyers)	3.70
860	Let It Be/Turn Back The Hands Of Time – Nicky Thomas	5.70
861	La La/Reggae Fever – The Inspirations	1970
862	The Train Is Coming/Man Oh Man – The Inspirations	6.70
863	Danzella/Danzella (Version) – Nicky Thomas/Joe Gibbs' All Stars	7.70
864	NYT*	
865	Hi Jacked/Life Is Down In Denver – Joe Gibbs' All Stars (B-side also on Amalgamated AMG 866B)	8.70
866	Money Raper (actually Plays 'Turn Back The Hands Of Time (Version)')/Mother Matty – Joe Gibbs & The Destroyers/The Slickers (A-side also on AMG 865B/ B-side reissue of AMG 852A)	9.70
867	Movements (The Joe Gibbs Way)/Caesar – Joe Gibbs (A-side actually by Count Machuki & The Destroyers/B-side actually by The Destroyers)	1970
868	Gift Of God/The Raper – Joe Gibbs (A-side actually Lizzy/B-side actually The Joe Gibbs' All Stars)	10.70
869	Perfect Born Yah/Red Red Wine – Joe Gibbs All Stars (actually by The Immortals)	1970
870	Seeing Is Believing/Ghost Capturer – Caly Gibbs/Joe Gibbs' All Stars	1970
871	Pumpkin Eater/Pumpkin Eater (Version) – Johnny Lover/Joe Gibbs' All Stars	3.71
872	Ghost Walk/Joy Stick – Caly Gibbs [Carlton Gibbs]/Joe Gibbs' All Stars	1971
873	Two Edged Sword/Two Edged Sword (Version) – Johnny Lover/Joe Gibbs' All Stars	1971

* Not yet traced.

Note: All issues produced by Joe Gibbs except where stated otherwise.

AMALGAMATED (PREFIX AMG CSP)
003   What Moma No Want She Get/Jackpot – Stranger Cole/The Pioneers

Note: A one-off issue and quite why this came out is a mystery. The 'CSP' prefix was used by Trojan only once, on the Coxsone label Reggae Special *compilation album, issued in 1969. It may have been intended as a promotional vehicle for Amalgamated (ie a double A-side featuring two of the labels' top sellers).*

AMALGAMATED 'SACRED' SERIES (PREFIX AMGSS)
001   We Are Not Divided/He Is So Real To Me – The Marvettes   1968
002   We Shall Have A Grand Time/Let The Power Fall On Me – The Marvettes   1968
003   I Was Once Lost In Sin/What A Wonderful Thing – The Marvettes   1968

Note: These three releases were all Joe Gibbs productions and saw issue on his JA Testimony imprint.

ATTACK (FIRST SERIES: 1969-70) (PREFIX ATT)
8000   Gentle On My Mind/Music Box – Pat Sandy/Big L (prod Philligree)   12.69
8001   Phoenix Reggae/Music Box – Family Circle [Symarip]/Big L (prod Philligree)   12.69
8002   Reggae Krishna/Official – Family Circle [Symarip]/Family Circle [Symarip] With Reco Rodriguez (prod Philligree)   1969
8003   Consider Me/Family Man – Pat Sandy/Big L (prod Philligree)   1969
8004   By The Time I Get To Phoenix/Hungry Man – Family Circle [Symarip] & Karl Griffiths/Big L (prod Philligree)   1969
8005   Stagger Back/The Show Boat – Family Circle [Symarip]/Big L (prod Philligree)   1969
8006   NYT
8007   NYT
8008   NYT
8009   NYT
8010   NYT
8011   Su, Su, Su/Better Herring – The Soul Directions (actually The Pioneers) (prod Byron Lee)   1.70
8012   NYT
8013   I'm A Puppet/Vindication – The Pyramids (prod Philligree)   4.70
8014   Hey Little Girl/Why Don't You Try Me – Dave King Reggae Band (prod Philligree)   4.70
8015   Loving Lover/Cora – Ray Martell (prod Philligree)   5.70
8016   Nyah Bingewe/Message – Nyah Earth (prod Philligree)   1970
8017   Dual Heat/Night Of The Long Knives – Nyah Earth (prod Philligree)   5.70
8018   I Can't Go On/Only You – Winston Groovy (prod Laurel Aitken)   1970

'Young, Gifted And Black', Bob (Andy) & Marcia (Griffiths), 1970, used on TBL122

Bob Andy, 2002 (picture: 'Spinello')

Trojan single 'all orange' design, first (Duke Reid) series, 1967

Trojan single 'orange and white' design, 1971

Trojan single 'brown' label design, Kensal Road sleeve, 1978

Trojan single 'brown' label design, 1971

'Hot Shot' sleeve design, 1969

Demo single aimed at the pop charts, 1971

GPW pre-release single with the centre pushed out for use on a sound system (GPW77 is 'Java' by Augustus Pablo, which, although a sizable hit on import, Trojan never issued); issued on 16 February 1971

Reggae Party sleeve shot, taken at Chalk Farm Studio, used on TBL172, 1971. Clockwise from top left: Sonny 'SS' Binns (cigar), The Rudies/Greyhound (keyboards), Errol Denvers (Greyhound, guitarist), Dandy Livingstone, George Decker (head only), Bruce Ruffin, Danny Bowen Smith (Greyhound, drummer). Centre: Honey Boy (Keith Williams, stout in hand), Alex Hinds (Marvels), unknown guy in black and Maurice Ellis (wearing tam), Cimarons drummer. Front: Nicky Thomas, Franklyn Dunn (Cimarons, bass), Locksley Gichie (Cimarons, guitar)

NICKY THOMAS

TROJAN
Recording Artist

KIETH HUDSON

TROJAN
Recording Artist

JOHN HOLT

TROJAN
Recording Artist

THE PIONEERS

JUDGE DREAD

TROJAN
Recording Artist

TROJAN
Recording Artist

A selection of Trojan publicity pictures from 1972

Shot taken outside Music House, used on TBL170, 1971.
L-r: unknown, Webster Shrowder, Desmond Bryan, Dandy Livingstone

MUZIK CITY

WE ARE THE LEADERS IN BLACK MUSIC

For the best in Reggae, Soul, Jamaican imports, Jazz imports and Pop

WE HAVE BRANCHES THROUGHOUT LONDON

5a SHEPHERDS BUSH MARKET W12	Tel: 743 2332
11a MODEL MARKET, LEWISHAM SE13	Tel: 852 5964
44 HIGH STREET, LEWISHAM SE13	Tel: 852 1223
21 HIGH STREET, DEPTFORD SW8	Tel: 692 8225
23 RIDLEY ROAD, DALSTON E8	Tel: 247 1548
30 STATION APPROACH, KENSAL RISE NW10	Tel: 969 2800
32 GOLDHAWK ROAD W9	Tel: 749 3515
55 ATLANTIC ROAD, (DESMONDS HIP CITY) SW9 ..	Tel: 733 6270
72 GRANVILLE ARCADE, BRIXTON SW9	Tel: 274 3274
93 GRANVILLE ARCADE, BRIXTON SW9	Tel: 274 4310
206 UXBRIDGE ROAD W12	Tel: 743 0462
530 HARROW ROAD W9	Tel: 969 2560
BALHAM KIOSK, BALHAM HIGH STREET SW12	Tel: 675 3153

Head Office: **MUSIC HOUSE, 12 NEASDEN LANE NW10** *Tel: 459 5222*

Magazine ad from 1973

Skinhead Moonstomp album sleeve, TBL102, 1970

Dalston Market, January 1973

London sound system, 1973

Trojan staff outing, 1968, used on TRL1. L-r: 'Lenky' Bryan, Webster Shrowder, Desmond Bryan

Producer Derrick Harriott's studio band, The Crystalites, used on TBL114.
The musicians were from a relatively small pool of session men who would work for a variety of producers. They would work under a different group name for each producer. Back row (l-r): Wallace Wilson, Paul Douglas, Derrick Harriott, Jackie Jackson, Winston Wright, Larry McDonald, Gladstone Anderson. Front (l-r): Hux Brown (pushing), Les Davis ('Bongo Les'), Herman Davis ('Bongo Herman')

Producer Clancy Eccles' studio band The Dynamites, used on TBL124.
Back (l-r): Hux Brown, Paul Douglas, Winston Wright, Gladstone Anderson.
Centre: Jackie Jackson. Front: Clancy Eccles

Magazine ad, March 1976

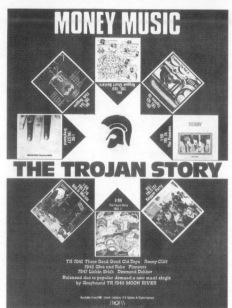

Advert from 11 December 1971

Rico Rodriguez, London, January 1973

Dandy Livingstone, 1972,
used on TRLS45

The Maytals, 1970,
used on TBL107

Ken Boothe, 1974, photographer
unknown

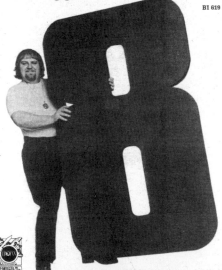

JUDGE DREAD
"I'm feeling great...So here's Big Eight"

BI 619

Ad from April 1973

Following his two smash singles Big Six & Big Seven
Judge releases his next hit single ... Big Eight. On this one
you can follow the fortunes of the Grand Old Duke of York,
Little Bo Peep and many others.
Also watch out for the Judge's new album 'Dreadmania'
(It's all in the Mind) TRLS 60

TR🔱JAN TOP 50 & New Releases.

W/E 10th MARCH 1972
****

LAST WEEK	THIS WEEK			TITLE	ARTIST
1	1	TR	7848	MOON RIVER	GREYHOUND
3	2	TR	7852	MOTHER AND CHILD REUNION	THE UNIQUES
2	3	TRM	9001	CHOPSTICKS/I'VE GOT IT/PUT IT ON	THE DELTONES
6	4	GD	4020	HYPOCRITE	THE HEPTONES
7	5	GD	4022	LIVELY UP YOURSELF	BOB MARLEY
4	6	TE	915	KARATE	DAVE AND ANSEL COLLINS
5	7	DYN	428	JUST A DREAM	SLIM SMITH
8	8	US	380	BET YOU DON'T KNOW	SHENLEY DUFFUS
20	9	SUM	8535	STORY BOOK CHILDREN	SIDNEY, GEORGE AND JACKIE
10	10	DYN	427	ALCAPONE GUNS DON'T BARK	DENNIS ALCAPONE
11	11	TR	7850	YESTERDAY MAN	NICKY THOMAS
18	12	PB	5510	SKANKY DOG	BUNNY FLIP
9	13	BR	1107	JOHNNY GUNMAN	JACKIE EDWARDS
16	14	BI	598	A SOMETIMES GIRL	THE CABLES
15	15	US	377	ALPHA AND OMEGA	DENNIS ALCAPONE
14	16	SUM	8533	NEVER YOU CHANGE	THE MAYTALS
19	17	US	381	WONDER MAN	THE UPSETTERS
12	18	SB	1065	HAVE YOU SEEN HER	DERRICK HARRIOTT
17	19	JP	786	I NEED YOUR LOVING	SLIM SMITH
13	20	RAN	521	IT'S NOW OR NEVER	JIMMY LONDON
32	21	GD	4021	RIOT	SOUL SYNDICATE
22	22	GG	4530	DONKEY FACE	THE MAYTONES
41	23	TR	7854	BUT I DO	BOB AND MARCIA
26	24	DU	129	ONLY LOVE CAN MAKE ME SMILE	GABY AND THE CABLES
31	25	US	376	GIVE ME POWER	THE UPSETTERS
24	26	HS	057	ONE NIGHT OF SIN	JACKIE BROWN
39	27	HS	058	PRAY FOR ME	MAX ROMEO
45	28	TI	7068	MIGHTY REDEEMER	JUSTIN HINDS
29	29	GD	4008	FLYING MACHINE	TEDDY MAGNUS
30	30	DU	127	LAST CALL	SIR HARRY
25	31	PB	5509	THEM A FI GET A BEATIN	PETER TOUSH
21	32	SB	1068	OVER THE RIVER	DERRICK HARRIOTT
-	33	DYN	430	I BELEIVE IN MUSIC	THE JAMAICANS
34	34	DU	125	MEDLEY VERSION	DENNIS ALCAPONE
43	35	SUM	8532	MY LIFE, MY LOVE	THE MELODIANS
36	36	GG	4529	KEEP IT UP	JOHN HOLT
49	37	BI	600	IT'S NOT WHO YOU KNOW	TWINKLE BROTHERS
38	38	GD	4019	BREAKING YOUR HEART	THE SCORPIONS
27	39	BI	595	DANCING WITH MY BABY	LAUREL AITKEN
40	40	GD	4017	I'M SORRY	THE MATADORS
23	41	TRM	9000	SONGS OF PEACE	BRUCE RUFFIN
-	42	JP	787	COME ON	THE CABLES
35	43	US	375	EARTHQUAKE	THE UPSETTERS
44	44	GD	4015	LIVING IN SWEET JAMAICA	JACKIE BROWN
28	45	TR	7846	GIVE AND TAKE/PRIDE AND PASSION	THE PIONEERS
46	46	BI	602	I'M TRYING	ALTON ELLIS
47	47	GD	4007	MISS LABBA LABBA	TWINKLE BROTHERS
48	48	JP	772	STICK BY ME	JOHN HOLT
37	49	GD	4016	JAMAICAN HILITE	THE GAYTONES
50	50	BI	601	YOU DON'T CARE	LLOYD SPARKS

Trojan Top 50, week ending 10 March 1972

'Young, Gifted And Black' sheet music, 1970

8019   You Can't Turn Your Back On Me/The Worm – Winston Groovy/Pama Dice
(prod Laurel Aitken)   6.70

8020   Let Me Out/I Belong To You – Concorde (prod Philligree)   5.70

8021   Get Lost Boss/I'll Be There – The Prodigal Sons with The Cimarons/Theresa &
Catherine with The Cimarons (prod Philligree)   1970

8022   You, Yes You/Version Be There – The Reaction/The Cimarons (prod Philligree) 10.70

8023   I'm A Drifter/Drifting Version – Tubal Caine/The Cimarons (prod Philligree)   10.70

Note: Most, or all, of the above releases were put out during the time Attack was administered by Doctor Bird. Trojan took over the label at some point but it is not clear when, particularly given that Philligree productions continued to be released on it. Attack had slightly changed its label design and was using 'standard' B&C/Trojan pressings by the time ATTT 8013 was put out, so the switch to Trojan may have occurred at that point.

8024   What's Going On – Pat Satchmo/Tubby's In Full Swing – Lloyd & Kerry
(actually Lloyd Young & Carey Johnson) (prod Tony Robinson)   7.72

8025   This Beautiful Land/Beautiful Version – The Melodians/Melodious Rhythms
(prod Tony Brevett)   9.72

8026   Feel Good (actually 'Feel Good All Over')/Feel Good Version – H Handy
(actually Horace Andy)/Phil Pratt All Stars (prod Phil Pratt)   9.72

8027   Fine Style/On The Track – Dennis Alcapone/Winston Scotland
(prod Tony Robinson)   9.72

8028   Sylvia's Mother (Reggae)/Sylvia's Mother – John Jones (actually unidentified
male vocalist) & The Now Generation (prod Richard Khouri)   9.72

8029   Scorpion/Hands & Feet – Lloyd & Carey (actually Lloyd Young & Carey
Johnson) & The GG All Stars/The Maytones (prod Alvin Ranglin)   9.72

8030   This A Pepper/Justice – U Roy Junior/John Holt (prod Phil Pratt)   1972

8031   Without You (What Would I Do)/Without You (Instrumental) – The Melodians/
The Dynamites (prod Tony Brevett)   10.72

8032   Do It Again/Watch It – Carey/Lloyd (actually Lloyd Young & Carey Johnson)/
Gary Ranglin (prod Alvin Ranglin)   10.72

8033   Blue Moon/After Midnight – The Platonics/Sidney, George & Jackie
[The Pioneers] (prod Sydney Crooks & Dennis Lemon [Judge Dread])   10.72

8034   Take It Easy/How I Want To Love You – The Reggae Boys (actually
The Pioneers)/Sidney, George & Jackie (prod Sydney Crooks)   1972

8035   Starting All Over Again/Instrumental Version – Hopeton Lewis/The Dynamites
(prod Tommy Cowan & Warwick Lyn)   1972

8036   Save The Last Dance For Me/Be The One – The Heptones (prod Joe Gibbs)   1972

8037   Ganja Free/Ganja (Version) – Clancy Eccles/The Dynamites (prod Clancy Eccles) 1972

8038   Don't Believe Him Donna/Beyond The Reef – Johnny Lynch (prod Sonny Roberts) 1972

8039   Bound In Chains/Chains Version – The Clarendonians/Stud All Stars
(prod Dennis Brown & Peter Austin)   1972

8040   Standing In The Rain/Stand Up (Version) – Rad Bryan (actually Neville Grant)
(prod Rad Bryan)   1972

8041	Feel Nice (Version)/Quick & Slick – Bongo Herman, Les & Bunny/Winston Scotland (prod Tony Robinson)	1972
8042	It Was Written Down/Sweet & Dandy – The Maytals (prod Warwick Lyn/ Leslie Kong)	1972
8043	Musical Goat/Stinging Dub – Winston Grennon & J [Jackie] Jackson (prod Alvin Ranglin)	1972
8044	This World/Same Thing – The Soulettes (prod Lee Perry)	1973
8045	Time & The River/Time & The River (Version) – John Holt (prod Arthur 'Duke' Reid)	3.73
8046	Da Doo Ron Ron/Da Doo Ron Ron (Instrumental) – Winston Heywood (prod Winston Heywood & Tony King)	3.73
8047	Aily I/Aily I (Version) – Cynthia Richards/Reid's All Stars (prod Arthur 'Duke' Reid)	3.73
8048	Derrick's Big Eleven/My Ding-A-Ling – Derrick Morgan (prod Edward 'Bunny' Lee)	3.73
8049	Multiplication/Morning Rises – The Thoroughbreds (prod Lloyd Coxson)	3.73
8050	Space Flight/Burning Wire – I Roy/Jerry Lewis (prod Lee Perry)	1973
8051	Nice One Cyril/Nice One Cyril (Version) – The Breadcrumbs (prod H Bowen)	1973
8052	People Got To Be Free/Come Together – Denzil Dennis (prod Pat Rhoden)	1973
8053	Give Me A Chance/King Of Zion – The Cables/Jah Fish (prod Keble Drummond)	1973
8054	Papa Was A Rolling Stone/Feeling High – Sydney, George & Jackie [The Pioneers] (prod Sidney Crooks, George Agard & Jackie Robinson)	1973
8055	Live To Love/Hearts Desire – Sid Cook (actually Sidney Crooks) (prod Sidney Crooks)	1973
8056	Brown Baby/Brown Baby (Version) – Derrick Harriott/The Crystalites (prod Derrick Harriott)	1973
8057	Crowded City/Thula Thula – The Messengers (prod Lloyd Charmers)	1973
8058	Baby Don't Get Hooked On Me/Harry Hippy – Neville Grant (prod Sidney Crooks)	1973
8059	One Of A Kind/Ace Blank – Happy Junior & The Iqs/The Shondell All Stars (prod Sidney Crooks)	1973
8060	Without You In My World/It's Flowing (actually 'It's Growing') – Audley Rollen (prod Sonia Pottinger)	10.73
8061	Thinking Of You/Thinking Of You Version – King Sporty (prod Noel Williams)	1973
8062	Girl I've Got A Date/We've Got To Make Love – King Sporty (prod Noel Williams)	1973
8063	Kiss An Angel In The Morning/Inez – Ken Parker/Tommy McCook (actually with Lester Sterling) (prod Arthur 'Duke' Reid)	1974
8064	At The Club/Reggae Fever – Sidney, George & Jackie [The Pioneers] (prod Dandy [Robert Thompson])	1974
8065	I See You/Pass It On – The Hanneseys (actually The Pioneers) (prod Sidney Crooks)	1974
8066	Love Is Overdue/Love Is Overdue (Part 2) – Gregory Isaacs (prod Alvin Ranglin)	1974
8067	Heartaches/PEO 111 – Annetta Jackson & Bobby Stephen (prod Webster Shrowder, Des Bryan & Joe Sinclair)	1974

8068	All On The House/Cold Blood – Boy Wonder (actually Eugene Paul) (prod Sidney Crooks)	1974
8069	Frankie & Johnny/Frankie & Johnny (Version) – Al Cook (actually Sidney Crooks) (prod Sidney Crooks)	1974
8070	Hold My Hand/Hold My Hand (Part 2) – The Starlites/The GG All Stars (prod Alvin Ranglin)	1974
8071	Duppy Gunman/Duppy Gunman Version – Ernie Smith (prod Ernie Smith)	1974
8072	Living For The City/Just Wanna Live – Pat Rhoden (prod Pat Rhoden)	6.74
8073	Count Your Blessings/Count Your Blessings (Version) – Ken Parker (prod DC Anderson)	6.74
8074	Labour Day/Labour Day (Version) – Tropic Sunlight (prod DC Anderson)	6.74
8075	Atlantic One (Part 1)/Atlantic One (Part 2) – Ansel Collins/The GG All Stars (prod Alvin Ranglin)	1974
8076	NYT	
8077	Changing Partners/Changing Partners (Part 2) – Barbara Jones/The GG All Stars (prod Alvin Ranglin)	9.74
8078	Sweet Rebel Woman (Vocal)/Sweet Rebel Woman (Instrumental) – Sonny Popkiss (prod Dandy [Robert Thompson])	9.74
8079	Oh Carol (Vocal)/Oh Carol (Instrumental) – Freddy McKay (prod Lloyd Campbell)	1974
8080	A Noh Me Trouble You/A Noh Me Trouble You (Instrumental) – The Willows/The GG All Stars (prod Alvin Ranglin)	1974
8081	Don't Go/Dub Wise – Gregory Isaacs/The GG All Stars (prod Alvin Ranglin)	1974
8082	The Same Folks/Dubwise – Ronnie Davis/The GG All Stars (prod Alvin Ranglin)	1974
8083	I'm Gone/I'm Gone (Instrumental) – Derrick [Morgan] & Hortense [Ellis] (prod Edward 'Bunny' Lee)	1974
8084	Love Vibration/Rock A Bye Woman – The Uniques (actually by Freddy McKay) (prod Sidney Crooks)	12.74
8085	Arise Selassie I Arise/(Sitting On) The Dock Of The Bay – Freddy McKay (prod Sidney Crooks)	12.74
8086	I Feel Sorry/I Feel Sorry (Instrumental) – Brad Lundy (prod Sidney Crooks)	11.74
8087	The Monkey/110th Avenue – Count Prince Miller/Love Children Band (prod RD Livingstone [Dandy])	11.74
8088	I Lost My Lover/Bula Dub – Ronnie Davis/Matador All Stars (prod Lloyd Campbell)	1.75
8089	NYT	
8090	Kiss Me Neck/Da Ba Day – The Upsetters (prod Lee Perry)	1.75
8091	Share The Good Times/Share The Good Times (Version) – Brent Dowe & The Gaytones (prod Sonia Pottinger)	1.75
8092	How Glad I Am/How Glad I Am (Part 2) – The Tidals (prod Alvin Ranglin)	1.75
8093	Dread Out Deh/Dread Dub – Joy White (prod Lloyd Campbell)	1975
8094	Ok Carol/Dub – Lennox Brown/Spiderman (actually by The Matador All Stars) (prod Lloyd Campbell)	1975
8095	Bad Da/Ad Dab – Gregory Isaacs (prod Winston 'Niney' Holness)	2.75

| 8096 | House Of Dreadlocks/Tangle Locks – Big Youth/The Groove Master (prod Tony Robinson) | 3.75 |

8096 House Of Dreadlocks/Tangle Locks – Big Youth/The Groove Master (prod Tony Robinson) 3.75

8097 Nothing Is Impossible/Black Out – The Interns/The Hardy Boys (prod Winston Riley) 3.75

8098 I'm Falling In Love/Love Dub – Ranchie [McLean]/Skin, Flesh & Bones (prod Panschly) 1975

8099 Walk Through This World/Instrumental – Barbara Jones/The GG All Stars (prod Alvin Ranglin) (A-side reissued on Attack ATT 8114B) 3.75

8100 Rock With Me Baby/A Crabit Version – Johnny Clarke/King Tubby's & The Aggrovators (prod Edward 'Bunny' Lee) 4.75

8101 Don't Cut Off Your Dreadlocks/Don't Cut Off Your Dreadlocks (Instrumental) – Linval Thompson/King Tubby's (prod Edward 'Bunny' Lee) 4.75

8102 Outformer Parker/Natty Down There – I Roy (prod George Agard & Sidney Crooks) 4.75

8103 NYT

8104 Mummy Hot & Daddy Cold/Some Like It Dread – Big Youth/The Groovemaster (prod Tony Robinson) 5.75

8105 Just Be Jolly/Dub With I – U Roy (prod Edward 'Bunny' Lee) 6.75

8106 Fly Little Silver Bird/Fly Little Silver Bird (Dub) – Gregory Isaacs (prod Tony Robinson) 1975

8107 Bushweed Corntrash/Callying Butt – Bunny & Ricky/The Upsetters (prod Lee Perry) 1975

8108 Jah Jah Bless The Dreadlocks/Jah Jah Version – The Diamonds (prod Edward 'Bunny' Lee) 1975

8109 Too Bad Bull/Bad Cow – Bunny & Ricky/The Upsetters (prod Lee Perry) 1975

8110 Natty Dread Don't Cry/The Medusa – Tapper Zukie/Tommy McCook (prod Edward 'Bunny' Lee) 1975

8111 Seven Letters/Seven Letters Version – Delroy Wilson/The Aggrovators (prod Edward 'Bunny' Lee) 1975

8112 Saturday Night Special/Saturday Night Version – Michael Dyke/Chinna [Earl Smith] (prod Earl 'Chinna' Smith) 1975

8113 Just Can't Figure Out/Just Can't Figure Out (Version) – The Diamonds (prod Edward 'Bunny' Lee) 1975

8114 Slim Boy/Walk Through This World – Barbara Jones (prod A Ranglin) (B-side reissue of Attack ATT 8099A) 1975

8115 NYT

8116 Tradition/Tradition (Version) – Ronnie Davis (prod Edward 'Bunny' Lee) 1975

8117 Nice & Easy/Nice & Easy (Version) – Horace Andy (prod Edward 'Bunny' Lee) 1975

8118 Cold I Up/Cold I Up (Version) – Johnny Clarke (prod Edward 'Bunny' Lee) 1975

8119 Rainbow/Rainbow (Version) – Michael Dyke (prod Earl 'Chinna' Smith) 1975

8120 Honey Child (aka 'You Won't See Me')/Time Is Running Out – Delroy Wilson (prod Keith Anderson [Bob Andy]) 1975

8121 World Class/World Class (Version) – Jah Lloyd (prod Glen Lee) 1976

312	Burning Fire/Burning Fire (Version) – Joe Higgs/The Rupie Edwards All Stars	1970
313	Uncle Charlie/When You Got To A Party (Version) – Froggy Ray/Froggy Ray (actually by Rupie Edwards All Stars)	1970
314	Half Moon/Full Moon – FroGGy Ray/The Rupie Edwards All Stars (B-side also issued on Explosion EX 2030A)	1970
315	Musical Attack/Shack Attack – Keith Cole/The Rupie Edwards All Stars	2.71
316	Music Alone Shall Live Version 3/Behold Another Version – Keith Cole/The Rupie Edwards All Stars	2.71
317	You Must Believe Me/You Must Believe Version – Niney & The Observers (prod Winston 'Niney' Holness)	1971
318	Jamaican Boy/Brainwash – The Conscious Minds (prod Harris BB Seaton & Rupie Edwards)	1971
319	Can't Hide The Feeling/Can't Hide The Feeling (Version) – The Gaylads/The Rupie Edwards All Stars (prod Harris BB Seaton & Rupie Edwards)	1971
320	Soulful Stew/Version 2 – Rupie Edwards All Stars	5.71
321	Weary Version 3/Hills & Valleys – Glen Adams/Tony Brevett (prod Tony Brevett)	6.71
322	Ain't Misbehavin'/Genuine Love – Ken Parker	1971
323	Love Is What I Bring/Love Is What I Bring Part 2 – Dave McClaren (actually by Dave Barker & The Uniques)/The Rupie Edwards All Stars (B-side actually U Roy Junior/A-side produced by Lloyd Charmers)	8.71
324	Deep Meditation/Deep Meditation (Part 2) – Errol Dunkley/The Rupie Edwards All Stars	9.71
325	Ba Da Doo Ba Dey/Ba Da Doo Ba Dey (Version) – The Itals/The Rupie Edwards All Stars	1971
326	Girl You Are Too Young/Girl You Are Too Young (Version) – The Diamonds/The Rupie Edwards All Stars	9.71
327	Three In One (Medley)/One In Three – Errol Dunkley/The Rupie Edwards All Stars	1971
328	NYT	
329	Popacito/I'm Gonna Live Some Life – U Roy Junior/Rupie Edwards	1972
330	Solid As A Rock/Solid (Version) – The Ethiopians/The Rupie Edwards All Stars	1972
331	Three Tops Time (Medley)/Part 2 – Dion Cameron & The Three Tops/Underground People	1972
332	Eternal Drums/Darling Ooh Wee – Bongo Herman & Les/Errol Dunkley (both sides actually by U Roy Junior)	1972
333	Press Along/Press Along (Version) – Rupie Edwards All Stars (actually by Max Romeo)/Rupie Edwards All Stars	1972
334	Are You Sure/Are You Sure (Version) – Max Romeo/The Rupie Edwards All Stars	1972
335	Jimmy As Job Card (actually titled 'Jimmy Has A Job Card')/Riot – The RupieEdwards All Stars	1972
336	I Want Justice/Justice (Version) – BB Seaton/The Rupie Edwards All Stars	1972
337	Christmas Parade/Santa – The Rupie Edwards All Stars/Underground People	1972

BIG SHOT (PREFIX BI)

501	Reggae Girl/Donkey Trot – The Tennors/Clive's All Stars (prod Albert Gene Murphy)	12.68
502	If You Can't Be Good Be Careful/Something About My Man – The Gaylets (prod: A-side Federal/B-side Lynford Anderson)	12.68
503	Chattie Chattie/Magic Touch – Junior Soul [Murvin] (prod Derrick Harriott)	1.69
504	It's Reggae Time/The Clamp Is On – Don Tony Lee/ Errol Dunkley (prod Edward 'Bunny' Lee) (reissue from Island label WI 3160)	1969
505	Standing In/Bumble Bee – Derrick Harriott (prod Derrick Harriott)	1.68
506	Shower Of Rain/It Might As Well Be Spring – Derrick Morgan/Val Bennett (prod Edward 'Bunny' Lee)	2.69
507	Forest Gate Rock/Rock, Rock & Cry – Lester Sterling/The Raving Ravers (prod Edward 'Bunny' Lee)	2.69
508	Sufferer/Kiss A Finger – The Kingstonians (prod Derrick Harriott)	1.69
509	John Jones/Place Called Happiness – Rudy Mills (prod Derrick Harriott)	1.69
510	Biafra/Drop Pon – The Crystalites (prod Derrick Harriott) (B-side reissued on Song Bird SB 1030B)	2.69
511	Another Lonely Night/Been So Long – Derrick Harriott (prod Derrick Harriott)	2.69
512	You're My Girl/Ooh-Pa-Pa-Py (actually titled 'Let Them Say') – Eddie Lovette (prod Federal)	1969
513	Say I'm Back/Deportation – Monty Morris (prod Albert Gene Murphy)	4.69
514	You're No Good/Do The Reggae – The Tennors (prod Albert Gene Murphy)	4.69
515	Is It Because?/Take Life Like It Is – Sugar Simone (prod Les Foster) (soul)	3.69
516	Son Of A Preacher Man/That's How Strong My Love Is – The Gaylets (prod Ken Lazarus/Richard Khouri for Federal)	3.69
517	Another Scorcher/My Baby – The Tennors (actually with Jackie Bernard)/ The Tennors (prod Albert Gene Murphy)	4.69
518	Parapinto/Cool Hand Luke – Cannonball King [Karl Bryan] & Johnny Melody (prod Albert Gene Murphy)	5.69
519	You're My Girl/Let Them Say – Eddie Lovette (prod Federal) (essentially a reissue of BI 512 with the same B-side but with correct title)	4.69
520	Worries A Yard/Hound Dog Special – The Versatiles/Val Bennett (prod Lee Perry/ E Barnett)	5.69
521	Suzy Wong/Deebo – Keelyn Beckford/The Swinging Kings (prod A. Barnett)	5.69
522	Windy/Windy, Part 2 – The Saints (prod Les Foster)	7.69
523	You Belong To My Heart/Bless You – The Demons (prod Melmouth Nelson)	7.69
524	Make It Easy On Yourself/I've Tried Before – The Impersonators (prod Melmouth Nelson)	7.69
525	Old Man Dead/Reggae Me – Vern (Buckley) & Alvin (Ranglin)/GG Rhythm Section (prod Alvin Ranglin)	7.69
526	Nice Nice/I'll Be Around – The Kingstonians (prod Derrick Harriott	8.69
527	Hustler/Magic Touch – Junior Mervin [Murvin] (prod Derrick Harriott) (B-side reissue of BI 503B)	9.69
528	Mr Tambourine Man/Old Fashioned Way – Keith Hudson (actually by Ken Boothe) (prod Keith Hudson)	9.69

529	Do It Nice/Because You're Mine – Les Foster (prod Les Foster)	9.69
530	NYT	
531	NYT	
532	Sweeter Than Honey/Son Of Reggae – Sylvan Williams (prod Hawk)	10.69
533	This Old Man/When The Morning Comes – Sylvan Williams (prod Hawk)	1970
534	Dirty Dog/Round & Round The Moon – Amor Vivi (prod Unaccredited)	1.70
535	I'm So Afraid/Mother Nature – The Escorts (actually The Mad Lads) (prod Winston Riley)	1970
536	He Who Keepeth His Mouth/One Day You'll Need My Kiss – Johnny Osborne And The Sensations (prod Winston Riley)	1970
537	Sweet Soul Special/Memories Of Love – Boris Gardiner & The Love People (prod Winston Riley)	2.70
538	Darkness/Watch This Music (actually 'Keep Out' aka 'Pork Chops') – Boris Gardiner/The Love People (prod Winston Riley)	3.70
539	Hot Shot/Watch This Music – Boris Gardiner & The Love People (prod Winston Riley)	3.70
540	Hot Shot/Memories Of Love – Boris Gardiner & The Love People (prod Winston Riley) (A-side issued on BI 539/B-side not the same as that issued on BI 537B)	3.70
541	NYT	
542	NYT	
543	Come Back Darling/Move Over – Techniques All Stars (A-side actually by Johnny Osbourne & The Sensations)/Techniques All Stars (prod Winston Riley)	4.70
544	NYT	
545	Elfrego Bacca/Iron Joe – Techniques All Stars (A-side actually by Dave Barker & Ansel Collins)/The Techniques (actually by Dave Barker) (prod Winston Riley)	5.70
546	Queen Of The World/Top Of The World (Version) – Lloyd & Claudette/The Prophets (B-side actually by The Cimarons) (prod Des Bryan & Webster Shrowder)	3.70
547	I Don't Want To Love You/Your Love Is Pure – Errol English [Junior English] (prod Larry Lawrence)	3.70
548	Once In My Life/Rabbit In A Cottage (actually titled 'In A Cottage In A Wood') – Errol English [Junior English] (prod Larry Lawrence)	5.70
549	See & Blind/Scar Face – Johnny Osbourne/The Techniques (B-side actually by Boris Gardiner & The Happening) (prod Winston Riley)	4.70
550	Return Of The Pollock/Concorde – Patrick & Lloyd/The Prophets (prod Swan) (B-side reissued on Trojan TR 7763B/A-side reissued on Horse HOSS 18B)	4.70
551	/Sycidilic – Sir Collins All Stars (prod Clancy Collins) (probably unissued)	1970
552	African Train/Do Good – Sir Collins All Stars/unknown male vocalist (prod Clancy Collins) (probably unissued)	1970
553	Bush Beat/Please Come Home – Lloyd & The Prophets with The Cimarons/Patrick & The Prophets with The Cimarons (prod Des Bryan & Webster Shrowder for Grape)	5.70
554	Crystal Blue Persuasion/Crystal Blue Persuasion (Version 2) – The Prophets & The Cimarons (prod Grape)	5.70

555	Tumble Time/Part 2 – The Prophets & The Cimarons (actually with Claudette)/ The Prophets (with The Cimarons) (prod Grape)	5,70
556	Jaco/Soul Reggae – Jaco & The Prophets/The Prophets (B-side actually by The Cimarons) (prod Swan) (A-side reissued on Big Shot BI 611B)	5.70
557	Revenge Of Eastwood/Revenge Of Eastwood, Version II – The Prophets (prod Swan)	6.70
558	Once A Man/Soul Mood – Billy Jack & The Cimarons/Candy & The Cimarons (prod Swan)	1970
559	Bet Yer Life I Do/Ace Of Hearts – Billy Jack & The Cimarons/Candy The Cimarons (prod Swan)	7.70
560	NYT	
561	Put It On/Rasta Isies – The Hi-Tals (prod Swan)	1970
562	Funky Fight/You Turned Me Down – The Cimarons (prod Carl Levy) (label States 'CIM 3')	11.70
563	NYT	
564	NYT	
565	Shades Of Hudson/Spanish Amigo – Keith Hudson (actually by Dennis Alcapone) (prod Keith.Hudson)	12.70
566	Freedom Sound/Last Love – Lloyd Sievright & Barry Howard (prod Bruce White/Creole)	1970
567	Bongo Man/Creation Version – The Linkers/Fud Christian All Stars (prod Fud Christian)	2.71
568	Blood & Fire/Mud & Water – Niney (prod Winston 'Niney' Holness)	3.70
569	He's Not A Rebel/Rebel Version – The Ethiopians/JJ All Stars (prod Karl JJ Johnson)	2.71
570	Perseverence/Perseverence Version – Carl Dawkins/JJ All Stars (prod Karl JJ Johnson)	1971
571	Never Fall In Love Again (actually 'I'll Never Fall In Love With You Again')/ Never Fall Version – Fud Christian All Stars (actually with Winston Heywood)/ The Fud Christian All Stars	3.71
572	Out The Light Baby/Mosquito One – El Paso (actually by Dennis Alcapone) (prod Byron Smith)	3.71
573	El Fishy/Nightmare (actually 'In The Spirit') – Herman/Herman's All Stars (actually by Lloyd Charmers) (prod Herman Chin-Loy/Lloyd Charmers)	4.71
574	The Selah/Don't Let Me Go – The Ethiopians (prod Karl JJ Johnson)	1971
575	Brimstone & Fire/Lightning & Thunder – The Observers (prod Winston 'Niney' Holness)	4.71
576	Wig Wam/Peace & Love – Sonny Bradshaw & Young Jamaica (prod Premiere) 1971	
577	Tar Baby (actually 'Crazy Baby')/Archie [Version of A-side] – Herman (actually by U Roy Junior)/Tommy McCook (prod Herman Chin-Loy)	5.71
578	New Love/The Mood – Herman Chin-Loy/Augustus Pablo (prod Herman Chin-Loy)	5.71
579	East Of The River Nile/River Nile Version – Augustus Pablo & Herman's All Stars (prod Herman Chin-Loy)	5.71

580	Voodoo/Hard Fighter – The Hippy Boys/Little Roy (prod Lloyd Daley)	6.71
581	I'm Moving On/Version Two – Cynthia Richards/The Hippy Boys (prod Lloyd Daley)	6.71
582	Two In One/Rock A Boogie – The Teardrops/Larry's All Stars (prod Larry Lawrence)	1971
583	Worried Over You/Worried Over You (Version) – Ruby & Gloria/Lloyd's All Stars (prod Lloyd Campbell)	7.71
584	Lonely Man/Lonely Man Version – Gregory Isaacs/Rupie Edwards All Stars (prod Rupie Edwards)	8.71
585	Psalm 9 To Keep In Mind/Mood Of The Observers – Tommy McCook & The Observers/The Observers (prod Winston 'Niney' Holness)	1971
586	Message To The Ungodly/Isiah Version – Niney & The Observers (prod Winston 'Niney' Holness)	9.71
587	Sister Big Stuff/Free Man – Danny Raymond (actually by Danny Ray & Dandy)/Boy Friday [Dandy](prod Dandy [Robert Thompson])	1971
588	Keep Pushing/Hot Tip – The Observers (prod Winston 'Niney' Holness)	9.71
589	Be True To Yourself/Version – Alton Ellis/Luna Funk (prod Sylvan Williams & Des Bryan)	1971
590	So Nice (aka Thinking)/So Nice (Version) – Ken Boothe (prod Herman Chin-Loy)	10.71
591	I'll Be Right There/Hot Pants Rock – Rad Bryan/The Playboys (A-side actually by The Sensations) (prod Rad Bryan for Bush)	1971
592	My Best Girl/My Best Girl (Version) – Rad Bryan (prod Rad Bryan for Bush)	1971
593	You Took Me By Surprise/You Took Me By Surprise Version – The Twinkle Brothers (actually by Tony Brevett) (prod Martin Riley)	1971
594	Nyah Festival/Brixton Serenade (actually 'What Am I Living For') – The Matador (actually by Lloyd [Campbell] The Matador)/The Matador (actually by Derrick Morgan) (prod Lloyd Campbell)	11.71
595	Dancing With My Baby/Do The Boogaloo – Laurel Aitken (prod Laurel Aitken for Bush)	12.71
596	Know Your Friend/Know Your Friend (Version) – Sketto (actually Sketto Richards)/Three Sevens (prod Bush)	11.71
597	Waterloo Rock (aka 'Jericho Rock')/Walls Soul – Don Reco (actually Reco Rodriguez & Lloyd Campbell's All Stars)/Lloyd Campbell's All Stars (prod Lloyd Campbell For Bush)	1971
598	A Sometime Girl/Version – The Cables/In-Crowd Band (prod Hugh Madden)	1971
599	Just Do The Right Things/Corporal Jones – Rad Bryan (actually by Lloyd Parks) (prod Rad Bryan for Bush)	1971
600	It's Not Who You Know/I Need Someone – The Twinkle Brothers (B-side actually by The Ethiopians) (prod Martin Riley) (reissued on Horse Hoss 51)	1971
601	You Don't Care/Must Care (Version) – Lloyd Sparks (actually Lloyd Parks)/Prince Tony's All Stars (prod Tony Robinson)	1972
602	I'm Trying/Luna's Mood – Alton Ellis/Luna Funk (prod Sylvan Williams & Des Bryan)	1972
603	Our Anniversary/Version – The Tropic Shadow (prod Phil Pratt)	1972
604	Va Va Voom/Rebel – Carl Masters/The God Sons (prod Glen Brown & G Mahtani)	1972

605	Take Me In Your Arms/Two Timing Woman – Laurel Aitken (prod Laurel Aitken)	1972
606	Tubby's Control/More Music – Tommy McCook & Ron Wilson (prod Glen Brown)	1972
607	Hiding By The Riverside/The Red Sea – Niney/The Observers (prod Winston 'Niney' Holness)	1972
608	Big Six/One Armed Bandit – Judge Dread (B-side actually by The Judge Dread Sound) (prod Bush)	1972
609	Beg In The Gutter/Beg In The Gutter (Version) – Niney (prod Winston 'Niney' Holness)	1972
610	Everyday Music/Observing The Av – The Observers/Niney (prod Winston 'Niney' Holness)	1972
611	Night Food Reggae/Jaco – Nora Dean/The Prophets (prod Bush) (B-side reissue of BI 556A)	1972
612	Dr Spock/Joe Kidd – The Vulcans (prod Bush)	1972
613	Big Seven/Dread – Judge Dread (prod Bush)	1972
614	Are You Sure/I Don't Know Why – Dave Barker (B-side actually by The Sensations) (prod Larry Lawrence for Bush)	1972
615	Red Herring/Vulcanised – The Vulcans (prod Bush)	1972
616	Ain't It Groovy/My Children Favourite – Buster Pearson (prod Buster Pearson for Bush)	3.73
617	Housewives Choice/Don't You Worry – Derrick Morgan & Hortense Ellis (prod Edward 'Bunny' Lee for Bush)	3.73
618	English Chicken/Material – Lascelles Perkins (prod Sid Bucknor/Clancy Collins)	1973
619	Big Eight/Mind The Doors – Judge Dread (prod Joe Sinclair, Des Bryan & Webster Shrowder)	1973
620	Ding-A-Ling, Ting-A-Ling/Run Rhythm Run – Steve Collins (prod Clancy Collins for Bush)	1973
621	Don't Throw Stones/Toughness (actually titled 'Lucifer') – Sidney Rodgers & The Fighters/The Fighters (actually by Winston Wright) (prod Larry Lawrence) (A-side also issued on Techniques TE 923)	1973
622	La La At The End/Sound Track La La La – Norman Brown/Prince Tony's All Stars (prod Tony Robinson)	1973
623	Stop Baby/Version – Millie & Winston/The Gaytones (prod Sonia Pottinger)	1973
624	White Rum & Salvation/Jam Dung – L Charmers (A-side actually by Lloyd Charmers/B-side actually by Murphy Romeo) (prod Lloyd Charmers)	1973
625	Jill's On The Pill/Pill Control – The Jays (prod Sidney Crooks)	1973
626	Big Nine/Nine & A Bit Skank – Judge Dread (prod Des Bryan, Webster Shrowder & Bush)	1974
627	You Can't Get/Showcase – Kingston Four Combo (prod Dandy [Robert Thompson]) & Shady Tree)	1974
628	Grandad's Flannelette Nightshirt/Dance Of The Snods – Judge Dread (prod Alted)	11.74
629	Mama Dee/Mama Dee, Part 2 – The Starlites/The GG All Stars (prod Alvin Ranglin)	1.75
630	If You're Ready, Come Go With Me (The People's Champion)/If You're Ready (Dub Ali Dub) – Vin Gordon/Skin, Flesh & Bones (prod Lloyd Parks)	1.75

BLACK SWAN (TROJAN SERIES, PREFIX BW)

1401	Bongo Bongo/Ramba – Young Satch [Ferdinand Dixon]/The Boys (prod Bryan, Shrowder & Sinclair)	10.70
1402	Mo'bay (Montego Bay)/Going West – Selwyn Baptiste/Reco Rodriguez (prod Bryan, Shrowder & Sinclair For Grape Productions)	1970
1403	I Got It/I Got It Version – The Lowbites (prod Bryan, Shrowder & Sinclair)	1971
1404	Dawn Patrol/Whisky Bonga – The Itals (prod Swan)	3.71
1405	Love You The Most/Love You The Most Version – Lloyd Clarke/The Lowbites (B-side actually by Morgan's All Stars) (prod Derrick Morgan)	4.71
1406	Tomorrow's Dreams/Hot Pants Reggae – Lee Bogle/The Swans (prod Bryan, Shrowder & Sinclair)	4.71
1407	Judgement Rock/Night West – The Itals (actually by Charlie Ace)/The Itals (prod Bryan, Shrowder & Sinclair)	1971
1408	If It's Hell Down Below (We're All Gonna Go)/Just A Little Bit Of Love – Laurel Aitken (prod Laurel Aitken)	5.71
1409	Talk To Me Baby/Talk To Me Baby (Version) – Ruby & Gloria/Lloyd's All Stars (prod Lloyd Campbell)	7.71
1410	Girl You Rock My Soul/Girl You Rock My Soul (Version) – Rad Bryan (prod Rad Bryan)	1971

BLUE CAT (PREFIX BS)

100	Shake It Up/Goodies Are The Greatest (aka Rudies Are The Greatest) – The Pioneers With The Lyn Tait Band (prod Joe Gibbs)	2.68
101	I've Got Your Number/Hot Shot – Dermott Lynch (prod Charles Ross)	2.68
102	Musically/I'm Moving On – Keith Blake With The Lyn Tait Band (prod Joe Gibbs)	2.68
103	Give It To Me/Someday Someway – The Pioneers & Lyn Tait & The Jets/The Leaders (prod Joe Gibbs)	1968
104	Soul Glide/My Friends – Neville Irons (actually Neville Hinds)/The Dynamics (prod Joe Gibbs)	2.68
105	Whip Them/Some Having A Bawl – The Pioneers (With The Lyn Tait Band) (prod Joe Gibbs/Sidney Crooks)	3.68
106	Get Right/If I Did Look – The Wrigglers (With The Caribbeats) (prod Bobby Aitken)	3.68
107	7 11 Part 1/7 11 Part 2 – The Rudies (prod Charles Reid)	4.68
108	Way Of Life/I'm So Proud – Joe White (A-side actually by Karl Bryan & Lyn Tait's Band/B-side actually by Joe White, Glen Brown & Trevor Shield) (prod Charles Ross)	4.68
109	Cupid/Wise Message – The Rudies/Reco's All Stars (prod Charles Reid)	4.68
110	Go Away/Julie On My Mind – The Gaylads/The Soul Vendors (prod Clement Seymour Dodd)	5.68
111	Letter To Mummy & Daddy/Letter To Mummy & Daddy (Instrumental) – Duke All Stars (prod Charles Reid)	1968
112	Seven Letters/To Sir With Love – The Righteous Homes (actually by The Righteous Flames)/The Soul Vendors (prod Clement Seymour Dodd)	5.68
113	Pretty Blue Eyes/Pretty Blue Eyes (Part 2) – Roy & Duke All Stars (prod Charles Reid)	6.68

114   I Love You/I Can't Stand It – Carl Dawkins/Dermott Lynch (prod Charles Ross) 6.68

115   Sugar & Spice/Mercy, Mercy, Mercy – The Hamlins/The Soul Vendors
       (prod Clement Seymour Dodd)   6.68

116   Zigaloo/Wiser Than Solomon – Lester Sterling (prod Clement Seymour Dodd)   6.68

117   The Train Part 1/The Train Part 2 – Roy & Duke All Stars/Duke All Stars (prod
       Charles Reid)   7.68

118   Bye Bye Baby/Heart For Sale – Zoot Sims/The Thrillers (actually with
       Al Campbell) (prod Clement Seymour Dodd)   7.68

119   Try A Little Tenderness/Tender Arms – Joe White/Lyn Tait & Karl Bryan
       (prod Charles Ross)   1968

120   Good Girl/Musical Fever – Ed Nangle/The Enforcers (prod Clement Seymour
       Dodd)   7.68

121   Fat Fish/You're Gonna Lose – The Viceroys/The Octaves (prod Clement Seymour
       Dodd)   7.68

122   I've Got Everything/Echo – Dermott Lynch (prod Charles Ross)   7.68

123   These Foolish Things/This I Promise – Owen Gray (prod Clancy Collins)   8.68

124   Always/Big Man – The Gray Brothers (prod Clancy Collins)   8.68

125   The Fiddle/Shook (actually 'Something About My Man') – Nehemiah Reid/
       The Loveletts (actually by The Gaylets) (prod Nehemiah Reid/Lynford
       Anderson)   8.68

126   Girls Like Dirt/She Is Leaving – The Uniques/Glen Adams (actually by
       Alva Lewis) (prod Harry Robinson)   8.68

127   Khaki/Great Surprise – The Untouchables (actually by The Tennors)/Leroy Reid
       (prod Albert Gene Murphy/Nehemiah Reid)   1968

128   The Last Dance/Unworthy Baby – The Thrillers (actually with Al Campbell)/
       The Delta Cats (prod Clement Seymour Dodd)   8.68

129   Tender Arms/Something Is Worrying Me – Trevor (with Joe White & Glen Brown)/
       Dermott Lynch (prod Charles Ross) (A-side is vocal cut to BS 119B)   8.68

130   Pretty Girl/You Went Away – Trevor, Joe White & Glen Brown/Dermott Lynch
       (prod Charles Ross)   8.68

131   Way Of Life/I'm So Proud – Trevor, Joe White & Glen Brown/Lyn Tait &
       Karl Bryan (prod Charles Ross) (A-side is vocal cut to BS 108A/B-side is
       instrumental cut to BS 108B)   9.68

132   Intensified Girls/Jump & Shout – Anderson's All Stars (prod Gladstone
       Anderson)   9.68

133   Wala, Wala/Super Special – The Slickers/Lester Sterling (prod Eric Barnett/
       Bunny Lee)   10.68

134   Nana/I May Never See My Baby – The Slickers/Martin Riley (prod Slickers/
       Bunny Lee)   10.68

135   You Can Never Get Away/La La La Bamba – Enos McLeod/Enos & Sheila
       (prod Enos McLeod)   10.68

136   Young Love/Wall Flower – Lloyd Clarke/Ken Rose (B-side actually by
       The Untouchables) (prod Enos McLeod)   11.68

137   Prisoner In Love/True Love – The Untouchables/Edward Raphael
       (prod Enos McLeod)   11.68

138	Tonight Your Mine/Your Love – Enos & Sheila/The Untouchables (prod Enos McLeod)	11.68
139	Reggae Beat/Miss Eva – The Pioneers (prod Joe Gibbs)	12.68
140	Uncle Joe/Can't Understand – Austin Faithful (prod Nehemiah Reid/Rannie [Ronnie] Williams) (B-side reissued on BS 151B)	12.68
141	I Want It Girl/She Is Gone – Teddy Charmes (prod Tony Shabazz)	1.69
142	Issued on Trojan TR 628	
143	Mullo Reggae/Life Line – Amiel Mudie (& The Dandemites) (prod Amiel Mudie)	1.69
144	Belly Lick/The Game Song – Dennis Walks/Drumbago & The Blenders (prod Joe Gibbs)	12.68
145	Reggae Jeggae (actually titled 'Royal Reggae Jeggae')/Delilah – Drumbago & The Blenders/Tyrone Taylor (prod Joe Gibbs)	12.68
146	I Know A Place/I Dangerous – The Dee Set/Roy Bennett (prod Tony Shabazz)	1.69
147	You Stole My Money/Tell Me The Reason – Blue & Ferris/George Ferris (prod Charles Organaire)	1968
148	Read The News/Return Of The Bullet – Lance Hannibal [Tito Simon]/Reco And The Rhythm Aces (prod Joe Mansano)	1968
149	Billy Goat/Call You Up – The Maytones (prod Alvin Ranglin)	1968
150	Life On Reggae Planet/ZZ Beat – Joe Mansano/(Reco &) The Rhythm Aces (prod Joe Mansano)	1.69
151	Out Of The Fire/Can't Understand – Lloyd & Devon (B-side actually by Austin Faithful) (prod Joe Gibbs/Ronnie [Rannie] Williams) (B-side reissue of BS 140B)	2.68
152	Loving Reggae/Musical Beat – The Maytones/Roy Samuel (prod Alvin Ranglin)	2.69
153	Everyday Is Like A Holiday/Have You Time – Trevor & The Maytones (prod Alvin Ranglin)	2.69
154	Frying Pan/Code It – The Slickers/Ranfold [Rannie] Williams (prod Ronnie [Rannie] Williams)	3.69
155	Dig It Up/This Life Make Me (actually 'This Life Make Me Wonder') – The Sparkers/Delroy Wilson (prod Ronnie [Ranny] Williams)	4.69
156	I Can't Stop Loving You/Tell Me Darling – Owen Gray (prod Clancy Collins)	4.69
157	Drumbago's Dead/Song Of The Year – Sam Sham/The Sparkers (prod Nehemia Reid)	4.69
158	What A Sin Thing/Short Up Dress – Devon & Sedrick (prod Nehemia Reid)	4.69
159	Want It, Want It/Israel – Samuel Edwards/The Sparkers (prod Nehemia Reid)	5.69
160	The Bullet/Rhythm In – Reco & The Rhythm Aces (prod Joe Mansano)	5.69
161	Vietcong/Me Want Man – Al Reid/Max Romeo (prod Nehemiah Reid)	5.69
162	Leave Me To Cry/Warning – Carlton Reid (prod Nehemiah Reid)	6.69
163	It's Not The Way/Darling – Max Romeo/Al Reid (prod Nehemiah Reid)	6.69
164	Ratchet Knife/Bend The True – Amiel Moodie (prod Amiel Mudie)	6.69
165	2,000 Tons Of TNT/Botheration – GG Rhythm Section (actually by Vernon Buckley & The GG All Stars)/The Maytones (prod Alvin Ranglin)	6.69
166	Copper Girl/What Love – The Maytones (prod Alvin Ranglin)	7.69

167	Everybody Reggae/Another Fool – The GG All Stars/David & Bonnie (prod Alvin Ranglin)	1969
168	Wickeder/Stay In My Arms – Laxton [Ford] & Oliver [St David] (prod Alvin Ranglin)	7.69
169	The Magnificent Seven/Long Lost Love – The Soul Twins (actually by Winston Wright)/Rupie Edwards (Prod Rupie Edwards)	9.69
170	Buttoo/I Need Your Loving – The Concords (prod Rupie Edwards)	9.69
171	Strange/Your New Love – Dobby Dobson (prod Rupie Edwards)	9.69
172	Judas/World Come To An End – Gladstone [Adams] & The Followers (prod Alvin Ranglin)	1969
173	Mi Nah Tek You Lick/Dig Away De Money – The Maytones (prod Alvin Ranglin)	1969
174	If I Could Hear My Mother/Satan Can't Prevail – The Righteous Twins (prod Sonny Roberts) (Sacred)	11.69

BREAD (PREFIX BR)

1101	Susanne/I Need Your Love – Del Davis/Gene Laro (actually Gene Rondo) (prod Jackie Edwards)	
1101	Tell Me Why You Said Goodbye/I'll Make Him Believe In You – Bobby Foster/ Youth [I Jah Man Levi] (prod Jackie Edwards) (second issue unsubstantiated, possibly intended for release on BR 1102)	8.70
1102	NYT	
1103	Your Eyes Are Dreaming/Yes I Will – Danny Ray & Jackie Edwards/Victor Scott (prod Jackie Edwards)	1970
1104	Cum-Ba-Laa/I Want You Beside Me – Jackie's Boys/Jackie Edwards (prod Jackie Edwards) (A-side reissued on Bread BR 1110B)	1971
1105	Baby Don't Wake Me/Wishing & Hoping – Del Davis (prod Jackie Edwards) (B-side reissued on Trojan TR 7870B)	6.71
1106	NYT	
1107	Johnny Gunman/Johnny Gunman (Version) – Jackie Edwards/Jackie's Boys (prod Jackie Edwards)	1971
1108	I Do Love You/Who Told You So? – Jackie Edwards (prod Jackie Edwards)	1972
1109	NYT	
1110	Bewildered/Cum-Ba-Laa – Count Prince Miller/Jackie's Boys (prod Jackie Edwards) (B-side reissue of Bread BR 1104A)	1972
1111	Station Underground News/Better Days – Lee Perry/Carlton & The Shoes (prod Lee Perry)	1973
1112	The Youth Of Today/Close Observation – The Coolers/Tyrone Taylor (prod Clancy Eccles)	1973
1113	Pay For The Wicked/Pay For The Wicked (Version) – The Untouchables (prod Alvin Ranglin)	1973
1114	All Over The World, People Are Changing/Changing World (Dubwise) – The Maytones/The GG All Stars (prod Alvin Ranglin)	1973
1115	You Need Love/Love (Dub) – Billy Dyce & The Millions/The GG All Stars (prod Alvin Ranglin)	1973

1116	Cherry Baby/Summertime – The Messengers/BB Seaton (prod Lloyd Charmers)	1973
1117	Mama/Man A Walk & Talk – Nora Dean (prod Edward 'Bunny' Lee)	1973
1118	Just Enough/We Are Neighbours – David Isaacs (prod Lee Perry)	1973
1119	I Who Have Nothing/I'm Not Home – Derrick Morgan (prod Edward 'Bunny' Lee)	1973
1120	Don't Try To Use Me/Goddess Of Love – Horace Andy (prod Edward 'Bunny' Lee)	1973
1121	Musical Liquidator/Lorna Banana – Dennis Alcapone/Dennis Alcapone And Prince Jazzbo (prod Edward 'Bunny' Lee)	1973

CLANDISC (PREFIX CLA)

200	Skokiaan (Mr Midnight)/Who Yea – The Dynamites/King Stitt	10.69
201	The World Needs Loving/Dollar Train – Clancy Eccles & The Dynamites	1969
202	Vigorton 2/Mount Zion – King Stitt/Clancy Eccles	1969
203	Foolish Fool/On The Street – Cynthia Richards/King Stitt (A-side reissued on CLA 220A)	11.69
204	Soul Power/Rub It Down – Barrington Sadler	1969
205	NYT	
206	The Ugly One/Dance Beat – King Stitt/King Stitt & Clancy Eccles (B-side reissued on CLA 220B)	1970
207	Herbsman Shuffle/Don't Mind Me – King Stitt & Andy Capp/Higgs And Wilson [Joe Higgs & Roy Wilson] (B-side reissued on CLA 218A/A-side reissued on Trojan TRO 9064A)	4.70
208	Mademoiselle/Lion – Joe Higgs/The Dynamites	5.70
209	Open Up/Again – Clancy Eccles/Higgs & Wilson [Joe Higgs & Roy Wilson]	3.70
210	Conversations/Version – Cynthia Richards	4.70
211	Promises/Real Sweet – Cynthia Richards/Clancy Eccles & The Dynamites (A-side reissued on CLA 216B)	6.70
212	Black Beret/Love Me Tender – The Dynamites/Barry & The Affections	1970
213	Phantom/Skank Me – The Dynamites/Barry & The Affections	7.70
214	Africa/Africa Version 2 – Clancy Eccles & The Dynamites	7.70
215	See Me/Sound Of The '70s – Larry Lawrence (actually Earl Lawrence) [Earl George]/King Stitt	6.70
216	Can't Wait/Promises – Cynthia Richards (B-side reissue of CLA 211A)	8.70
217	Zion/Revival – The Westmorelites/Clancy Eccles & The Dynamites	1970
218	Don't Mind Me/Angel – Higgs & Wilson [Joe Higgs & Roy Wilson]/Glen & Roy (A-side reissue of CLA 207B)	1970
219	Sha La La La/Pop It Up – The Dynamites	4.70
220	Foolish Fool/Dance Beat – Cynthia Richards/King Stitt & Clancy Eccles (A-side reissue of CLA 203A/B-side reissue of CLA 206B)	5.70
221	Unite Tonight/Uncle Joe – Clancy Eccles & The Dynamites	7.70
222	Swanee River/The Past Time – The Baugh All Stars (A-side actually Gladstone Anderson/B-side actually 'Tonight' aka 'Feeling Inside' by Alton Ellis) (prod C Bough)	4.70
223	King Of Kings/Reggaedelic – King Stitt/The Dynamites	10.70

224	Holly Holy/Kingston Town – The Fabulous Flames/Lord Creator	11.70
225	I Was Just Thinking About You/Version – Cynthia Richards/The Dynamites (probably on blank label only)	1970
226	NYT	
227	Credit Squeeze (actually unknown instrumental)/Credit Version (actually unknown instrumental) – Clancy Eccles/The Dynamites (both sides actually by Carl Levy & The Cimarons) (prod unknown, possibly intended for release on Hot Rod) (A-side reissued on Trojan TR 7815)	12.70
228	Name Of The Game/Holly Version – Larry MacDonald & Denzil Laing/ The Fabulous Flames	1.71
229	Stand By Your Man/Version – Cynthia Richards/The Dynamites	3.71
230	Tomorrow (actually 'Where Will You Be Tomorrow')/Tomorrow Version 2 – Clancy & Cynthia (actually by Stranger Cole & Gladstone Anderson)/ The Dynamites (actually with Gladstone Anderson) (prod Clancy Eccles)	1971
231	Sweet Jamaica/Going Up West – Clancy Eccles/The Dynamites	5.71
232	NYT	
233	Rod Of Correction/Rod Of Correction Version – The Dynamites	7.71
234	Teardrops Will Fall/Teardrops Version – The Silvertones	8.71
235	John Crow Skank/Merry Rhythm – Clancy Eccles/King Stitt & The Dynamites	9.71
236	Power For The People/Power For The People (Version) – Clancy Eccles/ The Dynamites	10.71
237	Hello Mother/Hi-Di-Ho – The Dynamites/The Fabulous Flames	11.71
238	Don't Call Me Nigger/Joe Louis – The Soul Twins/The Dynamites	8.72
239	Hallelujah Free At Last/Sha La La – Clancy Eccles/The Dynamites	8.72

Note: All recordings produced by Clancy Eccles, except where otherwise stated.

DOCTOR BIRD (SECOND SERIES, PREFIX DB)

1501	Just Wait & See/Message To Mary – Al Barry/The Markonians (prod Al Barry/Philigree)	1970
1502	Morning Sun/Over & Over – Al Barry & The Cimarons/The Markonians with The Nyah Shuffle (prod Al Barry/Philigree)	1970
1503	Rum Bum A Loo/Drummer Bird – The Message (prod Philigree)	1970

DOWNTOWN (PREFIX DT)

401	Move Your Mule/Reggae Me This, Reggae Me That – Dandy	1968
402	Come Back Girl/Shake Me Wake Me – Dandy	12.68
403	Dream/Sincerely – Denzil [Dennis] & Pat [Rhoden]	12.68
404	Tell Me Darling/Cool Hand Luke – Dandy/Brother Dan All Stars	1.69
405	Copy Your Rhythm/Lovely Lady – Dandy/Brother Dan All Stars	12.68
406	Doctor Sure Shot/Put On Your Dancing Shoes – Dandy	1969

407	Sweet Chariot/Let's Go Downtown – The Dreamers	1.69
408	I Second That Emotion/Dear Love – The Dreamers	1969
409	Pushwood/Reggae Train – Mr Most [Dandy]	2.69
410	Reggae In Your Jeggae/Reggae Shuffle – Dandy/The Dreamers	2.69
411	You Don't Care/Tryer – Dandy & Audrey [Hall]	3.69
412	NYT	
413	Moma Moma/Melody For Two – The Israelites	1969
414	Love Me Tonight/Shoot Them Amigo – Audrey [Hall]/Brother Dan All Stars	1969
415	Rock Steady Gone/Walking Down – Dandy	1969
416	I'm Your Puppet/Watch Boy – Dandy	3.69
417	Quando Quando/Reg 'A' Jeg – Reco [Rodriguez] & The Rudies	1969
418	Lover's Concerto/Along Came Roy – Audrey [Hall]/Herbie Grey & The Rudies	4.69
419	Red Red Wine/Blues – Tony Tribe/The Rudies (actually with Reco Rodriguez)	4.69
420	The Untouchables/Lazy Boy – Sonny Binns & The Rudies/The Rudies	4.69
421	Games People Play/One Fine Day – Dandy/Audrey [Hall]	1969
422	Lover's Question/One Fine Day – Gene Rondo/Herbie Grey & The Rudies	1969
423	Groovin'/These Memories – Owen Gray/Herbie Grey & The Rudies	1969
424	Wheels/Night Train – Sonny Binns & The Rudies	5.69
425	NYT	
426	Everybody Feel Good/Downtown Jump – Downtown All Stars/The Rudies	6.69
427	I Don't Wanna Lose That Girl/Train From Vietnam – Freddie Notes & The Rudies	7.69
428	Lovey Dovey/Kitty Wait – Owen [Gray] & Dandy/Herbie Grey & The Rudies	1969
429	People Get Ready/Near East – Dandy/The Rudies	5.69
430	NYT	
431	Sentimental Reason/Then You Can Tell Me Goodbye – Gene Rondo	6.69
432	Tear Them/Chaka Grind – Desmond Riley/George Lee & The Rudies	6.69
433	Seven Books/Chaka Beat – The Israelites	7.69
434	Be Natural, Be Proud/Who You Want To Run To – Dandy	6.69
435	Tears On My Pillow/Man Pon Spot – Desmond Riley/The Rudies	6.69
436	You'll Lose A Good Thing/If I Had Wings – Audrey [Hall]/Desmond Riley	7.69
437	Come On Home/Love Is All You Need – Dandy	8.69
438	Out Your Fire/No Return – Desmond Riley	8.69
439	I'm Gonna Give Her All The Love I Got/Why Wait – Tony Tribe/Herbie Grey	1969
440	Boss Sound/Everything Is Alright – Dessie [Desmond Riley] & John (actually Lyndon Johns)	9.69
441	Burial Of Longshot (Part 1)/Burial Of Longshot (Part 2) – Prince Of Darkness [Dandy]/George Lee	1969
442	Everybody Loves A Winner/Try Me One More Time – Dandy	1969
443	Talking Boss/Jungle Fever – George Lee (actually with Prince Of Darkness [Dandy])/George Lee	1969
444	Don't Gamble With Love/Songbird – Lyndon Johns	10.69

445	Come Together/Music Fever – The Israelites (actually with Dandy)/Jake Wade	1969
446	Give Me Love/Daddy's Home (actually 'Ghost Rider') – The Emotions/Horace Faith (actually by The Music Doctors)	11.69
446	Give Me Love/Daddy's Home – The Emotions/Horace Faith (duplicate issue of DT 446 with correct B-side, but existence unconfirmed)	1969
447	Music Doctor, Chapter 1/Music Doctor, Chapter 2 – The Music Doctors	1969
448	Meeting Over Yonder/Ghost Rider – Prince Of Darkness (credit should actually be Dandy)/The Music Doctors (see also DT 446B)	1969
449	Pop Your Corn/Pledging My Love – Audrey [Hall]	1969
450	Skinhead A Message To You/Going Strong – Desmond Riley/The Music Doctors	1969
451	Oh Mama, Oh Papa/Bring Back The Night – Lyndon Johns	1969
452	Sweeter Than Sugar/The Way You Move – Audrey [Hall]	1.70
453	Won't You Come Home/Baby Make It Soon – Dandy	1969
454	Oh I Was Wrong/Let's Try Again – Audrey [Hall]/Dandy & Audrey {Hall}	1.70
455	Gumption Rock/Bounce Down – The Soul Explosion	1.70
456	Raining In My Heart/First Note – Dandy/Dandy (actually by The Music Doctors)	2.70
457	Someday We'll Be Together/Sunset Rock – Audrey [Hall]/The Music Doctors	2.70
458	Build Your Love On A Solid Foundation/Baby, Let's Talk It Over – Dandy	3.70
459	Spreading Peace/Guitar Riff – Gene Rondo/The Music Doctors	5.70
460	I'm Gonna Keep On Trying ('Til I Win Your Love)/Girl I Need You – Count Prince Miller	5.70
461	Goodnight My Love/I Don't Want To Be Hurt – Winston Laro (actually Gene Rondo)/Boysie	5.70
462	Morning side Of The Mountain/Show Me Baby – Dandy & Audrey [Hall]/Audrey [Hall]	6.70
463	How Glad I Am/I'm So Glad – Audrey [Hall]/Dandy & Audrey [Hall]	7.70
464	Take It Easy/Funk The Beat – The Megatons	11.70
465	What's Your Name/Mr Lockabe – Dennis Lowe/The Music Doctors	1970
466	unknown instrumental/unknown instrumental – The Music Doctors (found on blank label only)	1970
467	Sound Of Today/Red Red Wine Version – Prince Of Darkness/The Music Doctors	1.71
468	Stand Up For The Sound/Old Man Trouble – Dennis Lowe/Owen [Gray] And Dennis [Lowe]	12.70
469	Militant Man/Reggae Jeggae Version – The Megatons/The Music Doctors	1970
470	Version Girl/Grumble Man – Boy Friday [Dandy]	1.71
471	Music So Good/Right Track – Boy Friday [Dandy] & The Groovers/The Groovers	2.71
472	Sound I Remember/Reconsider Our Love – Boy Friday [Dandy]/Joan Long	1971
473	Take A Message Ruby/Second Note – Boy Friday [Dandy]	1971
474	NYT	
475	NYT	
476	There'll Always Be Sunshine/Sunshine Track – Boy Friday [Dandy]	5.71
477	Hot Pants Girl/Raunchy – Boy Friday [Dandy]	1971

478	Not issued on Downtown; issued on Trojan TR 7828	
479	Val/Bank Raid – Tammi Dee	7.71
480	The Pliers/The Pliers (Part 2) – The Music Doctors	1971
481	El Raunchy/Making Conversation – Boy Friday [Dandy]	1971
482	Only The Strong Survive/Survival – Dave Barker/Committee All Stars (prod Paul Khouri)	1971
483	Could It Be True/Your Eyes Are Dreaming – Dandy & Jackie [Edwards]	1971
484	Daddy's Home/Everyman – Dandy	10.71
485	Under The Boardwalk/Double Barrel Version – Down To Earth (actually Dandy)/Ansel Collins (prod Dandy [Robert Thompson])/Ansel Collins	1971
486	Oh Mammy Blue/Oh Mammy Blue Version – The Cimarons	12.71
487	Holy Christmas/Silent Night – The Cimarons	1971
488	Forever Music/The Boy I Love – John Shaft/Blossom Johnson	1972
489	Give Me Some More/Some More Version – Studio Sound (actually by Dandy)	1972
490	Wanna Be Like Daddy/A Little More – Gene Rondo/Studio Sound	1972
491	Herb Tree/Holy Poly – Family Man [Aston Barrett]/Studio Sound (prod Aston Barrett/Dandy)	1972
492	True True To My Heart/Ace Ninety Skank (actually 'S90 Skank') – Keith Hudson/Big Youth (prod Keith Hudson)	12.72
493	Meet The Boss/Musical Right – Sir Harry (prod Ken Wilson)	1972
494	Get Out Of My Life/Get Out Of My Life (Version) – Niney (actually with The Observers) (prod Winston Holness)	1972
495	Hi Diddle (actually 'Beardman Feast')/Hi Diddle (actually 'Beardman Feast [Version]') – Niney (actually by Max Romeo)/Niney All Stars (actually by The Observers) (prod Winston Holness)	1972
496	Swinging Along/My Baby Is Gone – Dennis Alcapone/Delroy Wilson (prod Edward 'Bunny' Lee)	1972
497	Dock Of The Bay/Dock Of The Bay(Version) – Big Youth/The Crystalites (prod Derrick Harriott)	1973
498	There Is Something On Your Mind/Something On Your Mind (Version) – Hubert Lee/Impact All Stars (prod Vincent Chin)	1973
499	Black Ipa/Black Ipa Skank – The Upsetters (actually with Lee Perry) (prod Lee Perry)	1973
500	Dreadlocks Man/Rasta Want Peace – The Aggrovators (actually by The Rasta Twins) (prod Edward 'Bunny' Lee)	3.73
501	Pretty Girl/Face Girl (Version) – Delroy Wilson/The Professionals (prod Joe Gibbs)	1973
502	You Are A Wanted Man/Back To Dubwise – The Starlites/The GG All Stars (prod Alvin Ranglin)	1973
503	Blackman Time/Hi Jacking – I Roy (prod Augustus Clarke)	1973
504	Apollo 17/Uptown Rock – Sir Harry (actually with The Cables) (prod Hugh Madden)	1973
505	Why Do People Have To Cry/Why Do People Have To Cry (Version) – Branton King (prod B Barnes)	1973

506	Sunshine Showdown/Sunshine Showdown Version – The Upsetters (actually with Lee Perry)/The Upsetters (prod Lee Perry)	1973
507	Two Wedden Skank/A Whole Lotta Sugar Down Deh – Glen Brown/ Berry Simpson (prod Glen Brown)	1973
508	What Did You Say/What Did You Say (Version) – Dennis Alcapone/ Prince Tony's All Stars (prod Tony Robinson)	1973
509	Sick & Tired/Hot Tip – Neville Grant/Prince Django (prod Lee Perry)	1973
510	The Meaning Of One/Let Me In Your Heart – Prince Jazzbo/Suzanne Prescod (prod Glen Brown)	1973
511	Rastafari Ruler/Yesterday – The Twins/Tyrone Taylor (prod Clancy Eccles)	1973
512	Tighten Up Skank/Mid East Rock – The Upsetters (actually with Dillinger) (prod Lee Perry)	1973
513	Bucky Skank/Yucky Skank – The Upsetters (actually with Lee Perry) (prod Lee Perry)	1973
514	Sugar Plum/Sugar Plum (Version) – Bellfield [Stanley Beckford] (prod Alvin Ranglin)	1973
515	The Meaning Of Life/The Meaning Of Life Version – The Heptones/Morwell Esq (prod Morice Wellington)	1973
516	Love Of Jah Jah Children/Jah Jah Children Version – The Millions/The GG All Stars (prod Alvin Ranglin)	1973
517	Dedicated To Illiteracy/Illiteracy Dub – Stranger [Cole] & Gladdy [Anderson] With Shorty Perry/The GG All Stars (prod Alvin Ranglin)	1973
518	Try Me/Rhythm Style – Roman Stewart/Simplicity People (prod Augustus Clarke)	1973
519	Clapper's Tail/Live & Learn – I Roy (prod Augustus Clarke)	1973
520	Hey Little Girl/Don't Blame The Man – Derrick Morgan (prod Edward 'Bunny' Lee)	1973

Note: All releases produced by Dandy unless otherwise stated (issues 401 to 484 inclusive were all produced by him). Also, just to clarify, the production credits 'Thompson/Mulby', 'Downtown Music' and 'R Thompson' are all Dandy. He later (on other Trojan labels) used the credit Shady Tree Music.

DUKE (PREFIX DU)

1	I Wish It Would Rain/There Comes A Time – The Techniques (prod Arthur 'Duke' Reid)	1968
2	Those Guys/I'll Never Fall In Love Again – The Sensations (prod Arthur 'Duke' Reid)	12.68
3	I'll Make It Up/One Dollar Of Music – Carl Dawkins/JJ All Stars (prod Karl JJ Johnson)	12.68
4	Happy Time/Smashville – Herbie Carter (actually Keble Drummond)/The Boys (actually The Jay Boys) (prod Harry Johnson)	12.68
5	Cuss Cuss/Lavender Blue – Lloyd Robinson (prod Harry Johnson)	1.69
6	Man Of My Word/The Time Has Come – The Techniques (prod Winston Riley)	1.69
7	Left With A Broken Heart/Got To Get Away – The Paragons (prod The Paragons)	1968

8	Penny Reel/Soul Tonic – Whistling Willie (actually Neville Willoughby) (prod Neville Willoughby)	1969
9	Auntie Lulu/Bag-A-Boo (actually 'Don't Brag, Don't Boast') – The Slickers (actually by Clancy Eccles)/Clancy Eccles (prod Clancy Eccles)	1969
10	What A Botheration/Stand By Me – The Upsetters (actually with Lee Perry)/The Upsetters (prod Lee Perry) (A-side also issued on Trojan TR 612B)	1969
11	Eight For Eight/You Know What I Mean – The Upsetters/The Inspirations (prod Lee Perry) (also issued on Upsetter US 300)	1969
12	Reggae Dance/I Know – Owen Gray (prod Owen Gray)	3.69
13	Soul Pipe/Overproof – King Cannon [Karl Bryan] (& Anderson's All Stars) (prod Lynford Anderson)	3.69
14	Diana/Personality – Alton Ellis (prod Arthur 'Duke' Reid)	1969
15	Cuyah/Forever – Lloyd Tyrell [Lloyd Charmers]/The Uniques (prod Lloyd Charmers for Winston Lowe)	3.69
16	Follow That Sound/Love In Summer – Lloyd Tyrell [Lloyd Charmers] (actually with The Hippy Boys) (prod Lloyd Charmers for Winston Lowe)	3.69
17	Home Without You/Why Pretend – The Beltones (prod Harry Johnson)	4.69
18	Life/I Like Your Smile – Roy Shirley (prod Karl JJ Johnson)	4.69
19	Easy Sound/Freedom Sound – The Boys (actually The Jay Boys)/The Afrotones (prod Harry Johnson)	4.69
20	Suffering Stink/The Break – Band Of Mercy & Salvation/Bob Melody (actually Winston Francis) (prod Disclick)	1969
21	Never My Love/The Bold One – Boris Gardiner (prod Boris Gardiner)	4.69
22	You're My Everything/What Am I To Do – The Techniques (prod Winston Riley)	5.69
23	Friends & Lovers (actually 'Friends & Lovers Forever')/Hot Line – Patti La Donne/Joe's All Stars (prod Joe Mansano) (Joe label)	5.69
24	Hey Jude/Musical Feet – Joe's All Stars (prod Joe Mansano) (Joe label)	1969
25	Five To Five/Come See About Me – Lloyd Charmers (actually with The Hippy Boys)/The Soul Stirrers (actually Lloyd Charmers) (prod Lloyd Charmers for Winston Lowe) (B-side also issued on Song Bird SB 1002B)	5.69
26	Hear Ya/Live Life – The Scorchers/The Vibrators (prod Karl JJ Johnson)	6.69
27	Glad You're Living/Help Wanted – Stranger Cole (prod Karl JJ Johnson)	6.69
28	Battle Cry Of Biafra/Funky Reggae Part 1 – Joe's All Stars (prod Joe Mansano) (Joe label)	6.69
29	Never Gonna Give You Up/Don't Mix Me Up – The Royals (prod L Edwards)	7.69
30	John Public/Fire Corner – The Dynamites/King Stitt (actually with The Dynamites) (prod Clancy Eccles)	6.69
31	I Don't Care/Shoo Be Doo – The Dingle Brothers/Clancy Eccles (prod Clancy Eccles)	7.69
32	Mother Hen/Chastise Them – The Harmonisers (actually George & Steve)/Winston Sinclair (A-side prod George 'Regent' King/B-side prod Winston Sinclair)	8.69
33	Seven Lonely Days/He Don't Love You Like I Do – Owen Gray (prod Robert Thompson)	8.69

34	Dracula Prince Of Darkness/Honky – King Horror/Joe's All Stars (prod Joe Mansano) (Joe label)	8.69
35	My Girl [Soul]/Bigger Boss – The Ethiopians/Ansel Collins (actually with Count Sticky) (prod Karl JJ Johnson)	1969
36	Safari/Last Laugh – Lloyd Charmers (prod Lloyd Charmers)	8.69
37	Everybody Bawling/Come Look Here – Vincent Gordon/The Silvertones (prod Arthur 'Duke' Reid)	
38	NYT	
39	Soul Serenade/Elizabethan Reggae – Byron Lee & The Dragonaires (actually with Winston Wright)/Byron Lee & The Dragonaires (actually Boris Gardiner & The Love People) (prod Byron Lee/Junior Chung/Boris Gardiner) (some copies correctly credit 'Elizabethan Reggae' to Boris Gardiner) (A-side reissued on Horse HOSS 56A)	2.70
40	Organism/Itch – Anonymously Yours (prod Bart Sanfilipo)	9.69
41	The Judge/Soul Of Jomel (actually 'Soul Of Joel') – Hot Rod/Ron (prod Joe Mansano) (Joe label)	9.69
42	African Meeting/Higher & Higher – Girlie & Jomo (actually Girlie & Joe Mansano)/Josh (prod Joe Mansano) (Joe label)	1969
43	NYT	
44	NYT	
45	NYT	
46	Black Panther/I Want To Be Loved – Sir Collins (prod Clancy Collins)	10.69
47	Black Diamonds/I Remember – Sir Collins & The Diamonds/The Diamonds (prod Clancy Collins)	1969
48	Bye Bye Love/It's Love – The Diamonds (prod Clancy Collins)	1969
49	Love Is A Treasure/I Want To Be – The Dials (prod Clancy Collins)	11.69
50	Brixton Cat/Solitude – Dice The Boss/Joe's All Stars (prod Joe Mansano) (Joe label)	1969
51	Gun The Man Down/The Thief – Dice The Boss/Joe Mansano (prod Joe Mansano) (Joe label)	1969
52	But Officer/Reggae On The Shore – Dice The Boss/Joe's All Stars (prod Joe Mansano) (Joe label)	1.70
53	It's Not Impossible/Dynamite Line – Joe's All Stars (actually by Tito Simon)/Joe's All Stars (prod Joe Mansano) (Joe label)	1969
54	Pair Of Wings (actually titled 'Muriel')/I Can't Stop Loving You – The Diamonds (prod Clancy Collins)	1969
55	Brother Moses/Funny Familiar Forgotten Feelings – Sir Collins & The Earthquakes (prod Clancy Collins)	1969
56	Earthquake/Simmering – The Earthquakes (prod Clancy Collins)	1969
57	Your Boss DJ/Read The News – Dice The Boss/Tito Simon (prod Joe Mansano) (Joe label)	1.70
58	My Girl/You Were To Be – Glen Adams/The Gladiators (prod Arthur 'Duke' Reid)	2.70
59	Lick A Pop/Treasure – Hot Rod All Stars (prod Hot Rod)	1970
60	Where Were You/Just A Smile – The Techniques (prod Winston Riley)	1970

61	Mek You Go On So/Neck Tie – The Ethiopians/Winston Wright (& The JJ All Stars) (prod Karl JJ Johnson)	2.70
62	This World And Me (actually 'Satisfaction')/Poppy Cock – Carl Dawkins/Winston Wright & The JJ All Stars (prod Karl 'JJ' Johnson) (A-side also issued on Trojan TR 7765A)	2.70
63	The Bull/River Ben Come Up – Freddie Notes & The Rudies (prod Joe Sinclair)	2.70
64	NYT	
65	Paint Your Wagon/Organ Man – The Setters (actually by The Hot Rod All Stars) (prod Hot Rod)	2.70
66	Return Of The Bad Man/Caysoe Reggae – Hot Rod All Stars (prod Hot Rod)	4.70
67	Drink Milk/Everywhere I Go – Justin Hinds & The Dominoes (prod Arthur 'Duke' Reid)	3.70
68	Chicken Inn/Scratchin' Chicken (actually titled 'Chicken Scratch') – Freddie Notes & The Rudies/Count Suckle With Freddie Notes & The Rudies (prod Joe Sinclair/Count Suckle)	2.70
69	The Law/The Law (Instrumental) – Andy Capp/Winston Wright & The Dragonaires (prod Byron Lee)	1970
70	It's A Shame/Desertion – Al T. Joe (prod Al T. Joe)	5.70
71	Poppy Show/Pop A Top – Andy Capp (prod Lynford Anderson)	3.70
72	Remember That Sunday/Last Lick – Alton Ellis (actually with Phyllis Dillon)/Tommy McCook (prod Arthur 'Duke' Reid)	3.70
73	Stealing Stealing/Stealing (Instrumental Version) – John Holt/Winston Wright (actually with The Supersonics) (prod Arthur 'Duke' Reid)	4.70
74	Funky Reggae/I Love My Baby – Dave Barker/The Yard Brooms (actually by The Versatiles) (prod Arthur 'Duke' Reid)	5.70
75	Black Street/Nobody Knows – Rico/unidentified vocalist (prod Clancy Collins) (probably not issued)	
76	The Rooster/Walk Through This World – Jeff Barnes/Phyllis Dillon (prod Arthur 'Duke' Reid)	6.70
77	Open Jaw/Working Kind – Tommy McCook/John Holt (prod Arthur 'Duke' Reid)	5.70
78	The Key To The City/Give It To Me – Tommy McCook/Dorothy Reid (prod Arthur 'Duke' Reid)	5.70
79	I Can't Hide/Kansas City – Ken Parker/Tommy McCook (prod Arthur 'Duke' Reid)	6.70
80	Geronimo/Feel Alright – The Pyramids (prod Bruce Anthony)	6.70
81	Ooh Wee/Hold It Baby – Al Barry (prod Al Barry for Philligree)	1970
82	Death Rides/Destruction – The Good Guys (prod Byron Lee)	1970
83	Wreck It Up/Dynamic Groove – The Good Guys (prod Byron Lee)	7.70
84	Happiness/Latissimo – The Good Guys (prod Byron Lee)	10.70
85	Hard On Me/Please Don't Stop The Wedding – Tommy Cowan & The Jamaicans (prod Tommy Cowan)	1970
86	Going In Circles/Doggone Right – Bobby Blue (actually Bobby Davis) (prod Lloyd Charmers) (A-side reissued on Explosion EX 2054A And Trojan TR 7936B)	8.70
87	Colour Him Father/Colour Him Father (Version) – The Charmers/Lloyd Charmers (prod Lloyd Charmers)	7.70

88	You Can't Wine/Bee Sting – The Kingstonians/Rupie Edwards All Stars (prod Rupie Edwards)	8.70
89	You Broke My Heart/Tell Me The Reason – Domino Johnson & The Champions (prod Domino Johnson)	10.70
90	Eye For An Eye/You Broke My Heart (Version) – Tony (actually Tony Sexton) & The Champions/The Champions (prod Domino Johnson)	1970
91	Cashbox/Strolling In The Park – Byron Lee & The Dragonaires/Winston Wright (prod Byron Lee)	8.70
92	Cloudburst/Message From A Blackman – The Hippy Boys/Lloyd Charmers (prod Lloyd Charmers)	8.70
93	Get Together/Instalment Plan – Carl Dawkins/Aston 'Family Man' Barrett (prod Karl JJ Johnson)	10.70
94	Collecting Coins/Cabbage Leaf – JJ All Stars (prod Karl JJ Johnson)	1970
95	This Land/This Land (Version) – Carl Dawkins/JJ All Stars (prod Karl JJ Johnson)	12.70
96	Surprise Package/I'm Sorry – Rico (actually Reco Rodriguez) & Satch (actually Ferdinand Dixon)/Pete Johnson (prod Larry Lawrence)	1.71
97	Come Along/Try To Be Happy – The Clarendonians (prod Karl JJ Johnson)	1970
98	Funny/Sugar Cane – Rupert Cunningham (prod Charles Ross)	1970
99	Sometimes/Girl Like You – Errol English [Junior English] & The Champions (prod Domino Johnson)	2.71
100	NYT	
101	Coolie Man/Coolie Version – The Cambodians/The JJ All Stars (prod Karl JJ Johnson)	12.70
102	Drop Him/Version Drop – The Ethiopians/The JJ All Stars (prod Karl JJ Johnson)	12.70
103	Pharoah's Walk/Little Caesar – Exodus/Exodus (actually by Sammy Jones) (prod Jack Price)	1.71
104	Single Girl/Together We'll Be – Silkie Davis [TT Ross] (prod [Calva] Les Foster)	1970
105	Love I Tender/When The Lights Are Low – U Roy/Joya Landis (prod Byron Smith)	1.71
106	Donkey Skank/Donkey Track – Scotty & The Tennors (actually by The Tennors)/Murphy's All Stars (prod Albert Gene Murphy)	1971
107	To The Fields/To The Fields (Version) – Herman [Chin-Loy] & The Aquarians (prod H Chin-Loy)	2.71
108	Rim Bim Bam/Rim Bim Bam (Version) – The Ethiopians/Randy's All Stars (prod V Chin)	2.71
109	Be Loving To Me/Judgement Rock – The Tillermen (actually Greyhound) (prod Big G)	1971
110	One Bad Apple/Poop-A-Poom – Barry Biggs/Byron Lee & The Dragonaires (prod Byron Lee)	4.71
111	Silhouettes/That Did It – Winston Wright & The Upsetters (prod Lee Perry)	4.71
112	Grooving Out On Life/Fire Fire – Hopeton Lewis/Byron Lee & The Dragonaires (prod Byron Lee & Winston Blake/Byron Lee)	4.71
113	Big Bamboo/King Ja Ja – Emile Straker & The Merrymen (prod Emile Straker) (Calypso reissue from Trojan TR 692)	1971

114	Maria/Only A Fool (Breaks His Own Heart) – Mighty Sparrow (prod Byron Lee) (Calypso reissue from 1969. reissued on Trojan TRO 9046)	5.71
115	Dr Kitch/Love In The Cemetery – Lord Kitchener (prod WIRL Records) (Calypso reissue from 1963/2, respectively)	5.71
116	Babylon A Fall/Version Buggy – The Maytones/Tony King (actually by unidentified DJ) (prod Alvin Ranglin)	5.71
117	NYT	
118	Put It Good/Put It Good (Version) – The Bleechers/The JJ All Stars (prod Karl JJ Johnson)	6.71
119	Bend Down/Heaven Help Us All – Ernie Smith (prod Ernie Smith for Federal)	1971
120	Remember/Madhouse – The Sensations/Larry's All Stars (prod Larry Lawrence)	1971
121	What Are You Doing Sunday/Sweet Dream – The Sensations/The Ruffians (prod Larry Lawrence)	10.71
122	Reggae In The Fields/Love Brother (Instrumental) – Augustus Pablo/Tommy McCook (prod Herman Chin-Loy)	10.71
123	Come On Home Girl/You Are Mine – Bill & Pete Campbell (prod Bill Campbell)	11.71
124	Mixing/In Orbit – The Cables/The In Crowd Band (prod Keble Drummond)	1971
125	Medley Version/Part 2 – Dennis Alcapone & The Gaytones (prod Sonia Pottinger)	1971
126	Lion's Den/Lion's Den (Version) – The Kingstonians (prod Karl JJ Johnson)	1971
127	Last Call/Hot Call – Sir Harry/Organ D (prod Morice Wellington)	1972
128	The Sensational Melodians (Medley)/Part 2 – The Melodians (prod Sonia Pottinger)	1972
129	Only Love Can Make You Smile/Only Love (Version) – Gaby (actually Gaby Wilton) & The Cables (prod Glen Brown)	1971
130	The Mighty Melodians (Medley)/Part 2 – The Melodians (prod Sonia Pottinger)	1972
131	The Sky's The Limit/The Sky's The Limit (Version) – Dennis Alcapone (prod Keith Hudson)	1972
132	Bald Headed Teacher/Bald Headed Teacher (Version) – Trevor Lambert (actually Max Romeo)/The Headmasters (prod Tony Robinson)	1972
133	My Whole World/How Can You Mend A Broken Heart – Carl Dawkins (prod Karl JJ Johnson)	1972
134	Rebel Train/Babylon Version – Jago (prod Morice Wellington)	1972
135	Soup/Soup (Version) – JJ All Stars (actually with Lloyd Young)/The JJ All Stars (prod Karl JJ Johnson)	1972
136	Apples To Apples/Good Life – Sir Harry/Drumbeat All Stars (prod Ken Wilson)	1972
137	Live It Up/Baby Don't Do It – U Roy Junior/Dennis Brown (prod Lloyd Daley)	1972
138	NYT	
139	What About The Half/What About The Half (Version) – Dennis Brown (prod Lloyd Daley)	1972
140	Wheel & Tun Me/Hey Mama – Whistling Willie (actually Neville Willoughby) (prod Neville Willoughby)	7.72
141	Boat To Progress/Boat To Progress (Version) – Ritchie MacDonald & Glen Brown (prod Glen Brown)	8.72
142	I Forgot To Be Your Lover/I've Got To Settle Down – Denzil Dennis (prod Denzil Dennis & Pat Rhoden)	1972

143 Save The Last Dance For Me/Be The One – The Heptones (prod Joe Gibbs) 1972

144 Reggae Limbo/Broken Contract – The Chuckles/Zap Pow (prod Keith Hudson) 1972

145 Satan Side/Evil Spirit – Keith Hudson & The Chuckles/Don D Junior
(prod Keith Hudson) 1972

146 Runaway Child/Wedding March – Roy Bailey (prod Lloyd Campbell) 1972

147 Get In The Groove/Get In The Groove (Version) – Dennis Alcapone & Dennis
Brown/The Dynamites (prod Dennis Alcapone) 1972

148 Vision/Young & Unlearned – Al T Joe (prod Al T Joe) 1972

149 Headquarters/Black Girl In My Bed – Dillinger/Shenley Duffas (prod Lee Perry) 1973

150 Rastaman Going Back Home/Barble Dove Skank – Flowers & Alvin
(actually Lloyd Flowers & Alvin Ranglin)/Little Youth (prod Alvin Ranglin) 3.73

151 Africa Want Us All/Liberation – Allan King/Joe Gibbs All Stars (prod Joe Gibbs) 1973

152 Wipe Them Out/Go Back Home – Matumbi (prod Dennis Bovell) (A-side also
issued on Horse HOSS 39B) 1973

153 Words Of My Mouth/Words Of My Mouth (Version) – The Gatherers/
The Upsetters (prod Lee Perry) 1973

154 Murmuring/Donkey Face Skank – The Millions/Tommy McCook & Bobby
Ellis (prod Alvin Ranglin) 1973

155 Suspicion/Suspicion (Version) – Jimmy Green (actually Jimmy London)/
The Rhythm Rulers (prod Lloyd Campbell) 1973

156 Buck & The Preacher/Buck & The Preacher (Version) – I Roy/Pete Weston
All Stars (prod Pete Weston) 1973

157 The Higher The Mountain/The Higher The Mountain (Version) – U Roy/
Old Boys Inc (prod Ewart Beckford [U Roy]) 1973

158 Shotgun Wedding/Girl Of My Dreams – Cornel Campbell (prod Edward
'Bunny' Lee) 1973

159 The Very Best I Can/Heading For The Mountains – Cornel Campbell
(prod Edward 'Bunny' Lee) 1973

160 Blackbirds Singing/Always – Roslyn Sweat & The Paragons (prod Arthur
'Duke' Reid) 1973

161 Love Is A Treasure/Love Is A Treasure (1967) – Lizzy & Freddy McKay/
Freddy McKay (prod Arthur 'Duke' Reid) 1973

162 Children Of The Night/For The Good Times – The Chosen Few (actually by
Norman Brown & Lloyd Charmers)/Lloyd Charmers (prod Lloyd Charmers) 10.73

163 Stoned In Love With You/Stoned In Love (Version) – The Chosen Few (actually
by Norman Brown & Lloyd Charmers) (prod Lloyd Charmers) 10.73

164 It's Too Late/It's Too Late (Version) – The Chosen Few (actually by Norman Brown
& Lloyd Charmers)/Micky Chung (prod Lloyd Charmers) 10.73

165 Beef Sticker/Ten Commandments – Fud & Del/Prince Heron (prod Fud Christian) 1973

DUKE REID (PREFIX DR)

2501 What Does It Take/Reggae Merengue – Alton Ellis/Tommy McCook &
The Supersonics 8.70

2502 Hopeful Village/White Rum – The Tennors/Earl Lindo 1970

2503	Sunday Gravy/Write Her A Letter – Neville Hinds/John Holt	10.70
2504	Sugar Pantie/Ballafire – Ken Parker (actually by Andy Capp)/Tommy McCook & The Supersonics	2.71
2505	Boom Shacka Lacka/Dynamite – Hopeton Lewis (actually with The Chosen Few)/Tommy McCook & The Supersonics	1970
2506	Come Out Of My Bed/Hide & Seek – John Holt/Winston Wright	10.70
2507	Mother's Tender Care/Soldier Man – The Ethiopians/Tommy McCook & The Supersonics	1970
2508	If Your Name Is Andy/Skavoovie – Dorothy Reid	1970
2509	Wake The Town/Big Boy & Teacher – U Roy	9.70
2510	Rule The Nation/Angel A La La – U Roy/Nora Dean	10.70
2511	Say Me Say/I Want It – Justin Hinds	1970
2512	You Made Me So Very Happy/Mighty As A Rose (actually titled 'Continental') – Alton Ellis/Tommy McCook & The Supersonics	1970
2513	Wear You To The Ball/The Ball – U Roy & The Paragons/Earl Lindo	1970
2514	You'll Never Get Away/Rock Away – U Roy & The Melodians/Tommy McCook Quintet	12.70
2515	Version Galore/Nehru – U Roy & The Melodians/Tommy McCook & The Supersonics	1970
2516	Testify/Super Soul – Hopeton Lewis/Smokey 007 & The Supersonics	1.71
2517	Tom Drunk/Wailing – U Roy & Hopeton Lewis/Tommy McCook & The Supersonics	2.71
2518	True True True/On The Beach – U Roy & Ken Parker/U Roy & The Paragons	1971
2519	Flashing My Whip/On The Beach – U Roy & The Paragons (duplicate issue, has 'DR 2519A1/DR 2519A' respectively in runout grooves)	1971
2519	Flashing My Whip/Do It Right – U Roy & The Paragons/U Roy & The Three Tops (duplicate issue, has 'DR 2519B1/DR 2519B2' respectively in runout grooves)	1971
2520	Rock To The Beat (actually titled 'Number One Station')/Love Is Not A Gamble – U Roy (actually by Dennis Alcapone & The Duke Reid All Stars)/U Roy (actually by Dennis Alcapone & The Techniques)	1972
2521	Jimmy Brown/Jimmy Brown (Version) – Ken Parker/Tommy McCook And The Supersonics	1972
2522	Hurt (actually titled 'Your Enemy Can't Hurt You')/Hurt (Version) (actually 'Your Enemy Can't Hurt You (Version)') – Reid's All Stars (actually by The Eagles)/Reid's All Stars	1973
2523	Guess I This Riddle/Guess I This Riddle (Version) – Eddy Ford/Reid's All Stars	1973
2524	You're The One I Love/You're The One I Love (Version) – Dorothy Russell/Reid's All Stars	1973

Note: All releases produced by Arthur 'Duke' Reid.

DYNAMIC (PREFIX DYN)

401	Got To Be Mellow/Love Grows – Barry Biggs (prod Dynamic Sounds)	9.70
402	Out Of Time/Love For Everyone – Henry III [Henry Buckley] & Hubcap And Wheels/The Viceroys (prod Dynamic Sounds)	11.70

403	One Pound Weight/Come Dance – Henry III [Henry Buckley] & Hubcap And Wheels (prod Dynamic Sounds)	1970
404	Commanding Wife/Band Of Gold – Boris Gardiner & The Happening (prod Boris Gardiner for Dynamic Sounds)	1970
405	Hitching A Ride/Hitching A Ride (Version) – Al T. Joe/Byron Lee & The Dragonaires (prod Al T Joe)	1.71
406	Johnny Too Bad/Saucy Hoard – The Slickers/Roland Alphonso (prod Sid Bucknor)	2.71
407	6345789/Warm & Tender Love – Austin Faithful (prod Sid Bucknor)	1971
408	Each One, Teach One/Thinking Of You – The Blues Busters (prod Dynamic Sounds) (B-side also issued on Trojan TR 7819A)	3.71
409	Shock Attack/My Sweet Lord – Busty Brown (actually with Lee Perry)/Byron Lee & The Dragonaires (actually with Keith Lyn) (prod Lee Perry/Dynamic Sounds)	3.71
410	Love Uprising/My Love For You – The Jamaicans (prod Tommy Cowan)	4.71
411	Hallelujah/Trying To Reach My Goal – Ken Boothe (prod Ken Boothe)	4.71
412	NYT	
413	Never Gonna Give You Up/Never Gonna Give (Version) – The West Indians/Rebellious Subjects (prod Sid Bucknor)	5.71
414	Way Back Home/Way Back Home (Version) – Byron Lee & The Dragonaires (prod Winston Blake)	1971
415	Bed Of Roses/Forgive Me – Jo Spencer (prod Dynamic Sounds)	1971
416	NYT	
417	Mary/Soldier Boy – The Jamaicans/The Conscious Minds (prod Tommy Cowan)	1971
418	Rich Man, Poor Man/You Don't Know – The Cables/The Dingle Brothers (prod Sid Bucknor)	7.71
419	You Can't Win/Don't Fight The Law – The Slickers (prod Sid Bucknor)	7.71
420	Cherry Oh Baby/Sir Charmers Special – Eric Donaldson/Lloyd Charmers (prod Edward 'Bunny' Lee)	1971
421	Horse & Buggy/Buggy & Horse – Dennis Alcapone/Roland Alphonso & Denzil Laing (prod Edward 'Bunny' Lee)	11.71
422	Ripe Cherry/Red Cherry – Dennis Alcapone/Inner Circle (prod Edward 'Bunny' Lee)	10.71
423	Love Of The Common People/Dragon's Net – Eric Donaldson/Denzil Laing (prod Dynamic Sounds)	11.71
424	Bam So Bo/Bam So Bo (Version) – Winston Heywood & The Hombres (prod Winston Heywood)	11.71
425	Just Can't Happen This Way/Just Can't (Version) – Eric Donaldson/The Dragonaires (prod Dynamic Sounds)	1971
426	Carry That Weight/More Weight – Dobby Dobson/Hubcap & Wheels (prod Dynamic Sounds)	1971
427	Al Capone's Guns Don't Bark/Guns Don't Bark – Dennis Alcapone/The Dynamites (prod Edward 'Bunny' Lee)	1971
428	Just A Dream/Send Me Some Loving – Slim Smith (prod Edward 'Bunny' Lee)	2.72
429	What A Price/The Prisoner's Song – Al T Joe (prod Al T Joe)	2.72
430	I Believe In Music/I Believe In Music (Version) – The Jamaicans/The Dynamites (prod Tommy Cowan)	1972

431 I'm Indebted (To You)/I'm Indebted (Version) – Eric Donaldson/The Dynamites
(prod Dynamic Sounds) 1972

432 Pharaoh Hiding/Hail To Power – Junior Byles/The Upsetters (prod Lee Perry) 1972

433 Geraldine/Reverend Heray (actually 'Reverend Leroy') – Tommy
(actually Tommy Cowan) (prod Tommy Cowan) 1972

434 Man No Dead/Man No Dead (Version) – KC White (prod KC White) 1972

435 Make It Reggae (aka Hot Reggae)/Go Johnny Go – Byron Lee & The
Dragonaires/Dennis Alcapone (prod Byron Lee/Bunny Lee) 1972

436 Come Together/Going Back To My Home Town – Hopeton Lewis (prod Lee Perry) 1972

437 Everybody Needs Help/Everybody Needs Help (Version) – Derrick Morgan
(prod Edward 'Bunny' Lee) 1972

438 Redemption Song/Redemption Song (Version) – The Maytals/The Dynamites
(prod Warrick Lyn) 1972

439 Miserable Woman/The Lion Sleeps – Eric Donaldson (prod Dynamic Sounds) 1972

440 Kenyatta/Kenyatta (Version) – Joe White/Joe White Recording Band
(prod Joe White) 1972

441 Stop The War/Stop The War (Version) – Winston Heywood & The Hombres/
The Hombres (prod Winston Heywood) 1972

442 Are You Sure/Are You Sure (Version) – The Jamaicans (prod Warwick Lyn) &
Tommy Cowan 1972

443 Throw Away Your Gun/Sad Song – Busty Brown & The Warners/The Twinkle
Brothers (prod Sid Bucknor) 6.72

444 We Love Jamaica/We Love Jamaica (Version) – Max Romeo/The Soul Rhythms
(prod Max Romeo) 1972

445 Blue Boot/Blue Boot (Version) – Eric Donaldson/The Dynamites (prod Dynamic
Sounds) 9.72

446 My Confession/My Confession (Version) – Eric Donaldson/The Aggrovators
(prod Edward 'Bunny' Lee) 9.72

447 Good Together/Good Together (Version) – Hopeton Lewis (prod Dynamic Sounds) 1972

448 Festival Wise/Festival Wise – U Roy/The Dynamites (prod Dynamic Sounds) 1972

449 Family Man/Family Man (Version) – Ricky Slick [Richard Grant] (prod Dynamic
Sounds) 10.72

450 Last Night I Didn't Get To Sleep At All/Last Night (Version) – Chris Leon/
The Dynamites (prod Dynamic Sounds) 1972

451 Peace/Peace (Version) – Shenley Duffas/The Upsetters (prod Lee Perry) 12.72

452 Little Did You Know/Little Did You Know (Version) – Eric Donaldson/
The Dynamites (prod Dynamic Sounds) 1972

453 Tears From My Eyes/Tears From My Eyes (Version) – Ken Boothe/The Conscious
Minds (prod Ken Boothe & BB Seaton) 1972

454 Talk About Love/Don't Forget To Remember – Adinah Edwards (prod Tommy
Cowan) 1972

455 Life Is The Highest/Reincarnate – Tesfa Macdonald (prod Tesfa MacDonald) 1972

456 Sunshine Love/Sunshine Love (Version) – The Jamaicans (prod Tommy Cowan) 1972

457 Seek & You'll Find/Seek & Find (Version) – Winston Heywood/The Hombres
(prod Winston Heywood) 1972

EXPLOSION (PREFIX EX)

2001 Death A Come/Zylon – Lloyd Charmers (actually by Lloyd Robinson)/
Lloyd Charmers (prod Lloyd Daley) 1969

2002 Doctor Who/Part 2 – Bongo Herman & Les Chen (prod Derrick Harriott) 1969

2003 Barefoot Brigade/Slippery – Winston Wright & The Crystalites/(Bobby Ellis &)
The Crystalites (prod Derrick Harriott) 1969

2004 NYT

2005 Bombshell/Bag A Wire – Bobby Ellis & The Crystalites (prod Derrick Harriott) 12.69

2006 A Fistful Of Dollars/The Emporer – The Crystalites/Bobby Ellis & The
Crystalites (prod Derrick Harriott) 1969

2007 Lemi Li/Goody Goody – Rudy Mills (prod Derrick Harriott) 1970

2008 Tighten Up Your Gird (actually 'Tighten Up Your Guard')/Look To The Sky
(aka Let Me Be The One aka This Is My Song) – Keith & Tex & The Crystalites
(prod Derrick Harriott) 1.70

2009 She's Gone/Old Old Song – Tinga [Stewart] & Ernie [Smith] (prod Derrick
Harriott) 1.70

2010 The Bad/The Bad (Version 2) – The Crystalites (prod Derrick Harriott) 2.70

2011 Flight 404/Darling Come Down – Winston Wright & The GG All Stars/Lloyd
& Robin (prod Alvin Ranglin) 2.70

2012 Funny Man/Champion – The Maytones/The GG All Stars (prod Alvin Ranglin) 3.70

2013 Sentimental Reason/Lover Girl – The Maytones (prod Alvin Ranglin)
(possibly unissued) 3.70

2014 Barabus/King Of Life (actually This Kind Of Life) – The Maytones (A-side actually
The GG All Stars) (prod Alvin Ranglin) 4.70

2015 Funny Girl/Funny Girl (Version) – Winston Wright & The GG All Stars
(prod Alvin Ranglin) 4.70

2016 Higher Than The Highest Mountain/Musical Shot – Eric 'Monty' Morris/
The GG All Stars (prod Alvin Ranglin) 5.70

2017 Funky Monkey/Funky Monkey (Version 2) – Dice The Boss (prod Laurel Aitken) 5.70

2018 Chinee Brush/Real Collie – Trevor Lloyd/Dice & Cummie (prod Laurel Aitken) 6.70

2019 Give Me Back Your Love/Hold Me – Trevor Lloyd (prod Laurel Aitken) 6.70

2020 Funky Duck/Funkier Than Duck – Dice The Boss (prod Laurel Aitken) 1970

2021 Stick By Me/The Designer – Bob Roberts/Tommy McCook (prod uncredited) 1970

2022 In The Summertime/Apollo Moon Rock – Billy Jack/Nat Cole (prod Nat Cole) 7.70

2023 Man From Carolina/Gold On Your Dress – The GG All Stars/The GG All Stars
(actually by The Slickers) (prod Alvin Ranglin) 7.70

2024 African Melody/Serious Love – The Maytones (actually by The GG All Stars)
(prod Alvin Ranglin) 7.70

2025 Ganga Plane/Deep River – The GG All Stars/The GG All Stars (actually by
Aston Barratt) (prod Alvin Ranglin) 8.70

2026 Can I Get Next To You/Big Five – The Charmers (prod Lloyd Charmers) 8.70

2027 Cecilia/Chariot Without Horse – The Maytones (A-side actually by Keeling Beckford/
B-side actually by Nyah Hunter & The GG All Stars) (prod Alvin Ranglin) 1970

2028 Too Late/Each Day – Joel Marvin (actually Gregory Isaacs) (prod Rupie Edwards) 7.70

2029   Groovy Jo Jo/Ten Steps To Soul – Joe Joe Bennett & Mudies All Stars
(prod Harry Mudie)   7.70

2030   Full Moon/Baby – Rupie Edwards All Stars/Rupie Edwards All Stars (actually by
unidentified male vocalist) (prod Rupie Edwards) (A-side also issued on Big label
BG 314B)   1970

2031   Love At First Sight/I Need Your Care – Rupie Edwards All Stars/Rupie Edwards
(prod Rupie Edwards)   1970

2032   Vengeance/Look A Py-Py – The Hippy Boys (actually with Lloyd Charmers)/
The Hippy Boys (prod Lloyd Charmers)   8.70

2033   Another Festival/Happy Time – The Maytones (prod Alvin Ranglin)   1970

2034   Ready Talk/There Is Something About You – Lloyd Charmers/Lloyd Charmers
(actually with Busty Brown) (prod Lloyd Charmers)   1970

2035   Sweet Back/Music Talk – Lloyd Charmers (prod Lloyd Charmers)   10.70

2036   Ring The Bell/Ring The Bell (Version 2) – Trevor & Keith (prod Alvin Ranglin)   1970

2037   Blue Moon/Oh Me Oh My (Version) – Guts McGeorge (prod Rupie Edwards)   11.70

2038   NYT

2039   Revelation Version/Marka Version – Dennis Alcapone (prod Keith Hudson)   11.70

2040   Whisper A Little Prayer/Rain A Fall – Hugh Roy (actually by Audley Rollen)/
Hugh Roy (actually by Merlene Webber) (prod Keith Hudson)   1970

2041   California Dreaming/One Woman – Hugh Roberts (actually by Lloyd Charmers)
(prod Lloyd Charmers)   12.70

2042   All Kinds Of Everything/Cool & Easy – Wayne Howard/Lloyd Charmers
(prod Lloyd Charmers)   12.70

2043   Delivered/Especially For You – Neville Hinds (A-side actually 'Especially For
You' by Winston Blake/B-side actually Delivered by Neville Hinds & The
Matadors) (prod Lloyd Daley)   2.71

2044   Love I Madly/Musical Shower – Tony Binns (prod Lloyd Charmers)   2.71

2045   Skinhead Train/Everstrong – The Charmers/Tony Binns (prod Lloyd Charmers)   2.71

2046   Humpty Dumpty/Got To Get A Message To You – Tony Binns/Johnny Barker
(B-side actually by Dave Barker & The Charmers) (prod Lloyd Charmers)   1971

2047   Back To Africa/Born To Lose – Lloyd & Joy (actually by Alton Ellis)/Lloyd &
Joy (prod Lloyd Daley)   2.71

2048   Never Fall In Love With You Again (Version 3)/Jet 747 (Version 4) – Glen Adams/
The Jet Scene (prod Fud Christian)   4.71

2049   Love Brother/Uganda – Herman Chin-Loy (actually with The Aquarians)
(prod Herman Chin-Loy)   1971

2050   Starvation/Starvation (Version) – The Ethiopians/The JJ All Stars (prod Karl JJ
Johnson)   1971

2051   I Feel Good/I Feel Good (Version) – Carl Dawkins/The JJ All Stars (prod Karl JJ
Johnson)   6.71

2052   Hold On Girl/Hold On (Version) – Randy's All Stars (prod Vincent Chin)   7.71

2053   Oh Lord/Raindrops (actually titled 'My Baby') – Errol Dunkley & The Impact
All Stars/Keith & The Impact All Stars (B-side actually by Lloyd Charmers)
(prod Keith Chin/Lloyd Charmers)   7.71

2054	Going In Circles/Just My Imagination – The Charmers (actually by Bobby Blue [Bobby Davis])/The Charmers (actually by Dave Barker & The Charmers) (prod Lloyd Charmers) (A-side reissued on Duke label DU 86A and Trojan TR 7936B)	7.71
2055	Reggae In Wonderland/Wonder (Version) – The Charmers (actually by Byron Lee & The Dragonaires) (prod Lloyd Charmers)	7.71
2056	Girl/Sister Big Stuff – Ken Lazarus/Tomorrow's Children (prod Federal)	8.71
2057	I Love Jamaica/Marry Me Marie – Neville [Willoughby] (prod Neville Willoughby)	1971
2058	Life Is Rough/Life Is Rough (Version) – Shout (prod Federal)	1971
2059	Make It Great/Make It Great (Version) – Carl Dawkins/JJ All Stars (prod Karl JJ Johnson)	1972
2060	Stagger Lee/Musical Version – John Lee (actually by John Holt)/The Aggrovators (prod Edward 'Bunny' Lee)	1972
2061	Bounce Me Johnny/Bounce Me (Version) (B-side actually titled 'Say You') – The Slickers (prod Federal)	1972
2062	Repatriation/Repatriation Version – Audley Rollen/U Roy Junior (prod Lloyd Daley)	1972
2063	Samba Girl/Samba Girl (Version) – England Cook/Now Generation (prod Lloyd Daley)	1972
2064	Hail The Man/Where Do I Go? – Ken Lazarus (prod Federal)	1972
2065	Not Another Woman/Don't Go Wrong – Carl Dawkins (prod Karl JJ Johnson)	1972
2066	Soul & Inspiration/Trying My Faith – Paddy Corea/The Stags (artist possibly The Versatiles) (prod Bush)	7.72
2067	Sprinkle Some Water/Howdy & Tenky – Shorty Perry/Lloyd [Flowers] & Alvin [Ranglin] (prod Alvin Ranglin)	9.72
2068	Black Magic Woman/Black Magic Woman (Version) – Phil Pratt (actually by Dennis Brown)/Phil Pratt All Stars (prod Phil Pratt)	9.72
2069	Long Long Road/Long Long Road (Version) – Milton Hamilton & The Classics (actually Milton Hamilton & Denzil Dennis)/The Classics [Milton Hamilton & Denzil Dennis] (prod Pat Rhoden)	1972
2070	The Killer Passing Through/Show Some Loving – The Swans (actually possibly by U Roy Junior)/The Swans (prod Bush)	1972
2071	Let Me Down Easy/Easy (Version) – Derrick Harriott/The Crystalites (prod Derrick Harriott)	12.72
2072	Memories Of Love/In Peace – The Orbitones/Sonny Earl (prod Sonny Roberts)	1972
2073	Chirpy Chirpy Cheep Cheep/Chirpy Chirpy Cheep Cheep – The Jay Boys (prod Harry Johnson)	1972
2074	The Time Has Come/Blessed Is The Man – Slim Smith (prod Edward 'Bunny' Lee)	1972
2075	Forward Up/Forward (Version) – The Stingers/The Upsetters (prod Lee Perry)	1972
2076	Brown Girl/Halfway Tree Rock – The Maytones/Shorty Perry (prod Alvin Ranglin)	1972
2077	Rhythm Pleasure/Doctor Seaton – Jerry Lewis/The Aggrovators (prod Edward 'Bunny' Lee)	1972
2078	Stand Up & Fight/Sunny Side Of The Sea – Dennis Alcapone & Slim Smith (prod Edward 'Bunny' Lee)	1973

2079	Weather Report/Weather Report (Version) – The Tennors/Duke Reid's All Stars (prod Arthur 'Duke' Reid)	3.73
2080	I'll Never Find Another You/Another You (Version) – Jimmy London/Impact All Stars (prod Vincent Chin)	1973
2081	Seven Little Girls Sitting In The Back Seat/Give A Little Love – The Peaches (actually by Winston Groovy & The Peaches) (prod Sidney Crooks)	1973
2082	Sha La La La Lee/No Matter What You Do – The Clem Bushay Set (prod Clement Bushay)	1973
2083	I'm A Believer/You'll Be Mine – Winston Tucker [Winston Tucker] (prod Winston Tucker)	1973
2084	My Island/My Island (Version) – Paulette Williams/The GG All Stars (prod Alvin Ranglin)	1973
2085	That Lady/Sonia – The Paris Connection (prod C Troutt, aka Mike Dorane)	1973
2086	Nose For Trouble/Version – Winston Groovy/Rhythm Rulers (prod Winston Tucker)	1973
2087	Single Girl/Version – Barbara Thompson (B-side actually by Dandy & Count Prince Miller) (prod Dandy [Robert Thompson]) & Shady Tree)	1974
2088	Please Don't Make Me Cry/So Easy – Winston Groovy (prod Sidney Crooks/ Winston Tucker)	1974
2089	None Shall Escape The Judgement/Every Rasta Is A Star – Johnny Clarke (prod Edward 'Bunny' Lee)	1974
2090	The Man Who Sold The World/The Man Who Sold The World (Version) – The Wally Brothers/Wally's All Stars (prod Webster Shrowder & Des Bryan)	1974
2091	Mockingbird/Mockingbird (Instrumental) – The Tulips (actually The Marvels)/ Des All Stars (prod Webster Shrowder & Des Bryan)	1974

GAYFEET (GS PREFIX)

FIRST SERIES

201	Fatty/Landlord – Bim & Bam	1969
202	If It Don't Work Out/Ki Salavoca [ska] – Joe White/Baba Brooks Band	1969
203	By The Time I Get To Phoenix/Lover Boy – Lou Sparks (actually Lloyd Parks)/ Lou Sparks (actually by Roland Alphonso)	12.69
204	Little Donkey/Hope & Joy – Eric Boswell (actually by Lloyd Parks & Maxine)/ Eric Boswell (actually by Lloyd Parks)	1.70
205	Jennifer/Slipping – Junior Soul [Murvin]	1970
206	NYT	
207	You Are Not My Kind/You Are Not My Kind (Version 2) – Naomi/ The Gaytones	6.70
208	We Will Make Love/Sticker – Lou Sparks (actually Lloyd Parks)/Roland Alphonso	7.70

Note: All productions by Mrs Sonia Pottinger.

SECOND SERIES

206	Medicine Doctor/Facts Of Life – Big Youth	1973
207	Emergency Call/Emergency Call (Version) – Judy Mowatt/The Gaytones (reissued on Trojan TR 7912)	1973
208	You Make Me Cry/You Make Me Cry (Version) – Winston Jones/The Gaytones	1973
209	My Baby Just Cares For Me/Jah Jah Me No Horn Yah – Cornel Campbell (prod Edward 'Bunny' Lee)	1973
210	Hard Feeling/Regular Style – U Roy (prod Alvin Ranglin)	1973

Note: All productions by Mrs Sonia Pottinger except where otherwise stated.

GG (PREFIX GG)

4501	Music Keep On Playing/Keep On Playing Version – The GG All Stars (A-side actually by Cornel Campbell/B-side actually by Bucknor's All Stars (prod Sidney Bucknor)	1.70
4502	NYT	
4503	NYT	
4504	It's Been A Long Time/Feel It More & More – Winston Wright/Paulette And Gee	1970
4505	I Don't Like To Interfere/Interfere Version – The Maytones/The GG All Stars	1970
4506	Hold On Tight/Hold On Tight Version – Paulette & Gee/The GG All Stars	1970
4507	Ontarius Version/Ontarius Version 2 (actually 'Want Money') – Charlie Ace/Winston Wright	1.70
4508	Cleanliness/Cleanliness Version – The Maytones/The GG All Stars	1.70
4509	NYT	
4510	Rocking On The GG Beat/Rocking On The GG Beat (Part 2) – The GG All Stars (actually by Clifton Smith & Winston)	3.71
4511	Lonely Nights/Let The Version Play – The GG All Stars (actually by Eric Donaldson)/The Maytones	3.71
4512	Mr Brown/Minna Hear Me Now – Trevor Brown/Winston Wright & Clifton (A-side reissued on GG 452B)	3.71
4513	All One Nation/Judgement Warrant – The GG All Stars/Val Bennett	2.71
4514	Groove Me/Groove Me Version – Keelyn Beckford/The GG All Stars	2.71
4515	Shook & Shake (Version 3) (actually titled 'Shook, Shimmy & Shake [Version 3]')/ Roll On Version 2 (actually 'Reaping Version') – Charlie [Ace], Paulette & Gee/Winston Wright (B-side also on GG 4516B)	4.71
4516	False Reaper/Reaping Version – Gerald McKleish/The GG All Stars (B-side also on GG 4515B)	3.71
4517	My Love & I/Lover's Affair Version 2 – Winston Wright/Charlie Ace And The Maytones	1971
4518	Do Something/Groove Me – Charlie Ace/The Maytones	4.71
4519	Sounds Of Our Forefathers/Love Bug – The Ethiopians	4.71
4520	Jordan River/Jordan River Version – Maxie [Max Romeo] & Glen [Adams]/Glen Adams	1971

4521	Devil's Angel/Devil's Angel Version – Bunny & The Klemanaires/The GG All Stars	1971
4522	Black & White/Mr Brown – The Maytones/Trevor Brown	9.71
4523	Little Boy Blue/Little Boy Blue Version – Vern & Son (actually by The Maytones)/The Typhoon All Stars	10.71
4524	Oh My Baby/Change Of Lover (actually 'Oh My Baby') – The Slickers/Winston Wright (actually by The Slickers) (the same track appears on both sides)	10.71
4525	Bongo Man Rise/Remember – The Maytones/Roy & Bim	11.71
4526	Rod Of Righteousness (actually titled 'Stretch Forth His Hand')/King Of Kings (actually titled 'King Of Glory') – The GG All Stars (actually by Prince Huntley)/Dennis Alcapone	1971
4527	Got To Go Home/How Long Will You Stay – The Invaders/Paulette & Gee	11.71
4528	Place In My Heart (actually titled 'Is There A Place In Your Heart For Me')/You've Got A Friend – Cynthia Richards/Irving Brown [Al Brown] And Cynthia Richards	12.71
4529	Keep It Up/A Love Like Yours – John Holt	1972
4530	Donkey Face/Donkey Face (Version) – The Maytones/The GG All Stars	1972
4531	As Long As You Love Me/As Long As You Love Me (Version) – The Maytones/The GG All Stars	1972
4532	Be My Guest/Way Down South – Billy Dyce/U Roy	1972
4533	Israel Want To Be Free/Israel (Version) – The Ethiopians/The Typhoon All Stars	1972
4534	Take Warning/Warning (Version) – Billy Dyce/The Typhoon All Stars	1972
4535	Is It Really Over?/Born To Be Loved – Max Romeo/The Maytones	1972
4536	Undying Love (actually 'Unity Is Love')/Piccadilly Hop (actually 'The Harder They Come') – Billy Dyce/Charlie Ace	1972
4537	Time Is Still Here/Time Is Still Here (Version) – Billy Dyce/The Typhoon All Stars	1972
4538	Musical Alphabet/Things Gonna Change (actually titled 'Things Gonna Change') – Dennis Alcapone/Buckley All Stars (actually by Vernon Buckley)	1972
4539	Bad Cow Skank/Drummer Roach – Tommy McCook & Bobby Ellis/Gladstone Anderson	3.73
4540	Brother Louie/Brother Louie (Version) – Matumbi/Blackbeard All Stars (prod Dennis Bovell)	1973

Note: All issues produced by Alvin Ranglin except the first and final issue.

GRAPE (GR PREFIX)

3000	Belittle Me/Keep Your Love – Carlton Alphonso (prod Sid Bucknor)	1969
3001	Moon Walk/Think – Sprong & The Nyah Shuffle (prod Joe Sinclair)	1969
3002	Darling It Won't/Moon Train – Johnny Youth & Nyah Shuffle/The Hip City Boys (prod Joe Sinclair)	1969
3003	Cutting Blade/The Vampire – King Horror (prod Laurel Aitken)	1969
3004	Casa Boo Boo/My Girl – Tony (A-side actually by Count Sticky) (prod Tony Robinson)	1969
3005	Leaving Me Standing/Little Girl – Winston Groovy (prod Laurel Aitken)	1969

3006   The Hole/Lover Come Back – King Horror/Winston Groovy (B-side actually by
Lloyd & The Slim Twins) (prod Laurel Aitken/unknown)   1969

3007   Lochness Monster/Zion I – King Horror (actually with Reco)/The Visions
(prod Laurel Aitken/Winston Riley)   1.70

3008   Merry Xmas/I Am Lonely – Winston Groovy (B-side actually by Barry Bailey)
(prod Laurel Aitken/unknown)   1969

3009   Captain Hook/The Girl [I Love] – The Visions (A-side actually by Riley's All Stars)
(prod Winston Riley)   1970

3010   Guns Of Naverone/Yester-Me, Yester-You, Yesterday – Freddie Notes & The
Rudies (B-side actually by Winston Francis) (prod Joe Sinclair)   1.70

3011   Babylon/Girl I've Got A Date – Freddie Notes & The Rudies (B-side actually
by Winston Francis) (prod Joe Sinclair)   1.70

3012   True Love (actually titled ('If You Cry) True Love, True Love')/Another Saturday
Night – Terry, Carl & Derrick/Roy [Junior] Smith (prod Calva L [Les] Foster)   1970

3013   See Through Craze/I'm The One – Roy [Junior] Smith/Terry, Carl & Derrick
(prod Calva L [Les] Foster)   5.70

3014   Night Food Reggae/Walk With Des – Des All Stars (actually The Rudies)
(prod Des Bryan & Webster Shrowder)   3.70

3015   If I Had A Hammer/Hammer Reggae – Des All Stars (actually The Rudies)
(prod Des Bryan & Webster Shrowder)   3.70

3016   Henry The Great/Black Scorcher – Des All Stars (actually The Rudies)
(prod Des Bryan & Webster Shrowder)   4.70

3017   Ace Of Hearts/Bet Yer Life I Do – Candy/Billy Jack (prod Grape)   1970

3018   Let's Work Together/Jam Monkey – Billy Jack/The Corporation (prod Grape)   7.70

3019   Boot Lace (actually titled 'Simmer Down')/Honey Won't You Stay (actually
titled 'Sylvie You're No Good') – Nyah Shuffle (prod Grape)   1970

3020   Skinhead A Bash Them/Walking Through Jerusalem – Claudette & The
Corporation/The Corporation (prod Grape) (B-side reissued on GR 3022B)   7.70

3021   Stingray (actually titled 'Get Up Edina')/Paradise – Nyah Shuffle (prod Grape)   '9.70

3022   Sweet Musille (actually titled 'Sweet Mademoiselle')/Walking Through Jerusalem –
The Corporation (actually by The Dynamites)/The Corporation (prod Clancy
Eccles/Grape)   8.70

3023   NYT

3024   NYT

3025   Come Down (Part 1)/Come Down (Part 2) – Carey [Johnson] & Lloyd [Young]/
The Dynamites (prod Warrick Lyn for Dynamic Sounds)   1972

3026   On Top Of The Peak/Rack-A-Tack – U Roy/Typhoon All Stars (prod Alvin
Ranglin)   10.72

3027   Searching For Your Love/Searching (Version) – Del Williams/The GG All Stars
(prod Alvin Ranglin)   1972

3028   If Loving You Is Wrong (I Don't Want To Be Right)/In De Pum Pum –
The Maytones/[Lloyd] Flowers & Alvin [Ranglin] (prod Alvin Ranglin)   1972

3029   Big Bad Boy/Big Bad Version – Alton Ellis/Hudson's All Stars (prod Keith Hudson)   1972

3030   The Exile Song/In The Burning Sun (Ya Ho) – Skiddy & Detroit/Bunny Gayle
(prod Keith Hudson)   1972

3031   Sincerely/Sincerely (Version) – Shenley Duffas/The Upsetters (prod Lee Perry)   1972

3032   Send A Little Rain (actually 'I'm Just A Sufferer')/Version – Derrick Morgan/Morgans' All Stars (prod Derrick Morgan)   1972

3033   You're A Big Girl Now/You're A Big Girl Now (Version) – The Chosen Few (prod Derrick Harriott) (B-side also issued on Trojan TR 7882B)   1972

3034   Vampire Rock/El Sisco Rock – Jah Fish/The Mod Stars (prod Keble Drummond)   1972

3035   Rasta Dub/Rasta Version – Dennis Alcapone/The Upsetters (prod Lee Perry)   1973

3036   Be Faithful Darling/Be Faithful Version – Clancy Eccles All Stars (actually by Unidentified Male Vocalist)/Clancy Eccles All Stars (prod Clancy Eccles)   1973

3037   Babylon Gone/Speak No Evil – Zeddie Bailey/Tony King (actually by Prince Tony) (prod Fud Christian)   1973

3038   Can I Change My Mind/Just Because – Delroy Wilson (prod Edward 'Bunny' Lee)   3.73

3039   Why Did You Do It/One Love – Errol Dunkley (prod Edward 'Bunny' Lee)   3.73

3040   Foreman Versus Frasier/Round Two – Big Youth (prod Joe Gibbs)   1973

3041   Warrika Hill/Battlefield – Love Generation (actually by The Versatiles)/Third & Fourth Generation (prod Joe Gibbs)   1973

3042   Let Me Dream/Let Me Dream (Version) – The Hoffner Brothers (prod Larry Lawrence)   1973

3043   Change Partners/Pleading For Your Love – Cynthia Richards/The Selectors (prod Larry Lawrence)   1973

3044   JA To UK/JA To UK Version – Big Youth (prod L Campbell)   1973

3045   Dear Lonely Hearts/I Tried To Love You – Lloyd & Barbara/Lloyd Bantam (actually Lloyd Banton) (prod Lloyd Bantam)   1973

3046   Money Raper/Three In One Medley (Baby/Why Must I/Why Did You Leave) – The Heptones & The Love Generation (prod Joe Gibbs)   1973

3047   Free From Chains/Papa Do It Sweet – Prince Jazzbo/Lloyd & Patsy (prod Tony Robinson)   1973

3048   George Foreman/Version – Bacca (prod Neville Hinds & Harry Johnson)   1972

3049   Backslider/Mosquito Dub – The Untouchables/The GG All Stars (prod Alvin Ranglin)   1973

3050   Blackula/Blackula Version – The Crystalites (prod Derrick Harriott)   1973

3051   Opportunity Rock/Double Attack – Big Youth (prod Glen Brown & M Miller)   1973

3052   Abusing & Assaulting/Food Control – Shorty Perry (prod Alvin Ranglin)   1973

3053   Old Time/Dub – The Heptones/The GG All Stars (prod Alvin Ranglin)   1973

3054   One Wife/One Wife (Version) – Junior Soul [Murvin]/The Crystalites (prod Derrick Harriott)   1973

3055   Morning Has Broken/Don't Take Love For A Game – You & I (prod C Troutt aka Mike Dorane)   1973

3056   Be True/Navajo Trail – Tony Gordon (A side actually by Alton Ellis) (prod Stanley Pemberton, Sylvan Williams & Des Bryan)   1973

3057   Mr Softhand/Dub – Vernon Buckley/The GG All Stars (prod Alvin Ranglin)   1973

3058   Ital Queen/Dub – Vernon Buckley/The GG All Stars (prod Alvin Ranglin)   1973

3059   People Got To Be Free/Ups & Downs – Denzil Dennis (prod Pat Rhoden)   1973

3060	Our Rendezvous/Our Rendezvous (Version) – Freddy McKay/Soul Dynamites (prod Warwick Lyn)	1973
3061	Concrete Jungle/Screaming Target – Big Youth & Simplicity People (prod Augustus Clarke)	1973
3062	Murderer/The Killer – Simplicity People/Big Youth (prod Augustus Clarke)	1973

GREEN DOOR (PREFIX GD)

4000	Rasta Never Fails/Rasta Never Fails (Version) – The Charmers (actually Ken Boothe & Lloyd Charmers) (prod Lloyd Charmers)	9.71
4001	One Big Unhappy Family/Africa Is Paradise – The Charmers/The Conscious Minds (prod Lloyd Charmers)	9.71
4002	Medley (Part 1)/Medley (Part 2) – Ken Boothe (prod Herman Chin-Loy)	10.71
4003	Carroll Street/Version – Winston Blake & The M Squad/Ansel Collins (prod Winston Blake)	10.71
4004	Drums Of Passion/Love & Emotion Version – B Leggs (actually by Bongo Herman & Les Chen with Morgan's All Stars) (prod Derrick Morgan)	10.71
4005	Trenchtown Rock/Grooving KGN. 12 – Bob Marley & The Wailers (prod Bob Marley) (A-side reissued on Trojan TR 7979A)	10.71
4006	You've Got A Friend/Cheep – Zimm & Dee Dee (actually Winston Francis & Donna Hinds)/The Groovers (prod Bush)	11.71
4007	Miss Labba Labba/Best Is Yet To Come – Twinkle Brothers (prod Edward 'Bunny' Lee)	1971
4008	Flying Machine/Machine Version – Teddy Magnus/The Version Boys (B-side actually by Lynford 'Hux' Brown) (prod Upset)	1971
4009	Seven In One Medley/Part 2 – The Clarendonians (prod L Hanson)	11.71
4010	Chopsticks/Belmont Street – The Deltones (prod Des Bryan for Bush)	1971
4011	Heads Or Tails/Raunchy – Winston Wright/The Roasters (prod Lynford Anderson)	1971
4012	Girl Called Clover/Girl Called Clover (Version) – Young Al Capone (possibly Dillinger) (prod Tony Robinson)	12.71
4013	NYT	
4014	Harbour Shark/Harbour Shark Version – Wailing Souls (prod Keith Cole)	1971
4015	Living In Sweet Jamaica/Living In Sweet Jamaica Version – Jackie Brown/Tony's All Stars (prod Tony Robinson)	1.72
4016	Jamaican Hi-Lite (Part 1)/Jamaican Hi-Lite (Part 2) – The Gaytones (prod Sonia Pottinger)	1971
4017	I'm Sorry (actually titled 'So Ashamed')/Melodica Version – The Matadors (actually by Tony Brevett)/The Rhythm Rulers (prod Tony Brevett)	1972
4018	NYT	
4019	Breaking Your Heart/Breaking Your Heart – The Scorpions/The In Crowd (prod Hugh Madden)	1972
4020	Hypocrite/Straight To The Head – The Heptones/Johnny Lover (actually Charlie Ace) (prod Joe Gibbs)	1972
4021	Riot/Smoke Without Fire – Soul Syndicate (actually with Johnny Moore) (prod Keith Hudson)	2.72

4022 Lively Up Yourself/Live – Bob Marley & The Wailers/Tommy McCook (prod Bob Marley) 1972

4023 High School Serenade/On The Track – Lennox Brown/Winston Scotland (prod Tony Robinson) 1972

4024 Merry Up/Merry Up (Version) – The Godsons (prod Glen Brown) 1972

4025 Guava Jelly/Redder Than Red – Bob Marley & The Wailers (prod Bob Marley) 1972

4026 A Sugar/A Sugar (Part 2) – Roy Shirley/Altyman Reid (prod Roy Shirley) 1972

4027 My Little Filly/My Girl – Winston Scotland/Bunny Brown (prod Tony Robinson) 1972

4028 I Can't Forget/I Can't Forget (Version) – Lloyd Robinson & The Now Generation (prod Lloyd Daley) 1972

4029 Jamaican Skank/Bings Comes To Town – Pomphey/G. Moore (actually Johnny 'Dizzy' Moore) (prod The Rohoism) 1972

4030 Hot Bomb/The Bomb (Version) – I Roy & The Jumpers/The Jumpers (prod Derrick Morgan) 1972

4031 Have I Sinned/Have I Sinned (Version) – Ken Boothe (actually with Lloyd Charmers)/The Charmers Band (prod Lloyd Charmers) 1972

4032 Breezing/Breezing Version – Mickie Chung & The Now Generation (prod Lloyd Charmers) 1972

4033 Loving You/Loving You Version (prod Glen Brown & M. G. Mahtani) 1972

4034 Hudson Affair/Hot Stick Version – U Roy/Keith Hudson (prod Keith Hudson) 1972

4035 Bringing In The Sheaves/Version – Hortense Ellis & Stranger Cole/Bunny Lee's All Stars (prod Edward 'Bunny' Lee) 1972

4036 Cheer Up/Version – Rue Lloyd (prod Glen Brown & M. G. Mahtani) 1972

4037 Shalimar Special/Shalimar Version – Lloyd Young/G. Mahtani All Stars (prod Glen Brown & M. G. Mahtani) 1972

4038 Night Owl/Night Owl (Version) – The Clarendonians/Tony's All Stars (prod Tony Robinson) 7.72

4039 The Kingman Is Back/Version – The Hoffner Brothers/Shalimar All Stars (prod Glen Brown & MG Mahtani) 8.72

4040 The Harder They Come/Time Is Still Here (Version) – The Carifta All Stars/ Typhoon All Stars (prod Alvin Ranglin) 9.72

4041 Rub Up A Daughter/Daughter (Version) – Dennis Alcapone/Tony's All Stars (prod Tony Robinson) 9.72

4042 Dearest Darling/Stardust – Cornel Campbell (prod Edward 'Bunny' Lee) 9.72

4043 President Mash Up The Resident/President (Part 2) – Shorty The President (prod Rupie Edwards) 1972

4044 Make Love/Tic Toc Bill – I Roy/The Stags (prod Bush) 1972

4045 Summertime/Grazing – Domino Johnson/The Swans (Domino Johnson for Bush Productions/Bush) 1972

4046 Big Boy/Big Boy (Version) – Junior Soul [Murvin] (prod Derrick Harriott) 1972

4047 Life/Life (Version) (B-side actually Bob Andy Medley) – Bob Andy/Harry J All Stars (actually Bob Andy) (prod Harry Johnson) 12.72

4048 Honey Baby/Chalk Farm Special – Niney & Ken Elliott (prod Bush) 1972

4049 African Breakfast/Chairman Of The Board – Bongo Herman/Bongo Herman, Les Chen & Bingy Bunny (prod Harry Johnson) 1972

4050   High School Dance/Dance Version – Hubert Lee/Tony's All Stars (prod Tony Robinson)   1972

4051   Cool Breeze/Windstorm – Big Youth With Keith & Tex/The Crystalites (prod Derrick Harriott)   1972

4052   King Tubby's Special/Here Come The Heartaches – U Roy/Delroy Wilson (prod Edward 'Bunny' Lee)   1972

4053   Silver Words/Rasta God Version – Ken Boothe/The Now Generation (prod Winston 'Niney' Holness)   3.73

4054   Lonely Soldier/Lonely Soldier (Version) – Gregory Isaacs/The Impact All Stars (prod Vincent Chin)   3.73

4055   Alone Again Naturally/My Part – The Now Generation/Mind, Body & Soul (prod Lloyd Charmers)   3.73

4056   The First Cut Is The Deepest/No Good Girl – KC White (prod KC White)   3.73

4057   Give Me Love/Help Them Oh Lord – Cornel Campbell (prod Edward 'Bunny' Lee)   1973

4058   Let Me Love You/If It Don't Work Out – Slim Smith (prod Edward 'Bunny' Lee)   1973

4059   You Don't Know/The Border Song – Bob Andy (prod Harry Johnson)   1973

4060   Ain't That Peculiar/What Is Man – Delroy Wilson (prod Douglas Williams)   1973

4061   Reggae Makossa/Reggae Makossa (Version) (actually 'No Nola') – Brent Dowe/The Gaytones (B-side actually by The Melodians) (prod Sonia Pottinger) (B-side reissue of High Note label HS 044B)   1973

4062   I'll Be Standing By/I'll Be Standing By (Version) – Jimmy Green [Jimmy London]/Lloyd's All Stars (prod Lloyd Campbell)   1973

4063   Yearful Of Sundays/Version – King Sporty (prod King Sporty)   1973

4064   Save The People/Salvation Train – Lloyd Charmers/Scotty (prod Lloyd Charmers)   1973

4065   Rock & Roll Lullaby/Rock & Roll Version – Jimmy Green [Jimmy London] (prod Lloyd Campbell)   1974

HARRY J LABEL (HJ PREFIX)

6601   Big Three/Lavender – Harry J All Stars (B-side actually by Lloyd Robinson) (B-side reissue of Duke DU-5B)   2.70

6602   The Dog/The Dog (Part 2) – Harry J All Stars   2.70

6603   Feel A Little Better/I'll Be Your Man – Lloyd Parks (prod Lloyd Parks)   2.70

6604   Fire/Fire (Part 2) – The Jamaicans (prod Tommy Cowan)   1970

6605   Young, Gifted & Black/Young, Gifted & Black (Instrumental) – Bob [Andy] & Marcia [Griffiths]/The Jay Boys (reissued on Trojan TR 7925A)   2.70

6606   NYT

6607   Jack The Ripper/Don't Let Me Down (correct title: Operamatic) – Harry J All Stars   5.70

6608   Reach For The Sky/Interrogator – Harry J All Stars   5.70

6609   Jay Moon Walk/Elcong – The Jay Boys   3.70

6610   Je'Taime/It Ain't Me Babe – The Jay Boys   3.70

6611   Hang My Head & Cry/Hang My Head & Cry (Instrumental) – Bob Andy/The Jay Boys (possibly not issued)   1970

6612   Peace Of Mine/Weep – Bob Andy (A-side reissued on Trojan TR 7809B)   4.70

6613	Put A Little Love In Your Heart/Bah Oop Ah – Marcia Griffiths/The Jay Boys (B-side actually Lloyd, Freddie & The Des All Stars) (B side prod Des Bryan for Bush) (A-side also issued on Trojan TR 693A, without orchestration)	5.70
6614	Didn't I (Blow Your Mind This Time)/Tilly – The Cables/The Jay Boys	7.70
6615	We've Got To Get Ourselves Together/Festival Spirit – Bob [Andy] And Marcia [Griffiths]/Glen [Adams] & Dave [Barker] (B-side actually by The Jamaicans)	1970
6616	Salt Of The Earth/Name Ring A Bell – The Cables (also issued on Trojan TR 7792)	1970
6617	Del Gago/Killer Version – The Jay Boys	1970
6618	I Can't Get Next To You/Part 2 – The Jay Boys (actually by The Charmers) (prod Lloyd Charmers)	9.70
6619	Cambodia/Cambodia Version – Blake Boy (actually Winston Blake)/The Jay Boys (prod Winston Blake)	1970
6620	Feel Alright/Equal Rights – The Cables	1970
6621	Return Of The Liquidator (aka 'Tons Of Gold')/All Day – Harry J All Stars (A-side actually by Val Bennett & The Harry J All Stars)	1970
6622	NYT	
6623	Band Of Gold/Cowboy (Version 2) – Marcia Griffiths/The Jay Boys	10.70
6624	The Same Old Life/Life Version – Roy Panton/The Jay Boys	1970
6625	More Heartaches/More Heartaches Version – Lizzie/The Harry J All Stars	1970
6626	Holy Moses/Version – Bob Andy/The Jay Boys (possibly not issued)	1970
6627	NYT	
6628	The Arcade Walk/Version 2 – The Jay Boys	2.71
6629	NYT	
6630	NYT	
6631	United We Stand/unknown – Bob [Andy] & Marcia [Griffiths]/Bob [Andy] & Marcia [Griffiths] (probably not issued)	1971
6632	NYT	
6633	NYT	
6634	Set Me Free/Free Version – Uriel Aldridge/Lloyd Willis	1971
6635	NYT	
6636	NYT	
6637	NYT	
6638	NYT	
6639	Issued on Explosion Ex 2073	
6640	Come Back And Stay/Come Back And Stay Version – The Fabulous Five Inc/ The Peter Ashbourne Affair	1972
6641	Down Side Up/Version – Harry J All Stars (actually by Carey Johnson & Lloyd Young)/Harry J All Stars	1972
6642	Skank In Bed/African Breakfast – Scotty/Bongo Herman & Les	10.72
6643	Have You Ever Seen The Rain/Spanish Harlem – Honey Boy Martin	1972
6644	African People/Version – The Jay Boys Harry J All Stars (A-side actually by Winston Jarrett & The Flames)	1972

6645	UFO/Version – Geoffrey Chung & The Harry J All Stars/Harry J All Stars	1972
6646	The Word Is Love/Version – The Ethiopians/Harry J All Stars (prod Keith Anderson [Bob Andy])	3.73
6647	Zion Iah/Zion Iah Version – Giginri	1973
6648	Me & Mrs Jones/Melodica Version – Joe White	1973
6649	Time Is Getting Harder/Hardest Version – The Simplicity People	1973
6650	Lottery Spin/Lottery Spin Version – Zap Pow (A-side also issued on Trojan TR 7886B)	1973
6651	Treasure Isle Skank/Words Of Wisdom – U Roy (prod Arthur 'Duke' Reid)	1973
6652	Yim Mas Gan/Crankshaft Version – The Abyssinians/The Now Generation (prod Lloyd Daley)	10.73
6653	Deliver Us To Africa (Lord Deliver Us/Back To Africa)/Nyah Medley – Alton Ellis/Little Roy (prod Lloyd Daley)	10.73
6654	What's Your Name/What's Your Name Version – Audley Rollen/The Now Generation (prod Lloyd Daley)	10.73
6655	Musical Drum Sound/Version – I Roy/The Now Generation (prod Lloyd Daley)	10.73
6656	Glitter Not Gold/Version – Big Joe/Matador All Stars (prod Lloyd Daley)	10.73
6657	Musical Splendour/Musical Drum & Bass – Neville Hinds/Matador All Stars (prod Lloyd Daley)	190.3
6658	Chucky/Version – The Viceroys (prod Sidney Crooks)	1973
6659	NYT	
6660	Pussy Cat/Skanky Pussy – Lloydie [Charmers] & The Lowbites (prod Lloyd Charmers)	1973
6661	Country Living/Version – The Jamaican Eagles (prod Federal)	1973
6662	I'm Gonna Love You Just A Little Bit More/Have I Sinned – Lloyd Charmers (prod Lloyd Charmers)	1974
6663	Buy You A Ring/Pray Moma – The Ethiopians (prod Rupie Edwards)	1974
6664	Brighter Days Will Be Coming/Version – Clancy Eccles/The Dynamites (prod Clancy Eccles)	1974
6665	Big Splish Splash/Hail Rasta Brother Hail – The Ethiopians (prod Rupie Edwards)	1974
6666	Sorry Harry/Party Time – Dennis Alcapone (prod Sidney Crooks)	1974
6667	What Happen To The Youth Of Today/Baby Don't Do It – Delroy Wilson (prod Edward 'Bunny' Lee)	1974
6668	Eddie My Love/What Is Your Plan – Nora Dean/Jackie Brown (prod Edward 'Bunny' Lee)	1974
6669	Wheel & Jig/Version – The Viceroys (prod Sidney Crooks)	1974
6670	Butter Fe Fish/Bammie Fe Fish – Skin, Flesh & Bones (prod Dickie Wong)	1974
6671	Why Do Falls Fall In Love?/Version – Derrick Harriott/The Crystalites (prod Derrick Harriott) (A-side reissued on Trojan label TR 7981A)	5.74
6672	Let's Get It On/Version – Lloyd Charmers (prod Lloyd Charmers)	1974
6673	Keep Those Records Playing/Star Apple – Al Cook (actually Sidney Crooks) (prod Sidney Crooks)	1974

6674 Homely Girl/Thunderball (Beard Man) – Jackie Robinson (prod Robert Thompson (Dandy)/Des Bryan & Webster Shrowder) — 1974

6675 Some Guys Have All The Luck/Version – Derrick Harriott/The Crystalites (prod Derrick Harriott) — 1974

6676 Burning Fire/Burning Drums – Bob Andy (prod Keith Anderson [Bob Andy]) — 1974

6677 Skanking Monkey/Skanking Monkey (Version) – Ken Parker (actually by Stranger Cole & Gladstone Anderson) (prod DC Anderson) — 7.74

6678 Lord A Massie Massie/Version – Danny D & The Shadows (prod DC Anderson) — 1974

6679 Let's Ride On/Version – Bobby Lawrence (prod Ellis Breary) — 1974

6680 Please Don't Make Me Cry/So Easy – Winston Groovy (prod Winston Tucker/Sydney Crooks) (also issued on Explosion EX 2088) — 7.74

6681 I Need Your Love/Version – Gregory Isaacs/The GG All Stars (prod Alvin Ranglin) — 1974

6682 Ride On Ride On/Wild Goose Chase – Dennis Brown & Big Youth/Observer All Stars (prod Winston 'Niney' Holness) — 1974

6683 Rock Your Baby/Rozcy Dozcy – The Maroons [Cimarons] (prod Des Bryan & Webster Shrowder) — 8.74

6684 Sitting On The Sidewalk/Version – Ansel Linkers/The GG All Stars (prod Alvin Ranglin) — 8.74

6685 Drift Away/Upside Down – George Dekker (prod Sidney Crooks) — 1974

6686 A Walking Miracle/Version – Baby Bertie (prod Bertie Chin) — 8.74

6687 Saturday Night/Instrumental – Lorenzo [Laurel Aitken] (prod Laurel Aitken) (tracks recorded in 1969) — 1974

6688 Irie Festival/Instrumental – Turnel McCormack & The Cordells/Fabulous Five Inc (prod Tommy Cowan) — 1974

6689 Black Pepper/Pepper Rock – Heavy Jeff (actually by Skin, Flesh & Bones) (prod Dickie Wong) — 1974

6690 Solitary Man/Instrumental – Skin, Flesh & Bones (prod Dickie Wong) — 1974

6691 Together/Version – Jimmy London/Lloyd's [Campbell's] All Stars (prod Lloyd Campbell) — 1974

6692 Oh Pa Pa/Boneyard Skank – The Drifting Blenders/Lloyd [Charmers] All Stars (prod Lloyd Charmers) — 1974

6693 I'm Leaving It Up To You/Teach The Children – Winston & The Zion Boys/Locksley Gitchie & The Zion Boys (prod Kush) — 11.74

6694 Kung Fu Fighting/The Teacher – The Maroons [Cimarons] (prod Des Bryan for Kush/Des Bryan & Webster Shrowder For Kush) — 1974

6695 My Love For You/Smokey Mountains – Jackie Robinson/The RD Livingstone All Stars (prod Robert Thompson [Dandy] for Trojan/Robert Thompson [Dandy] For Shady Tree) — 11.74

6696 Nosey Parker/Nosey Parker (Instrumental) – George Dekker/George Dekker Band (prod George Dekker) — 1974

6697 Lee's Dream/So Long Baby – Derrick (Morgan) & Paulette (prod Edward 'Bunny' Lee) — 1974

6698 Country Boy/Give The Little Man A Hand – Cornel Campbell (prod Edward 'Bunny' Lee) — 11.74

6699	Lonely Woman/Lonely Woman (Instrumental) – Horace Andy/The Crystalites (prod Derrick Harriott) (reissue of Song Bird SB 1085)	11.74
6700	Why Don't You Do Right/Version – Dimples Hinds/Dandy Livingstone All Stars (aka The Love Children) (prod Robert Thompson [Dandy] & Shady Tree)	11.74
6701	Natty Dread/Collie Burning – Sambo Jim (actually Judge Dread & The Cimarons) (prod Kush)	12.74
6702	Lee Goofed (So Long Baby)/Ruff Ready – Love Children (prod Dandy [Robert Thompson]) & Shady Tree)	11.74
6703	Feel So Good/Instrumental – Derrick Morgan & Hortense Ellis/The Aggrovators (prod Edward 'Bunny' Lee)	1.75
6704	A Message To Martha/Tears Won't Help – Treasure Boy (A-side actually by Freddie McKay/B-side actually by Dennis Brown) (prod Sidney Crooks)	12.74
6705	Take These Chains From My Heart/If You Want To Be Happy – Bill Walker (prod Sidney Crooks)	12.74
6706	Move Out A Babylon/Move Out A Babylon (Instrumental) – Johnny Clarke/The Aggrovators (reissued on Horse HOSS 86)	1.75
6707	NYT	
6708	Blue Moon/Greensleeves – George Larnyoh & The Love Children/The Love Children (prod Robert Thompson [Dandy] & Shady Tree)	1.75
6709	NYT	
6710	NYT	
6711	NYT	
6712	How Glad I Am/How Glad I Am Part 2 – The GG All Stars (A-side actually by The Tidals) (prod Alvin Ranglin)	1975

Note: All tracks from HJ-6601 to 6650 produced by Harry Johnson, unless otherwise stated.

HIGH NOTE (PREFIX HS)

001	ABC Rock Steady/Soul Drums – The Gaylads/Count Ossie & Leslie Butler	1968*
002	Not used	
003	Lady With The Starlight/Gay Drums – Ken Boothe/Count Ossie & Leslie Butler	11.68
004	Dance With Me/Let's Have Some Fun – Delano Stewart	11.68
005	Check Up/I'll Come Back – Al & The Vibrators	1968
006	NYT	
007	Fire In Your Wire/Move Up Calypso – Patsy (with Byron Lee & The Dragonaires)/Al & The Vibrators (A-side prod Byron Lee)	1968*
008	Top Cat/Stars Above – Leslie Butler/Webber Sisters	11.68
009	Revival/Over The Rainbow's End – Leslie Butler/The Gaylads	12.68
010	Lucky Is The Boy/Bobby Sox To Stockings – Boris Gardiner (prod Boris Gardiner)	1.69
011	Put Yourself In My Place/It Hurts – Delroy Wilson	1.69
012	We Were Lovers/Give Me A Chance – Patsy/Patsy & Delano Stewart	1.69
013	National Lottery/Round Seven – The Soul Rhythms	1969
014	Rocking Sensation/One Look – Delano Stewart/The Gaysters (actually The Originals Orchestra aka The Gaytones)	1969

015	I'm The One Who Loves You/If I'm In A Corner – Delroy Wilson/The Afrotones	4.69
016	If You Can't Beat Them Join Them/Anywhere You Want To Go – The Conquerors	4.69
017	Mary, Mary/Going Away – The Beltones	5.69
018	The Storm/You Can't Stop Me – The Emotions	7.69
019	Reggae Buddy/Easy Squeeze – The Victors	7.69
020	Oh What A Glory/The Morning In The Sky – The Creary Sisters (gospel)	8.69
021	Dr No Go/Sailing (actually 'Faberge') [ska] – The Hippie Boys (The Hippy Boys) (B-side actually by Baba Brooks)	8.69
022	Your Number One/I've Tried My Best – Delroy Wilson	8.69
023	Broken Heart/All For One – The Beltones/The Afrotones	8.69
024	Wailing Festival/Me & My Baby (actually titled 'By The River') – The Federals (A-side prod David Scott)	9.69
025	Mr DJ/National Dish – The Conquerors	1969
026	Rumbay (aka Rum Bay)/I Held Your Hand (aka Find Someone) – The Emotions/Patsy	1969
027	Got To Come Back/Don't Believe In Him – Delano Stewart	1969
028	Good To Me/What Do You Want Me To Do – Delroy Wilson	10.69
029	Talk (actually titled 'Toil')/Talk (Part 2) (actually 'Toil (Part 2)') – Marcia Griffiths	1969
030	Chicken Licken/Our Man Flint – The Hippy Boys/Baba Brooks	10.69
031	NYT	
032	Rasta/Like Dirt – The Tadpoles (prod Peter Ashbourne)	11.69
033	The Man Of Galilee/Take Up The Cross – Otis Wright (gospel)	1969
034	Hallelujah/I Wish It Could Last – Delano Stewart	1969
035	Reggae Pressure/It Hurts (Inst.) – The Hippy Boys	12.69
036	NYT	
037	Target (actually 'Musical Fight')/Find Someone (actually 'True Love') – The Gaytones (actually The Crashers)/Patsy (B-side reissue from HS 026B)	2.70
038	Piccadilly Hop/Nigeria – The Hippy Boys	3.70
039	Wherever I Lay My Hat/Don't Believe In Him – Delano Stewart (B-side reissue of HS 027B)	5.70
040	Soul Pressure/Seed You Sow [ska] – Winston Wright & The Gaytones/Winston Wright & The Gaytones (actually by Bonnie Frankson)	5.70
041	Stay A Little Bit Longer/Stay A Little Bit Longer (Version 2) – Delano Stewart/(Gladstone Anderson &) The Gaytones	5.70
042	Praise Fari/Cherrie, Part 2 – The Ethiopians/The Gaytones	8.70
043	Little Suzie/Cherrie – The Soul Twins	8.70
044	Love Is A Good Thing/No Nola – The Melodians (B-side reissued on Green Door GD 4061B)	1970
045	When/Chapter – First Generation/The Gaytones	1970
046	Your Destiny/Lock Love Away – The Gentles (actually The Melodians)	1970
047	Natural Woman/Woman Version – Naomi/The Gaytones	1970

048   Ten To One/Another Version – The Gaytones (actually with Busty Brown)/
The Gaytones   1970

049   She Want It/Give Him Up – Dave Barker (actually with The Gaylads)/
First Generation (A-side prod Ansel Collins)   1970

050   Must Get A Man/The Valet – Nora Dean (mento)   3.71

051   Creation Version/Version 3 – Charlie Ace & The Gaytones/The Gaytones   1970

052   Run To The Rock/Run To The Rock (Version) – The Righteous Flames/
The Gaytones (prod Lee Perry)   2.71

053   Home Bound/Chapter 3 – Teddy & The Conquerors/The Gaytones   1971

054   Joy To The World/Joyful (Version) – Julie Anne (actually Judy Mowatt) &
The Chosen Few with The Gaytones/The Gaytones   7.71

055   Heart Of Knights/One Toke Over The Line – The Gaytones (actually by Lennox
Brown)/The Gaytones (actually by Stranger Cole & Gladstone Anderson)   11.71

056   Unbelievable Sounds/Unbievable Sounds Version – Scotty & Hucks Brown/
The Gaytones (B-side actually 'Going Back Home' by Al & The Vibrators)   1971

057   One Night Of Sin/One Night (Version) – Jackie Brown (actually with
The Gaytones)/The Gaytones   1.72

058   Pray For Me/Pray For Me (Version) – Max Romeo & The Gaytones/The Gaytones   1972

059   She Kept On Talking/Talking (Version) – Julie Anne (actually Judy Mowatt)
& The Gaytones/The Gaytones   1972

060   Last Dance/Version – Jackie Brown & The Gaytones/The Gaytones   1972

061   Skavito/Savito – The Undergrounds (calypso)*   1972

*Note: All tracks produced by Sonia Pottinger except where othwise stated. Items marked * were
issued on both Hi-Note and High Note labels.*

HORSE (PREFIX HOSS)

1   I Must Go Back/I Want To Be Near You – Jackie Edwards (prod Jackie Edwards)   5.71

2   Summer Is The Season/Riding My Bicycle – Riverbank (prod Dandy [Robert
Thompson])   7.71

3   Bouncing All Over The World/Tell Me – Tony Gregory (prod Count Prince Miller)   7.71

4   Chick-A-Boom/Sunflower Wine – Big Gee (prod Kool Records)   7.71

5   Jesus Is Just Alright/You Knew How To Hurt A Man – Bourbon Street Mission
(prod Stanney Pemberton for September Productions Ltd)   1971

6   Sunday Morning/One Three – Ernie Smith (prod Federal)   1971

7   Brandy/Lead Me Back – Scott English (prod Dave Bloxham)   1971

8   Skinny Dippin'/Sweet Bread – The Zooms (prod Ken Howard & Alan Blakely)   8.71

9   Act Like A Man/Back On My Feet – Roger Holman (prod Holman & May)   10.71

10   Hey Mama/Ride Baby Ride – Rick Whitehead (prod Richard Whitehead)   10.71

11   Who Turned The World Around?/I Love You So – Tony Gregory (prod Tony
Gregory)   1972

12   I Feel So Bad/I'll Make Them Believe In You – Danny Ray (prod Jackie Edwards)   1972

13   Love Sweet Love/Open The Door – Del Davis (prod Jackie Edwards)   1972

14	Willie Come Home/Heaven Knows – Chris Parie (prod Trojan)	
15	Baby Don't Wake Me/A Little Story – Jackie Edwards (prod Jackie Edwards)	1972
16	Suzanne Beware Of The Devil/Right On Brother – Dandy Livingstone (prod Dandy [Robert Thompson])	8.72
17	Tchaikovsky Piano Concerto No. 1/Cool Shade – Neasden Connection (prod Dandy [Robert Thompson]) & Shady Tree	1972
18	Struggling Man/Return Of The Pollock – The Cimarons/The Prophets (actually by Patrick & Lloyd) (prod Bush/Swan) (B-side reissue of Big Shot BI 550A)	9.72
19	Easy Come, Easy Go/I'll Be True To You – Tito Simon (prod Clancy Eccles)	9.72
20	Nose For Trouble/Times Have Changed – Pat Rhoden (prod Pat Rhoden)	9.72
21	White & Wonderful, Black & Beautiful/Peace & Love – Danny Ray (prod Jackie Edwards) (A-side reissued on Horse HOSS 33A)	1972
22	The Further You Look/I Wanna Dance – John Holt (prod Tony Ashfield & Mike Berry)	1972
23	How Could I Let You Get Away/How Could I Let You Get Away (Version) Barry Biggs (prod Dynamic Sounds)	1972
24	Lord Pity Us All/Beautiful Feeling – Martin Reilly (actually Martin Riley) (prod Mike Berry & Tony Ashfield)	1972
25	Big City/Brand New Day – Dandy Livingstone (prod Dandy [Robert Thompson] & Shady Tree) (first pressing)	1972
25	Big City/Think About That – Dandy Livingstone (prod Dandy [Robert Thompson] & Shady Tree) (second pressing, double A-side)	1972
26	World Without Love/Bucket – Del Davis (prod Bush)	3.73
27	NYT	
28	Come Back Liza/Got To Say I'm Sorry – Dandy Livingstone (prod Dandy [Robert Thompson])	1973
29	Images Of You/Doing The Moonwalk – Nicky Thomas (prod Nicky Thomas/Joe Gibbs) (A-side also issued on Trojan TR 7878A)	1973
30	Build It Up/You Can't Be Serious – Tito Simon (prod Clancy Eccles)	1973
31	One Woman/Secondhand Love – Bob Andy (prod Keith Anderson [Bob Andy])	1973
32	Loving Her Was Easier/Ling Tong Ting – Lloyd Charmers (prod Lloyd Charmers)	1973
33	White & Wonderful, Black & Beautiful/On The Run (With A Gun) – Danny Ray (prod Jackie Edwards) (A-side reissue of Horse HOSS 21A)	1973
34	Loop-De-Loop/In Style – Happy Junior & The IQs (prod Sidney Crooks)	1973
35	Snake In The Grass/Snake In The Grass (Version) – Jimmy Shondell (actually Eugene Paul)/Ron Stewart (prod Sidney Crooks)	1973
36	Build Me Up/Close To You – Brent Dowe & The Gaytones (prod Sonia Pottinger)	10.73
37	Lonely For Your Love/Message To Maria – Nicky Thomas (prod Tony King & Nicky Thomas)	10.73
38	She Ain't Nothin' But The Real Thing/Oh What A Feeling (prod unknown)	1973
39	Can't Get Enough (Of That Reggae Stuff)/Wipe Them Out – Matumbi (prod Dennis Bovell) (B-side also issued on Duke DU 152A)	1973
40	Mellow Mood/Mellow Mood (Version) – Judy Mowatt (actually with The Gaytones) (prod Sonia Pottinger)	1973

LIVERPOOL JOHN MOORES UNIVERSITY
LEARNING SERVICES

41	We Can Make Sweet Music/Stoned Out Of My Mind – Winston Groovy (prod Winston Tucker [Winston Groovy])	1974
42	I Shall Sing/Close (Instrumental) – Judy Mowatt & The Gaytones/The Gaytones (prod Sonia Pottinger) (A-side reissue of Trojan TR 7817A)	1974
43	Love Is A Hurting Thing/Gladness – Brent Dowe/The Gaytones (prod Sonia Pottinger)	1974
44	You Are Everything/For The Good Times – The Chosen Few/Lloyd Charmers (prod Lloyd Charmers)	1974
45	Caribbean Rock/All Strung Out On You – Dandy Livingstone (prod Dandy [Robert Thompson] & Shady Tree)	1974
46	Life Is Just For Living/To Be With You – Lloyd Charmers (prod Lloyd Charmers)	5.74
47	Sweet Harmony/Sweet Organ (Version) – Lloyd Charmers (prod Lloyd Charmers)	5.74
48	I'm Only Here For The Beer/Sober Up – The Artistic League (prod Dandy [Robert Thompson] & Shady Tree)	1974
49	Black Oppressor/Black Oppressor (Version) – Leo Simpson (prod Leo Simpson)	5.74
50	Personality/Stone Cold – Jackie Robinson/Pioneer All Stars (prod Sidney Crooks)	1974
51	It's Not Who You Know/I Need Someone – The Twinkle Brothers/The Ethiopians (prod Martin Riley) (reissue of Big Shot BI 600)	7.74
52	Sweet Bitter Love/Boneyard Skank – Marcia Griffiths (prod Lloyd Charmers)	7.74
53	Warm & Tender Love/Love Is A Game – Jackie Robinson/The Pioneers (prod Jackie Robinson)	7.74
54	Something's Gotten Hold Of My Heart/Tenod – Jenny Taylor/Des All Stars (prod Webster Shrowder)	1974
55	Rock The Boat/Curfew – The Inner Circle (prod Tommy Cowan)	1974
56	Soul Serenade/Bond In Bliss – Winston Wright & The Dragonaires (prod Byron Lee) (A-side reissue of Duke DU 39A/B-side reissue of Trojan TR 7747A)	9.74
57	This Monday Morning Feeling/Count The Hours – Tito Simon (prod Keith Foster [Tito Simon])	1974
58	The Best Time Of My Life/What Am I To Do – Pat Kelly (prod Pat Kelly)	1974
59	Boogie On Reggae Woman/Boogie On Reggae Woman (Version) – Pat Rhoden (prod Pat Rhoden)	11.74
60	When Will I See You Again/When Will I See You Again (Version) – Marcia Griffiths/Onika (prod Lloyd Charmers)	11.74
61	Do It 'Til Your Satisfied/Collie Dub – Soul Messengers [The Cimarons] (prod Kush)	1.75
62	Hey There Lonely Girl/Grasshopper – J D Alex [Judge Dread] (prod Alted)	12.74
63	Marie's Song/Marie's Song (Dub) – Fitz Major/The GG All Stars (prod Alvin Ranglin)	1.75
64	Bongo Natty/Look What You Done – Owen Gray (prod Edward 'Bunny' Lee)	2.75
65	Never Fall In Love Again/Hey Girl, Don't Bother Me – Johnny Clarke (prod Edward 'Bunny' Lee)	1975
66	Rasta Don't Fear/Version – Derrick Morgan/Bunny Lee All Stars (prod Edward 'Bunny' Lee)	2.75
67	Black Superman (Muhammed Ali)/Black Superman Instrumental – Derrick Morgan/Bunny Lee All Stars (prod Edward 'Bunny' Lee)	2.75

68   Duke Of Earl/Duke Of Earl (Version) – Cornel Campbell/Bunny Lee All Stars
(prod Edward 'Bunny' Lee)   1975

69   In My Life/In My Life (Version) – Jackie Robinson/Pioneer All Stars (prod Jackie
Robinson)   2.75

70   Let Locks Grow/Natty Locks – Barrington Spence (prod Tony Robinson)   1975

71   Nyah Nyah/Nyah Nyah (Version) – Jerry Morris (prod Jerry Morris)   2.75

72   Face Dog/Face Dog (Version) – Derrick Harriott/The Crystalites (prod Derrick
Harriott)   1975

73   Bump Me Baby/Kush Maroons – The Maroons [The Cimarons] (prod Kush)   1975

74   No Jestering/Part 2 Dub – Carl Malcolm (B-side actually by Skin, Flesh & Bones)
(prod Clive Chin)   1975

75   Nine Pound Steel/Money Day (Version) – Sidney, George & Jackie [The Pioneers]
(prod Sidney Crooks, George Agard & Jackie Robinson [The Pioneers])   4.75

76   At The End Of The Rainbow/At The End Of The Rainbow (Version) – Johnny
Clarke/Rupie's All Stars (prod Rupie Edwards)   4.75

77   Jah Jah Train/Move Jah – Barrington Spence/Skin, Flesh & Bones (prod Tony
Robinson)   4.75

78   I Hear My Train/I Hear My Train (Instrumental) – Junior English (prod Ellis
Breary)   5.75

79   God Bless Jamaica/God Bless Jamaica (Instrumental) – Max Romeo (prod Randy
Chin)   4.75

80   Talking Blues/Talking Blues (Version) – The Maroons [The Cimarons] (prod Des
Bryan)   4.75

81   Dr Honey/Honey Dub – Norris Weir (prod Norris Weir)   4.75

82   NYT

83   Je'taime Moi Non Plus/Look A Pussy – Judge Dread (prod Alted)   5.75

84   The End Of The World/Escape From The Planet Of The Apes – Jason Sinclair/
The Baboons (prod Alted)   5.75

85   Skank Indigo/Expression In Dub – Harry J All Stars (actually with Joe White)/
Harry J All Stars (prod Harry Johnson)   5.75

86   Move Out A Babylon/Move Out A Babylon (Instrumental) – Johnny Clarke/
The Aggrovators (prod Edward 'Bunny' Lee) (reissue of Harry J HJ 6706)   5.75

87   On The Beach/On The Beach (Version) – Owen Gray/The Aggrovators Stars
(prod Edward 'Bunny' Lee)   5.75

88   Soldering/Soldering Part 2 – The Starlites/The GG All Stars (prod Alvin Ranglin)   5.75

89   I'm Your Puppet/Uptown Skank – Jimmy London/Skin, Flesh & Bones
(prod Lloyd Campbell)   5.75

90   Who Knows I Love You/Who Knows I Love You – Dimples Hinds/The All Stars
(prod Shady Tree)   5.75

91   Mama/Mama (Version) – The Soul Syndicate (prod unknown)   6.75

92   You Are Mine/You Are Mine (Version) – Johnny Clarke & Paulette/
The Aggrovators (prod Edward 'Bunny' Lee)   6.75

93   I Don't Want To See You Cry/I Don't Want To See You Cry (Version) –
Cornel Campbell/The Aggrovators (prod Edward 'Bunny' Lee)   6.75

94 I Shall Not Remove/I Shall Not Remove (Version) – Cornel Campbell/
The Aggrovators (prod Edward 'Bunny' Lee)   6.75

95 Heavenly/Heavenly (Version) – The Starr Bounds (prod Trevor Starr)   6.75

96 Wherever I Lay My Hat/Wherever I Lay My Hat (Version) – Cornel Campbell/
The Aggrovators (prod Edward 'Bunny' Lee)   6.75

97 Check It Out/Check It Out Version – Bob Andy (prod Keith Anderson [Bob Andy])
(possibly not issued)   1975

98 Say You/Say You Version – Jackie Robinson/Pioneer All Stars
(prod Jackie Robinson)   6.75

99 Darling Dry Your Eyes/Darling Dry Your Eyes (Version) – Barrington Spence
(prod Tony Robinson)   1975

100 Too Much War/War Version – Johnny Clarke/The Aggrovators (prod Edward
'Bunny' Lee)   1975

101 I Want To Stay Here & Love You/I Want To Stay Here (Version) – Derrick And
Paulette (prod Edward 'Bunny' Lee)   1975

102 Back In My Arms/Back In My Arms (Version) – Jackie Edwards/The Aggrovators
(prod Edward 'Bunny' Lee)   1975

103 Since I Fell For You/Since I Fell For You (Version) – Johnny Clarke/The
Aggrovators (prod Edward 'Bunny' Lee)   1975

104 Behold/Behold (Version) – Derrick Morgan & Johnny Clarke/The Aggrovators
(prod Edward 'Bunny' Lee)   1975

105 Some Woman Must Cry/Some Woman Must Cry (Version) – Derrick Morgan/
The Aggrovators (prod Edward 'Bunny' Lee)   1975

106 Move Out/Dance With Me – Tommy McCook & The Aggrovators (prod Edward
'Bunny' Lee)   1975

107 Rebel Soldering/Revel Soldering (Version) – Johnny Clarke/The Aggrovators
(prod Edward 'Bunny' Lee)   1975

108 Do You Love Me/Do You Love Me (Version) – Johnny Clarke/The Aggrovators
(prod Edward 'Bunny' Lee)   1975

109 Everybody Needs Love/In The Middle Of The Night – Honey Boy
(prod Sid Bucknor & Keith Williams [Honey Boy])   1975

110 Let's Have Some Fun/'Cos I Love You – Honey Boy (prod Sid Bucknor &
Keith Williams [Honey Boy])   1975

111 Fatty Bum Bum Gone To Jail/Fatty Bum Bum Gone To Jail (Version) – Laurel
Aitken (prod Laurel Aitken)   1975

112 Sounds Of A Good Song/Sounds Of A Good Song (Version) – Clinton Taylor
And Dansak (prod Sonny Binns & Trevor Starr)   1975

113 How Could You Do This?/Album Of My Life – Nora Dean & Dansak
(prod Sonny Binns & Trevor Starr)   1975

114 Moving Away/Moving Away (Version) – Dennis Brown (prod Winston Holness)   1975

115 Tell Me Baby/Tell Me Baby (Version) – Mike Dorane (prod Mike Dorane)   1975

116 Your Cheating Heart/News For My Baby – Winston Groovy (prod Winston
Tucker [Winston Groovy])   1975

117 Rock Away/Rock Away (Version) – Gregory Isaacs (prod Winston 'Niney'
Holness)   1975

118	NYT	
119	Free Up Jah Jah Children/Free Up Jah Jah Children (Version) – Owen Gray/ Bunny Lee All Stars (prod Edward 'Bunny' Lee)	1975
120	Take A Little Time To Know Me/Take A Little Time (Version) – Junior Tucker (prod unknown)	1976
121	Sha-La-La/Sha-La-La (Version) – The Maytones/The GG All Stars (prod Alvin Ranglin)	1976
122	I Say 'Super Jaws'/Super Jaws (Version) – Owen Gray/The Trojans (prod Eddie Airey)	1976
123	Everybody's Got A Song To Sing/We've Got To Part – The Cables/Trevor Shield & The Beltones (prod Harry Johnson)	1976
124	Cool Rasta/Dreadlocks – The Heptones (prod Harry Johnson)	1976
125	Oh Patricia/Read The News – Tito Simon (prod Clancy Eccles/Keith Foster [Tito Simon]) (also issued on Trojan TRO 9002/B-side reissue of Trojan TR 7964B)	1976
126	My Love For You Is Over Now/My Love For You Is Over Now (Version) – Doreen Murray (prod Jerry Morris)	1976
127	I Don't Want To Be A Beggar/Lynda – Rudolph [Rudy] Mowatt (prod Harry Johnson)	1976
128	Peacemaker/Mellow Up Yourself – Jam Now Generation/Bonnie Gayle (prod Clive Hunt)	1976
129	My Sweet Ceceile/He'll Have To Go – Lloyd Banton (prod Lloyd Banton)	1976
130	Ching Lue/Ching Lue (Version) – Cliff. St Lewis (prod Cliff St Lewis)	1976
131	Everybody Needs Love/Everybody Needs Love (Version) – Lloyd Parks/ Bunny Lee All Stars (prod Edward 'Bunny' Lee)	1976
132	Run Joe/Mr Bojangles – Lloyd Charmers (prod Lloyd Charmers)	1977
133	(Sitting On) The Dock Of The Bay/Change Your Style – Dennis Brown (prod Sidney Crooks)	1977
134	Mr Fixit/Mr Fixit (Version) – Max Romeo (prod Edward 'Bunny' Lee)	1977
135	Let The World Unite/Let The World Unite (Version) – Paulette Walker (prod Barry Gruber)	1977
136	Banana/Banana (Version) – Cliff St. Lewis (prod Cliff St Lewis)	1977
137	Slow Down/Slow Down (Version) – Floyd Lloyd Seivreight (prod Floyd Lloyd Seivreight)	1977
138	Dignity & Principle/Dignity & Principle (Version) – Big Joe (prod Linval Thompson) (A-side also issued on Attack ATT 8136B)	1977
139	Jah Jah Forgive You/Jah Jah Forgive You – Jah Stitch (prod Cecil Smith)	1977
140	Lead On Jah Jah/Lead On Jah Jah (Version) – Cecil 'Guitar' Smith (prod Cecil Smith)	1977
141	I'm Still In Love With You Girl/Muriel – Alton Ellis (prod Alton Ellis)	1977
142	Back In My Arms/Back In My Arms (Version) – Doreen Shaeffer (prod Barrington Dunn)	1977
143	Opportunity/Opportunity (Version) – George Faith (prod Barrington Dunn)	1977
144	Up Park Camp/Up Park Camp (Version) – John Holt/The Aggrovators (prod Edward 'Bunny' Lee)	1977

145 Mother & Father/Songs Of Distress – Michael Robinson & XLR (prod Mike Robinson) 1977

146 No Chance/No Chance (Version) – Johnny Orlando (prod Winston Tucker [Winston Groovy]) 1977

147 Going Over Yonder/Going Over Yonder (Version) – Rocky Delvar [Les Foster]) (prod Les Foster) 1977

148 Wailing Of Black People/Wailing Of Black People (Version) – Velvet Shadows (prod Alton Ellis) 1977

149 Some Helping Up/Some Helping Up (Version) – Owen Gray (prod uncredited) 1978

150 Don't Stay Away/Don't Stay Away Dub – Dudley (prod Winston Groovy [Winston Tucker]) 1978

151 Sweet Memories/Sweet Memories (Version) – Winston Groovy & Sandra Brightly (prod Winston Groovy [Winston Tucker]) 1978

152 Babylon A Fall Down/Downfall Rock – Velvet Shadows (prod Alton Ellis) 1978

153 Segregation/Segregation (Version) – Tony Sexton/Super Star (prod Clement Bushay) 1978

154 Love Plea/Rocker's Plea – Pancho Alphonso (prod Pancho Alphonso) 1978

155 NYT

156 Just Like A River/The Same One – Danny Ray (prod JO Christie) 1978

157 Walk Away/Walk Away (Version) – Marie Pierre (prod Dennis Bovell) (reissued on Trojan TRO 9066) 1978

158 Reggae Man/Heavy Reggae Man (Version) – Teddy Davis (prod Stan Biederbeck) 1978

HOT ROD (PREFIX HR)

100 Walk The Hot Streets/You Say You Don't Love Me – Carl Levy & The Cimarons/Peggy & The Cimarons 5.70

101 Remember Easter Monday/Pum Pum Lover – Peggy & Jimmy/Carl Levy 5.70

102 Not issued on Hot Rod (issued on Torpedo TOR 19: 'Why Why Why'/'Fistful Of Dollars' – Betty Sinclair/The Hot Rod All Stars)

103 I Shall Follow The Star/Gifted At The Top – Peggy/Carl Levy 6.70

104 Skinhead Speaks His Mind/Carnaby Street – The Hot Rod All Stars/Carl Levey [Levy] 6.70

105 Grandfather Clock/Kick Me Or I Kick You – The Cimarons 1970

106 Prison Sentence/Darling I Need You – Winston James & The Cimarons/Janet Ferron & The Cimarons 6.70

107 Strictly Invitation/Dog Your Woman – Patsy & Peggy 6.70

108 Beautiful World/Shocks Of A Drugs Man – The Hot Rod All Stars 7.70

109 I Wish You Well/Impossible Love – Delroy Dunkley/Tony [Nash] & Delroy [Dunkley] 7.70

110 Keep On Trying/Just Can't Do Without Your Love – Tony Nash/Winston James 8.70

111 Leaving Everything/Psychedelic Bird – Josh/The Hot Rod All Stars 1970

112 NYT

113 I Don't Want To/I Don't Want To (Version 2) – The Merritts/The Hot Rod All Stars 1970

Note: All recordings produced by Lambert Briscoe, operator of the Brixton-based Hot Rod Sound System.

JJ RECORDS (PREFIX JJ)

3302	Wreck It Up/Don't Go – The Ethiopians (prod Leonard Dillon for JJ Records)	1970
3303	Hong Kong Flu/Everything Crash – The Ethiopians (prod Karl 'JJ' Johnson)	1970

J-DAN LABEL (PREFIX JDN)

4400	Somebody's Baby/I Spy – Little Des [Desmond Riley]	1.70
4401	Cock Robin/Seven Zero – Ansel Collins/King Dennis (prod Ansel Collins)	3.70
4402	Electric Shock/Black Robin – The Music Doctors/King Dennis	2.70
4403	Bush Doctor/Lick Your Stick – The Music Doctors	2.70
4404	Preaching Love/Iron Man – The Music Doctors/George Lee & The Music Doctors	1970
4405	My Mother's Eyes/Gum Pot – The Soul Explosions	4.70
4406	NYT	
4407	Johnny Dollar/Touch Of Poison – George Lee & The Music Doctors	4.70
4408	NYT	
4409	NYT	
4410	Can't Help From Crying/Can't Get Used To Losing You – The Israelites	4.70
4411	The Wild Bunch/Born To Be Strong – The Music Doctors/The Music Doctors (actually by The Israelites)	5.70
4412	Consider Me/You Walked Away – Roy Gee	5.70
4413	Try To Understand/I'd Rather Go Blind – Roy Gee	7.70
4414	In The Summertime/Foundation Track – The Music Doctors	7.70
4415	I Want To Tell The World/Underground Man – The Mother's Sons	8.70
4416	I Don't Want No More/Third Note Swing – Boy Friday [Dandy]	2.71
4417	Discretion Version/Doctor Dan – The Music Doctors	1971
4418	Situation Version/Keeping Tracking – Boy Friday [Dandy]/Our Band	2.71

Note: All tracks produced by Dandy (Robert Thompson) unless othwise stated.

JACKPOT (PREFIX JP)

700	Seven Letters/Too Bad – Derrick Morgan (prod Edward 'Bunny' Lee/ Harry Robinson)	7.69
701	Dark End Of The Street/Apple Blossoms – Pat Kelly/Mr Versatile (actually Lester Sterling) (prod Lee Perry/Bunny Lee)	7.69
702	Having A Party/Devil's Disciples – Errol Dunkley/Mr Versatile (actually Lester Sterling) (prod Edward 'Bunny' Lee)	8.69
703	Sweeten My Coffee (actually titled 'Then You Can Tell Me Goodbye')/Cherry Pink – Pat Kelly/Mr Miller (possibly Roland Alphonso) (prod Edward 'Bunny' Lee)	8.69

704 Zapatoo The Tiger/Music House – Rolo Poley (actually Roland Alphonso & Unidentified Dj) (prod Edward 'Bunny' Lee) 8.69

705 Love Power/Since You Are Gone – Wonder Boy (actually Slim Smith)/Little Boy Blue (actually Pat Kelly) (prod Edward 'Bunny' Lee/Lee Perry) 10.69

706 The Crimson Pirate/Moon Duck (actually 'Moon Dusk') – Peter Touch (actually Peter Tosh) (prod Edward 'Bunny' Lee) 10.69

707 Feel It (aka Feel The Crumpet)/Kiss Me Quick – Mr Miller (actually by Bunny Lee)/Mr Miller (actually by Keeling Beckford) (prod Edward 'Bunny' Lee) 1969

708 Funky Chicken/Funky Chicken Part 2 (actually 'Dallas, Texas [Instrumental]') – Winston Groovy/The Cimarons (prod Laurel Aitken) 4.70

709 Funny/Funny Version – Winston Groovy/The Cimarons (prod Laurel Aitken) 4.70

710 Memory Of Don Drummond/Resting – Don D Junior (actually by Rico)/ The Tobies (prod Clancy Collins) 4.70

711 Too Late/Late Night – Vincent McLeod/Sir Collins (B-side actually by Clancy Collins' All Stars) (prod Clancy Collins) 1970

712 Let's Fall In Love/Purple Moon – Claudette & The Cimarons/The Prophets (prod Grape) 5.70

713 Wood In The Fire/The Naked City – King Horror & The Cimarons (prod Laurel Aitken) 8.70

714 Police/Honky Tonk Popcorn – King Horror/Pama Dice (prod Laurel Aitken) 1970

715 Bongo Man/Bear The Pussy – Pama Dice (prod Laurel Aitken) 1970

716 Sin, Sun & Sex/Reggae Reggae Popcorn – Pama Dice (prod Laurel Aitken) 8.70

717 Pack Of Cards/Spread Joy – Nat Cole/Nat Cole (actually with Sonny Binns) (prod Nat Cole) 1970

718 Love Making/My Love (Part 1) – Rita (actually Rita Alston with Nat Cole & Sonny Binns)/Sonny Binns (prod Nat Cole) 6.70

719 Riot/Boys & Girls – Moffat All Stars/The Impersonators (prod Melmouth Nelson) 6.70

720 NYT

721 NYT

722 Sugar Sugar/Sign Off – Nat Cole/Sonny Binns & Rita Alston (prod Nat Cole) 6.70

723 The Wedding/Air Balloon – Roy Smith [Junior Smith] (prod Roy Smith) 7.70

724 If You Want Me Girl/Confusion – Roy Smith [Junior Smith] (prod Roy Smith) 1970

725 NYT

726 NYT

727 Brotherly Love/Old Kent Road – Channel Five (actually by Martin Riley & The Uniques)/Channel Five (actually by Martin Riley) (prod Martin Riley) 1970

728 Look Over Your Shoulder/The Kiss – Nora [Dean] & Vern/Tommy McCook (prod Tommy McCook) 1970

729 See You At Sunrise/Just Out Of Reach (Of My Two Empty Arms) – The Interns/ Little Wonder (actually John Holt) (prod Edward 'Bunny' Lee) 9.70

730 Mr Chatterbox/Walk Through This World – The Interns (actually Bob Marley & The Wailers)/Little Wonder (actually by Doreen Shaeffer) (prod Edward 'Bunny' Lee) 10.70

731 You Can Do It Too/All My Enemies Beware – The Twinkle Brothers/The Twinkle Brothers (actually by Eric Morris) (prod Edward 'Bunny' Lee) 1970

732   Lonely Boy/Oo Boo – Errol The Champion (actually by Errol English &
      The Champions) (prod Larry Lawrence) (A-side reissued on Jackpot JP 738A)   1970

733   Dj's Choice/Can't Do Without It (actually 'Lesson Of Love') – Winston Williams/
      Slim Smith (actually with The Uniques) (prod Edward 'Bunny' Lee)   1970

734   I Just Don't Know What To Do (With Myself)/Lorna (actually titled 'Laura
      (What's He Got That I Ain't Got)') – Pat Kelly (prod Edward 'Bunny' Lee)   10.70

735   Get In The Groove/A Little Tear – Jeff Barnes/John Holt (prod Edward 'Bunny'
      Lee)   10.70

736   The Fastest Man Alive/Bloodshot Eyes – Dave Barker/Norman Grant
      (prod Edward 'Bunny' Lee)   1970

737   NYT

738   Lonely Boy/All Of My Life – Errol [English] & The Champions/Tony [Sexton]
      & The Champions (prod Larry Lawrence) (A-side reissue of Jackpot JP 732A)   10.70

739   NYT

740   Miss World/Take What You've Got – The Twinkle Brothers (prod Edward
      'Bunny' Lee) (issued on Pink Jackpot label)   11.70

741   Sweet Young Thing/Grandma – The Twinkle Brothers (prod Edward 'Bunny' Lee) 12.70

742   Wet Version/I've Got To Get Away – Dave Barker (prod Edward 'Bunny' Lee)   10.70

743   The People's Choice/Let Me Go Girl – Winston Williams/Bobby James (actually
      by Bill Gentles) (prod Edward 'Bunny' Lee)   1970

744   Top Of This World/Everybody Reggae – Mcbean Scott & The Champions/Larry
      Lawrence & The Champions (prod Larry Lawrence)   1970

745   Girl Of My Dreams/On Broadway – Dave Barker (prod Edward 'Bunny' Lee)   12.70

746   The Same Song/Groovin' – Domino Johnson & The Champions (prod Larry
      Lawrence)   1970

747   NYT

748   Cut Throat/Left The Water (actually 'You Left The Water Running') –
      Phil Pratt's All Stars/Ken Boothe (prod Phil Pratt)   1971

749   Released on Smash, SMA 2307

750   The Truth Hurts/My Life Goes On (No More) – Ernest Wilson (prod Edward
      'Bunny' Lee) (A-side reissued on Jackpot JP 765B)   1970

751   Sex Machine/You Left & Gone – The Aggrovators (actually with Dave Barker)
      (prod Edward 'Bunny' Lee)   1970

752   Give Me Some Light/Don't Turn Your Back On Me – Dave Barker (prod Edward
      'Bunny' Lee)   1971

753   Not issued (released on Smash SMA 2307)

754   The Boy Was Mine/? – Maxine (prod Edward 'Bunny' Lee) (probably unissued) 1971

755   Judge Aggro/Don't Rock The Boat – The Aggrovators/Satch (prod Larry Lawrence) 1971

756   NYT

757   Love Version/Ball Of Confusion – Winston Williams/Darker Shades Of Black
      (prod Edward 'Bunny' Lee)   1.71

758   War/People's Version – Darker Shades Of Black/Jeff Barnes (prod Edward
      'Bunny' Lee)   1971

759   I Won't Hold It Against You/King Of Hearts – Dave Barker/Bobby James
      (prod Edward 'Bunny' Lee)   1971

760	NYT	
761	Hear My Heart/Puppet On A String – Rob Walker (actually by Derrick Morgan)/ Rob Walker (prod Edward 'Bunny' Lee)	4.71
762	Midnight/Midnight Version – Lloyd [Clarke] & Doreen [Schaeffer]/Bunny Lee's All Stars (prod Edward 'Bunny' Lee)	4.71
763	Better Must Come/Version – Delroy Wilson/Bunny Lee All Stars (prod Edward 'Bunny' Lee)	4.71
764	Just For A Day/He Ain't Heavy, He's My Brother – Pat Kelly (prod Edward 'Bunny' Lee)	1971
765	Let Them Talk/The Truth Hurts – Ernest Wilson (prod Edward 'Bunny' Lee) (B-side reissue of Jackpot JP 750A)	1971
766	My Desire/Bring It Up – The Soulettes (prod Bob Marley)	1971
767	All Of Your Loving (aka Bring It Up)/Love Me – The Soulettes/Lloyd Clarke (A-side prod Bob Marley/B-side prod Edward 'Bunny' Lee) (A-side reissue of Jackpot JP 766B)	5.71
768	Do Your Own Thing/Talk About Love – The Twinkle Brothers/Pat Kelly (prod Phil Pratt)	6.71
769	Cool Operator/I'm Yours – Delroy Wilson (prod Edward 'Bunny' Lee)	1971
770	Try Again/Version 3 – Delroy Wilson/The Aggrovators (prod Edward 'Bunny' Lee)	8.71
771	Double Attack/The Sniper – Lizzie & Delroy Wilson/The Aggrovators (actually with Augustus Pablo) (prod Edward 'Bunny' Lee)	1971
772	Stick By Me/It's A Pleasure – John Holt (prod Edward 'Bunny' Lee)	10.71
773	Jumping Jack/King Of The Track – Dennis Alcapone (actually with John Holt)/ The Aggrovators (actually with Dennis Alcapone) (prod Edward 'Bunny' Lee)	10.71
774	It's A Jam In The Street/A Man Needs A Woman – John Holt (prod Edward 'Bunny' Lee)	10.71
775	Togetherness (Black & White)/Live Good – Dennis Alcapone And John Holt/ Delroy Wilson (prod Edward 'Bunny' Lee)	10.71
776	Tell It Like It Is/Come Along – Dennis Alcapone/Delroy Wilson (prod Edward 'Bunny' Lee)	11.71
777	Not issued (issued on Green Door GD 4007)	
778	Room Full Of Tears/? – Alton Ellis (prod Edward 'Bunny' Lee) (probably unissued)	1971
779	Keep Walking/Will You Still Love Me Tomorrow – Slim Smith (prod Edward 'Bunny' Lee)	1971
780	Keep Your True Love Strong/Nice To Be Near – John Holt/Delroy Wilson (prod Edward 'Bunny' Lee)	11.71
781	Peace & Love/Who Is Your Brother – Delroy Wilson/Jeff Barnes (prod Edward 'Bunny' Lee)	12.71
782	Nice To Be Near/Doing My Own Thing – Delroy Wilson (prod Edward 'Bunny' Lee) (release unconfirmed)	1971
783	Oh Girl/The Clock – John Holt (prod Edward 'Bunny' Lee) (probably issued only with blank label)	1971
784	Any More/Lost Love – John Holt (prod Edward 'Bunny' Lee)	1971
785	NYT	

786   I Need Your Loving/You Got What It Takes – Slim Smith (prod Edward 'Bunny' Lee)   2.72

787   Come On/Come On Version – The Cables/The Aggrovators (prod Edward 'Bunny' Lee)   1972

788   Take Me Back/Where Do I Turn? – Slim Smith (prod Edward 'Bunny' Lee)   1972

789   You're No Good/Rain From The Skies – Slim Smith (prod Edward 'Bunny' Lee) 1972

790   Don't You Know/Riding For A Fall – John Holt (prod Edward 'Bunny' Lee)   1972

791   The Mighty Organ/My Confession – Lascelles Perkins & Hortense Ellis/Stranger Cole (prod Edward 'Bunny' Lee)   1972

792   Who Cares/Who Cares Version – Delroy Wilson/U Roy Junior (prod Lee)   1972

793   Let Them Talk/Bringing In The Guns – Derrick Morgan (prod Edward 'Bunny' Lee) 1972

794   Won't Be This Way/Ain't No Love – Derrick Morgan (prod Derrick Morgan (prod Edward 'Bunny' Lee)   1972

795   The Same Old Song/Stay By Me – Delroy Wilson (prod Edward 'Bunny' Lee)   1972

796   Play It Cool/King Of The Zozas – Alton Ellis/The Aggrovators (prod Edward 'Bunny' Lee)   1972

797   Me Naw Run/All Night Long – Derrick Morgan (prod Edward 'Bunny' Lee)   1972

798   Closer Together/Blinded By Love – Slim Smith (prod Edward 'Bunny' Lee)   1972

799   Turning Point/Money Love – Slim Smith (prod Edward 'Bunny' Lee)   1972

800   My Baby Is Gone/This Old Heart Of Mine – Delroy Wilson (prod Edward 'Bunny' Lee)   1972

801   The Minstrel (actually 'Queen & The Minstrel')/Put Yourself In My Place – Cornel Campbell (prod Edward 'Bunny' Lee)   1972

802   Festival 10/Version – Derrick Morgan/The Aggrovators (prod Edward 'Bunny' Lee) 1972

803   You'll Be Sorry/Green Grow The Lilacs – Dave Barker (prod Edward 'Bunny' Lee for Bush Productions)   8.72

804   Cheer Up/Loving You – Delroy Wilson (prod Edward 'Bunny' Lee)   8.72

805   Guilty/Version – Ken Parker/The Aggrovators (prod Edward 'Bunny' Lee for Bush Productions)   8.72

806   Two Ton Gulleto/Gulleto Version – U Roy Junior (prod Edward 'Bunny' Lee)   9.72

807   Looking Back/I'll Be There – John Holt (prod Edward 'Bunny' Lee for Bush Productions)   10.72

808   Cassius Clay/Love & Affection – Dennis Alcapone/Slim Smith (actually with The Uniques) (prod Edward 'Bunny' Lee) (issued on light-blue label)   3.73

809   Pity The Children/You're No Good – Cornel Campbell & The Eternals (prod Edward 'Bunny' Lee)   3.73

810   Your Pretty Face/Your Pretty Face Version – Keble Drummond (prod Hugh Madden) 3.73

811   Ration/Things Not Easy – Joe Gibbs All Stars (actually by Bongo Herman & Bingy Bunny)/Joe Gibbs All Stars (actually by The Meditators) (prod Joe Gibbs) (also issued on Smash SMA 2331, with correct credits)   1973

812   Justice To The People/Justice To The People Verse 2 – Lee Perry & The Upsetters (prod Lee Perry)   1973

813   He Can't Spell/Acid Version – Dennis Brown/The Crystalites (prod Derrick Harriott) 1973

814   Harry Hippy/Just One Kiss – Cornel Campbell (prod Edward 'Bunny' Lee)   1973

JOE (PREFIX JRS)
1   Behold/Tea, Patty, Sex & Ganja – The Critics With The Nyah Shuffle/Sexy Frankie   3.70
2   Since I Met You Baby/Jughead – Paula Dean & The Nyah Shuffle/Paula Dean & The Nyah Shuffle (actually without Paula Dean)   4.70
3   She Caught The Train/Teahouse From Emperor Roscoe – Ray Martell/Pama Dice   5.70
4   NYT
5   Trial Of Pama Dice/Jughead Returns Version 1 – Lloyd, [PamA] Dice & Mum With The Nyah Shuffle/The Nyah Shuffle   4.70
6   Son Of Alcapone/All My Enemies – Joe The Boss [Joe Mansano]   5.70
7   Small Change/Mind Your Business – Girlie/Girlie & Joe [Mansano]   5.70
8   People Are Running/Schooldays – Pamela Brown/The Critics (actually by Pamela Brown)   5.70
9   Skinhead Revolt/Tony B's Theme – Joe The Boss [Joe Mansano]/Joe's All Stars   5.70
10   If Life Was A Thing/Daisy Bothering – Joe The Boss [Joe Mansano]/Lloyd Kingpin   7.70
11   Don't Play That Song/Just One Look – Delroy Williams & The Reaction/Boss All Stars   7.70
12   NYT
13   unknown instrumental/Young & Strong Version 1 – Joe's All Stars/Joe The Boss [Joe Mansano] (probably on blank label only)   1970
14   Appeal Of Pama Dice/Young & Strong Version 2 – Lloyd, Mum & Barrister/Boss All Stars   1970
15   NYT
16   Lazarus/Brixton Is Free – Dice The Boss & Joe Mansano/Joe The Boss [Joe Mansano] & Reco Rodriguez (probably on blank label only)   1970
17   The Informer/Cool It – Dice The Boss/Joe's All Stars   1970

Note: All releases in this series produced by Joe Mansano, who operated Joe's Record Shack in Brixton's Granville Arcade. Also see the Duke label, which issued 11 singles with a Joe label under its own DU prefix. The numbers concerned are 23, 24, 28, 34, 41, 42, 50, 51, 52, 53 and 57.

JUMP UP (PREFIX JU)
540   Muhammed Ali/Undemocratic Rhodesia – Mr Calypson/Sampson The Lark (prod Ed Shaw)   1971
541   Mr Walker/Mae Mae – Mighty Sparrow (prod WIRL)   1971

MOODISC (PREFIX MU)
3501   Musically Red/Bratah – Winston Wright & Mudie's All Stars   9.70
3502   Back Door/Too Much Fire – Lloyd Charmers & Mudie's All Stars/Freddy Mclean (actually Freddy McKay)   9.70
3503   Wha Who Wha Version/Wha Who Wa – Mudie's All Stars/Count Sticky   1970
3504   On The Water/Cash Register – The Jolly Boys/Mudies All Stars   1.70
3505   Time Is The Master/I'll Run Away – John Holt/Winston Shand   1.71

3506	Let's Start Again/Christmas Joy – Don Cornel (actually Cornel Campbell) & The Eternals	1970
3507	Push Me In The Corner/Mudie's Madness – The Eternals/Mudie's All Stars	4.71
3508	Keep On Dancing/My Jealous Eyes – The Eternals/Hazel Wright	6.71
3509	Musical Pleasure/Hot Pop – I Roy/Joe Joe Bennett & Mudie's All Stars	5.71
3510	Heart Don't Leap/Snow Bird – I Roy & Dennis Walks/Joe Joe Bennett & Mudie's All Stars (B-side reissued on Moodisc MU 3514A)	6.71
3511	I'll Never Believe In You/Black Attack – The Dynamic Gang (prod Sid Bucknor)	5.71
3512	Let Me Tell You Boy/Let Me Tell You Boy (Version) – I Roy & The Ebony Sisters/Mudie's All Stars	6.71
3513	It May Sound Silly/It May Sound Silly (Version) – John Holt/Mudie's All Stars	1971
3514	Snow Bird/Change The Tide – Joe Joe Bennett & Mudie's All Stars/Mudie's All Stars (A-side reissue of Moodisc MU 3509B)	1971
3515	Whispering Drums/Give Me Some More Loving – Count Ossie & Mudie's All Stars/Slim Smith & The Uniques	1971

Note: *All releases produced by Harry Mudie, except MU 3511. It should be mentioned that there was a further series of Moodisc (in 1972) issued by R&B Discs from November 1971 and a later version of the imprint around 1975 issued by another concern. The above listing however is the series issued by Trojan/B&C.*

PEOPLE REGGAE SERIES (PREFIX PEO)

101	NYT	
102	NYT	
103	Natty Dread Girl/Version – Linval Thompson (prod Edward 'Bunny' Lee)	1975

PRESSURE BEAT (PREFIX PB)

5501	No Honey, No Money/This Message To You – Niney & The Destroyers (actually with Slim Smith)/The Inspirations	2.70
5502	Mad Rooster/As Far As I Can See (actually titled 'The Wicked Must Survive') – Lloyd Willis/Niney & The Destroyers (actually by The Reggae Boys)	2.70
5503	Walk By Day, Fly By Night/Unknown Tongue – The Reggae Boys/The Destroyers	3.70
5504	News Flash/News Flash (Part 2) – Desi Young/The Destroyers	1970
5505	Pressure Tonic/Machuki's – The Destroyers/The Destroyers (actually with Count Machuki)	3.70
5506	Pussy Catch A Fire/Follow This Beat (actually 'Secret Weapon') – The Soul Brothers/The Destroyers (actually by Ansel Collins) (B-side reissue of Amalgamated AMG 832A)	1970)
5507	Jack Of My Trade/United We Stand – Lord Comic/Cynthia Richards (actually duet with Irving 'Al' Brown)	1970
5508	Ten Feet Tall (actually titled 'Wear You From The Ball')/Chapter Two (actually titled 'Harmony Hall') – Lizzy/The Destroyers (actually by Nicky Thomas)	1970

5509	Them A Fi Get A Beatin'/Them A Fi Get A Beatin' (Version) – Peter Tosh/Third & Fourth Generation	1972
5510	Shanky Dog (actually titled 'Skanky Dog')/Boney Dog – Winston Scotland/ The Destroyers	2.72
5511	Hammering (Version)/Medicine Man – Nicky & Cat Campbell (actually Nicky Thomas & Cap Campbell)/First Generation	9.72
5512	Yuh Wrong Fe Trouble Joshua/Joshua Row Us Home – Eddy Ford/Carey [Johnson] & Lloyd [Young]	9.72
5513	Money In My Pocket/Money In My Pocket (Version) – Dennis Brown/Joe Gibbs All Stars	1972
5514	Tipatone/Do It To Me – Joe Gibbs All Stars (actually by Keith Smiley)	1972
5515	More Dub/More Dub (Version) – Johnny Lover/The Professionals	1973

PYRAMID (PREFIX PYR)
SECOND SERIES

7000	Money Never Built A Mountain/My World – The Tennors (prod Edward 'Bunny' Lee)	1973
7001	Tip From The Prince/Fat Beef Skank – I Roy/Dillinger (prod Tony Robinson)	1973
7002	Ba-Ba-Ri-Ba Skank/Buck & The Preacher – Dennis Alcapone & Lizzy/Tommy McCook (prod Arthur 'Duke' Reid)	10.72
7003	Truly/Cruising – Alton Ellis (prod Lloyd Coxson)	10.72
7004	Waxy Doodle/Go Away – Leo Graham (prod Leo Graham)	10.72
7005	Can You Keep A Secret/Peter & Judas – Big Youth & Keith Hudson/Earl Flute & Horace Andy (prod Keith Hudson)	10.72
7006	I Could Never Have Another/It Ain't Always What You Do – Brad Lundy (prod Sydney Crooks)	1973
7007	Baby Don't Do It/You'll Never Know – The Now Generation (prod Federal)	1973
7008	Belch It Off/Jack Horner – Dennis Alcapone (prod Sydney Crooks)	1974
7009	New Situation/New Situation (Version) – Rocking Horse (prod Lloyd Campbell)	1974
7010	Great Messiah/Nana Nana – The Meditations (prod Alvin Ranglin)	1974
7011	No Work, No Pay/No Work No Pay (Version) – The Tellers (prod Rupie Edwards)	1974
7012	Innocent People Cry/Innocent People Cry – Gregory Isaacs/The GG All Stars (prod Alvin Ranglin)	1974
7013	My Desire/Lemon Tree – Johnny Clarke (prod Edward 'Bunny' Lee)	1974
7014	Butter Fe Fish/Bammie & Fish – Skin, Flesh & Bones (prod Dickie Woung)	1974

Note: The first Pyramid series was issued by Doctor Bird Records, 1966–9.

Q (PREFIX Q)

2200	Lavender Blue/Humpty Dumpty – Count Suckle (prod Count Suckle)	1970
2201	Please Don't Go/Bread On The Table – Count Suckle with Freddie Notes & The Rudies (prod Count Suckle)	1970
2202	NYT	

| 2203 | Peace To You Brother/Tribute To Jimi Hendrix – Jimmy Lindsay & The Beans (prod Freddie Notes) | 1970 |
| 2204 | Moving Train/Sweet Louise – Hughie & Huyitis [The Rudies] (prod Freddie Notes) | 1970 |

RANDYS (PREFIX RAN)

500	I'm The One, You're The One/End Us (correct Ja title 'Endust') – Randy's All Stars	7.70
501	Pepper Pot/The Same Thing – Randy's All Stars (actually with Count Machuki)/The Soul Twins (actually The Gaylads)	8.70
502	Dixie/Five Cents (actually 'A Lover's Question') – Randy's All Stars/Max Romeo (actually Winston Samuels)	9.70
503	October/Time Out – Dave Barker/Randy's All Stars	8.70
504	Give Thanks & Praise/Get Ready – The Lyrics/Tommy McCook And Randy's All Stars	1970
505	Emperor Waltz/War (Version 1) – Randy's All Stars	1970
506	Blue Danube Waltz/Together – Randy's All Stars/Delroy Wilson	1970
507	Bridge Over Troubled Water (Instrumental)/Waterfall – Randy's All Stars	1970
508	Want Man/Want Man (Version) – Nora Dean/Randy's All Stars	1.71
509	Me Want Girl/Me Want Girl (Version) – The Ethiopians/Randy's All Stars	1971
510	True Man/Truthful (actually 'Mr Tom (Version)') – The Ethiopians/Randy's All Stars (actually by Herman Marquis)	1971
511	Give Thanks/Give (Version) – The Lyrics/Randy's All Stars	4.71
512	Mr Tom/Sad News – The Ethiopians & Randy's All Stars	3.71
513	NYT	
514	Shake A Hand/Lick I Pipe – Jimmy London & The Impact All Stars/Karl Murphy & The Impact All Stars	7.71
515	Down By The Riverside/Riverside Version – Keith Poppin & The Impact All Stars/Impact All Stars	7.71
516	Close To Me/Close To Me (Version) – Max Romeo/Impact All Stars (possibly issued on white label only)	1971
517	Bridge Over Troubled Waters/War (Version 2) – Jimmy London & The Impact All Stars/Randy's All Stars	8.71
518	Hip Hip Hooray/Hip Hip Hooray Version – Jimmy London & The Impact All Stars/Impact All Stars	1971
519	Go Back Version 4/Go Back Version 3 – Impact All Stars	1971
520	A Little Love/A Little Love (Version) – Jimmy London & The Impact All Stars	10.71
521	It's Now Or Never/It's Now Or Never (Version) – Jimmy London & The Impact All Stars	2.72
522	Hard Time/Change Your Ways – Rocking Horse & The Impact All Stars	1972
523	King Of Babylon/Nebuchadnezzar – Junior Byles/The Upsetters (actually by Dennis Alcapone) (prod Lee Perry)	1972
524	Stars/Stars (Version) – Lloyd Parks/Dennis Alcapone (prod Tony Robinson)	1972
525	Sing A Song Of Freedom/Freedom (Version) – The Freedom Group/The Impact All Stars	1972

526	Cheater/Harvest In The East – Dennis Brown/Tommy McCook & The Impact All Stars	1972
527	Jamaican Festival '72/Jamaican Festival '72 (Version) – Jimmy London & The Rocking Horse/The Impact All Stars	1972
528	Meet Me At The Corner/Meet Me (Version) – Dennis Brown/The Impact All Stars	1972
529	Sweet Caroline/Sweet Caroline – C Donovan (actually Don Carlos)/The Impact All Stars	1972
530	Passion Love/Love Makes The World Go Round – The Melodians (prod Arthur 'Duke' Reid)	1972
531	Kick The Bucket/I'm A Man Of My Word – Keith Poppin (prod Tony Robinson)	1973
532	Froggie/Froggie (Version) – U Roy Junior/The Rhythm Rulers (prod Lloyd Campbell)	10.73
533	Don't Think About Me/Skin Him Alive – Horace Andy & Earl Flute/Dino Perkins (prod Keith Hudson)	1973
534	Silver Platter/Jean You Change Everything – Keith Hudson & I Roy/Keith Hudson (prod Keith Hudson)	1973
535	I'm So Fed Up/Fed Up (Version) – Rocking Horse	1973
536	Bedroom Mazurka/Melodica Version 2 – Augustus Pablo & Fay Bennett/Augustus Pablo & The Crystalites (prod Derrick Harriott)	1973

Note: All recordings produced by Vincent Chin unless otherwise stated.

SMASH (PREFIX SMA)

2300	NYT (possibly not used)	
2301	My Boy Lollipop/Everybody Needs Love – Maxine (prod Edward 'Bunny' Lee)	11.70
2302	Big Red Ball/Big Red Ball – Vers II – The Aggrovators (A-side actually 'Bum Ball Chapter II' by Delroy Jones/B-side actually with Lloyd [Robinson] & Devon [Russell]) (prod Errol Thompson)	12.70
2303	My Heart Is Gone/My Heart Is Gone (Version) – John Holt/Phil Pratt's All Stars (prod Phil Pratt)	1970
2304	Skankey/Skankey – Vers II – Niney All Stars/Bunny Lee All Stars (prod Winston 'Niney' Holness)	1970
2305	In Reach/Life Is Not The Same Anymore – Bunny Lee All Stars/Maxine (prod Edward 'Bunny' Lee)	1970
2306	I Had A Talk With My Woman/Life Is Not The Same Anymore – John Holt/Maxine (prod Edward 'Bunny' Lee)	1970
2307	Stop Them/I Don't Care (What They Say) – Bill Gentles/Maxine (prod Edward 'Bunny' Lee)	11.70
2308	NYT	
2309	NYT	
2310	NYT	
2311	Don't Get Me Confused/Ball Of Confusion – Keith Hudson/D Smith (actually by Dennis Alcapone) (prod Keith Hudson)	12.70

2312	One More Bottle Of Beer/Beer Version – The Aggrovators (actually with Dave Barker)/The Aggrovators (prod Edward 'Bunny' Lee)	1970
2313	Wake The Nation/One Thousand Tons Of Version – U Roy & Jeff Barnes/Jeff Barnes (actually with Roland Alphonso) (prod Edward 'Bunny' Lee)	1970
2314	You Said It/Hot Sauce – Bobby (James) & Dave (Barker)/The Aggro Band (prod Edward 'Bunny' Lee)	1970
2315	The Wizard (aka 33–66)/Sweet Like Candy – The Aggrovators (A-side actually by Roland Alphonso)/The Aggro Band (actually by Winston Williams & Pat Kelly) (prod Edward 'Bunny' Lee)	1970
2316	NYT	
2317	I Am Trying/I Am Trying Version – Delroy Wilson/Collins All Stars (prod Clancy Collins)	1970
2318	Satisfaction/Satisfied Version – Delroy Wilson/Alton Ellis & Delroy Wilson (prod Clancy Collins)	1971
2319	A Little Loving/A Little Loving (Part 2) – Alton Ellis/Collins All Stars (prod Clancy Collins)	1971
2320	I'll Be There/Rude Boy Train – Alton Ellis/The Hi-Tals (prod Clancy Collins)	1971
2321	Sir Collins' Special/Conqueror (actually titled 'Heart Of Knights') – Collins All Stars (actually by Lester Sterling & Sir Collins)/Collins All Stars (actually by Lennox Brown) (prod Clancy Collins/Sonia Pottinger) (B-side also issued on High Note HS 055A)	1971
2322	Hard Life/Version Life – Merlene Webber/Collins' All Stars (prod Des Bryan & Clancy Collins)	1971
2323	What It Was/Chicken Thief – Delroy Wilson/Lloyd Clarke (prod Edward 'Bunny' Lee/Derrick Morgan)	1971
2324	Mother & Father Love/Mother Love Version – John Holt/The Aggrovators (prod Edward 'Bunny' Lee)	1971
2325	Need No Whip/Grine Grine – Charlie Ace (prod Theo Beckford)	1971
2326	Light Of Day/I Thought You Knew – Keith Hudson (prod Keith Hudson)	1973
2327	Concentration/Concentration Version 2 – Dennis Brown/The Crystalites (prod Derrick Harriott)	1973
2328	Soul Sister/Soul Sister (Version) – The Heptones/Impact All Stars (prod Lee Perry)	1973
2329	Don't Break Your Promise/I've Been Admiring You – John Holt (prod Edward 'Bunny' Lee)	1973
2330	Black Man Kingdom Come/Swing & Dine – The Gaytones (both sides actually by The Melodians) (prod Sonia Pottinger) (B-side is original 1968 cut)	1973
2331	Things Not Easy/Ration – The Meditators/Bongo Herman & Bingy Bunny (prod Joe Gibbs) (also issued on Jackpot JP, with A- and B-sides reversed and with erroneous credits)	1973
2332	Hello My Little Queen/African Queen – Mickey Lee (actually Ken Parker)/ Augustus Pablo (prod Joe Gibbs)	1973
2333	Rock & Cry/September Rose – Sugar Simone (prod C Troutt aka Mike Dorane)	1973
2324	How You Gonna Get Control/Dubbing Control – Bellfield (Stanley Beckford)/ The GG All Stars (prod Alvin Ranglin)	1973
2335	I'm Just A Rover/Version – You & I (prod C Troutt aka Mike Dorane)	1973

2336	Trying To Wreck My Life/Live & Learn – Delroy Wilson (prod Edward 'Bunny' Lee)	1973
2337	Magnificent Seven/LeGGo Beast – I Roy (prod Augustus Clarke)	1973
2338	Rose Of Sheron/Slip Out – I Roy (prod Augustus Clarke)	1973
2339	Never Give Up/Fooling Me – Derrick Morgan (prod Edward 'Bunny' Lee)	1973

SONG BIRD (PREFIX SB)

1001	Ling Tong Ting/Sweet Sweet – Lloyd Charmers/Lloyd Robinson (prod Lloyd Charmers)	1969
1002	Long About Now/Come See About Me – Bruce Ruffin & The Temptations (A-side actually Bruce Ruffin & The Techniques/B-side actually by Lloyd Charmers) (prod Winston Lowe/Lloyd Charmers) (B-side also issued on Duke DU 25B)	1969
1003	Grooving Reggae/They Got To Move – Lloyd Charmers/Lloyd Robinson (prod Lloyd Charmers) (possibly not issued)	1969
1004	NYT	
1005	Biddy Biddy/It's A Wonderful Time – The Eagles (prod Joe Sinclair)	1969
1006	Rudam Bam/Prodigal Boy – The Eagles (B-side actually 'Any Little Bit' by The Techniques) (A-side prod Joe Sinclair/B-side prod Lloyd Charmers)	1969
1007	In The Spirit/Duckey Luckey – Lloyd Charmers (prod Lloyd Charmers for Winston Lowe/	10.69
1008	Darling Please/I've Got Plans – Stranger Cole (prod Stranger Cole)	1969
1009	I've Been Loving You/Memphis Reggae – The Megatons (actually The Rudies) (prod Joe Sinclair)	1969
1010	Ging Gang Goolie/I'm Thirsty – The Megatons (actually The Rudies) (prod Joe Sinclair)	1969
1011	The Clip/Little Miss Muffet – The Kingstonians/Tony (actually Tony Binns)	1969
1012	By The Time I Get To Phoenix/Heartbreak Girl – Noel Brown	1969
1013	Riding For A Fall/I'm Not Begging – Derrick Harriott	1.70
1014	Sitting On Top/You Were Meant For Me – Derrick Harriott	1.70
1015	Musical Madness/Musical Madness (Version 2) – The Crystalites	1970
1016	NYT	
1017	The Undertaker/Stop That Man – The Crystalites	3.70
1018	True Grit/True Grit Version 2 – Bongo Herman, Les & The Crystalites	5.70
1019	Singer Man/Singer Man, Version 2 – The Kingstonians/The Crystalites	3.70
1020	Lady Madonna/Version 2 – The Crystalites	4.70
1021	Love I/Heavy Load – Glen Brown/The Crystalites	4.70
1022	Go Bye Bye/Laugh It Off – Derrick Harriott	5.70
1023	Come A Little Closer/Come A Little Closer (Part 2) – The Prunes (actually with Eric Donaldson)/The Crystalites	5.70
1024	Isies/Isies (Version 2) – The Crystalites	7.70
1025	Stranger In Town/Version 2 – The Crystalites	7.70

1026	I'm The One Who Loves You/Suffering In The Land – Clyde McPhatter & The Rudies (prod Sidney Crooks) (possibly unissued)	1970
1027	Use What You've Got/Only Yesterday – Clyde McPhatter & The Rudies (prod Sidney Crooks) (possibly unissued)	1970
1028	Message From A Blackman/Message From A Blackman (Version 2) – Derrick Harriott/The Crystalites	6.70
1029	Psychedelic Train/Psychedelic Train (Part 2) – Derrick Harriott & The Chosen Few/Derrick Harriott & The Crystalites	7.70
1030	Sic Him Rover (aka Dog Taker)/Drop Pon – The Crystalites (B-side is reissue from Big Shot BI 510B)	6.70
1031	Time Is Hard/Time Is Hard, Part 2 – The Chosen Few	8.70
1032	Going Back Home/Part 2 – The Chosen Few/The Crystalites	1970
1033	No Man Is An Island/No Man Is An Island (Part 2) – Derrick Harriott/The Crystalites	8.70
1034	Overtaker/Version 2 – The Crystalites	8.70
1035	Undertaker's Burial/Ghost Rider – The Crystalites	1970
1036.	Short Story/No Baptism (Version 2) – The Crystalites	1970
1037	NYT	
1038	NYT	
1039	Handful Of Friends/Handful Of Friends Version – Pat Satchmo/The Crystalites	10.70
1040	No Baptism/Version 2 – The Ethiopians/The Crystalites	10.70
1041	Rumble Rumble/Rumble Version – The Kingstonians/The Crystalites	1970
1042	Groovy Situation/The Crystal Groove – Derrick Harriott/The Crystalites (A-side reissued on Trojan TR 7887A)	10.70
1043	Psychedelic Train, Chapter 3/Groovy Situation, Version 3 – Derrick Harriott/The Crystalites	1970
1044	Sesame Street/Sesame Version – Scotty/The Crystalites	1970
1045	Out There/Out There Version – The Kingstonians/The Crystalites	12.70
1046	Why Can't I Touch You?/Version – The Chosen Few/The Inner Circle Band	12.70
1047	Good Ambition/Ambition Version – The Ethiopians/The Crystalites	1970
1048	Hear That Train/Hear That Train (Version) – Tinga Stewart/The Crystalites	1971
1049	Riddle I This/Musical Chariot – Scotty & Derrick Harriott/Scotty & The Crystalites	1971
1050	Home Sweet Home/Hail I – Bongo Herman & Les	2.71
1051	Jam Rock Style/Rock Style Version – Scotty & The Crystalites/The Crystalites	1.71
1052	Candy/Candy Version – Derrick Harriott/The Crystalites	1.71
1053	Golden Chickens/Stranger In Town Version – Ramon & The Crystalites/The Crystalites	1.71
1054	Medicine Stick/Short Cut – Denzil Laing & The Crystalites/The Crystalites	1971
1055	Lollipop Girl/Lollipop Version – Derrick Harriott/The Crystalites	1971
1056	Penny For Your Song/Penny (Version) – Scotty/The Crystalites	1971
1057	Earthly Sounds/Earthly Sounds Version – The Crystalites (actually with Hux Brown)/The Crystalites	1971

1058	NYT	
1059	What A Pain/Pain Version – The Ethiopians/The Crystalites	1971
1060	Know Far I/Know Far I Version – Bongo Herman & Bunny/The Crystalites	1971
1061	Shaft/Shaft Version – The Chosen Few/The Crystalites	1971
1062	Lot's Wife/Slave – The Ethiopians/Derrick Harriott	1971
1063	Medley In Five (actually 'The Sensational Derrick Harriott')/Part 2 – Derrick Harriott	1971
1064	Best Of Five/Part 2 – The Ethiopians	1971
1065	Have You Seen Her?/Have You Seen Her Version – Derrick Harriott/The Crystalites	1971
1066	Salaam (Peace)/Scra-Per – Bongo Herman, Les & Bunny/The Crystalites	1971
1067	Everybody's Just A Stall/Everybody (Version) – The Chosen Few/The Crystalites	1971
1068	Over The River/River (Version) – Derrick Harriott/The Crystalites	1972
1069	We Are Praying/Praying (Version) – Bongo Herman & Bunny/The Crystalites	1972
1070	Do Your Thing/Your Thing (Version) – The Chosen Few/The Crystalites	1972
1071	Since I Lost My Baby/Version – Derrick Harriott/The Crystalites	1972
1072	Call Me Trinity/Monkey Drop – The Crystalites (actually with Joe White)/Scotty	1972
1073	Fat Boy/Boy Version – Bunny Brown/The Crystalites	1972
1074	Silhouettes/Silhouettes Version – Dennis Brown/The Crystalites	1972
1075	Changing Times/Changing Times Version – Roman Stewart & Dave/The Crystalites	1972
1076	Not issued	
1077	Not issued	
1078	Being In Love/Love Version – Derrick Harriott/The Crystalites (reissued on Trojan TR 7970)	1972
1079	Mash Up/Mash Up (Version) – The Diamonds/The Dynamites (prod Derrick Harriott)	1972
1080	Clean Race/Version Train – Scotty & The Crystalites/The Crystalites	1972
1081	Smokey Eyes/Smokey Eyes Version – Glen Brown & The Crystalites/The Crystalites	9.72
1082	People Make The World Go Round/People Version – Errol Brown & The Chosen Few/The Crystalites	10.72
1083	International Pum/Reggaematic – Niney/The Observers (prod Max Romeo & Winston 'Niney' Holness)	1972
1084	Don't Rock The Boat/Rock Version – Derrick Harriott/The Crystalites	1972
1085	Lonely Woman/Lonely Woman Version – Horace Andy/The Crystalites (reissued on Harry J HJ 6699B)	1973
1086	Dr Fud/La-Fud-Del-Skank – Fud & Del/Fud Christian All Stars (prod Fud Christian)	1973

Note: All releases produced by Derrick Harriott unless otherwise stated.

SPINNING WHEEL (SW PREFIX)

100	Haunted House/Double Wheel – The Upsetters (prod Lee Perry)	6.70
101	The Miser/Do It Madly – The Upsetters/Chuck Junior (prod Lee Perry)	6.70
102	Choking Kind/Penny Wise (actually 'Penny Wise & Pound Foolish') – The Upsetters (prod Lee Perry)	7.70
103	Land Of Kinks/This Man – (Hugh Hendricks) & The Upsetters/Oniel Hall (prod Lee Perry)	7.70
104	NYT	
105	Bush Jacket/Soul Face – The In Crowd (prod Earl White)	3.71
106	My Sweet Lord/Devil's Lead Soup (prod Rudies & Joe Sinclair)	1971
107	Bogusism/Soul For Sale – The Cimarons (prod Carl Levy)	1971
108	Voice Of The People/People Version – Jimmy [Martin] Riley (prod Martin Riley)	6.71
109	Crying Every Night/Crying Every Night Version – Herman Marquis (A-side actually by Stranger Cole) (prod Byron Smith)	6.71
110	Stupid Doctor/Groovin' In Style (Groovin' Out On Life) – Tommy McCook/Rob Walker (actually by Ken Parker) (prod Byron Smith)	6.71

SUMMIT (PREFIX SUM)

8501	Everything Is Beautiful/Give Up – Beverley's All Stars (A-side actually by BB Seaton)/Beverley's All Stars	10.70
8502	Collie & Wine/Collie & Wine Version – Glenmore [Glen] Brown/Beverley's All Stars	1970
8503	Got To Get Away/Got To Get Away Version – Delroy Wilson/Beverley's All Stars	1970
8504	NYT	
8505	Walking In The Rain/Walking In The Rain Version – The Melodians/Beverley's All Stars	1970
8506	Staircase Of Time/Staircase Of Time Version – Tony Brevett/Beverley's All Stars	1970
8507	NYT	
8508	Rivers Of Babylon/Babylon Version – The Melodians/Beverley's All Stars	11.70
8509	Bitterness Of Life/Ooh Child – Bruce Ruffin & Beverley's All Stars	12.70
8510	Peeping Tom/Peeping Tom Version – The Maytals/Beverley's All Stars	1970
8511	Starvation/Starvation Version – The Pioneers/Beverley's All Stars	1.71
8512	It Took A Miracle/Miraculous Version – The Melodians/Beverley's All Stars	2.71
8513	Monkey Girl/Monkey Girl Version – The Maytals/Beverley's All Stars	1971
8514	My Jamaican Girl/My Jamaican Girl Version – The Gaylads/Beverley's All Stars	1971
8515	Sounds Of Babylon/Sounds Of Babylon (Version) – Samuel The First [Philip Samuels]/Beverley's All Stars	2.71
8516	Candida/Are You Ready – Bruce Ruffin & Beverley's All Stars	2.71
8517	Get Ready/Get Ready Version – The Pioneers/Beverley's All Stars	1971
8518	I Wish It Could Be Peaceful Again/I Wish It Could Be Peaceful Again (Version) – Ken Boothe/Beverley's All Stars	3.71
8519	Your Feeling & Mine/Your Feeling (Version) – Ken Boothe/Conscious Minds	1971

8520	One Eye Enos/One Eye Enos Version – The Maytals/Beverley's All Stars	4.71
8521	Knock Three Times/This Time I Won't Hurt You – Brent Dowe/The Gaylads	4.71
8522	Come Ethiopians Come/Come Ethiopians (Version) – The Melodians/Beverley's All Stars	5.71
8523	Bongo Man/Now I Know – James Chambers [Jimmy Cliff]/Ken Boothe	6.71
8524	Free The People/Free The People (Version) – Bruce Downer (actually Bruce Ruffin)/Beverley's All Stars	7.71
8525	Put Your Hand In The Hand/Miracle Version (actually 'It's Gonna Take A Miracle (Version)') – Brent Dowe (actually with Hortense Ellis)/Beverley's All Stars (first pressing with 'SUM 8525B1' in B-side runout)	1971
8525	Put Your Hand In The Hand/Miracle Version (actually 'It Took A Miracle [Version]') – Brent Dowe (actually with Hortense Ellis)/Beverley's All Stars (second pressing with 'SUM 8525B2' in B-side runout)	8.71
8526	Stop The Train/Caution – The Wailers & Beverley's All Stars	1971
8527	It's You/It's You (Version) – The Maytals/Beverley's All Stars	9.71
8528	Lady Of My Complexion/No Sad Song – The Pioneers (prod Sidney Crooks)	10.71
8529	Walk With Love/Walk With Love (Version) – The Maytals/Beverley's All Stars	10.71
8530	Freedom Train/Freedom Train (Version) – Brent Dowe/Beverley's All Stars	11.71
8531	Games People Play/Games People Play (Version) – The Melodians/Beverley's All Stars	1971
8532	Rivers Of Babylon/My Life, My Love – The Melodians & Beverley's All Stars (first pressing, has 'SUM 8532A1'/'A2' respectively in runouts/A-side reissue of SUM 8508A)	1971
8532	My Life, My Love/My Life, My Love (Version) – The Melodians/Beverley's All Stars (second pressing, has 'SUM 8532B1'/'B2' respectively in runouts)	1971
8533	Never You Change/Never Change (Version) – The Maytals/Beverley's All Stars	1972
8534	The Time Has Come/No Sins At All – The Melodians & Beverley's All Stars (duplicate issue with 'SUM 8534B1' in B-side runout)	1972
8534	The Time Has Come/McIntosh – The Melodians & Beverley's All Stars/Brent Dowe & Beverley's All Stars (duplicate issue with 'SUM 8534B2' in B-side runout)	2.72
8535	Storybook Children/Gorgeous, Marvellous – Sidney, George & Jackie [The Pioneers]	2.72
8536	Thy Kingdom Come/Thy Kingdom Come (Version) – The Maytals/Beverley's All Stars	1972
8537	It Must Be True Love/It Must Be True Love (Version) – The Maytals/Beverley's All Stars	1972
8538	Haile Selassie/Old Man River – Mello & The Mellotones (prod Clancy Eccles)	1972
8539	Three Blind Mice/Three Blind Mice (Version) – Leo Graham/The Upsetters (prod Lee Perry)	1973
8540	Memories By The Score/Memories By The Score (Version) – Ansel Linkers [Ansel Cridland]/Fud Christian All Stars (prod Fud Christian)	1973
8541	Melody Maker/Uncover Me – Keith Hudson & The Mafia All Stars (prod Keith Hudson)	3.73
8542	A So We Stay/Scarface – Big Youth & Dennis Brown/Winston Scotland (prod Joe Gibbs)	1973

8543   Everyday Is The Same Kind Of Thing/Sweat Of Your Brow – Paulette
(actually Paulette Williams)/Shorty Perry (prod Alvin Ranglin)   1973

Note: All releases produced by Leslie Kong except where stated (SUM 8527 and last six issues).

TECHNIQUES (PREFIX TE)

900   Something Tender/Bewitch – Techniques All Stars (actually by Winston Wright)/
Techniques All Stars   7.70

901   Double Barrel/Double Barrel (Version 2) – Dave [Barker] & Ansel Collins   8.70

902   War Boat/War Boat (Version) (actually titled 'Mr Blue') – Techniques All Stars
(actually by The Sensations)   9.70

903   You'll Get Left (actually 'You'll Get Left (Version)')/It's Your Thing –
The Coons (actually by The Techniques All Stars)/Alton Ellis   1970

904   Lonely Man/I Feel Alive – The Techniques   1970

905   I'll Be Waiting (actually 'Don't Know Why I Love You')/I'll Be Waiting (Version)
(actually 'Don't Know Why I Love You (Version)') – Alton Ellis (actually by
The Sensations)/Techniques All Stars   10.70

906   Feel A Little Better/You'll Get Left (Organ Version) – The Coons (actually by
The Techniques All Stars)/Winston Wright   1970

907   Top Secret/Crazy Rhythm – Winston Wright   11.70

908   To The Other Woman/To The Other Woman (Version) – Hortense Ellis/
Techniques All Stars   1971

909   Jumping Jack/Point Blank – Rad Bryan/Ansel Collins   1971

910   NYT

911   unknown/8.5 Special – unknown artist/Techniques All Stars (label for this release
featured on sleeve of *Trojan Story Volume 1*, but existence not confirmed)   1971

912   NYT

913   Nuclear Weapon/La La La – Ansel Collins/The Techniques (actually by
The Techniques All Stars)   1971

914   Monkey Spanner/Monkey Spanner (Version 2) – Dave [Barker] & Ansel Collins/
Ansel Collins (B-side reissued on Trojan TR 7875B)   1971

915   Karate/Doing Your Own Thing – Dave [Barker] & Ansel Collins   1971

916   See & Blind/Rema Skank – Johnny Osbourne/Techniques All Stars   1972

917   High Explosion/High Explosion (Version) – Lloyd Young/Ansel Collins   1972

918   Look Into Yourself/Look Into Yourself (Version) – Dennis Alcapone/Techniques
All Stars)   1972

919   Promises/Promises (Version) – The Ethiopians/The Tivolies   1972

920   Horns Of Paradise/Grass Roots – Trammy [Ron Wilson]/Techniques All Stars   1973

921   Mr Harry Skank/Telavid Drums – Prince Jazzbo/Glen Brown All Stars
(prod Glen Brown)   1973

922   Woman Don't You Go Astray/Travelling Man – Winston Wright/(Dave Barker &)
The Techniques   1973

923   Don't Throw Stones/Toughness (actually titled 'Lucifer') – Sidney Rodgers &

	The Fighters/The Fighters (actually by Winston Wright) (prod Larry Lawrence) (also issued on Big Shot BI 621)	1973
924	That's When It Hurts/I'll Take You Home – The Silvertones (prod Lee Perry)	1973
925	Just One Look/Sinner Man – Annette Clarke (prod Lee Perry)	1973
926	Pauper & The King/Loving Pauper – I Roy & Gregory Isaacs/Gregory Isaacs (prod Augustus Clarke)	1973
927	Rub It Down/Rub It Down (Version) – The Eagles/Tommy McCook All Stars (prod Arthur 'Duke' Reid)	10.73
928	Aunt Kereba/Waterloo Rock (Version) – U Roy Junior/Don Reco (actually Reco Rodriguez & Lloyd Campbell's All Stars) (prod Lloyd Campbell)	10.73
929	Anywhere But Nowhere/Anywhere But Nowhere (Version) – KC White/Impact All Stars (prod KC White)	1973
930	Monkey Fashion/Medley Mood – I Roy (prod Roy Cousins)	10.73
931	Tonight I'm Staying Here With You/Lady Love – Romey Picket (actually Ronnie Davis & The Tennors) (prod Edward 'Bunny' Lee)	1974

Note: *All tracks produced by Winston Riley unless otherwise stated.*

TREASURE ISLE (PREFIX TI)

7050	Skinhead Moonstomp/Must Catch A Train – Symarip (prod Graeme Goodall/Philligree) (A-side reissued on Trojan TRO 9062A)	1969
7051	NYT	
7052	Pop A Top/The Lion Speaks – Andy Capp/Reco [Rodriguez] (prod Lynford Anderson/Philligree)	3.70
7053	Boss Cocky/Musical True – Claudette/Live Shocks (prod Philligree) (issued on blank label only)	1970
7054	Parson's Corner/Redeem – Symarip (prod Philligree)	2.70
7055	La Bella Jig/Holidays By The Sea – Symarip (prod Philligree)	3.70
7056	Hooked On A Feeling/Turn Round Twice – Boris Gardiner/The Message (prod Junior Chung/Philligree)	7.70
7057	NYT	
7058	One Life To Live, One Love To Give/My Best Dress – Phyllis Dillon/Tommy McCook	6.71
7059	Drive Her Home/Drive Her Home (Part 2) – Hopeton Lewis & U Roy/Tommy McCook & The Supersonics	6.71
7060	To The Other Man/Stampede – Hopeton Lewis & Tommy McCook & The Supersonics/Tommy McCook & The Supersonics	6.71
7061	Lets Build Our Dreams/Testify Version – John Holt/Tommy McCook & The Supersonics	7.71
7062	Behold/Way Back Home – U Roy With Tommy McCook & The Supersonics/Tommy McCook & The Supersonics	7.71
7063	Botheration/Mouth Trombone – Justin Hinds & The Dominoes/Tommy McCook	1971
7064	Everybody Bawlin'/Ain't That Loving You – U Roy & The Melodians/U Roy & Alton Ellis	7.71

| 7065 | Sister Big Stuff/Black River – John Holt/Tommy McCook & The Supersonics | 9.71 |

7065   Sister Big Stuff/Black River – John Holt/Tommy McCook & The Supersonics   9.71

7066   Paragons Medley/Medley Version – John Holt (& The Paragons)/Tommy McCook & The Supersonics   11.71

7067   Pirate/Depth Charge – The Ethiopians/Tommy McCook & The Soul Syndicate   1971

7068   Mighty Redeemer/Redeemer Version – Justin Hinds/Duke Reid's All Stars   1972

7069   The Great Woggie/Buttercup Version – Dennis Alcapone/Tommy McCook And The Supersonics   1972

7070   Midnight Confession/Midnight Confession (Version) – Phyllis Dillon/Tommy McCook & The Soul Syndicate   1972

7071   Judgement Day/Judgement Day (Version) – Hopeton Lewis & Dennis Alcapone/Earl Lindo & Tommy McCook & The Soul Syndicate   1972

7072   Jungle Fever/Clean Up Woman – Cynthia Richards & The Soul Syndicate   1972

7073   Help Me Make It Through The Night/Help Me Make It (Version) – Ken Parker/Tommy McCook All Stars   1972

7074   Wake Up Jamaica/Wake Up (Version) – Dennis Alcapone (actually with Joya Landis)/Tommy McCook All Stars   1973

Note: Releases prior to 7050 were issued during the time when Treasure Isle was a subsidiary of Island records and have not been included here for that reason. Those releases between 7050 and 7056 were issued during the time the label was administered by Graeme Goodall and his Doctor Bird group but have been included here for the sake of completeness. Numbers 7058 to 7074 inclusive were produced by Duke Reid.

TROJAN (PREFIX TR)
First Series (001–015)

001   Judge Sympathy/Never To Be Mine – Duke Reid (actually by The Freedom Singers & The Duke Reid All Stars)/Roland Alphonso   1967

002   Folk Song/Starry Night – Tony & Dennis/Tommy McCook & The Supersonics   7.67

003   It's Raining/Sound Of Music – The Treetops (actually The Three Tops)   7.67

004   Ain't That Loving You/Comet Rock Steady – Alton Ellis/Tommy McCook   8.67

005   I Want To Be Loved By You/Tulips – Oliver St. Patrick & The Diamonds (actually by Boris Gardiner & The Diamonds)   8.67

006   This Is A Lovely Way/Things Of The Past (actually titled 'A Thing Of The Past') – Phyllis Dillon   8.67

007   Dedicated To You/Things I Said To You – The Jamaicans   8.67

008   NYT

009   Why Birds Follow Spring/Soul Rock – Alton Ellis/Tommy McCook & The Supersonics   12.67

010   Love Is A Treasure/Zazuka – The Treasure Isle Boys (actually by Freddy McKay)/The Treasure Isle Boys   1.68

011   Loving Pauper/Sir Don – Tommy McCook & The Supersonics   12.67

012   Not used

013   Not used

014   Not used

233

015   Make Me Yours/We Have Happiness – Shirley Kaye (actually by Phyllis Dillon) 12.67

Note: All the above issues were produced by Duke Reid.

TROJAN (600 SERIES)

601	Donkey Returns/Tribute To Sir KB – Brother Dan All Stars (prod Dandy [Robert Thompson])	7.68
602	Eastern Organ/Our Love Will Last – Brother Dan All Stars/The Jivers (actually with Pat Rhoden) (prod Dandy [Robert Thompson])	7.68
603	Hold Pon Them/Answer Me – Brother Dan All Stars/Owen Gray (prod Dandy [Robert Thompson])	1968
604	Wear My Crown/Down On The Beach – The Jivers (actually with Pat Rhoden) (prod Dandy [Robert Thompson])	8.68
605	Pony Ride/Baby You Send Me – Winston & Pat [Rhoden] (prod Dandy [Robert Thompson])	8.68
606	Woman Is Greedy/Endlessly – Pat Rhoden/Junior Smith [Roy Smith] (prod Pat Rhoden)	1968
607	Read Up/Gallop – Brother Dan All Stars (prod Dandy [Robert Thompson])	1968
608	Another Saturday Night/Bee's Knees – Brother Dan All Stars (prod Dandy [Robert Thompson])	7.68
609	Possibly not used	
610	Bookie Man/More Love – The Race Fans/The Uniques (prod Lynford Anderson/Bunny Lee)	10.68
611	Spanish Harlem/If I Did Know (actually 'If I Didn't Know') – Val Bennett/Roy Shirley (prod Lee Perry/Bunny Lee)	9.68
612	Uncle Charlie (aka Uncle Charley)/What A Botheration – The Mellotones (prod Lee Perry) (B-side also issued on Duke DU 10A)	10.68
613	Tighten Up/Good Ambition – The Untouchables (aka The Inspirations)/Roy Shirley (prod Lee Perry/Bunny Lee)	1968
614	Donkey Train/Down By The Riverside – Denzil Dennis (prod Dandy [Robert Thompson])	10.68
615	Me Nah Worry/Hush Don't You Cry – Denzil Dennis (prod Dandy [Robert Thompson])	11.68
616	Place In The Sun/Handi-Cap – David Isaacs/The Upsetters (prod Lee Perry)	1968
617	Stir It Up/This Train – Bob Marley & The Wailers (prod Bob Marley)	11.68
618	The Toast/Kicks Out – Dandy (prod Dandy [Robert Thompson])	11.68
619	Watch This Sound/Out Of Love – The Uniques (prod Winston Lowe/Lloyd Charmers)	1968
620	Kansas City/Out The Light – Joya Landis (prod Arthur 'Duke' Reid)	1968
621	Rent Too High/Everytime – Glen Adams (A-side actually by Ranny Williams & George Regent/B-side actually titled 'Ace Of Spades' by Ranny Williams) (prod George 'Regent' King)	1968
622	Angel Of The Morning/Love Letters – Joya Landis/Alton Ellis & Phyllis Dillon (prod Arthur 'Duke' Reid)	11.68

623	In Like Flint/Nobody's Business – Byron Lee & The Dragonaires (prod Byron Lee)	11.68
624	Soul Limbo/Whistling Song – Byron Lee & The Dragonaires (prod Byron Lee)	1968
625	Win Your Love/All In The Game – George A Penny/Val Bennett (prod Lynford Anderson)	11.68
626	Fat Man/South Parkway Rock – Derrick Morgan/Val Bennett (prod Lynford Anderson)	11.68
627	Mix It Up/I'll Be Around – The Kingstonians (prod Karl JJ Johnson)	11.68
628	No More Heartaches/I'll Follow You – The Beltones (prod Harry Johnson)	12.68
629	You Crummy/Sentance – Lee Perry/Danny [Simpson] & Lee [Perry] (prod Lee Perry)	12.68
630	I Can't Stand It/Trying To Reach My Goal – Alton Ellis (A-side actually by Alton Ellis & Lloyd Williams) (prod Arthur 'Duke' Reid)	1968
631	Mr Walker/Sunset Jump-Up – Byron Lee & The Dragonaires (prod Byron Lee)	12.68
632	Lovey Dovey/Grooving – Owen Gray (prod Clancy Collins)	12.68
633	I'll Be Lonely/Second Fiddle – Jay & Joya (actually John Holt & Joya Landis)/The Supersonics (prod Arthur 'Duke' Reid)	12.68
634	Labba Labba Reggae (actually 'Reggae (Lonely Goat Herd)')/Love Up Kiss Up – Alton Ellis (actually by The Supersonics)/The Termites (prod Arthur 'Duke' Reid)	12.68
635	Rudy The Red Nose Reindeer/White Christmas – Steam Shovel (prod J Simpson) (issued on Big Bear label)	12.68
636	Honey Love/Thunderstorm – Burt Walters/King 'Cannonball' Bryan [Karl Bryan] (prod Lynford Anderson)	12.68
637	Time Marches On/Party Tonight – The Race Fans/The Silvertones (prod Lynford Anderson)	12.68
638	Dulcemania/Chinaman – Drumbago & The Dynamites/Clancy Eccles (prod Clancy Eccles)	1.69
639	Sweet Africa/Let Us Be Lovers – Clancy Eccles (prod Clancy Eccles)	1.69
640	Baby Baby/Barbara – Val Bennett (prod Lee Perry)	1.69
641	Moonlight Lover/I Love You True – Joya Landis (prod Arthur 'Duke' Reid)	1.69
642	Breaking Up/Party Time – Tommy McCook (actually by Alton Ellis with Tommy McCook & The Supersonics) (prod Arthur 'Duke' Reid)	2.69
643	Tonight/Maybe Someday – John Holt with Tommy McCook & The Supersonics (prod Arthur 'Duke' Reid)	1969
644	Uncle Desmond/Bronco – Lee Perry (actually by The Mellotones)/The Upsetters (actually with Sir Lord Comic) (prod Lee Perry) (reissued on Upsetter US 326A)	1969
645	A-Yuh (actually 'Hey You')/Just A Mirage – The Uniques (prod Winston Lowe/Lloyd Charmers)	2.69
646	Old Man Say/Promises – The Silverstars (prod Clancy Eccles)	2.69
647	Bangarang Crash/Rahtid – Clancy Eccles/The Dynamites (actually with Drumbago) (prod Clancy Eccles)	3.69
648	Constantinople/Deacon Son (actually 'Deacon Don') – Clancy Eccles (prod Clancy Eccles)	3.69
649	Demonstration/My Girl – Clancy Eccles/Val Bennett (prod Clancy Eccles)	4.69
650	I Can't Stop Loving You/Tell Me Darling – Owen Gray (prod Owen Gray)	3.69

651 Love Is All I Had/Boys & Girls Reggae – Phyllis Dillon (prod Arthur 'Duke' Reid) 1969

652 You Should've Known Better/Third Figure – Justin Hinds & The Dominoes/
Tommy McCook (prod Arthur 'Duke' Reid) 4.69

653 Out Of Sight/I Want You Closer – Danny Simpson/John Holt (prod Arthur 'Duke' Reid) 4.69

654 Hang `Em High/Candy Lady – Richard Ace/[Hugh] Black & [George] Daley (prod Harry Johnson) 3.69

655 Since You've Been Gone/Things I Love – Eric Fatter (actually Eric Fratter)/
The Afrotones (prod Harry Johnson) 4.69

656 Sweet Chariot/Far Far Away – Max Romeo & The Hippy Boys (prod Max Romeo) 5.69

657 The Saint/Ease Me Up Officer – Tommy McCook/Soul Ofrous (B-side actually by Winsaton Jarrett) (prod Arthur 'Duke' Reid) 5.69

658 Fattie Fattie/Last Call (actually titled 'Tribute To Drumbago') – Clancy Eccles/
The Silverstars (actually by The Dynamites) (prod Clancy Eccles) .5.69

659 Dollars & Cents/Popcorn Reggae – Gladstone Adams/Tommy McCook (prod Arthur 'Duke' Reid) 6.69

660 Everybody Bawlin'/Killowatt – The Melodians/Tommy McCook (prod Arthur 'Duke' Reid) 6.69

661 Ali Baba/I'm Your Man – John Holt with Tommy McCook & The Supersonics (prod Arthur 'Duke' Reid) 6.69

662 Pick Out Me Eye/Think You Too Bad – The Royals (prod L Edwards) 6.69

663 Soul Scorcher/Lucky Boy – King Cannon [Karl Bryan]/Glen [Brown] And Dave [Barker] (prod Harry Johnson) (issued on Harry J label) 7.69

664 The Moon Is Playing Tricks On Me/Soul Special – Trevor Shield/King Cannon [Karl Bryan] (prod Harry Johnson) (issued on Harry J label) 1969

665 Splender Splash/Please – The Jay Boys/Trevor Shield (prod Harry Johnson) (issued on Harry J label) 7.69

666 Woman Capture Man/One (actually 'One Heart, One Love') – The Ethiopians (prod Karl JJ Johnson) 6.69

667 Proud Mary/My Devotion – Tony King & The Hippy Boys (actually without Tony King) (prod Bart San Filipo) 7.69

668 Love/The Whole Family – The Hippy Boys (actually with Max Romeo)/
The Hippy Boys (prod Bart San Filipo) 7.69

669 Michael Row The Boat Ashore/Guess Who's Coming To Dinner – The Hippy Boys (prod Bart San Filipo) 7.69

670 Too Experienced/I Really Love You Baby – Owen Gray (prod Owen Gray) 7.69

671 Get On The Right Track/Moonshot – Phyllis Dillon (actually with Hopeton Lewis)/Tommy McCook (prod Arthur 'Duke' Reid) 8.69

672 Long Shot Kick The Bucket/Jumping The Gun – The Pioneers/Reco [Rodriguez] (prod Leslie Kong/Robert Thompson [Dandy]) (issued on both all-orange and orange-and-white labels/A-side reissued on Trojan TR 7968A and TRO 9063A) 8.69

673 Red Ash/Bluebird – Karl Bryan/The Silvertones (prod Arthur 'Duke' Reid) 8.69

674 What You Gonna Do/Have You Ever Been To Heaven – John Holt (prod Arthur 'Duke' Reid) 8.69

675 Liquidator/La La Always Stay (actually 'Rich In Love') – Harry J All Stars (actually

with Winston Wright)/Glen & Dave (actually Glen Adams) (prod Harry Johnson) (issued on Harry J label and A-side reissued on Trojan TRO 9063B) — 8.69

675 The Liquidator/Festive Spirit – Harry J All Stars (actually with Winston Wright)/ Glen & Dave (actually by The Harry J All Stars) (prod Harry Johnson) (issued on Harry J label and A-side reissued on Trojan TRO 9063B) — 8.69

676 Take You For A Ride/I'm Coming Home – Girl Satchmo & Tommy McCook (prod Arthur 'Duke' Reid) — 9.69

677 You Done Me Wrong/If This World Were Mine – Tyrone Evans (prod Arthur 'Duke' Reid) — 1969

678 Memory Of Don/Darling I Love You – Don Drummond/John Holt (prod Arthur 'Duke' Reid) — 1969

679 Ease Up/You're Gonna Feel It – The Bleechers (prod Lee Perry) — 1969

680 Get Back/I'm Not For Me – Anonomously Yours/Ernie Smith (prod Trojan [JA] Productions) — 1969

681 It's Your Thing/'69 – Anonymously Yours (B-side actually by Wallace Wilson) (prod Trojan [JA] Productions) — 1969

682 NYT

683 Double Shot/Gimme Gimme Gal – Beverley's All Stars/Beverley's All Stars (actually by The Mellotones) (prod Leslie Kong) — 1969

684 NYT

685 Black Bud/Too Late – The Pioneers (B-side actually Harmonisers) (A-side prod Leslie Kong/B-side prod by Hippy Boy) — 10.69

686 Tribute To Rameses/Lipstick On Your Collar – Tommy McCook/Phyllis Dillon (B-side actually by unknown female vocalist) (prod Arthur 'Duke' Reid) — 10.69

687 NYT

688 You Had Your Chance/Wha' She Do Now – The Gaylads (prod Lynford Anderson) 1969

689 Sound Of Silence/Walk On By – St. Andrew's Girls Choir (prod Trojan Records) 1969

690 Wonderful World, Beautiful People/Hard Road To Travel – Jimmy Cliff (prod Jimmy Cliff & Leslie Kong) — 10.69

691 Memphis Underground (Part 1)/Memphis Underground (Part 2) – The JJ All Stars (prod Karl JJ Johnson) — 1969

692 Big Bamboo/King Ja Ja – The Merrymen (prod Emile Straker) (reissued on Duke DU 113) — 1969

693 Put A Little Love In Your Heart/Jay Fever (aka Shining) – Marcia Griffiths/ The Jay Boys (actually with Karl Bryan) (prod Harry Johnson) (issued on Harry J label) — 10.69

694 Have Sympathy/Spyrone – John Holt/Harry J All Stars (prod Harry Johnson) (issued on Harry J label) — 1969

695 Sweet Sensation/It's My Delight – The Melodians (prod Leslie Kong) — 12.69

696 Got To Be Free/Situation – The Rulers (prod Karl JJ Johnson) — 12.69

697 Well Read/Robert F Kennedy (actually 'Feel The Spirit') – The Ethiopians/ The JJ All Stars (actually by The Ethiopians) (prod Karl JJ Johnson) — 1969

698 Poor Rameses/In Orbit – The Pioneers/Beverley's All Stars (prod Leslie Kong) 12.69

699 Night Of Love/Copy Cat – Ansel Collins/Derrick Morgan (prod Leslie Kong) 1969

7700 SERIES

7700	One Way Love/No More Heartaches – The Coloured Raisins (prod Joe Sinclair)	3.70
7701	Moonlight Groover/Everyday Is Just A Holiday – Winston Wright/The Sensations (prod Arthur 'Duke' Reid)	1969
7702	Wooden Heart/All My Life – John Holt (prod Arthur 'Duke' Reid)	1.70
7703	There's A Fire/Last Time – The Gaylads (prod Leslie Kong)	1.70
7704	Dry Up Your Tears/One Way Street – Bruce Ruffin/Beverley's All Stars (prod Leslie Kong)	1.70
7705	Intensified Change/Marie – The Silvertones (prod Arthur 'Duke' Reid)	1969
7706	Black Coffee/Heartaches – Tommy McCook & The Supersonics/Vic Taylor (prod Arthur 'Duke' Reid)	1969
7707	Little Drummer Boy/Mary's Boy Child – The Merrymen (prod Emile Straker)	1969
7708	I'll Need You Tomorrow/I'm Gonna Make It – The Kingstonians (prod Leslie Kong)	1.70
7709	Pressure Drop/Smoke Screen – The Maytals/Beverley's All Stars (prod Leslie Kong)	1.70
7710	Samfie Man/Mother Rittie – The Pioneers (prod Leslie Kong)	1.70
7711	Monkey Man/Night & Day – The Maytals (prod Leslie Kong)	2.70
7712	Cotton Dandy/Don't Get Weary – Ansel Collins/Carl Dawkins (prod Leslie Kong)	1.70
7713	Shanghai/Rome Wasn't Built In A Day (B-side actually 'Honey Don't Go') – Freddie Notes & The Rudies (B-side actually by Winston Francis) (prod Joe Sinclair)	1.70
7714	Lick It Back/Busy Bee – The Clarendonians/Beverley's All Stars (prod Leslie Kong)	1970
7715	Moon Invader/You Got To Love Me – Winston Wright/Radcliffe Ruffin (prod Arthur 'Duke' Reid)	1970
7716	Why Baby Why/Keep My Love From Fading – Ken Boothe (prod Leslie Kong)	2.70
7717	Lock Jaw/My Desire – Dave Barker (actually with The Supersonics)/The Yard Brooms (prod Arthur 'Duke' Reid)	1.70
7718	Run Fattie/Hoola Bulla – The Slickers (prod Leslie Kong)	2.70
7719	Baby Don't Do It/Touchdown – The Clarendonians/Beverley's All Stars (prod Leslie Kong)	2.70
7720	A Day Seems So Long/Project – The Melodians/Beverley's All Stars (prod Leslie Kong)	2.70
7721	Wiggle Waggle/Jaga Jaga War – The Wanderers (prod Leslie Kong)	1970
7722	Vietnam/She Does It Right – Jimmy Cliff (prod Leslie Kong & Jimmy Cliff)	1970
7723	Boss Festival/Lucky side – The Pioneers (prod Leslie Kong)	1970
7724	Rocco/Don't Tell Your Mama – Freddie Notes & The Rudies (prod Joe Sinclair)	2.70
7725	Lucianna/I Really Like It – The Jubilee Stompers (prod Brian Daley)	2.70
7726	Sweet & Dandy/54–46 [1968 Rocksteady version] – The Maytals (prod Leslie Kong)	3.70
7727	Suffering/Crazy Elephant – The Revelations/The Megatons (B-side actually by The Rudies) (prod Joe Sinclair)	2.70
7728	Eldora/If It's Not True – Techniques All Stars (prod Winston Riley)	2.70
7729	Moon Dust/Fat Cat – Ansel Collins (prod Leslie Kong)	1970

7730   High Voltage/High Voltage (Version 2) – Ansel Collins (prod Leslie Kong)   2.70

7731   Squeeze Up/Squeeze Up (Version 2) – Byron Lee & The Dragonaires
(prod Byron Lee)   3.70

7732   Strong Man/Sentimental – The Hot Rod All Stars (prod Lambert Briscoe)   2.70

7733   Virgin Soldier/Brixton Reggae Festival – The Hot Rod All Stars/The Setters
(actually by The Hot Rod All Stars) (prod Lambert Briscoe)   3.70

7734   Down On The Farm/Easy Street – Freddie Notes & The Rudies (prod Joe Sinclair)   2.70

7735   Barbwire/Calypso Mama – Nora Dean/The Barons (prod Byron Smith)   3.70

7736   Birth Control/Love At First Sight – Byron Lee & The Dragonaires (prod Byron Lee)   1970

7737   I'm The One/Who's Gonna Be Your Man – Bruce Ruffin (prod Leslie Kong)   4.70

7738   That's What Love Will Do/This Time I Won't Hurt You – The Gaylads
(prod Leslie Kong)   5.70

7739   Driven Back/Trouble Deh A Bush – The Pioneers (prod Leslie Kong)   4.70

7740   Show Me The Way/The Monster – Delroy Wilson/Beverley's All Stars (actually
with unidentified DJ) (prod Leslie Kong)   1970

7741   Bla, Bla, Bla/Reborn – The Maytals (prod Leslie Kong)   4.70

7742   Maybe Now/So Much Love – Joe White (prod Leslie Kong)   1970

7743   Young, Gifted & Black/Moonglow – The Gaylads/Beverley's All Stars   3.70

7744   Mayfair/Enoch Power – Millie (actually with Symarip) (prod Philigree)   3.70

7745   Suffering In The Land/Come Into My Life – Jimmy Cliff (prod Leslie Kong &
Jimmy Cliff)   3.70

7746   Simmer Down Quashie/Caranapo – The Pioneers (prod Leslie Kong)   5.70

7747   Bond In Bliss/Musical Scorcher – Winston Wright & The Dragonaires (prod Byron
Lee) (A-side reissued on Horse HOSS 56B)   5.70

7748   Family Man/Mellow Mood – The Upsetters (prod Bruce Anthony) (B-side reissued
on Trojan TR 7823B)   5.70

7749   Capo/Mama Look – The Upsetters (prod Bruce Anthony)   5.70

7750   Love Of The Common People/Compass – Nicky Thomas/The Destroyers
(prod Joe Gibbs) (reissued on Trojan TRO 9067A)   5.70

7751   Popcorn Funky Reggae (Title actually Seems To Be 'Reggae Chicken')/My Love –
Rita Alston/Nat Cole (actually with Rita Alston) (prod Nat Cole)   5.70

7752   All Kinds Of Everything/All Kinds Of Everything (Instrumental Version) –
Peggy/Carl Levy (prod Lambert Briscoe)   5.70

7753   Dynamic Pressure/Reggae Me Dis, Reggae Me Dat – Boris Gardiner (prod Boris
Gardiner)   1970

7754   Party Time/Party Time (Part 2) – Bim, Bam & Clover (prod Laurel Aitken)   5.70

7755   Feel Alright/Telstar – The Pyramids (prod Bruce Anthony)   5.70

7756   Freedom Street/Freedom Version – Ken Boothe/Beverley's All Stars (prod Leslie
Kong)   5.70

7757   Water Melon/She's My Scorcher – The Maytals (prod Leslie Kong)   1970

7758   Al Capone/Kaiser Bill – Emporer Rosko (prod M Colombia) (A-side reissued on
Trojan TR 7949)   6.70

7759   Soul Shakedown Party/Soul Shakedown Party (Version II) – Bob Marley & The

	Wailers/Beverley's All Stars (prod Leslie Kong) (A-side reissued on Trojan TR 7911A)	8.70
7760	Battle Of The Giants/Message To Maria – The Pioneers (prod Leslie Kong)	6.70
7761	Julianne/We Five – Byron Lee & The Dragonaires (prod Byron Lee)	7.70
7762	ABC Reggae/Be Yours – The Rockstones (actually by The Gaylads)/Beverley's All Stars (prod Leslie Kong)	6.70
7763	Tell The Children The Truth/Something Is Wrong Somewhere – The Gaylads (prod Leslie Kong)	1970
7764	Say Darling Say/Come Rock It With Me – The Melodians (prod Leslie Kong)	8.70
7765	Satisfaction/Things A Get Bad To Worse – Carl Dawkins/The Ethiopians (prod Karl JJ Johnson) (A-side issued on Duke DU 62A)	1970
7766	Susie Is Sorrow/Don't Go – Horace Faith/Derrick Pepper (prod J Smith)	7.70
7767	You Can Get It If You Really Want/Beware – Jimmy Cliff (prod Leslie Kong)	7.70
7768	I'm Gonna Get There/Kinky, Funky Reggae – Joe White/Rupie Edwards' All Stars (prod Rupie Edwards)	1970
7769	Gave You My Love/Love Version – Delroy Wilson/Beverley's All Stars (prod Leslie Kong)	1970
7770	To Sir With Love/Reggae Shuffle – The Pyramids (prod Bruce Anthony)	7.70
7771	Soul Sister (actually titled 'God Loves You Soul Sister')/Soul Version – The Gaylads/Beverley's All Stars (prod Leslie Kong)	8.70
7772	It's Gonna Take A Miracle/Now I Know – Ken Boothe (prod Leslie Kong)	7.70
7773	Sweeter She Is/Fire Fire – The Charmers/Byron Lee & The Dragonaires (prod Lloyd Charmers/Byron Lee)	1970
7774	Leaving Rome/In The Nude – Joe Joe Bennett & Mudie's All Stars (prod Harry Mudie)	7.70
7775	Meshwire/Darling Please Return – Winston Wright/The Barons (prod Byron Smith)	7.70
7776	Cecilia/Stand Up – Bruce Ruffin/Beverley's All Stars (prod Leslie Kong)	1970
7777	You Can Get It If You Really Want/Perseverence – Desmond Dekker (prod Leslie Kong & Warwick Lyn)	8.70
7778	Everything Is Beautiful/Give Up – The Rockstones/Beverley's All Stars (prod Leslie Kong)	1970
7779	It's All In The Game/Easy Come – The Rebels (prod Sydney Crooks)	8.70
7780	Drums Of Freedom/Drums Version – Ken Boothe/Beverley's All Stars (prod Leslie Kong)	8.70
7781	Money Day/Ska Ba Do – The Pioneers (B-side actually by Beverley's All Stars) (prod Leslie Kong) (A-side reissued on Trojan TR 7968B & TRO 7995B)	8.70
7782	It's All In The Game/Game Version – The Gaylads/Beverley's All Stars (prod Leslie Kong)	8.70
7783	Issued on Summit SUM 8505	
7784	NYT	
7785	NYT	
7786	Dr Lester/Sun, Moon & Stars – The Maytals (prod Leslie Kong)	9.70
7787	This Little Light/Lover – Ray Martell With The Cimarons & The Reactions/Ray Martell & The Cimarons (prod Al Barry for Philigree/Philigree)	8.70

7788	Oh Me Oh My/I Did It – Lloyd Charmers (prod Lloyd Charmers)	1970
7789	issued on Duke DU 98	
7790	Black Pearl/Help Me Help Myself – Horace Faith (prod Pinpoint)	1970
7791	Montego Bay/Blue Mountain – Freddie Notes & The Rudies/The Rudies (prod Joe Sinclair)	9.70
7792	Salt Of The Earth/Name Ring A Bell – The Cables (prod Harry Johnson) (also issued on Harry J label HJ 6616)	10.70
7793	What Greater Love/Lady Love – Teddy Brown (prod Phillip Swern & Johnny Arthey for Pinpoint)	10.70
7794	Shamay Dray/Here – Draycopp (prod Best)	1970
7795	I Need Your Sweet Inspiration/Everything Nice – The Pioneers (prod Leslie Kong)	11.70
7796	God Bless The Children/Red Eye – Nicky Thomas (prod Joe Gibbs)	10.70
7797	Dancing In The Sun/Chick-A-Bow – Daniel In The Lion's Den/The Lion's Den (prod Webster Shrowder, Des Bryan & Joe Sinclair) (B-side reissued on Trojan TR 7866B)	1.71
7798	Patches/The Split – The Rudies (actually with Freddie Notes)/The Rudies (prod Bush)	11.70
7799	Fire & Rain/Cold & Lonely Night – The Gaylads (prod Leslie Kong)	11.70
7800	Take A Letter Maria/You're Coming Back – Dandy (prod Dandy [Robert Thompson]) (A-side reissued on Trojan Tro 7994A)	11.70
7801	Honey Hush/Sunday Morning – Millie (prod Jimmy Cliff)	11.70
7802	The Song We Used To Sing/Get Up Little Suzie – Desmond Dekker (prod Leslie Kong)	12.70
7803	All For You/All For You (Version) – The Pyramids (prod Bruce Anthony)	1.71
7804	You Got Me/1001 – James Miller (prod Philip Swern & Johnny Arthey in association with Pinpoint Productions)	12.70
7805	Stepping Out In The Lights/Beats There A Heart – Paul Tracy (prod Philip Swern & Johnny Arthey in association with Pinpoint Productions) (in Trojan *Pop* series)	1970
7806	Help Yourself/Why – Jimmy James (prod Trojan Productions)	1970
7807	If I Had A Hammer/Lonely Feelin' – Nicky Thomas (prod Joe Gibbs)	2.71
7808	54–46 Was My Number/54–46 Version – The Maytals/Beverley's All Stars (prod Leslie Kong)	1.71
7809	Green Green Valley/Peace Of Mind – Bob Andy (prod Clive Crawley/Harry Johnson) (B-side also issued on Harry J HJ 6612A)	2.71
7810	Walk A Mile In My Shoes/Reggae Rouser – Freddie Notes & The Rudies/Johnny Arthey Orchestra (prod Bush/Johnny Arthey)	2.71
7811	Rose Garden/Happiness Hasn't Hit Helen – Teddy Brown (prod Philip Swern & Johnny Arthey in association with Pinpoint Productions)	1971
7812	Young, Gifted & Black/Peace Of Mind/Green Green Valley/We've Got To Get Ourselves Together – Bob & Marcia/Bob Andy/Bob & Marcia/Bob Andy) (prod Harry Johnson/Harry Johnson/Bob Andy & Clive Crawley/Harry Johnson) (maxi single)	1971
7813	Down In The Boondocks/Baby Make It Soon – Delroy Williams (prod Philip Swern & Johnny Arthey in association with Pinpoint Productions)	3.71

7814   Rain/Off Limits – Bruce Ruffin/The Aquarians (prod Herman Chin-Loy)   1971

7814   Rain/Geronimo – Bruce Ruffin/The Pyramids (prod Herman Chin-Loy/
Bruce Anthony) (second pressing)   1971

7814   Rain/Stingo – Bruce Ruffin/The Pyramids (prod Herman Chin-Loy/Bruce Anthony)
(third pressing)   1971

7815   Stand By Your Man/Credit Squeeze – Marlene Webber/Clancy Eccles (prod Sid
Bucknor/Clancy Eccles) (B-side reissue of Clandisc CLA 227)   4.71

7816   Same Old Fashioned Way/Out Of Many, One People – Dandy (prod Dandy
[Robert Thompson])   4.71

7817   I Shall Sing/Target – Jean & The Gaytones (actually by Judy Mowatt &
The Gaytones)/The Gaytones (prod Sonia Pottinger) (A-side reissued on Horse
HOSS 42A)   4.71

7818   Pied Piper/Save Me – Bob [Andy] & Marcia [Griffiths] (prod Bob Andy)   1971

7819   Thinking Of You/Thinking Of You Version – The Blues Busters/Byron Lee &
The Dragonaires (prod Byron Lee) (A-side also issued on Dynamic DYN 408B) 1971

7820   Black & White/Sand In Your Shoes – Greyhound (prod Dave Bloxham)   5.71

7821   One Woman/Save Me Version – Bob Andy (prod Keith Anderson)
(A-side resissued on Trojan TR 7840A & Horse HOSS 31A)   5.71

7822   Growing Up/Lovitis – Fabulous Flames (prod Clancy Eccles)   6.971

7823   Funky Strip/Mellow Mood – Charlie Boy (unknown artist)/The Upsetters
(prod Herman Chin-Loy/Bruce Anthony) (B-side reissue of Trojan TR 7748B) 1971

7824   Mule Train/Mule Train Version – Count Prince Miller (prod Count Prince Miller) 6.71

7825   Let Your Yeah Be Yeah/More Love – The Pioneers (prod Jimmy Cliff &
Sidney Crooks)   7.71

7826   It's Too Late (To Say That You're Sorry)/Slow Rock – Laurel Aitken
(prod Laurel Aitken)   7.71

7827   Walk The World Away/Senorita Rita – Teddy Brown (prod Pinpoint)   7.71

7828   Salt Of The Earth/Salt Rock – Dandy (prod Dandy [Robert Thompson])   9.71

7829   NYT

7830   Tell It Like It Is/BBC – Nicky Thomas (prod Nicky Thomas)   7.71

7831   Hot Honolulu Night/Jane – Monsoon (prod Eddie Seaga)   7.71

7832   One Big Happy Family/Heaven Child – Bruce Ruffin (prod Bruce Anthony)   7.71

7833   In Paradise/Take Me As I Am – Jackie Edwards & Julie Ann (actually Judy
Mowatt)/Jackie Edwards (prod Jackie Edwards)   8.71

7834   Follow The Leader/Funky Jamaica – Greyhound (prod Dave Bloxham)   8.71

7835   Jamaica/Sea Wave – Honey Boy/The Hi-Tals (prod Des Bryan & Webster Shrowder) 9.71

7836   Come On Girl/So Many Ways – Jackie Edwards (prod Jackie Edwards)   9.71

7837   Help Me Make It Through The Night/Reconsider Our Love – Joyce Bond
(prod Dandy [Robert Thompson])   9.71

7838   Call Me Number One/Gypsy – The Aces (prod Carl Blake & Barry Howard) 10.71

7839   The Birds & The Bees/My Family – The Daytrippers (prod Roger Easterry &
Des Champ)   10.71

7840   One Woman/You Don't Know – Bob Andy (prod Bob Andy) (reissue of Trojan TR
7821A and reissued on Horse HOSS 31A)

7841 NYT

7842 Hysteriacide/One Dream – Count Prince Miller (prod Count Prince Miller)   11.71

7843 NYT

7844 issued on TR 7876

7845 Those Good, Good Old Days/Pack Up Hang-Ups – Jimmy Cliff (prod Jimmy Cliff) 11.71

7846 Give & Take/Pride & Passion – The Pioneers (prod Jimmy Cliff)   1971

7847 Licking Stick/Live & Learn – Desmond Dekker (prod Leslie Kong & Desmond Dekker)   11.71

7848 Moon River/I've Been Trying/The Pressure Is Coming On – Greyhound (prod Dave Bloxham) (maxi-single)   12.71

7849 Johnny Cool Man/Johnny Cool Man (Version) – The Maytals/Beverley's All Stars (prod Leslie Kong)   12.71

7850 Yesterday Man/I Can't Stand It – Nicky Thomas (prod Nicky Thomas)   1971

7851 Sex Machine/You Left & Gone – Dave Barker & The Aggrovators (prod Edward 'Bunny' Lee) (reissue of Jackpot JP 751, but existence unconfirmed)   1971

7852 Mother & Child Reunion/Corner Hop – The Uniques (actually The Pioneers) (prod Sidney Crooks for Bush)   2.72

7853 I Am What I Am/Sky High – Greyhound (prod Dave Bloxham) (reissued on Trojan TR 7927)   1972

7854 But I Do/I Don't Care – Bob [Andy] & Marcia [Griffiths] (prod Bob Andy & Clive Crawley)   1972

7855 You Don't Know Like I Know/Sometimes I'm Lonely – The Pioneers (prod Sidney Crooks & Clive Crawley)   1972

7856 For Your Precious Love/For Your Precious Love (Version) – Vic Taylor/Byron Lee & The Dragonaires (prod Byron Lee)   1972

7857 What Do You Want To Make Those Eyes At Me For?/Talking About Sally – Dandy (prod Robert Thompson)   1972

7858 Just Because/Yes I Will – Danny Ray (prod Jackie Edwards) (A-side reissued on Trojan TRO 7993B)   1972

7859 Pitter Patter/Litchfield Gardens – Ernie Smith (prod Richard Khouri)   1972

7860 Roll Muddy River/Auntie Roachie – The Pioneers (prod Sidney Crooks & Clive Crawley)   1972

7861 I'll Take You There/Tropical Lament – The Deltones (A-side actually by The Pioneers) (prod Bush)   1972

7862 Suzanne Beware Of The Devil/Doing The Moonwalk – Nicky Thomas (prod Shady Tree/Joe Gibbs) (B-side also issued on Horse Hoss 29B)   1972

7863 Star Trek/Concord – The Vulcans/The Prophets (prod Bush/Swan) (B-side reissue of Big Shot BI 550B)   1972

7864 Ebony Eyes/Ebony Eyes (Version) – The Chosen Few/The Crystalites (prod Derrick Harriott)   1972

7865 Louie Louie/Pressure Drop '72 – The Maytals (prod Chris Blackwell And Warwick Lyn)   1972

7866 Lonely For Your Love/Chick A Bow – The Uniques (actually The Pioneers)/The Lion's Den (A-side prod Bush/B-side prod Webster Shrowder, Des Bryan & Joe Sinclair) (B-side reissue of Trojan TR 7797B)   8.72

7867   Floating/I Troubles – Greyhound (prod Dave Bloxham)   8.72

7868   Come On Over To My Place/I'll Be Standing By – Jackie Robinson (prod Jackie Robinson)   8.72

7869   The World Needs Love/Destiny – The Pioneers (prod Sidney Crooks)   9.72

7870   Sugarloaf Hill/Baby Don't Wake Me – Del Davis (prod Count Prince Miller/Jackie Edwards (prod Jackie Edwards) (B-side reissue of Bread BR 1105A)   9.72

7871   Julie On My Mind/Miss Black & Beautiful – Danny Ray (prod Jackie Edwards)   9.72

7872   Then He Kissed Me/All The Day Long – The Marvels (prod Clive Crawley)   10.72

7873   Working On It Night & Day/Take A Look – The Aces (prod Carl Blake & Barry Howard)   10.72

7874   Pomps & Pride/Pomps & Pride (Part 2) – The Maytals/Byron Lee & The Dragonaires (prod Warrick Lynn)   1972

7875   Shocks Of Mighty/Monkey Spanner (Version) – Dave Barker & The Upsetters/Dave [Barker] & Ansel Collins (prod Lee Perry/Winston Riley) (A-side reissue of Upsetter US 331A/B-side reissued of Techniques TE 914B)   1972

7876   It Gotta Be So/The First Time For A Long Time – Desmond Dekker (prod Leslie Kong)   1972

7877   NYT

7878   Images Of You/I'll Be Waiting – Nicky Thomas (prod Nicky Thomas) (A-side also issued on Horse HOSS 29A/B-side reissued on Trojan TR 7885B & TRO 9026B)   1972

7879   Time Hard/Fall In Love – George Dekker/Sidney, George & Jackie [The Pioneers] (prod Sidney Crooks)   1972

7880   I Believe In Love/Habit – The Pioneers (prod Sidney Crooks)   10.72

7881   Reggae Christmas/Candy Man – The Gable Hall School Choir (prod Johnny Arthey) (reissued on Trojan TR 7943)   1972

7882   Everybody Plays The Fool/You're A Big Girl Now – The Chosen Few (prod Derrick Harriott) (B-side also issued on Grape GR 3033A)   1972

7883   White Christmas/My Love & I – Jackie Edwards (prod Chris Blackwell/Jackie Edwards)   1972

7884   Hat Trick/Wet Vision – U Roy (prod Edward 'Bunny' Lee)   1972

7885   Have A Little Faith/I'll Be Waiting – Nicky Thomas (prod Joe Gibbs) (B-side reissue of Trojan TR 7878B & Reissued on TRO 9026B)   1973

7886   Nice Nice Time/Lottery Spin – Zap Pow (prod Harry Johnson) (B-side also issued on Harry J HJ 6650B)   3.73

7887   Groovy Situation/The Loser – Derrick Harriott (prod Derrick Harriott) (prod Derrick Harriott) (A-side reissue of Song Bird SB 1042A)   3.73

7888   At The Discothèque/Step By Step – The Pioneers (prod Sidney Crooks)   1973

7889   What About You/Come Beside Me – Pat Rhoden (prod Pat Rhoden)   1973

7890   Check Out Yourself/Happy People – The Cimarons (prod Dandy [Robert Thompson] & Joe Sinclair)   1973

7891   Ton-Up Kids/Bandwagon – Dave [Barker] & Ansel Collins (prod Larry Lawrence)   1973

7892   You Can't Buy My Love/The First Cut Is The Deepest – Donna Dawson (prod Sidney Crooks)   1973

7893	Is It Because I'm Black?/Black, Gold & Green – Ken Boothe (prod Lloyd Charmers) (reissued on Trojan TRO 9052B)	1973
7894	Am I Black Enough For You?/Message From A Blackman – The Chosen Few (prod Derrick Harriott)	1973
7895	Theme From 'Peyton Place'/Do What You Wanna Do – Jackie Edwards (prod Jackie Edwards)	1973
7896	Keep Your Mouth Shut/Move Away – George Dekker (B-side actually The Sidney Crooks Band) (prod George Agard [George Dekker])	1973
7897	Bad To Be Good/Smoking – The Pioneers (prod Sidney Crooks, George Agard & Jackie Robinson [The Pioneers])	1973
7898	NYT	
7899	Big One/Oh She Is A Big Girl Now – Judge Dread (prod Joe Sinclair)	10.73
7900	Way Over Yonder/Way Over Yonder (Version) – Judy Mowatt/The Gaytones (prod Sonia Pottinger)	10.73
7901	The Whole World's Down On Me/For The Good Times (Instrumental) – BB Seaton & Ken Boothe/Mickie Chung & The Now Generation (prod Lloyd Charmers)	1973
7902	Reggae From The Ghetto/Light Your Fire – John Holt (prod Tony Ashfield & Mike Berry)	1973
7903	I'm Gonna Get Married/How Can I Control You? – Danny Ray (prod Jackie Edwards)	1973
7904	He's Got The Whole World In His Hands/Got To Get Away – The Marvels (prod Dandy [Robert Thompson])	1973
7905	Molly/Dr Kitch – Judge Dread (prod Joe Sinclair)	1973
7906	A Little Bit Of Soap/Hit Me With Music – The Pioneers (prod Sidney Crooks, George Agard & Jackie Robinson [The Pioneers]) (A-side reissued on Trojan TRO 9041A)	1973
7907	Let's Get It On/Mother Mary – Lloyd Charmers (prod Lloyd Charmers)	1973
7908	Pardon/Rub It Up – George Dekker (prod Sidney Crooks, George Agard And Jackie Robinson [The Pioneers])	1974
7909	Help Me Make It Through The Night/Tell Me Why – John Holt (prod Tony Ashfield)	1974
7910	(That's The Way) Nature Planned It/Nature Planned It (Version) – Ken Boothe/The Charmers (prod Lloyd Charmers) (A-side reissued on Trojan TR 7960A)	1974
7911	Soul Shakedown Party/Caution – Bob Marley & The Wailers (prod Leslie Kong) (A-side reissue of TR 7759A)	1974
7912	Emergency Call/Emergency Call Version – Judy Mowatt/The Gaytones (prod Sonia Pottinger) (reissue of Gayfeet GS 207)	1974
7913	I'm Gonna Knock On Your Door/Some Living, Some Dying – The Pioneers (prod Sidney Crooks)	1974
7914	The Lord's Prayer/PEO 111 – Annetta Jackson & Bobby Stephen/Des All Stars (prod Des Bryan & Webster Shrowder)	1974
7915	Here I Am Baby/Tit For Tat – Al Brown & Skin, Flesh & Bones/Skin, Flesh & Bones (prod Dickie Wong & Geoffrey Chung)	1974
7916	Play Me/Play Me (Version) – Marcia Griffiths/Lloyd Charmers (prod Lloyd Charmers)	1974

7917	Ain't It A Beautiful Morning/Make Me Your Number One – Danny Ray (prod Jackie Edwards)	1974
7918	You're My Future Wife/Do You Believe In Love – Jackie Edwards (prod Jackie Edwards)	5.74
7919	Over The Rainbow/We Are Not The Same – The Cimarons (prod Car Levy)	5.74
7920	Everything I Own/Drum Song – Ken Boothe/Ken Boothe (actually by Lloyd Charmers) (prod Lloyd Charmers)	5.74
7921	Get On Your Feet/Love Is Here – The Marvels (prod Dimple Hinds & Shady Tree)	1974
7922	If You're Ready, Come Go With Me/If You're Ready (Version) – Cynthia Richards/We The People Band (prod Lloyd Parks)	1974
7923	Honey Bee/Hot Blooded Man – The Pioneers (prod Sidney Crooks & Eddy Grant) (Trojan blue label)	1974
7924	I'd Love You To Want Me/I'm Dying For You – Ernie Smith (prod Federal)	1974
7925	Young, Gifted & Black/We Know – Bob [Andy] & Marcia [Griffiths] (prod Harry Johnson) (reissue of Harry J HJ 6605A)	1974
7926	Mr Brown/Dracula – Bob Marley & The Wailers/The Upsetters (prod Lee Perry) (both sides reissues of Upsetter label US 354/A-side reissued on Trojan TR 7979A)	1974
7927	I Am What I Am/Sky High – Greyhound (prod Dave Bloxham) (reissue of Trojan TR 7853)	7.74
7928	Back On The Scene/Newsboy – Junior English (prod Ellis Breary)	7.74
7929	Only A Child/Love Thy Neighbour – Nicky Thomas (prod Nicky Thomas & C Trout)	8.74
7930	You Can Get It If You Really Want/Reggae Time – The Cimarons (prod Carl Levy)	1974
7931	Jamaica Jerkoff/Grandma Grandpa – The Pioneers (prod Sidney Crooks)	1974
7932	NYT	
7933	You Make Me Feel Brand New/TSOP – The Inner Circle (prod Tommy Cowan)	8.74
7934	Play De Music/Play De Music Version – Tinga Stewart (prod Ernie Smith)	9.74
7935	I've Got To Go On Without You/I've Got To Go On Without You (Version) – Al Brown/Skin, Flesh & Bones (prod Dickie Wong & Geoffrey Chung)	11.74
7936	Play Me/Going In Circles – Marcia [Griffiths] & Lloyd [Charmers]/The Charmers (actually by Bobby Blue [Bobby Davis]) (B-side reissue of Duke DU 86A)	11.74
7937	Passing Strangers/Pick Yourself Up – The Marvels (prod Dandy [Robert Thompson])	1974
7938	Morning side Of The Mountain/Riding My Bicycle – Danny Ray (prod Dandy [Robert Thompson])	11.74
7939	Sweet Number One/Tall Oak Tree – The Pioneers (prod Sidney Crooks)	12.74
7940	Everybody Plays The Fool/Hard Feeling – The Chosen Few (prod Derrick Harriott)	12.74
7941	This Is Reggae Music/Break Down The Barriers (prod Tommy Cowan)	12.74
7942	Code Of Love/I'm Lonely No More – Teddy Brown (prod Sidney Crooks)	1974
7943	Reggae Christmas/Candy Man – The Gable Hall School Choir (prod Johnny Arthey) (reissue of Trojan TR 7881)	12.74
7944	Crying Over You/Now You Can See Me Again – Ken Boothe (prod Lloyd Charmers)	12.74
7945	Lover's Question/Question Sign – Lloyd Charmers (prod Lloyd Charmers)	12.74

7946	Oh My My/Puppet & Clown – Winston Groovy (prod Sidney Crooks)	12.74
7947	Lola/Mama's Song – Nicky Thomas (prod Nicky Thomas/Joe Gibbs)	1974
7948	Road Block/Forward Jah Jah Children – Inner Circle (prod Tommy Cowan)	2.75
7949	Al Capone/Anna – Emperor Rosko/The Main Men (prod Alted Productions) (A-side reissue of Trojan TR 7758A)	1.75
7950	Got To Have You Baby/Got To Have You Baby (Version) – Lord Tanamo (prod Joseph Gordon [Lord Tanamo])	2.75
7951	Sinner Man/Bend Down Low – Gregory Isaacs (prod Sidney Crooks)	3.75
7952	All For Jesus/All For Jesus – Ernie Smith (prod Federal)	3.75
7953	You Baby/Open The Door – John Holt (prod Tony Ashfield)	3.75
7954	Why Seek More/Version – Dennis Brown/The Observers (prod Winston 'Niney' Holness)	5.75
7955	I'll Take You Where The Music's Playing/All In The Family – The Melodians (prod Sonia Pottinger)	4.75
7956	Ramgoat Liver/Ramgoat Version – Pluto Shervington (prod Federal) (reissued on Trojan TR 7978 & TRO 9066)	4.75
7957	Midnight Train To Georgia/We Really Need Each Other – Teddy Brown (prod Jeff Calvert)	4.75
7958	Words Are Impossible/Bad Words – Cynthia Schloss/Now Generation All Stars (prod Winston Blake)	4.75
7959	Your Kiss Is Sweet/Judgement – Inner Circle (prod Tommy Cowan)	4.75
7960	(It's The Way) Nature Planned It/Sad & Lonely – Ken Boothe (prod Lloyd Charmers) (A-side reissue of Trojan TR 7910A)	3.75
7961	Touch Me Baby/Gambling Ain't No Good – The Marvels (prod Dandy [Robert Thompson]) And Shady Tree)	4.75
7962	I See You/Rainbow – Funky Brown (actually Al Brown) (prod Federal)	6.75
7963	Key Card/Key Card (Version) – Ernie Smith (prod Federal)	5.75
7964	Time Is The Master Of Man/Read The News – Tito Simon (prod Keith Foster [Tito Simon]) (B-side reissued on Trojan TRO 9002B & also issued on Horse HOSS 125B)	1975
7965	Can't Get Used To Losing You/Jane Anne – Danny Ray (prod Dandy [Robert Thompson] And Shady Tree) (A-side reissued on Trojan TRO 7993A)	5.75
7966	Let's Go/Let's Go (Version) – Ken Boothe (prod Lloyd Charmers)	1975
7967	For Your Love/For Your Love (Version) – Cynthia Richards (prod unknown)	6.75
7968	Long Shot Kick The Bucket/Money Day – The Pioneers (prod Leslie Kong) (A-side reissue of Trojan TR 672A & reissued on TRO 9063A/B-side reissue of Trojan TR 7781A & reissued on TR 7968B & TRO 7995B)	6.75
7969	Shaving Cream/Cream – Fabulous Five (prod Rahtid) (reissued on Trojan TRO 9047)	1975
7970	Being In Love/Being In Love (Version) – Derrick Harriott/The Crystalites (prod Derrick Harriott) (reissue of Song Bird SB 1078)	1975
7971	Help Me/Running Over – Freddy McKay (prod Sonny Binns & Trevor Starr)	1975
7972	Wolf In Sheep's Clothing/Wolf Run – Big Youth (prod Manley Buchanan [Big Youth])	1975

7973	Eighteen With A Bullet/Eighteen With A Bullet (Version) – Derrick Harriott (prod Derrick Harriott)	1975
7974	Baby Hang Up The Phone/I'll Be Your Man – Lloyd Parks (prod Lloyd Parks)	1975
7975	I'd Love You To Want Me/Morning Of My Life – John Holt (prod Ton Ashfield)	1975
7976	Run Johnny/Run Johnny (Version) – Lorna Bennett (prod Harry Johnson)	1976
7977	Hit The Road Jack/Hit The Road Jack (Version) – Big Youth (prod Manley Buchanan [Big Youth])	1976
7978	Ramgoat Liver/Ramgoat (Version) – Pluto Shervington (prod Federal) (reissue of Trojan TR 7956 and reissued on TRO 9066)	1976
7979	Mr Brown/Trenchtown Rock – Bob Marley & The Wailers (prod Lee Perry/ Bob Marley) (A-side reissue of Upsetter US 354A and Trojan TR 7926A/ B-side reissue of Green Door GD 4005A)	1976
7980	Ramblin' Man/Live The Life You Love – Gene Rondo (prod Keith Bonsoir)	1976
7981	Why Do Fools Fall In Love/Dancing The Reggae – Derrick Harriott (prod Derrick Harriott) (A-side reissue of Harry J label HJ 6671)	1976
7982	Mama Papa/Manuel Road – The Soul Syndicate (prod Harry Johnson)	1976
7983	If You Don't Know Me By Now/Wild Honey – Zap Pow (prod Harry Johnson)	1976
7984	Laugh & Grow Fat/Laugh & Grow Fat (Version) – Winston Groovy (prod Winston Tucker [Winston Groovy])	1976
7985	The Wonder Of You/The Wonder Of You (Version) – Lloyd Parks (prod Lloyd Parks)	1976
7986	Way Of Loving/Way Of Loving (Version) – Lloyd Miller (prod Lloyd Miller & Steve Wady)	1976

TROJAN (TRO SERIES, PREFIX TRO)

7987	I'll Take A Melody/Peace & Love – John Holt (prod Tony Ashfield)	1976
7988	What's Going On/Ten Against One – Big Youth (prod Manley Buchanan)	1976
7989	Reverand Lee/The Other Woman – Lorna Bennett (prod Harry Johnson)	1976
7990	Love Me For A Reason/Married Lady – Fab Five Inc [Fabulous Five] (prod Fab Five) (A-side reissued on Trojan TRO 9047B)	1976
7991	You'll Never Find/Mr Bojangles – John Holt (prod Edward 'Bunny' Lee)	1976
7992	Jah Bring I Joy/Joyful Dub – Bobby Melody (prod Alan Davidson)	1976
7993	Can't Get Used To Losing You/Just Because – Danny Ray (prod Dandy [Robert Thompson] And Shady Tree/Jackie Edwards) (A-side reissue of Trojan TR 7965A/B-side reissue of Trojan TR 7858A)	1976
7994	Take A Letter Maria/Version – Dandy (prod Dandy [Robert Thompson]) (A-side reissued on Trojan TR 7800A)	1976
7995	My Special Prayer/Money Day – The Pioneers (prod Sydney Crooks) (B-side reissue of Trojan TR 7781A & TR 7968B)	1976
7996	Run Away Pet/Version – Donna Dawson (prod Heavy Stone)	1977
7997	NYT	
7998	London/What Is Love? – Nicky Thomas (prod Nicky Thomas)	1977
7999	Soulful Lover Baby/Version – Floyd Lloyd [Seivreight] (prod Floyd Lloyd Seivreight & Harris Seaton)	1977

9000	Heavy Manners/Version – Prince Far I (prod Joe Gibbs) (on Lightning label)	1977
9001	Jah Jah Ital/Version – Diego & The Sons Of Jah (prod Trevor Starr)	1977
9002	Oh Patricia/Read The News – Tito Simon (prod Clancy Eccles/Keith Foster [Tito Simon] (reissue of Horse HOSS 125/B-side also issued on Trojan TR 7964B)	1977
9003	Silver Words/Speak Softly Love – Ken Boothe (prod Lloyd Charmers)	1977
9004	NYT	
9005	Keep It Like It Is/Fattie Bum Bum Gone To Jail – Louisa Marks/Laurel Aitken (prod Clement Bushay/Laurel Aitken)	1977
9006	Bonanza Ska/Napoleon Solo – Carlos Malcolm & His Afro Jamaican Rhythms/ Lyn Taitt & The Jets (A-side prod Carlos Malcolm/B-side prod Federal)	1977
9007	Why Must You Cry/Version – Barry Biggs (prod Mickie Chung & Neville Hinds)	1977
9008	Duppy Gunman/None Shall Escape The Judgement – Inner Circle (prod Cowan)	1977
9009	Long Time/Version – Winston Fergus (prod P Cann & Alan Davidson) (issued on Lightning label)	1977
9010	African Woman/Version – Winston Fergus (prod P Cann & Alan Davidson) (issued on Lightning label)	1977
9011	Feel Like Making Love/Version – Elizabeth Archer & The Equators (prod P Cann/Douglas/Carr) (issued on Lightning label)	1977
9012	Choking Kind/Playboy – Danny Ray (prod Jackie Edwards)	1977
9013	African Dub/Version – The Silvertones (prod Jerry McCarthy)	1977
9014	My Twenty Eight/My Twenty Eight Version – Thunderball (actually by The Silvertones) (prod Jerry McCarthy)	1977
9015	What A Situation/Version – The Silvertones (prod Jerry McCarthy)	1977
9016	NYT	1977
9017	Caribbean Way/Version – Lloyd Miller (prod Brian Carroll)	1977
9018	Let's Get It While It's Hot/Ungrateful Baby – John Holt (prod Edward 'Bunny' Lee)	1977
9019	Key Of Keys/Version – Michael 'Bammie' Rose (prod Melvurn Green)	1977
9020	I'll Be Free Some Day/Version – Candy Lewis (prod Clement Bushay)	1977
9021	Can't Satisfy/Version – Bagga (Matumbi) (prod Bevan Fagan)	1977
9022	Jah Jah No New/Satisfied Rock – Lambert Douglas (prod Bagga [Bevan Fagan])	1977
9023	Happiness/Dub – The Dingle Brothers (prod C. Francis)	1977
9024	When I Need You/Heavy Robbery – Owen Gray (prod Clement Bushay & Alan Davidson) (issued on Lightning label)	1977
9025	The Slave Trade/Roots – One Love (prod Bill Spencer) (issued on Lightning label)	1977
9026	Come Back Girl/I'll Be Waiting – Nicky Thomas (prod Nicky Thomas) (B-side reissue of Trojan TR 7878B & 7885B)	1977
9027	Man In Me/After Tonight – Matumbi (prod Dennis Bovell)	1977
9028	Nice & Easy/If You Need Me – Susan Cadogan (prod Lee Perry)	1977
9029	You Are Mine/Strange Thoughts – Honey Boy (prod Keith Williams [Honey Boy])	1977
9030	Everybody's Talking/Only A Smile – John Holt (prod Edward 'Bunny' Lee)	1977
9031	NYT	
9032	After Tonight/Go Back Home – Bagga Matumbi (prod Bevan Fagan)	1978
9033	Love Grows/Two Timer – Lloyd Miller (prod Tito Simon)	1978

9034 Right Road To Zion/Right Road To Dubland – The Jahlights (prod Bill Spencer) 1978
9035 Pie In The Sky/Version – Eugene Paul (prod Tito Simon) 1978
9036 Freedom Day/Love Don't Love Nobody – Ken Boothe (prod Lloyd Charmers) 1978
9037 Rivers Of Babylon/Give The Children Food – The Melodians/Owen Gray
(prod Leslie Kong/Clement Bushay) (A-side reissue of Summit SUM 8508 & 8532) 1978
9038 NYT
9039 The Greatest Love Of All/Version – Owen Gray/Jah Son (prod Clement Bushay) 1978
9040 Let's Spend The Night Together/Heavy Reggae Man – Teddy & The Discolettes
(prod OCR [Orbach & Chambers Ltd]) 1978
9041 A Little Bit Of Soap/Over & Over – The Pioneers (prod Sidney Crooks,
George Agard & Jackie Robinson) (A-side reissue of Trojan TR 7906A) 1978
9042 NYT
9043 Riot In A Notting Hill/Anuma – The Pioneers (prod Sidney Crooks) 1978
9044 Come Closer To Me/Sincerely – Jackie Edwards (prod Jackie Edwards/Bunny Lee) 1978
9045 Who Dun It? (Muhammed Ali)/Sweet Lorraine – Lloyd Miller (prod Tito Simon
[Keith Foster]) 1978
9046 Only A Fool Breaks His Own Heart/Maria – Mighty Sparrow (prod Byron Lee)
(calypso reissue of DU 114) 1978
9047 Shaving Cream/Love Me For Reason – Fab Five [Fabulous Five] (prod Rahtid/
Fab Five) (A-side reissue of Trojan TR 7969A/B-side reissue of Trojan TR 7990A) 1978
9048 Duppy Gunman/Key Card – Ernie Smith (prod Ernie Smith) 1978
9049 NYT
9050 Tell The Children The Truth/Seeing Is Believing – Jimmy Riley (prod Jimmy Riley) 1978
9051 Only issued as a 12" single
9052 Who Gets Your Love?/Is It Because I'm Black – Ken Boothe (prod Phil Pratt/
Lloyd Charmers) (B-side reissue of Trojan TR 7893A) 1979
9053 Barberman Bawling/Version – Well, Pleased & Satisfied (prod Paul Johnson) 1979
9054 Just The Way You Are/Fancy Make-Up – John Holt (prod Keith Bonsoir) 1979
9055 Nothing Gained (From Loving You)/Can't Go Through With Life – Marie Pierre
(prod Dennis Bovell) 1979
9056 Let Me Down Easy/Witchita Lineman – Dennis Brown (prod Derrick Harriott) 1979
9057 Walk Away/Nothing Gained (From Loving You) – Marie Pierre (prod Dennis
Bovell) 1979
9058 Liquid Horns/The Liquidator – Vin Gordon & The Corner Shots/Junior
The Corner Shots (prod Fat Man [Ken Gordon]) 1979
9059 Al Capone/Anna – Emperor Rosko/The Main Men (prod Alted Productions)
(A-side reissue of Trojan TR 7758 & TR 7949) 1979
9060 Choose Me/Someone Else's Man – Marie Pierre (prod Dennis Bovell) 1979
9061 Issued as a 12" single only
9062 Skinhead Moonstomp/Skinhead Jamboree – Symarip (prod Philigree) (A-side
reissue of Treasure Isle TI 7050A) 1980
9063 Long Shot Kick The Bucket/Liquidator – The Pioneers/Winston Wright & The
Harry J All Stars (prod Leslie Kong/Harry Johnson) (A-side reissue of Trojan TR

672A & TR 7968A/B-side reissue of TR 675A) 1980
9064 Issued as a 12" single only 1980
9065 Thank You Lord/Wisdom – Bob Marley & The Wailers (prod Bob Marley) 1981
9066 Walk Away/Version – Marie Pierre (prod Dennis Bovell) (reissue of Horse HOSS 157) 1981
9066 Ram Goat Liver/Version – Pluto Shervington (prod Federal) (reissue of Trojan TR 7956 & TR 7978 – duplicate issue on this number) 1981
9067 Love Of The Common People/Have A Little Faith – Nicky Thomas (prod Joe Gibbs) (reissue of Trojan TR 7750A) 1980
9068 Issued as a 12" single only
9069 Issued as a 12" single only
9070 Issued as a 12" single only
9071 Issued as a 12" single only
9072 Issued as a 12" single only
9073 The Ten Commandments – Judge Dread (prod Alted) 1980
9074 Soul Shakedown Party/Caution – Bob Marley & The Wailers (prod Leslie Kong) (reissue of Trojan TR 7911) 1981
9075 Cherry Oh Baby/Please Don't Make Me Cry/Red Red Wine (prod Edward 'Bunny' Lee/Winston Tuckjer [Groovy]/Robert Thompson [Dandy]) 1984
9076 54 46 Was My Number/Train To Skaville – The Maytals/The Ethiopians (prod Leslie Kong/Leonard Dillon)
9077 Too Much Love/Mr Bojangles – John Holt (prod Tony Ashfield) 1984
9078 Hippopotomus/007 – Desmond Dekker & The Aces (prod Leslie Kong) 1984
9079 Sensi For Sale/Depression Sandra Robinson (prod Ossie Ranks) 1985
9080 Merry Christmas, Happy New Year/Return Of Django – Lee Perry featuring Sandra Robinson/The Upsetters (prod Lee Perry) 1985
9081 Issued as a 12" single only
9082 Sexy Lady/All Things Are Possible – Lee 'Scratch' Perry & The Upsetters 1986
9083 Papers/Frozen Moments – Alan Price (prod Alan Price) 1986
9084 Do It Right/Opportunity – The Pioneers (prod Sidney Crooks) 1986
9085 Issued as a 12" single only
9086 Issued as a 12" single only
9087 Issued as a 12" single only
9088 You Make Me Feel Brand New/Elizabethan Reggae – Boris Gardiner/Boris Gardiner (& The Love People) (prod Lloyd Charmers/Junior Chung) 1986
9089 Reggae Me/Shub In – George Dekker (prod Sidney Crooks) 1986
9090 Reggae In London City/My Woman – The Pioneers (prod Sidney Crooks) 1986
9091 Heart Made Of Stone/Heart Made Of Stone (Version) – Audrey Hall (prod Edward 'Bunny' Lee & Joe Richards) 1986
9092 Bring It On Home To Me/He'll Understand – Ken Boothe (prod Lloyd Charmers) 1986
9093 Issued as a 12" single only
9094 A Sppace Man Came Travelling/My Oh My – John Holt (prod Edward 'Bunny' Lee & Joe Richards) 1986

9095   Merry Christmas, Happy New Year/The Perry Christmas Dub – Lee Perry
       featuring Sandra Robinson (prod Lee Perry)   1986

9096   Issued as a 12" single only

9097   Yodel Reggae/Yodel Dub – Leroy Gibbs (prod Desmond Rowe)   1987

9098   Issued as a 12" single only

9099   Do It Right/Honour Your Mother And Father – Desmond Dekker (prod Steve
       Grant & Delroy Wilson)   1987

9100   Not issued

9101   Wonderful World, Beautiful People/Licking Stick – Desmond Dekker
       (prod Steve Grant & Delroy Williams)   1987

9102   Not issued

9103   You Can Get It If You Really Want/If You Can't Do The Time – Mr Bojangles
       (actually by Delroy Williams) (prod Steve Grant & Delroy Williams)   1991

TROJAN 12" SERIES (PREFIX TROT)

9051   Rock With Me Baby/Lady Love – John Holt (prod Edward 'Bunny' Lee)   1978

9057   Walk Away/Nothing Gained (From Loving You) – Marie Pierre (prod Dennis
       Bovell)   1979

9061   Skinhead Moon/Stomp Skinhead Jamboree/Fung Shu – Symarip (prod Philigree) 1979

9063   Liquidator/Long Shot Kick De Bucket – Harry J All Stars/The Pioneers
       (prod Harry Johnson/Leslie Kong)   1979

9064   Herbsman Shuffle/Phantom/Fire Corner/Next Corner/Vigorton Two –
       King Stitt/Dynamites (prod Clancy Eccles)   1980

9067   Love Of The Common People/Have A Little Fairth – Nicky Thomas
       (prod Joe Gibbs)   1980

9068   Settle Down Girl/Settle Down Girl (Version) – Tristan Palmer (prod Linval
       Thompson)   1982

9069   Ghetto-Ology/Walking Through The Ghetto – Sugar Minott (prod Lincoln Minott) 1982

9070   Me Chat You Rock/It's Me – U Brown (prod Hugh Brown)   1982

9071   If I Didn't Want Your Loving/If I Didn't Want Your Loving (Version) –
       The Majesterians (prod Linval Thompson)   1983

9072   The Iron Lady (Maggie May)/Mr Reagan, President Of The United States –
       Ranking Trevor

9074   Soul Shakedown Party/Caution/Keep On Skanking – Bob Marley & The Wailers
       (prod Leslie Kong/Lee Perry)   1983

9075   Cherry Oh Baby/Please Don't Make Me Cry/Red, Red Wine/Many Rivers To
       Cross – Eric Donaldson/Winston Groovy/Tony Tribe/Jimmy Cliff (prod Edward
       'Bunny' Lee/Trojan/Robert Thompson/Leslie Kong)   1983

9077   Too Much Love/Mr. Bojangles/You'll Never Find Another Love Like Mine/Help
       Me Make It Through The Night – John Holt (prod Tony Ashfield/Bunny Lee)   1984

9078   Hippotamus/007/It Mek – Desmond Dekker & The Aces (prod Leslie Kong)   1984

9079   Sensi For Sale (Part 1)/Boogie Mix (Part 2)/Depression/Life's Riddle/Boogie Mix

       Sandra Robinson/The Tuff Tones/Sandra Robinson & The Tuff Tones/Dan
       Ambrassa & Tuff Tones (prod Ossie Ranks)   1985

9080   Merry Christmas, Happy New Year (The Perry Mix)/Merry Christmas, Happy
New Year (The Crossover/Radio Mix)/Return Of Django (Original Version)/
All Things Are Possible (Django '85) – Lee Perry & Sandra Robinson/The Upsetters/
Lee Perry (prod Lee Peery)   1985

9081   Let It Play/Digital Style/Having Fun/Rastafari/Mafia History – Akenzie Stevens
& The Tufftones/Winston Turner & The Tufftones/The Tufftones/Winston Turner
& The Tufftones/Isly Ren & The Tufftones (prod Ossie Ranks)   1986

9085   Pirate/Pirate (Version)/Pirate (Original Version) – The Ethiopians (prod Leonard
Dillon/Duke Reid)   1986

9086   War Ina South Africa/Vocal Dub version/Version – Killerman Jarrett (prod Tony
Shabazz & Patrick 'Scabba' Sutherland)   1986

9087   If You Leave Me (aka Don't Stay Away)/Jailhouse/Jailhouse (Version) –
Private Tabby (prod Tony Shabazz & Patrick 'Scabba' Sutherland)   1986

9091   Heart Made Of Stone/Heart Made Of Stone (Version)/It's Hard To Believe/It's
Hard To Believe (Version) – Audrey Hall/Don Evans (prod Edward 'Bunny' Lee) 1986

9092   Bring It On Home To Me/He'll Understand – Ken Boothe (prod Lloyd Charmers) 1986

9093   You're Everything To Me/You're Everything To Me Version/I'll Be Everything To
You/I'll Be Everything To You (Instrumental) – John Holt & The Hit Squad/June
Powell & The Hit Squad (prod Edward 'Bunny' Lee/Joe Richards)   1986

9096   What Is Man/Joe Blake/Hangin' On/Pull Up 88 – Vivian Withers (prod Viv,
John & Jimmy)   1987

9097   Yodel Reggae (Club Mix)/Yodel Reggae (Radio Mix)/Yodel Dub – Leroy Gibbs
(prod Desmond Rowe)   1987

9098   Israelites – Desmond Dekker/Israelites (Live Version) (prod unknown, existence
unconfirmed)   1988

TROJAN 12" (PREFIX TRD)
101A   Rock With Me Baby/Lady Love – John Holt (prod Edward 'Bunny' Lee)   1978

TROJAN MAXI SINGLES (PREFIX TRM)
3001   Young, Gifted And Black/Private Number/Pied Piper – Bob & Marcia
(prod Harry Johnson/Bob Andy)

3002   Double Barrel/Stone In Love/Monkey Spanner – Dave & Ansel Collins
(prod Winston Riley/Larry Lawrence)

3003   Love Of The Common People/Have A Little Faith/Yesterday Man – Nicky Thomas
(prod Joe Gibbs/Nicky Thomas)

3004   Liquidator/My Cherie Amour/Je Táime – The Harry J All Stars (prod Harry Johnson)

3005   Black And White/I Am What I Am/Moon River – Greyhound (prod Dave
Bloxham)

3006   Let Your Yeah Be Yeah/Sweet Inspiration/I Hear You Knocking – The Pioneers
(prod Jimmy Cliff/Sidney Crooks)

3007   Phoenix City/Guns Of Navarone/Guns Fever – Roland Alphonso/The Skatalites/
Baba Brooks (prod Coxsone Dodd/Duke Reid)

3008   No One Day Love/What Good Is Life/One More Chance – Winston Groovy
(prod Winston Groovy [Tucker])   1977

TROJAN MAXI SINGLES (PREFIX TMX)

4001 Trojan Explosion – Various (prod Various) 1979

To Be Young Gifted And Black/Black & White/Rivers Of Babylon/Ram Goat Liver – Bob & Marcia/Greyhound/The Melodians/Pluto Shervington

4002 Trojan Explosion 2 – Various (prod Various) 1979

Everything I Own/Song We Used To Sing/Montego Bay/You Can Get It If You Really Want – Ken Boothe/Desmond Dekker/Freddie Notes & The Rudies/ Desmond Dekker

4003 Trojan Explosion 3 – Various (prod Various) 1979

Help Me Make It Through The Night/This Monday Morning Feeling/Black Pearl/Pied Piper – John Holt/Tito Simon/Horace Faith/Bob & Marcia)

4004 Trojan Explosion 4 – Various (prod Various) 1979

Israelites/Long Shot Kick De Bucket/Monkey Spanner/Love Of The Common People – Desmond Dekker & The Aces/Pioneers/Dave & Ansel Colins/Nicky Thomas

4005 Trojan Explosion 5 – Various (prod Various) 1979

Liquidator/Return Of Django/Elizabethan Reggae/It Mek – Harry J & The All Stars/The Upsetters/Boris Gardiner (& The Love People)/Desmond Dekker & The Aces

4006 Trojan Explosion 6 – Various (prod Various) 1979

Let Your Yeah Be Yeah/007/Double Barrel/Suzanne Beware Of The Devil – The Pioneers/Desmond Dekker/Dave & Ansel Collins/Dandy Livingstone)

4007 Skinhead Moonstomp/Skinhead Jamboree/El Pussy Cat/Guns Of Navarone – Symarip/Symarip/Roland Alphonso/The Skatalites (prod Philligree/Clement 'Coxsone'; Dodd) 1979

4008 Rudy A Message To You/Tribute To The Prince/Bug City/Think About That – Dandy Livingstone (prod Robert Thompson [Dandy]) 1979

4009 Skinhead Classics – Various 1979

Train To Skaville/Monkey Man/Return Of Django/Phoenix City – The Ethiopians/The Maytals/The Upsetters/Roland Alphonso (prod Various) 1979

4010 Trojan Explosion – Various 1979

Israelites/Monkey Spanner/It Mek/Sideshow – Desmond Dekker & The Aces/ Dave & Ansel Collins/Desmond Dekker & The Aces/Barry Biggs (prod Various) 1979

4011 Big One/Big Six/Big Seven/Big Eight – Judge Dread (prod Bush) 1979

4012 Trojan Explosion Reggae Instrumental Hits – Various (prod Various) 1979

Tchaikovsky's Piano Concerto No 1/Take 5/Liquidator/Return Of Django – The Neasden Connection/Val Bennett/Harry J All Stars/The Upsetters

4013 Skinhead Classics Vol 2 – Various (prod Various) 1979

Barbwire/Skinhead Moonstomp/Wreck A Buddy/54–46 Was My Number – Nora Dean/Symarip/The Soul Sisters/Toots & The Maytals

4014 Trojan Explosion Vol 2 – Various (prod Various) 1979

Hurt So Good/Love Of The Common Pe ople/Crying Over You/Moon River – Susan Cadogan/Nicky Thomas/Ken Boothe/Greyhound 1979

TROJAN MAXI-SINGLES (PREFIX TRM)

9000	Songs Of Peace/You Are The Best/We Can Make It – Bruce Ruffin (prod Bruce Anthony)	2.72
9001	Chopsticks/I Got It/Put It On – The Deltones (prod Webster Shrowder, Des Bryan & Joe Sinclair)	1972
9002	NYT	
9003	Israelites/It Mek/007 – Desmond Dekker & The Aces (prod Leslie Kong)	1972
9004	Monkey Man/She's My Scorcher/One Eye Enos – The Maytals (prod Leslie Kong)	1972
9005	Sweet Sensation/Rivers Of Babylon/It Took A Miracle – The Melodians (prod Leslie Kong)	1972
9006	Are You Ready/Candida/Bitterness Of Life – Bruce Ruffin (prod Leslie Kong/ Herman Chin-Loy)	9.72
9007	NYT	
9008	Guns Of Navarone/Bonanza Ska/Napoleon Solo – The Skatalites/Carlos Malcolm & His Afro Jamaican Rhythms/Lynn Tait & The Jets (prod Coxsone Dodd/ Carlos Malcolm/Federal)	1972
9009	Pickney Gal/Peace In The Land/Hippopotamus – Desmond Dekker (prod Leslie Kong)	1972
9010	Phoenix City/El Pussy Cat Ska/Guns Fever – Roland Alphonso/Roland Alphonso/Baba Brooks (prod Coxsone Dodd/Duke Reid)	1972

UPSETTER (PREFIX US)

300	Eight For Eight/You Know What I Mean – The Upsetters/The Inspirations (also issued on Duke DU 11)	1969
301	Return Of Django/Dollar In The Teeth – The Upsetters (actually with Val Bennett)	1969
302	Good Father/What A Situation – David Isaacs/Slim Smith	1969
303	Ten To Twelve/People Funny Fi True – The Upsetters/The Upsetters (actually with Lee Perry)	1969
304	What A Price/How Can I Forget? – Busty Brown	1969
305	I've Got Memories/I'm Leaving – David Isaacs	1969
306	Mini Dress/Mad House – The Righteous Flames (actually with Winston Jarrett)/ The Upsetters (actually with Lee Perry)	1969
307	Night Doctor/I'll Be Waiting – The Upsetters/The Termites	5.69
308	To Love Somebody/Farmers In The Den – Busty Brown/The Bleechers	1969
309	Kiddyo/Endlessly – The Muskyteers (actually The Silvertones)	1969
310	Man From MI5/Oh Lord – The Upsetters/The West Indians	1969
311	He'll Have To Go/Since You're Gone – David Isaacs	1969
312	Badam Bam/Medical Operation – The Ravers/The Upsetters	7.69
313	Live Injection/Everything For Your Fun – The Upsetters/The Bleechers	8.69
314	Come Into My Parlour/Dry Your Tears – The Bleechers/The Mellotones	7.69
315	Cold Sweat/Pound Get A Blow – The Upsetters/The Upsetters (actually by The Bleechers)	1969
316	Hello Dolly/King Of The Trombone – Pat Satchmo/Busty Brown	1969

317	The Vampire/The Upsetter – The Upsetters/The Bleechers (first pressing with incorrect B-side credits)	1969
317	The Vampire/Check Him Out – The Upsetters/The Bleechers (second pressing with correct B-side credits)	1969
318	Soulful I/No Bread & Butter – The Upsetters/Milton Morris	1969
319	Who To Tell/I Can't See Myself Crying About You – David Isaacs (actually by Bruce Bennett)/Busty Brown	10.69
320	Dirty Dozen/Crying Too Long – The Shadows (actually The Jamaican Shadows)*	10.69
321	Drugs & Poison/Stranger On The Shore – The Upsetters	10.69
322	The Same Thing You Gave To Daddy/A Testimony – Nora Dean/Upsetter Pilgrims	1969
323	Same Thing/I Wear My Slanders – The Gaylads	11.69
324	Yakety Yak/Takio – The Upsetters (actually with Lee Perry)	1.70
325	Kill Them All/Soul Walk – The Upsetters (actually with Lee Perry)The Upsetters	3.70
326	Bronco (Old Man River)/One Punch – The Upsetters (actually with Sir Lord Comic)/The Upsetters (reissue of Trojan TR 644B)	2.70
327	Do You Like It/Touch Of Fire – Toots (actually Lee Perry)/The Upsetters	3.70
328	Consider Me/Consider Me (Version 2) – BB James [Busty Brown]	2.70
329	Melting Pot/Kinky Mood – The Heaters/The Upsetters	2.70
330	Spinning Wheel/Wheel Version 2 – Mel [Melanie Jonas] & Dave [Barker]	4.70
331	Shocks Of Mighty/Set Me Free – Dave Barker & The Upsetters (A-side reissued on Trojan TR 7875A)	3.70
332	Na Na Hey Hey/Pick Folk Kinkiest – The Upsetters	4.70
333	Granny Show/Granny Show Version – The Upsetters (actually with Dave Barker)	4.70
334	Fire Fire/Jumper – The Upsetters	5.70
335	The Pillow/Grooving – The Upsetters	5.70
336	Self-Control/The Pill – The Upsetters (actually by Martin Riley & Fay Bennett)/The Upsetters (actually by Martin Riley) ##	4.70
337	Let It Be/Big Dog Bloxie – The Soulettes/The Upsetters	6.70
338	Fresh Up/Toothaches – The Upsetters	9.70
339	Thanks We Get/Hurry Up – The Upsetters (actually by The Versatiles)	8.70
340	My Cup/Son Of Thunder – Bob Marley & The Wailers/The Upsetters (actually with Lee Perry)	8.70
341	Blood Poison/Thunder Version – The Upsetters	1970
342	Dreamland/Version Of Cup [My Cup Version] – The Upsetters	1970
343	Sipreano/Ferry Boat – The Upsetters (actually with Lee Perry)/The Upsetters	9.70
344	Some Sympathy/Tender Love – Dave Barker & The Upsetters/The Untouchables	10.70
345	Same Thing All Over/It's Over (Version) – The Untouchables/The Upsetters	1970
346	Bigger Joke/Return Of The Vampire – The Upsetters	1970
347	Sound Underground/Don't Let The Sun Catch You Crying – Dave Barker & The Upsetters/Dave Barker & The Wailers	11.70
348	Duppy Conqueror/Justice – Bob Marley & The Wailers/The Upsetters	10.70

349	Upsetting Station (actually Plays 'Duppy Conqueror')/Dig Your Grave – Bob Marley & The Wailers/The Upsetters (first pressing with wrong A-side)	10.70
349	Upsetting Station/Dig Your Grave – Dave Barker & The Upsetters/The Upsetters	1970
350	Tight Spot/Knock On Wood – Dave Barker & The Upsetters/The Untouchables	12.70
351	NYT	
352	Heart & Soul/Zig Zag – The Upsetters	1971
353	Elusion/Big John Wayne – Teddy (actually with The Upsetters)/The Upsetters	1.71
354	Mr Brown/Dracula – Bob Marley & The Wailers/The Upsetters (both sides reissued on Trojan TR 7926/A-side reissued on Trojan TR 7979A)	1.71
355	Confusion/Confusion Version – The Untouchables/The Upsetters	1971
356	Kaya/Kaya Version – Bob Marley & The Wailers/Bob Marley & The Wailers (actually by The Upsetters)	1971
357	Small Axe/All In One (Medley) – Bob Marley & The Wailers	2.71
358	Shocks '71/You've Got To Be Mine – Dave Barker (actually with Charlie Ace)/The Hurricanes (B-side reissued on Upsetter US 363A)	3.71
359	The Creeper/Creeping Version – Charlie Ace & The Upsetters/The Upsetters	3.71
360	NYT	
361	Copasetic/All Africans (actually titled 'Don't Cross The Nation') – The Upsetters (actually with U Roy)/The Upsetters (actually by Little Roy)	4.71
362	Groove Me/Screwdriver – Dave Barker/The Upsetters	4.71
363	You've Got To Be Mine/You've Got To Be Mine Version – The Hurricanes/The Upsetters (A-side reissue of Upsetter US 358A)	4.71
364	What A Confusion/Confusion Version 2 – Dave Barker (actually with Bunny Livingston)/The Upsetters	4.71
365	Earthquake/Place Called Africa – The Upsetters/Junior Byles	4.71
366	Run Up Your Mouth/Mouth Version – Rob Walker (actually by Stranger Cole)/The Upsetters	6.71
367	Never Had A Dream Come True/Never Had A Dream Come True Version – Glen Adams & The Upsetters	7.71
368	Picture On The Wall/Picture On The Wall Version – Rass [Karl] Dawkins & The Wailers/The Upsetters	7.71
369	More Axe/Axe Man – Bob Marley & The Wailers/The Upsetters (actually by Bongo Herman & Les Chen) (reissued on Upsetter US 372)	1971
370	Dark Moon/You'll Be Sorry – The Upsetters/David Isaacs	8.71
371	Dreamland/Dream Version – The Wailers (actually by Bunny Livingstone & The Upsetters)/The Upsetters	9.71
372	More Axe/Axe Man – Bob Marley & The Wailers/The Upsetters (actually by Bongo Herman & Les Chen) (reissue of Upsetter US 369)	9.71
373	Well Dread/Well Dread Version 2 – Dennis Alcapone/The Upsetters	1971
374	Piece Of My Heart/Piece Of My Heart Version – Mahalia Saunders (actually Hortense Ellis)/The Upsetters	1971
375	Earthquake (actually 'Earthquake Version')/Suspicious Minds – Hugh Roy (actually U Roy)/Mahalia Saunders (actually Hortense Ellis)	1971

376   Give Me Power/More Power – The Stingers/3rd & 4th Generation   1971

377   Alpha & Omega/Beat Down Babylon – Dennis Alcapone/Junior Byles   1971

378   Example Part 1/Example Part 2 – Winston Wright & 3rd & 4th Generation/
       3rd & 4th Generation With The Upsetters   12.71

379   Mighty Cloud Of Joy/Mighty Cloud Version – Mighty Sparks (actually by Lloyd
       Parks)   1971

380   Bet You Don't Know/Ring Of Fire (actually 'Babylon Chapter 5') – Chenley
       Duffus & The Soul Avengers/The Upsetters   1972

381   Wonder Man/Place Called Africa (actually titled 'Africa Stand') – Dennis
       Alcapone (actually with Dave Barker)/Dennis Alcapone   1972

382   Give Me Power Version 2/Public Enemy Number 1 – King Iwah & The Stingers/
       Max Romeo   1972

383   He Who Feels It/He Who Feels It (Chapter 2) – Prince Tallis & The Chalice/
       The Upsetters   1972

384   Blackman's Time/Black Supreme – Neville Grant/Ansel Collins & The Upsetters 1972

385   French Connection/French Connection Chapter 2 – Lee Perry & The Upsetters   1972

386   Babylon Burning/To Be Your Lover – Maxie [Romeo], Niney & Scratch/Chenley
       Duffus   1972

387   Festival Da Da/Da Da (Version) – Junior Byles/Lee Perry & The Upsetters   1972

388   Master Key/Key Hole – Dennis Alcapone/Dennis Alcapone & The Upsetters   8.72

389   Back Biter/Back Biter (Version) – Dennis Alcapone & Lee Perry/Lee Perry, Dennis
       Alcapone & The Upsetters   8.72

390   Whiplash/Whiplash Part 2 – Wesley ['Germs'] Martin/The Upsetters   9.72

391   Natty Natty/Natty Natty Version – ReGGie Lewis (actually Alva Lewis)/Alva
       Lewis & The Upsetters   9.72

392   Keep On Moving/African Herbsman – Bob Marley & The Wailers   1972

393   Crummy People (actually titled 'One Love, One Heart')/Moving Version –
       The Upsetters (actually by The Righteous Flames)/Big Youth   1972

394   Water Pump/Pumping Version – The Upsetters (actually with Lee Perry)   10.72

395   Preacher Man/Preacher Version – The Stingers/The Upsetters (actually with
       The Stingers)   10.72

396   Puss-See-Hole/I Want To Be Loved** – The Upsetters (actually with Lee Perry)/
       Winston Groovy   1972

397   Jungle Lion/Freakout Skank – Lee Perry & The Upsetters   1973

398   Cow Thief Skank.7 & Three Quarters Skank – Charlie Ace (actually with
       Lee Perry)/Charlie Ace & The Upsetters   3.73

399   News Flash/Flashing Echo – Leo Graham/Leo Graham & The Upsetters   1973

400   Stranger On The Shore/John Devour – David Isaacs/Dillinger   1973

*Note: All tracks produced by Lee Perry except * (Bobby Aitken productions), ## (Martin Riley
productions) and ** (a Winston Tucker [Groovy] production).*

REGGAE SINGLE RELEASES ON POP LABELS

B&C (PREFIX CB)
125 It Came Out Of The Sky/Oh Well – Freddie Notes & The Rudies (prod Joe
Sinclair & The Rudies) 1970

MOONCREST (PREFIX MOON) – REGGAE RELEASES ONLY
12 Battle Of New Orleans/Knocking On The Door – The Hot Shots (Clive Crawley
& The Cimarons) (prod Clive Crawley for Bush) 1973
13 Black Star/All Strung Out On You – Dandy Livingstone (prod Robert Thompson) 1973
20 Yesterday Man/Jerusalem Rock – The Hot Shots (Clive Crawley & The Cimarons)
(prod Clive Crawley) 1973
30 Caribbean/Caribbean (same title both sides) – The Hot Shots (Clive Crawley &
The Cimarons) (prod Clive Crawley) 1973

TROJAN PRE-RELEASES

The dates listed below indicate the year in which each recording was mastered by Trojan.

BZX SERIES
1 Chattie Chattie – Junior Murvin (prod Derrick Harriott) 1968
2 Magic Touch – Junior Murvin (prod Derrick Harriott) 1968
3 NYT
4 NYT
5 NYT
6 NYT
7 If You Can't Be Good Be Careful – The Gaylets (prod Federal) 1968
8 Something About My Man – The Gaylets (prod Federal) 1968
9 My Argument – Lloyd Charmers (prod Edward 'Bunny' Lee) 1968
10 Foey Man – George Dekker (prod Edward 'Bunny' Lee) 1968
11 The Prodigal Returns – Errol Dunkley (prod Edward 'Bunny' Lee) 1968
12 Nursery Rhyme Rocksteady – Errol Dunkley (prod Edward 'Bunny' Lee) 1968
13 What You Gonna Do – George Dekker (prod Edward 'Bunny' Lee) 1968
14 Great News – Alton Ellis & Flames (prod Edward 'Bunny' Lee) 1968
15 It's Alright Girl – Alton Ellis & Flames (prod Edward 'Bunny' Lee) 1968
17 Forest Gate Rock – Lester Sterling (prod Edward 'Bunny' Lee) 1968
18 It Might As Well Be Spring – Lester Sterling (prod Edward 'Bunny' Lee) 1968
19 NYT
20 Shower Of Rain – Derrick Morgan (prod Edward 'Bunny' Lee) 1968
21 NYT
22 The Clamp Is On – Errol Dunkley (prod Edward 'Bunny' Lee) 1968

23	Hold You Jack – Derrick Morgan (prod Edward 'Bunny' Lee)	1968
24	Too Bad – Derrick Morgan (prod Edward 'Bunny' Lee)	1968
25	One Morning In May – Derrick Morgan (prod Edward 'Bunny' Lee)	1968
26	It's Reggae Time – Don Tony Lee (prod Edward 'Bunny' Lee)	1968
27	Oh My Baby – The Harmonians (prod Albert Gene Murphy)	1968
28	Reggae Girl – The Tennors (prod Albert Gene Murphy)	1968
29	Gonna Make It – Cliff Smith (prod Albert Gene Murphy)	1968
30	Donkey Trot – Clive's All Stars (prod Albert Gene Murphy)	1968
31	Say I'm Back (He Is Back) – Monty Morris (prod Albert Gene Murphy)	1968
32	Go Your Way – The Harmonians (prod Albert Gene Murphy)	1968
31	In Like Flint – The Good Guys (prod Byron Lee)	1968
32	Nobody's Business – The Good Guys (prod Byron Lee)	1968
33	Power Cut – Abby Adams & His Boys (prod Edward 'Bunny' Lee)	1968
34	Robin Hood Rides Again – Abby Adams & His Boys (prod Edward 'Bunny' Lee)	1968
35	The Big Race (Adults Only) – Lord Power (prod Edward 'Bunny' Lee)	1968
36	Raw Calalue – Lord Power (prod Edward 'Bunny' Lee)	1968
37	NYT	
38	NYT	
39	NYT	
40	NYT	
41	NYT	
42	Sufferer – The Kingstonians (prod Derrick Harriott)	1968
43	Kiss A (Little) Finger – The Apostles/Kingstonians (prod Derrick Harriott)	1968
44	John Jones – Rudy Mills (prod Derrick Harriott)	1968
45	Place Called Happiness – Rudy Mills (prod Derrick Harriott)	1968
46	NYT	
47	Biafra – The Crystalites (prod Derrick Harriott)	1968
48	Drop Pan – The Crystalites (prod Derrick Harriott)	1968
49	NYT	
50	NYT	
51	Worries (A Yard) – The Versatiles (prod Lee Perry/E Barnett)	1969
52	Hound Dog Special – Val Bennett (prod Lee Perry/E Barnett)	1969
53	Suzy Wong – Keeling Beckford (prod A Barnett)	1969
54	Deebo – The Swinging Kings (prod A Barnett)	1969
55	Son Of A Preacher Man – The Gaylets (prod Federal)	1969
56	That's How Strong My Love Is – The Gaylets (prod Federal)	1969
57	NYT	
58	NYT	
59	NYT	
60	Deportation – Eric 'Monty' Morris (prod Albert Gene Murphy)	1969

61	You Are No Good – The Tennors (prod Albert Gene Murphy)	1969
62	Do The Reggae – The Tennors (prod Albert Gene Murphy)	1969
63	He Is Back (Say I'm Back) – Eric 'Monty' Morris (prod Albert Gene Murphy)	1969
64	NYT	
65	Another Scorcher – The Tennors (prod Albert Gene Murphy)	1969
66	My Baby – The Tennors (prod Albert Gene Murphy)	1969
67	Cool Hand Luke – Karl Bryan & Johnny Moore (prod Albert Gene Murphy)	1969
68	Parapinto – Karl Bryan & Johnny Moore (prod Albert Gene Murphy)	1969

GPW SERIES

1	Confusion – The Inspirations (prod Lee Perry)	1971
2	Confusion Version – The Upsetters (prod Lee Perry)	1971
3	Elusion – Teddy (prod Lee Perry)	1971
4	Big John Wayne – The Upsetters (prod Lee Perry)	1971
5	Mr Brown – Bob Marley & Wailers (prod Lee Perry)	1971
6	Dracula – The Upsetters (prod Lee Perry)	1971
7	Kayah – Bob Marley & Wailers (prod Lee Perry)	1971
8	Kayah Version – The Upsetters (prod Lee Perry)	1971
9	Heavy Load – Carl Dawkins (prod Lee Perry)	1971
10	Got To Be Mine/Down The Road – The Hurricanes The Upsetters (prod Lee Perry)	1971
11	NYT	
12	Small Axe – Bob Marley & Wailers (prod Lee Perry)	1971
13	NYT	
14	NYT	
15	NYT	
16	NYT	
17	NYT	
18	NYT	
19	NYT	
20	NYT	
21	NYT	
22	NYT	
23	NYT	
24	NYT	
25	NYT	
26	NYT	
27	NYT	
28	NYT	
29	NYT	
30	NYT	

31	NYT	
32	NYT	
33	NYT	
34	NYT	
35	NYT	
36	NYT	
37	NYT	
38	Take Me Baby (As I Am)/In Paradise – Jackie Edwards (prod Jackie Edwards)	1971
39	Walk With Love/Walk With Love Version – The Maytals/Beverley's All Stars (prod Leslie Kong)	1971
40	NYT	
41	NYT	
42	Musical Revolution/Trouble (tk.2) – Charlie Ace/The Green Busters (prod Theo Beckford)	1971
43	Give You All My Love/Trouble (tk.1) – The Green Busters (prod Theo Beckford)	1971
44	Teacher Teacher/Teacher Teacher Version – The Maytals/Beverley's All Stars (prod Leslie Kong)	1971
45	Poor Chubby/Better Days – Junior Byles/Carlton & The Shoes (prod Lee Perry)	1971
46	(Brand New) Second Hand/Second Hand Version – Peter Tosh & The Wailers (prod Lee Perry)	1971
47	My Girl/Coming Again – Busty Faith/Junior Byles (prod Lee Perry)	1971
48	Walking The Street/Jah Is Mighty – The Hurricanes/Bob Marley (prod Lee Perry)	1971
49	Jump And Rail/Trying My Faith (Got To Change) – The Bleechers (prod Lee Perry)	1971
50	Come On Over/Fancy Clothes – The Viceroys (prod Lee Perry)	1971
51	NYT	
52	NYT	
53	Bongo Man Rise/Remember – The Maytones/Roy & Bim (prod Alvin Ranglin)	1971
54	King Of Kings/Rod Of Righteousness – Dennis Alcapone/The GG All Stars (prod Alvin Ranglin)	1971
55	NYT	1971
56	Know Far I/Know Far I Version – Bongo Herman & Bingy Bunny (prod Derrick Harriott)	1971
57	Mr Big Stuff – The Crepsoles/The Aquarians (prod Herman Chin-Loy)	1971
58	Bye Bye Love/Valley Of The Dolls – The Fabulous Shoemakers/Roy & Dizzy (prod Fud Christian)	1971
59	Miss Annie Oh/Miss Annie Oh Version – Nora Dean/Fud Christian All Stars (prod Fud Christian)	1971
60	NYT	
61	Daddy Daddy Don't You Cry/I Like It – Tony King & Hippy Boys/The Hippy Boys	1971
62	NYT	
63	High And Dry/Love Is Blue/Moon River/Peace And Love – Greyhound (prod Dave Bloxham)	1971

64	NYT	
65	NYT	
66	NYT	
67	NYT	
68	Strange World/unknown – Bob & Marcia (prod Keith Anderson [Bob Andy])	1971
69	NYT	
70	NYT	
71	NYT	
72	NYT	
73	NYT	
74	NYT	
75	NYT	
76	Best Of Five Part One/Best Of Five Part Two – The Ethiopians (prod Derrick Harriott)	1971
77	Java/Version 2 – Augustus Pablo & The Impact All Stars (prod Vincent Chin)	1971
78	President In School/Walking Stick – Cat Campbell/Phillip Samuels (prod Alvin Ranglin)	1971
79	A Love Like Yours/Just Keep It Up – John Holt (prod Alvin Ranglin)	1971
80	Rosemarie/Version – Scotty/The Crystalites (prod Derrick Harriott)	1971
81	NYT	
82	Milk And Honey/Israel Want To Be Free – Dennis Alcapone/The Ethiopians (prod Alvin Ranglin)	1971
82	Hit Medley/You Got To Be Bad To Be Good – The Pioneers (prod Sidney Crooks)	1971

TMX SERIES

1	NYT	
2	NYT	
3	I'll Be Lonely – John Holt & Joya Landis (prod Arthur 'Duke' Reid)	1968
4	Second Fiddle – Tommy McCook & The Supersonics (prod Arthur 'Duke' Reid)	1968
5	NYT	
6	NYT	
7	NYT	
8	I Wish It Would Rain – The Techniques (prod Arthur 'Duke' Reid)	1968
9	There Comes A Time – The Techniques (prod Arthur 'Duke' Reid)	1968
10	NYT	
11	NYT	
12	Love Up Kiss Up – The Termites (prod Arthur 'Duke' Reid)	1968
13	Those Guys – The Sensations (prod Arthur 'Duke' Reid)	1968
14	I'll Never Fall In Love Again – The Sensations (prod Arthur 'Duke' Reid)	1968
15	NYT	
16	NYT	

17	Lonely Reggae – Tommy McCook & The Supersonics (prod Arthur 'Duke' Reid)	1968
18	NYT	
19	NYT	
20	NYT	
21	NYT	
22	NYT	
23	Dulcemania – Drumbago & The Dynamites (prod Clancy Eccles)	1968
24	Chinaman – Clancy Eccles (prod Clancy Eccles)	1968
25	Sweet Africa – Val Bennett & The Dynamites (prod Clancy Eccles)	1968
26	Let Us Be Lovers – Velma Jones & Clancy Eccles (prod Clancy Eccles)	1968
27	Mix It Up – The Kingstonians (prod Karl 'JJ' Johnson)	1968
28	I'll Be Around – The Kingstonians (prod Karl 'JJ' Johnson)	1968
29	I'll Make It Up – Carl Dawkins (prod Karl 'JJ' Johnson)	1968
30	One Dollar Of Music – JJ All Stars (prod Karl 'JJ' Johnson)	1968
31	NYT	
32	NYT	
33	Fat Man – Derrick Morgan (prod Lynford Anderson)	1968
34	South Parkway Rock – Val Bennett (prod Lynford Anderson)	1968
35	Thunderstorm – Karl Bryan (prod Lynford Anderson)	1968
36	Honey Love – Burt Walters (prod Lynford Anderson)	1968
37	Party Tonight – The Silvertones (prod Lynford Anderson)	1968
38	Time Marches On – The Race Fans (prod Lynford Anderson)	1968
39	Win Your Love – George A. Penny (prod Lynford Anderson)	1968
40	All In The Game – Val Bennett (prod Lynford Anderson)	1968
41	You Crummy – Lee Perry (prod Lee Perry)	1968
42	Sentence – Danny & Lee (prod Lee Perry)	1968
43	NYT	
44	NYT	
45	Baby Baby – Val Bennett (prod Lee Perry)	1968
46	Barbara – Val Bennett (prod Lee Perry)	1968
47	Farmer's In The Den – The Bleechers (prod Lee Perry)	1968
48	I'm Coming Home – unknown	1968
49	Mother Hen – The Harmonisers (prod George 'Regent' King)	1968
50	NYT	
51	Uncle Desmond – Lee Perry (prod Lee Perry)	1968
52	Bronco – The Upsetters (prod Lee Perry)	1968
53	Left With A Broken Heart – The Paragons (prod The Paragons)	1968
54	I've Got To Get Away – The Paragons (prod The Paragons)	1968
55	Freedom Sound – Lloyd Charmers (prod Lloyd Charmers)	1968
56	NYT	

57	Happy Time – Herbie Carter (prod Harry Johnson)	1968
58	Smashville – The Jay Boys (prod Harry Johnson)	1968
59	Lavender Blue – Lloyd Robinson (prod Harry Johnson)	1968
60	Cuss Cuss – Lloyd Robinson (prod Harry Johnson)	1968
61	Easy Sound – The Jay Boys (prod Harry Johnson)	1968
62	Candy Lady – Black & George (prod Harry Johnson)	1968
63	NYT	
64	A Man Of My Word – The Techniques (prod Winston Riley)	1968
65	The Time Has Come – The Techniques (prod Winston Riley)	1968
66	You're My Everything – The Techniques (prod Winston Riley)	1968
67	What Am I To Do – The Techniques (prod Winston Riley)	1968
68	NYT	
69	NYT	
70	NYT	
71	NYT	
72	Dollar In The Teeth – The Upsetters (prod Lee Perry)	1968
73	Return Of Django – The Upsetters (prod Lee Perry)	1968
74	NYT	
75	NYT	
76	Stand By Me – The Inspirations (prod Lee Perry)	1968
77	NYT	
78	Moonlight Lover – Joya Landis (prod Arthur 'Duke' Reid)	1968
79	I Love You True – Joya Landis (prod Arthur 'Duke' Reid)	1968
80	NYT	
81	Breaking Up – Alton Ellis (prod Arthur 'Duke' Reid)	1968
82	Party Time – Alton Ellis (prod Arthur 'Duke' Reid)	1968
83	Tonight – John Holt (prod Arthur 'Duke' Reid)	1968
84	Maybe Someday – The Paragons (prod Arthur 'Duke' Reid)	1968
85	Penny Reel – Whistling Willie (prod Neville Willoughby)	1969
86	Soul Tonic – Whistling Willie (prod Neville Willoughby)	1969
87	Good Father – David Isaacs (prod Lee Perry)	1969
88	What A Situation – Slim Smith (prod Lee Perry)	1969
89	What A Botheration – Lee Perry (prod Lee Perry)	1969
90	I'll Be Waiting – The Termites (prod Lee Perry)	1969
91	Big Boy – Ranny Williams (prod George 'Regent' King)	1969
92	NYT	
93	Seven Letters – Derrick Morgan (prod Edward 'Bunny' Lee)	1969
94	NYT	
95	NYT	
96	Just A Mirage – The Uniques (prod Lloyd Charmers for Winston Lowe)	1969

97	Ah Yuh – The Uniques (prod Lloyd Charmers for Winston Lowe)	1969
98	Soul Pipe – King Cannon (prod Lynford Anderson)	1969
99	Overproof – King Cannon (prod Lynford Anderson)	1969
100	Constantinople – Clancy Eccles (prod Clancy Eccles)	1969
101	NYT	
102	Deacon Don – Clancy Eccles (prod Clancy Eccles)	1969
103	NYT	
104	Old Man Say – The Silver Stars (prod Clancy Eccles)	1969
105	Promises – The Silver Stars (prod Clancy Eccles)	1969
106	Banganarng Crash – Clancy Eccles (prod Clancy Eccles)	1969
107	Rahtid – The Dynamites (prod Clancy Eccles)	1969
108	Bag-A-Boo – Clancy Eccles (prod Clancy Eccles)	1969
109	Auntie Lulu – Clancy Eccles (& Slickers) (prod Clancy Eccles)	1969
110	I Can't Stop Loving You – Owen Gray (prod Owen Gray)	1969
111	Reggae Dance – Owen Gray (prod Owen Gray)	1969
112	Tell Me Darling – Owen Gray (prod Owen Gray)	1969
113	I Know – Owen Gray (prod Owen Gray)	1969
114	What A Price – Busty Brown (prod Lee Perry)	1969
115	How Can I Forget – Busty Brown (prod Lee Perry)	1969
116	Ten To Twelve – The Upsetters (prod Lee Perry)	1969
117	People Funny Fi True – Lee Perry (prod Lee Perry)	1969
118	NYT	
119	NYT	
120	Diana – Alton Ellis (prod Arthur 'Duke' Reid)	1969
121	Personality – Alton Ellis (prod Arthur 'Duke' Reid)	1969
122	Love Is All I Had – Phyllis Dillon (prod Arthur 'Duke' Reid)	1969
123	Boys And Girls Reggae – Phyllis Dillon (prod Arthur 'Duke' Reid)	1969
124	You Should Have Known Better – Justin Hinds & The Dominoes (prod Arthur 'Duke' Reid)	1969
125	Third Figure – Tommy McCook & The Supersonics (prod Arthur 'Duke' Reid)	1969
126	NYT	
127	NYT	
128	Forever – The Uniques (prod Lloyd Charmers for Winston Lowe)	1969
129	Cuyah – Lloyd Charmers (prod Lloyd Charmers for Winston Lowe)	1969
130	NYT	
131	NYT	
132	NYT	
133	NYT	
134	Home Without You – The Beltones (prod Harry Johnson)	1969
135	Why Pretend – The Beltones (prod Harry Johnson)	1969

136	Life – Roy Shirley (prod Karl 'JJ' Johnson)	1969
137	I Like Your Smile – Roy Shirley (prod Karl 'JJ' Johnson)	1969
138	NYT	
139	NYT	
140	Hang 'Em High – Richard Ace (prod Harry Johnson)	1969
141	NYT	
142	Suffering Stink – Band Of Mercy & Salvation (prod Disclick)	1969
143	The Break – Winston Francis (prod Disclick)	1969
144	Never My Love – Boris Gardiner (prod Boris Gardiner)	1969
145	The Bold One – Boris Gardiner (prod Boris Gardiner)	1969
146	NYT	
147	NYT	
148	NYT	
149	NYT	
150	NYT	
151	NYT	
152	The Saint (Go Marching In) – Tommy McCook & The Supersonics (prod Arthur 'Duke' Reid)	1969
153	Ease Me Up Officer – Winston Jarrett & Flames (prod Arthur 'Duke' Reid)	1969
154	Fattie Fattie – Clancy Eccles (prod Clancy Eccles)	1969
155	Last Call – The Dynamites (prod Clancy Eccles)	1969
156	Friends And Lovers – Pattie La Donn (prod Joe Mansano)	1969
157	Hot Line – Joes All Stars (prod Joe Mansano)	1969
158	Hey Jude – Joes All Stars (prod Joe Mansano)	1969
159	Musical Feet – Joes All Stars (prod Joe Mansano)	1969
160	Battle Cry Of Biafra – Joes All Stars (prod Joe Mansano)	1969
161	Funky Reggae Part One – Joes All Stars (prod Joe Mansano)	1969
162	Five To Five – Lloyd Charmers (prod Lloyd Charmers)	1969
163	Come See About Me – Lloyd Charmers (prod Lloyd Charmers)	1969
164	Hear Ya – The Scorchers (prod Karl 'JJ' Johnson)	1969
165	Live Life – The Vibrators (prod Karl 'JJ' Johnson)	1969
166	Glad You're Living – Stranger Cole (prod Karl 'JJ' Johnson)	1969
167	Help Wanted – Stranger Cole (prod Karl 'JJ' Johnson)	1969
168	The Night Doctor – The Upsetters (prod Lee Perry)	1969
169	To Love Somebody – Busty Brown (prod Lee Perry)	1969
170	Everybody Bawlin' – The Melodians (prod Arthur 'Duke' Reid)	1969
171	Kilowatt – Tommy McCook & Winston Wright (prod Arthur 'Duke' Reid)	1969
172	Ali Baba – John Holt (prod Arthur 'Duke' Reid)	1969
173	I'm Your Man – John Holt (prod Arthur 'Duke' Reid)	1969
174	Pick Out Me Eye – The Royals (prod L Edwards)	1969

175	You Think You Too Bad – The Royals (prod L. Edwards)	1969
176	Dollars And Cents – Gladstone Adams (prod Arthur 'Duke' Reid)	1969
177	Popcorn Reggae – Tommy McCook & The Supersonics (prod Arthur 'Duke' Reid)	1969
178	NYT	
179	NYT	
180	NYT	
181	NYT	
182	NYT	
183	NYT	
184	NYT	
185	NYT	
186	NYT	
187	NYT	
188	NYT	
189	NYT	
190	Big Boy – Ranny Williams (prod Ranny Williams)	1969
191	Too Late – The Harmonisers (prod Ranny Williams)	1969
192	Sweet Things We Used To Do – The Harmonisers (prod Ranny Williams)	1969
193	House On Fire – The Harmonisers (prod Ranny Williams)	1969
194	Hog In A Minte – The Harmonisers (prod Ranny Williams)	1969
195	Dick Stiff And Shine – George Anthony (prod Ranny Williams)	1969
196	Never Gonna Give You Up – The Royals (prod L Edwards)	1969
197	Don't Mix Me Up – The Royals (prod L Edwards)	1969
198	NYT	
199	NYT	
200	Man From MI5 – The Upsetters (prod Lee Perry)	1969
201	Dry Up Your Tears – The Mellotones (prod Lee Perry)	1969
202	Oh Lord – The West Indians (prod Lee Perry)	1969
203	Come Into My Parlour – The Bleechers	1969
204	Everything For Fun – The Bleechers (prod Lee Perry)	1969
205	A Live Injection – The Upsetters (prod Lee Perry)	1969
206	Soulful I (Since You're Gone) – The Upsetters (prod Lee Perry)	1969
207	No Bread And Butter – Milton Henry (prod Lee Perry)	1969
208	Medical Operation – The Upsetters (prod Lee Perry)	1969
209	Badam Bam – The Ravers (prod Lee Perry)	1969
210	Thunderball – The Upsetters (prod Lee Perry)	1969
211	NYT	
212	NYT	
213	NYT	
214	What's Wrong With You – unknown (prod Lee Perry)	1969

215	Todal Wave – The Upsetters (prod Lee Perry)	1969
216	NYT	
217	He'll Have To Go – David Isaacs (prod Lee Perry)	1969
218	Since You Are Gone – David Isaacs (prod Lee Perry)	1969
219	NYT	
220	NYT	
221	NYT	
222	NYT	
223	NYT	
224	NYT	
225	Because You're Mine – Les Foster (prod Les Foster)	1969
226	Do It Nice – Les Foster (prod Les Foster)	1969
227	Windy Pt II – The Saints (prod Les Foster)	1969
228	NYT	
229	Windy Pt I – The Saints (prod Les Foster)	1969
230	NYT	
231	John Public – The Dynamites (prod Clancy Eccles)	1969
232	I Don't Care – The Dingle Brothers (prod Clancy Eccles)	1969
233	Shoo Be Do – Clancy Eccles (prod Clancy Eccles)	1969
234	Fire Corner – King Stitt (prod Clancy Eccles)	1969
235	I've Tried Before – The Impersonators (prod Melmouth Nelson)	1969
236	Make It Easy On Yourself – The Impersonators (prod Melmouth Nelson)	1969
237	You Belong To My Heart – The Demons (prod Melmouth Nelson)	1969
238	Bless You – The Demons (prod Melmouth Nelson)	1969
239	NYT	
240	NYT	
241	NYT	
242	I Can't See Myself Cry About You – Busty Brown (prod Lee Perry)	1969
243	Woman Capture Man – The Ethiopians (prod Karl 'JJ' Johnson)	1969
244	One – The Ethiopians (prod Karl 'JJ' Johnson)	1969
245	NYT	
246	NYT	
247	Proud Mary – Tony King & Hippy Boys (prod Hippy Boy)	1969
248	My Devotion – Tony King & Hippy Boys (prod Bart San Filipo)	1969
249	The Whole Family Is Here – The Hippy Boys (prod Bart San Filipo)	1969
250	Love – (Max Romeo &) The Hippy Boys (prod Bart San Filipo)	1969
251	Michael Row The Boat Ashore – Max Romeo & The Hippy Boys (prod Bart San Filipo)	1969
252	Who Is Coming To Dinner – The Hippy Boys (prod Bart San Filipo)	1969
253	Chastise Them – Winston Sinclair (prod Winston Sinclair)	1969

254	Apple Blossom – Mr Versatile (prod Edward 'Bunny' Lee)	1969
255	Devil's Disciples – Roland Alphonso (prod Edward 'Bunny' Lee)	1969
256	Having A Party – Errol Dunkley (prod Edward 'Bunny' Lee)	1969
257	NYT	
258	Love Power – Slim Smith (prod Edward 'Bunny' Lee)	1969
259	Since You Are Mine – Pat Kelly (prod Lee Perry)	1969
260	Too Experienced – Owen Gray (prod Owen Gray)	1969
261	I Really Love You Baby – Owen Gray (prod Owen Gray)	1969
262	Dark End Of The Street – Pat Kelly (prod Lee Perry)	1969
263	Cherry Pink – Mr Miller (prod Edward 'Bunny' Lee)	1969
264	Sweeten My Coffee – Slim Smith (prod Edward 'Bunny' Lee)	1969
265	Music House – Roland Alphonso (prod Edward 'Bunny' Lee)	1969
266	Zapatoo The Tiger – Roland Alphonso (prod Edward 'Bunny' Lee)	1969
267	Seven Long Days – Owen Gray (prod Owen Gray)	1969
268	He Didn't Love You Like I Love You – Owen Gray (prod Owen Gray)	1969
269	Long Shot Kick The Bucket – The Pioneers (prod Leslie Kong)	1969
270	(Too) Experienced – Owen Gray (prod Owen Gray)	1969
271	I Really Love You Baby – Owen Gray (prod Owen Gray)	1969
271	Get On The Right Track – Phyllis Dillon (& Hopeton Lewis) (prod Arthur 'Duke' Reid)	1969
272	Moon Shot – Tommy McCook & The Supersonics (prod Arthur 'Duke' Reid)	1969
273	NYT	
274	NYT	
275	NYT	
276	Itch – Anonymously Yours (prod Bart Sanfilipo)	1969
277	Organism – Anonymously Yours (prod Bart Sanfilipo)	1969
278	NYT	
279	NYT	
280	NYT	
281	NYT	
282	NYT	
283	NYT	
284	Lipstick On Your Collar – unknown female vocalist (prod Arthur 'Duke' Reid)	1969
285	Tribute To Rameses – Tommy McCook & The Supersonics (prod Arthur 'Duke' Reid)	1969
286	NYT	
287	NYT	
288	NYT	
289	NYT	
290	NYT	

291	NYT	
292	Soul Serenade – Byron Lee & The Dragonaires (prod Byron Lee)	1969
293	Elizabethan Reggay – Boris Gardiner & The Love People (prod Junior Chung/ Boris Gardiner)	1969
294	The Hustler – Junior Murvin (prod Derrick Harriott)	1969
295	The Magic Touch – Junior Murvin (prod Derrick Harriott)	1969
296	NYT	
297	NYT	
298	Nice Nice – The Kingstonians (prod Derrick Harriott)	1969
299	I'll Be Around – The Kingstonians (prod Derrick Harriott)	1969
300	NYT	
301	NYT	
302	Bigger Boss – Ansel Collins (prod Karl 'JJ' Johnson)	1969
303	My Girl – The Ethiopians (prod Karl 'JJ' Johnson)	1969
304	Tambourine Man – Ken Boothe (prod Keith Hudson)	1969
305	Old Fashioned Way – Ken Boothe (prod Keith Hudson)	1969
306	Safari – Lloyd Charmers (prod Lloyd Charmers)	1969
307	Last Laugh – The Jokers (prod Lloyd Charmers)	1969
308	In The Spirit – Lloyd Charmers (prod Lloyd Charmers)	1969
309	Duckey Luckey – Lloyd Charmers (prod Lloyd Charmers)	1969
310	Jumping The Gun – Rico (prod Robert Thompson [Dandy])	1969
311	Chicken Lickin' (Night Fall) – Lloyd Charmers & Hippy Boys (prod Lloyd Charmers)	1969
312	Dracula, Prince Of Darkness – King Horror (prod Joe Mansano)	1969
313	Honky – Joe's All Stars (prod Joe Mansano)	1969
314	Liquidator – Winston Wright (prod Harry Johnson)	1969
315	Feel The Festive Spirit – The Jamaicans (prod Harry Johnson)	1969
316	NYT	
317	NYT	
318	Get Back – Anonymously Yours (prod Trojan [JA] Productions)	1969
319	Not For Sale – Ernie Smith (prod Trojan [JA] Productions)	1969
320	'69 – Wallace Wilson (prod Trojan [JA] Productions)	1969
321	It's Your Thing – Anonymously Yours (prod Trojan [JA] Productions)	1969
322	Higher And Higher – Josh (prod Joe Mansano)	1969
323	African Meeting – Girlie & Jomo (prod Joe Mansano)	1969
324	The Judge – Josh (prod Joe Mansano)	1969
325	Soul Of Joe – Ron (prod Joe Mansano)	1969
326	Ease Up – The Bleechers (prod Lee Perry)	1969
327	You Gonna Feel It – The Bleechers (prod Lee Perry)	1969
328	Cold Sweat – The Upsetters (prod Lee Perry)	1969

329	Pound Get A Blow – The Bleechers (prod Lee Perry)	1969
330	Check Him Out – The Bleechers (prod Lee Perry)	1969
331	Who To Tell – David Isaacs (prod Lee Perry)	1969
332	NYT	
333	NYT	
334	NYT	
335	NYT	
336	La La Always Stay – Glen & Dave (prod Harry Johnson)	1969
337	Extn. 303 – Lloyd Charmers (prod Lloyd Charmers)	1969
338	Brixton – The Jokers (prod Lloyd Charmers)	1969
339	Real Real (aka Sweet Sweet) – Lloyd Robinson (prod Lloyd Charmers)	1969
340	African Zulu – Lloyd Charmers (prod Lloyd Charmers)	1969
341	Eko Craft – Lloyd Charmers (prod Lloyd Charmers)	1969
342	House In Session – Tommy Cowan (prod Tommy Cowan)	1969
343	Black Bud – The Pioneers (prod Leslie Kong)	1969
344	Come See About Me – Lloyd Charmers (prod Lloyd Charmers)	1969
345	NYT	
346	NYT	
347	NYT	
348	Who Yea – King Stitt (prod Clancy Eccles)	1969
349	Mr Midnight (aka Skokiaan) – The Dynamites (prod Clancy Eccles)	1969
350	Dollar Train – The Dynamites (prod Clancy Eccles)	1969
351	The World Needs Loving – Clancy Eccles (prod Clancy Eccles)	1969
352	On The Street – King Stitt (prod Clancy Eccles)	1969
353	Mount Zion – Clancy Eccles (prod Clancy Eccles)	1969
354	Vigerton Two – King Stitt (prod Clancy Eccles)	1969
355	Foolish Fool – Cynthia Richards (prod Clancy Eccles)	1969
356	NYT	
357	Rudam Bam – The Eagles (prod Joe Sinclair)	1969
358	NYT	
359	NYT	
360	NYT	
361	NYT	
362	Any Little Bit – The Techniques (prod Lloyd Charmers)	1969
363	NYT	
364	NYT	
365	NYT	
366	NYT	
367	NYT	
368	NYT	

369	Soul Power – Barrington Sadler (prod Clancy Eccles)	1969
370	Rub It Down – Barrington Sadler (prod Clancy Eccles)	1969
371	NYT	
372	NYT	
373	The Vampire – The Upsetters (prod Lee Perry)	1969
374	Dirty Dozen – The Shadows (prod Bobby Aitken)	1969
375	Crying Too Long – The Shadows (prod Bobby Aitken)	1969
376	Stranger On The Shore – Val Bennett (prod Lee Perry)	1969
377	Drugs And Poison – The Upsetters (prod Lee Perry)	1969
378	NYT	
379	NYT	
380	The Same Things – The Gaylads (prod Lee Perry)	1969
381	I Wear My Slanders – The Gaylads (prod Lee Perry)	1969
382	NYT	
383	NYT	
384	NYT	
385	NYT	
386	Double Shot – Beverley's All Stars (prod Leslie Kong)	1969
387	Coconut Water – The Mellotones (prod Leslie Kong)	1969
388	The Crimson Pirate – Peter Tosh (prod Edward 'Bunny' Lee)	1969
389	Moon Dusk – Peter Tosh (prod Edward 'Bunny' Lee)	1969
390	Kiss Me Quick – Keeling Beckford (prod Edward 'Bunny' Lee)	1969
391	Feel The Crumpet – Bunny Lee (prod Edward 'Bunny' Lee)	1969
392	Wonderful World, Beautiful People – Jimmy Cliff (prod Leslie Kong & Jimmy Cliff)	1969
393	Hard Road To Travel – Jimmy Cliff (prod Leslie Kong & Jimmy Cliff)	1969
394	This Old Man – Sylvan Morris (prod Hawk)	1969
395	Sweeter Than Honey – Sylvan Morris (prod Hawk)	1969
396	When The Morning Comes – Sylvan Morris (prod Hawk)	1969
397	Son Of Reggae – Sylvan Morris (prod Hawk)	1969
398	NYT	
399	NYT	
400	Bye Bye Love – The Dials (prod Clancy Collins)	1969
401	It's Love – The Dials (prod Clancy Collins)	1969
402	Love Is A Treasure – The Dials (prod Clancy Collins)	1969
403	I Want To Be – The Diamonds (prod Clancy Collins)	1969
404	NYT	
405	NYT	
406	I Want To Be Loved – Sir Collins & The Black Diamonds (prod Clancy Collins)	1969
407	Black Panther – Sir Collins & The Black Diamonds (prod Clancy Collins)	1969
408	Black Diamonds – Sir Collins & The Black Diamonds (prod Clancy Collins)	1969

409	I Remember – The Diamonds (prod Clancy Collins)	1969
410	NYT	
411	NYT	
412	NYT	
413	NYT	
414	NYT	
415	Read The News – Joe's All Stars (prod Joe Mansano)	1969
416	It's Not Impossible – Joe's All Stars (prod Joe Mansano)	1969
417	Reggae On The Shore – Joe's All Stars (prod Joe Mansano)	1969
418	Brixton Cat – Pama Dice (prod Joe Mansano)	1969
419	The Thief – Joe Mansano (prod Joe Mansano)	1969
420	Dynamite Line – Joe's All Stars (prod Joe Mansano)	1969
421	Your Boss DJ – Dice The Boss (prod Joe Mansano)	1969
422	But Officer – Dice The Boss (prod Joe Mansano)	1969
423	Solitude – Joe's All Stars (prod Joe Mansano)	1969
424	Gun The Man Down – Dice The Boss (prod Joe Mansano)	1969
425	NYT	
426	NYT	
427	I Can't Stop Loving You – The Earthquakes (prod Clancy Collins)	1969
428	Pair Of Wings – Sir Collins & The Earthquakes (prod Clancy Collins)	1969
429	Brother Moses – Sir Collins & The Earthquakes (prod Clancy Collins)	1969
430	Funny, Familiar Feeling – Sir Collins & The Earthquakes (prod Clancy Collins)	1969
431	Hot Shot (All Because I Need Your Loving) – Karl Bryan & Tommy McCook (prod Winston Riley)	1969
432	Diversion (aka Watch This Music) – Karl Bryan & Tommy McCook (prod Winston Riley)	1969
433	Memories Of Love – Boris Gardiner & The Love People (prod Winston Riley)	1969
434	Sweet Soul Special – Boris Gardiner & The Love People (prod Winston Riley)	1969
435	See And Blind – Boris Gardiner & The Love People (prod Winston Riley)	1969
436	Unknown – Boris Gardiner & The Love People (prod Winston Riley)	1969
437	Darkness – Ansel Collins & The Love People (prod Winston Riley)	1969
438	Pork Chops – Ansel Collins (prod Winston Riley)	1969
439	NYT	
440	Just One Smile – The Techniques (prod Winston Riley)	1969
441	The Workman Song – The Techniques (prod Winston Riley)	1969
442	Silhouettes – The Sensations (prod Winston Riley)	1969
443	I Never Knew (Make Believe) – The Sensations (prod Winston Riley)	1969
444	Where Were You (When The Lights Went Out) – The Techniques (prod Winston Riley)	1969
445	Mother Nature – The Mad Lads (prod Winston Riley)	1969
446	I Know A Girl – The Shades (prod Winston Riley)	1969

447	I'm So Afraid (Of Love) – The Mad Lads (prod Winston Riley)	1969
448	He Who Keepeth His Mouth – Johnny Osbourne & The Sensations (prod Winston Riley)	1969
449	One Day (You'll Need My Kiss) – Johnny Osbourne & The Sensations (prod Winston Riley)	1969
450	Red Sunset (Go Find Yourself A Fool) – Boris Gardiner & Love People (prod Winston Riley)	1969
451	I Need You Tomorrow – The Kingstonians (prod Leslie Kong)	1969
452	I'm Gonna Make It – The Kingstonians (prod Leslie Kong)	1969
453	NYT	
454	NYT	
455	NYT	
456	NYT	
457	NYT	
458	NYT	
459	I've Been Loving You – The Megatons (aka Rudies) (prod Joe Sinclair)	1969
460	Memphis Reggae – The Megatons (aka Rudies) (prod Joe Sinclair)	1969
461	Ging Gong Gollie – The Megatons (aka Rudies) (prod Joe Sinclair)	1969
462	I'm Thirsty – The Megatons (aka Rudies) (prod Joe Sinclair)	1969
463	Darling Please – Stranger Cole (prod Wilburn 'Stranger' Cole)	1969
464	I've Got Plans – Stranger Cole (prod Wilburn 'Stranger' Cole)	1969
465	Dirty Dog – Amor Vivi (prod Unaccredited)	1969
466	Round And Round The Moon – Amor Vivi (prod uncredited)	1969
467	Leaving Me Standing – Winston Groovy (prod Laurel Aitken)	1969
468	Little Girl – Winston Groovy (prod Laurel Aitken)	1969
469	The Hole – King Horror (prod Laurel Aitken)	1969
470	Merry X-Mas – Winston Groovy (prod Laurel Aitken)	1969
471	Lochness Monster – King Horror (prod Laurel Aitken)	1969
472	Zion I – The Visions (prod Laurel Aitken)	1969
473	Lover Come Back – Lloyd & The Slim Twins (prod unknown)	1969
474	I Am Lonely – Barry Bailey (prod unknown)	1969
475	NYT	
476	NYT	
477	NYT	
478	NYT	
479	NYT	
480	NYT	
481	NYT	
482	NYT	
483	NYT	
484	NYT	

485	NYT	
486	NYT	
487	NYT	
488	NYT	
489	NYT	
491	NYT	
492	NYT	
493	NYT	
494	NYT	
495	NYT	
496	NYT	
497	NYT	
498	NYT	
499	NYT	
500	Slow Motion (Ver 1) – The Upsetters (prod Lee Perry)	1970
501	Slow Motion (Ver 2) – The Upsetters (prod Lee Perry)	1970
502	Slow Motion (Ver 3) – The Upsetters (prod Lee Perry)	1970
503	Love Me Baby – The Upsetters (prod Lee Perry)	1970
504	Bab Thief – The Upsetters (prod Lee Perry)	1970
505	Take A Sip – The Upsetters (prod Lee Perry)	1970
506	Tank You – The Upsetters (prod Lee Perry)	1970
507	NYT	
508	Hurry Up – unknown (prod Lee Perry)	1970
509	NYT	
510	NYT	
511	Unknown – The Upsetters (prod Lee Perry)	1970
512	NYT	
513	Ferry Boat (Give It Up) – The Upsetters (prod Lee Perry)	1970
514	OK Carral – The Upsetters (prod Lee Perry)	1970
515	Sit Back – The Upsetters (prod Lee Perry)	1970
516	Bush Tea – The Upsetters (prod Lee Perry)	1970
517	Selassie Serenade – The Upsetters (prod Lee Perry)	1970
518	No Gwow – The Upsetters (prod Lee Perry)	1970
519	Lead Line – The Upsetters (prod Lee Perry)	1970
520	NYT	
521	NYT	
522	NYT	
523	NYT	
524	Squeeze Up (Part 1) – Byron Lee & The Dragonaires (prod Byron Lee)	1970
525	Squeeze Up (Part 2) – Byron Lee & The Dragonaires (prod Byron Lee)	1970

526	NYT	
527	NYT	
528	NYT	
529	NYT	
530	Rocko Psycho Delia – The Rudies (prod Joe Sinclair)	1970
531	The Bull – Freddie Notes & The Rudies (prod Joe Sinclair)	1970
532	The River Ben Come Up – Freddie Notes & The Rudies (prod Joe Sinclair)	1970
533	Don't Tell Your Mama – The Rudies (prod Joe Sinclair)	1970
534	Rudexodus – The Rudies (prod Joe Sinclair)	1970
535	Down On The Farm – The Rudies (prod Joe Sinclair)	1970
536	It Came Out Of The Sky – The Rudies (prod Joe Sinclair & The Rudies)	1970
537	Scratchin' Chicken – Freddie Notes & The Rudies (prod Joe Sinclair)	1970
538	Nationality – The Rudies (prod Joe Sinclair)	1970
539	Chicken Inn – Freddie Notes & The Rudies (prod Joe Sinclair)	1970
540	I Don't Want To Keep Up With The Jones – The Rudies (prod Joe Sinclair)	1970
541	Pick Folk Kinkiest – The Upsetters (prod Lee Perry)	1970
542	Na Na Hey Hey – The Upsetters (prod Lee Perry)	1970
543	Fire Fire – The Upsetters (prod Lee Perry)	1970
544	The Jumper – The Upsetters (prod Lee Perry)	1970
545	The Pillow – The Upsetters (prod Lee Perry)	1970
546	Grooving – The Upsetters (prod Lee Perry)	1970
547	Granny Show Version I – The Upsetters (prod Lee Perry)	1970
548	Granny Show Version II – The Upsetters (prod Lee Perry)	1970
549	This Man – O'Neil Hall (prod Lee Perry)	1970
550	Double Wheel – The Upsetters (prod Lee Perry)	1970
551	Haunted House – The Upsetters (prod Lee Perry)	1970
552	Land Of Kinks – The Upsetters (prod Lee Perry)	1970
553	The Miser – The Upsetters (prod Lee Perry)	1970
554	Choking Kind – The Upsetters (prod Lee Perry)	1970
555	Do It Madly – Chuck Junior (prod Lee Perry)	1970
556	Penny Wise – Chuck Junior (prod Lee Perry)	1970
557	Dreamland – The Upsetters (prod Lee Perry)	1970
558	Double Sip – The Upsetters (prod Lee Perry)	1970
559	Kangaroo Hop – The Upsetters (prod Lee Perry)	1970
560	No Love – The Upsetters (prod Lee Perry)	1970
561	Once In My Life – Errol English (prod Larry Lawrence)	1970
562	Rabbit In A Cottage – Errol English (prod Larry Lawrence)	1970
563	Love Is Pure – Errol English (prod Larry Lawrence)	1970
564	I Don't Want To Love You – Errol English (prod Larry Lawrence)	1970
565	NYT	

566	NYT	
567	NYT	
568	Day Dream – Betty Sinclair & The Hot Rod All Stars (prod Lambert Briscoe)	1970
569	Honey I Love You – Betty Sinclair & The Hot Rod All Stars (prod Lambert Briscoe)	1970
570	NYT	
571	NYT	
572	Mayfair – Millie Small (prod Philigree)	1970
573	Enoch Power – Millie Small (prod Philigree)	1970
574	Come Into My Life – Jimmy Cliff (prod Leslie Kong & Jimmy Cliff)	1970
575	Sufferin' In The Land – Jimmy Cliff (prod Leslie Kong & Jimmy Cliff)	1970
576	NYT	
577	NYT	
578	NYT	
579	This Man – O'Neil Hall (prod Lee Perry)	1970
580	NYT	
581	NYT	
582	Promises – Clancy Eccles & The Dynamites (prod Clancy Eccles)	1970
583	Real Sweet – Clancy Eccles & The Dynamites (prod Clancy Eccles)	1970
584	Black Beret – Clancy Eccles & The Dynamites (prod Clancy Eccles)	1970
585	Phantom – Clancy Eccles & The Dynamites (prod Clancy Eccles)	1970
586	Africa – Clancy Eccles & The Dynamites (prod Clancy Eccles)	1970
587	Africa Pt II – Clancy Eccles & The Dynamites (prod Clancy Eccles)	1970
588	See Me – Earl Lawrence (prod Clancy Eccles)	1970
589	Love Me Tender – Barry & The Affections (prod Clancy Eccles)	1970
590	Can't Wait – Cynthia Richards	1970
591	Promises – Cynthia Richards (prod Clancy Eccles)	1970
592	Sounds Of '70 – King Stitt & Clancy Eccles (prod Clancy Eccles)	1970
593	Zion – The Westmorlites (prod Clancy Eccles)	1970
594	Revival – The Dynamites (prod Clancy Eccles)	1970
595	Skank Me – Clancy Eccles & The Dynamites (prod Clancy Eccles)	1970
596	NYT	
597	NYT	
598	NYT	
599	NYT	
600	NYT	
601	NYT	
602	NYT	
603	NYT	
604	(I Need Your) Sweet Inspiration – The Pioneers (prod Leslie Kong)	1970
605	Israel – The Maytals (prod Leslie Kong)	1970

Trojan Albums Overview

In essence, Trojan Records used three main prefix systems to identify their album releases. Also over the course of time Trojan released albums on eight-track cartridge, cassette and latterly, of course, compact disc.

The three prefix systems were TTL, the budget-price album range that sold for 14/6d (77½p); TBL, which retailed at 19/11d (99p); and the prestige TRL(S) series that initially sold at 29/11d (£1.49) before climbing to the dizzy price of £1.99 by the middle of the 1970s. As mentioned elsewhere, Dandy launched both the TRL and TBL series in 1968, while the TTL series first saw action with the best-selling *Tighten Up* in 1969.

The TRL series was intended for prestige releases, mainly licensed in from Jamaican producers, with the later 'S' being added to the prefix indicating the recordings were in stereo, although quite a number of early TRL(S) albums have conflicting prefixes with the sleeve and label at odds with each other, as to whether the recording is in stereo or not. By late 1972, all TRL releases were in stereo – at least in theory – and could more or less accurately bear the S suffix, which continued until Trojan's takeover by Sanctuary in 2001.

A number of the early TRL albums appeared in the UK with American printed sleeves over-stickered with the Trojan catalogue number, while the vinyl disc was the normal Trojan UK pressing. These were the product of Byron Lee and his Dynamic recording set-up in Jamaica. Albums such as TRL8 *Sparrow Meets The Dragon* is found in a high quality US gatefold sleeve over-stickered, as is TRL28 *Reggae Splashdown* from bandleader Byron Lee which comes in a single sleeve design. These albums would be counterparts to existing albums in Jamaica, so the need to construct a new sleeve would be minimal, when the album was issued by Trojan in the UK. Particularly when, according to Rob Bell, Byron Lee's albums did not sell in large quantities, so Trojan would want to keep the production costs to a minimum.

The more wealthy Jamaican producers, such as Byron Lee, who had close ties with Trojan, purchased the sleeves in America due to the far higher quality of print and construction. He would then send the sleeves to London with an album master-tape, to be used by Trojan, replacing the Jamaican catalogue number with their own, via a sticker, as nothing else needed altering for the UK issue. Trojan would also print extra sleeves for an album release and export them to Jamaica for use with the locally pressed disc.

The TBL prefix series started slightly after the TRL and was intended as a range of budget priced albums. After the first album in 1968, the series issued four albums the following year and only really got in to its stride with the success Trojan were having both in the national charts and with the strong sales generated by the new skinhead audience.

These facts are reflected in the high number of various artists series issued, like *Tighten Up*, *Club Reggae* and *Reggae Chartbusters*, which all collect together many chart hits alongside more 'ethnic' material popular in the clubs.

The early 1970's DJ records' popularity was reflected in the *Version to Version* and *Version Galore* series which captured some of the finest recordings of that genre, while albums such as *Foolish Fool* and *Herbsman Reggae* underlined the sound of producer Clancy Eccles, and *The Undertaker* sold well, highlighting Derrick Harriott's Crystalites band.

The skinhead market was identified as a growth area and was particularly well catered for in 1970, with top names like The Maytals, Kingstonians and the ubiquitous Harry J All Stars all having their work issued on TBL albums. Many sold well in to the West Indian community as well, although Symarip's *Skinhead Moonstomp* was definitely angled straight at the new youth market. The TBL series was dropped in 1973.

Illustrating Trojan's somewhat inconsistent approach to releasing material, alternative versions of some early Trojan LPs can be found. Bob Marley's *Soul Rebels* album saw two pressings, initially appearing on Upsetter, albeit with the standard matrix number, and then a second pressing using the same number on the main Trojan label. Dave and Ansel Collins *Double Barrel* album also saw two pressings, both utilising the Trojan matrix TBL162 – initial copies were pressed using the Trojan version of producer Winston Riley's Techniques label, while slightly later the release was transferred to the main Trojan label.

The TTL series started in 1969 and issued bargain-priced collections, including *Tighten Up* and *Duke Reid Golden Hits*. Single artists were represented by albums such as *This Is Desmond Dekker* from the number one hit maker, and Derrick Morgan's *Seven Letters* collection. *Red Red Wine* cast the spotlight on Dandy's UK productions and was particularly boosted by Tony Tribe's national chart hit from which the album took its name. Original copies were pressed on the Downtown label while retaining the Trojan matrix, with slightly later pressings appearing on the normal Trojan label. All the sleeves showed a Downtown logo but retained the Trojan numbering. Similarly for Reco's *Blow Your Horn* LP, which found initial release on Downtown before being moved to the main Trojan imprint.

A whole host of attractive albums were issued, including producer Harry 'J' Johnson's work on *No More Heartaches*, Lloyd Charmers' work on *Reggae Is Tight* and Lee Perry's debut album for Trojan, *The Upsetter*. The bulk of the first thirty-five issues were first-rate, with a few retrospective albums offered alongside contemporary work, notably the *Guns Of Navarone* ska collection, the *Ride Your Donkey* ska and rocksteady set and the *You Left Me Standing* compilation, essentially a best of set featuring mid-'60s music from the Rio label. These LPs were the precursors of the revive albums that would bring Trojan back to prominence in the late '80s and early '90s.

After this initial burst of activity, the TTL series was confined mainly to out of date work, much of it originating from the Island label of the early to mid 1960's. Titles included Derrick Morgan's *Forward March*, a ska collection from 1963, *Keith And Enid Sing*, a collection of sentimental early-1960s ballads, and *Club Ska Volume One*, which had an original issue date of 1967, as *Club Ska '67*, again via Island on its WIRL imprint. Many of the titles were illustrated on the reverse of the TTL series albums. An extraordinary piece of cut-and-paste was executed on the *Club Ska* sleeve illustration, as the title is moved to the centre of the album and the "67' felt-penned over.

Several of the albums listed as TTL reissues that originated from the Island catalogue have never surfaced, such as Derrick Harriott, *Best Of Volume Two* and *Duke Reid Rock's Steady*. Whether they did find any form of release, possibly only to white label test-press, remains to be seen, although after such a length of time it would be thought that any titles that were going to turn up would have done so by now. Rob Bell recalls that they all reached at least the mastering stage.

The final TTL release was TTL58. It was a live recording from the Electric Living Trade Fair in Brighton, and featured The Pioneers on one side and Byron Lee & the Dragonaires on the other. *Caribbean Festival* was a limited edition promotional album issued in collaboration with the Electricity Council. The sleeve was a wrap-around paper affair with no joining at the top and bottom making it very vulnerable for the album simply to slide straight out of its cover. Judging by the number of copies that still appear, although a promotional item, the press run must have been in the thousands rather than a couple of hundred.

Tighten Up Volume Two and *Red Red Wine* were both originally to be issued on the Island label with different track listings and sleeves to the normal TTL releases. A track listing exists showing the alternative *Red Red Wine*, but beyond that and their inclusion in an Island catalogue nothing has ever been seen of these mysterious releases.

Beyond the normal TTL, TBL and TRL numbering systems Trojan issued triple albums such as *The Trojan Story* on TALL1 in a fold-over wallet-style sleeve, then repackaged it as a box set and renumbered it TALL100. Other triple album box sets followed all using the TALL prefix. Any double albums, the first of which was Desmond Dekker's *Double Dekker*, were prefixed TRLD and came in gatefold sleeves except Desmond's set which came in a standard cover.

Lee Perry, exceptionally, was granted his own prefix PERRY for the three triple box sets devoted to his work which Trojan assembled in the '80s. This unique accolade shows how collectable Scratch's music had become by that time.

Trojan also licensed recordings to mainstream budget labels such as Hallmark and MFP (Music For Pleasure), who no doubt were eager to cash in on the reggae boom of the early 1970's. These albums would be compiled from current or former hit records and packaged with the obligatory tasty West Indian young lady on the sleeve. Easily the best of these collections is *Reggae Party* on MFP from 1970, which consists of 12 top rate Leslie Kong produced tracks, the majority of which had been originally released on Trojan related labels. With a price sticker of 49p and none of the recordings being older than eighteen months, the set was an absolute snip for the enthusiast.

DISCOGRAPHICAL ODDITIES

TRL15 *Absolutely* by The Uniques vocal group exists both as a normal issue and as a Jamaican press using the Trojan metal stampers on the Splash label. In both instances the sleeve is a standard UK issue. Marley and Co's *Soul Rebels* (TBL126) from 1970 can also be found as a Jamaican-pressed Upsetter label in a UK sleeve. Once again the UK-manufactured metal stampers have been used bearing the Trojan matrix numbers.

It is known that Lee Perry would take the superior UK-manufactured metal stampers back to Kingston for the Jamaican pressings of his albums.

TBL145 issued as *Tighten Up Volume Three*, was also used for *That Wonderful Sound* from singer Dobby Dobson. This had the same track listing as a Pama Records album release, although a different sleeve. It was possibly deleted when Pama issued theirs, since very few copies have surfaced on Trojan.

TRL17 *I Need You* from Dandy And Audrey was briefly issued on the pink coloured Island label with a different sleeve. It had an Island catalogue number with the Trojan one in brackets.

Copies of TRL38 *Vic Taylor Does It His Way* from 1972 occasionally appear on an olive green Dynamic label as well as the standard Trojan imprint.

Tighten Up Volume Five. There are three pressings of this album: 1) with Peter Tosh's 'Memphis' in place of 'Duppy Conqueror'. 2) with 'Know Far I' appearing twice and 3) the conventional issue with the tracks as listed.

Jackpot of Hits (Amalgamated). There was another pressing with only 11 tracks (omitting 'Good Time Rock'). Probably this was because there are two pressing faults on the normal 12 track issue ('Catch the Beat' and 'Just Like A River'), so Trojan remastered it but left off the last track in error.

The Inspirations, *Reggae Fever* also included tracks by Ken Parker and Lloyd Willis so it could not be considered as exclusively Inspirations material.

Sufferer by The Kingstonians: the track 'Easy Ride Reggae' is by the Crystalites.

Man From Carolina by The GG All Stars: the track 'Gold On Your Dress' is by the Slickers and 'Chariot Without A Horse' is by Nyah Hunter and The GG All Stars.

Reggae Reggae Volume Two: unconfirmed if this was supposed to be *Vol 2* of *Reggae Reggae Reggae* (TBL 130).

Reggae Power Volume Two: there is a miscredit on 'Sylvia's Mother' which is the Eric Donaldson cut, not the version by John Jones (which was supposed to have been issued on Attack). Also there is no Vol. 1 of this, unless one was pressed but not put out. Of course there is the *Reggae Power* single-artist album by The Ethiopians, so possibly there was a mix-up with one or the other album titles – this seems likely as there is no track titled *Reggae Power* on The Ethiopians set.

Herbsman Reggae, The Dynamites: 'See Me' is by Earl Lawrence (Earl George), not Larry Lawrence.

Music House Volume Two: 'Beef Balls & Gravy' is the same as 'Bawling Baby' on a Pama Bullet single. 'Black Is Togetherness' is the same as 'Black Is Black' by Martin Riley, also on a Pama Bullet single. 'I Wish Someone' is the same as 'I Wish by' Basil Gail – yet again on a Pama Bullet single! (I Wish is also on the *Bob Marley and Friends* Trojan box set credited to Glen Adams).

Music House Volume Three: 'Molly' is by Lord Creator (Kentrick Patrick).

Tighten Up Volume Seven: unknown singer on 'Be Faithful Darling' – not Clancy Eccles as credited. 'I'm Feeling Lonely' is by Vernon Buckley solo rather than his vocal group The Maytones.

There are a number of gaps in all the numbering systems; some were never issued and a few have yet to be confirmed as having been pressed.

Trojan Albums Discography

1968–93

AMALGAMATED (PREFIX AMGLP)

2001	Fly Away To Glory – Al Stewart & The Marvetts (prod Joe Gibbs)	1968
2002	Explosive Rocksteady – Various Artists (prod Joe Gibbs)	1968
2003	Greetings from the Pioneers – The Pioneers (prod Joe Gibbs)	1968

AMALGAMATED (PREFIX CSP)

3	Jackpot Of Hits – Various Artists (prod Joe Gibbs)	1969

ATTACK (PREFIX ATLP)
FIRST SERIES

1001	The Heptones & Friends Volume 2 – Various Artists (prod Joe Gibbs)	1973
1002	Wake Up Jamaica – Dennis Alcapone (unissued)	
1003	Darling Ooh! – Errol Dunkley (prod Sonia Pottinger/Various)	1973
1004	Green Mango – Tommy McCook & Bobby Ellis (prod Winston Riley)	1973
1005	Belch It Off – Dennis Alcapone (prod Sidney Crooks)	1974
1006	U Roy – U Roy (prod Arthur 'Duke' Reid)	1974
1007	Tommy McCook – Tommy McCook/Various (prod Arthur 'Duke' Reid)	1974
1008	Musical Consortium – Various Artists (prod Sidney Crooks)	1974
1009	Officially – Lloyd Parks (prod Lloyd Parks)	1974
1010	A Love I Can Feel – John Holt (prod Clement Seymour Dodd)	1974
1011	Big Bamboo Sample – Various Artists (prod Clement Seymour Dodd)	1974
1012	Rave on Brother – Various Artists (prod Clement Seymour Dodd)	1974
1013	Picture On The Wall – Freddie McKay (prod Clement Seymour Dodd)	1974
1014	Natty Dub – The Aggrovators (prod Edward 'Bunny' Lee)	1975
1015	Enter Into His Gates With Praise – Johnny Clarke (prod Edward 'Bunny' Lee)	1975
1016	Feel So Good – Derrick Morgan (prod Edward 'Bunny' Lee)	1975
1017	Dubbing With The Observer – Niney & King Tubby (prod Winston 'Niney' Holness)	1975

SECOND SERIES

101	Various – Sufferer's Choice (prod Various)	1988

102	The Original Man – Andrew Tosh (prod Andrew Tosh)	1988
103	Do The Reggae, 1966–70 – The Maytals (prod Leslie Kong)	1988
104	Shocks Of Mighty, 1969–74 – Lee Perry & Friends (prod Lee Perry)	1988
105	Enter His Gates With Praise – Johnny Clarke (prod Edward 'Bunny' Lee)	1989
106	Johnny In The Echo Chamber: Dubwise Selection, 1975–1976 – The Aggrovators (prod Edward 'Bunny' Lee)	1989
107	Don't Trouble Trouble – Johnny Clarke (prod Edward 'Bunny' Lee)	1989
108	Public Jestering – Lee Perry & Friends (prod Lee Perry)	1990
109	Put On Your Best Dress, 1967–1968 – Various Artists (prod Sonia Pottinger)	1990
110	Dub Justice – The Aggrovators (prod Edward 'Bunny' Lee)	1990
111	Dub Jackpot – The Aggrovators & King Tubby's (prod Edward 'Bunny' Lee)	1990
112	Roots Reggae – Various Artists (prod Various)	1991
113	Reggae Attack – Various Artists (prod Various)	1990
114	Sufferer – The Kingstonians (prod Derrick Harrriott)	1991
115	Be Thankful (sampler) – Various Artists (prod Various)	1991
116	Darling Ooh – Errol Dunkley (prod Sonia Pottinger/Various)	1991

BIG SHOT (PREFIX BBTL)

3000	Reggae Girl – Various Artists (prod Albert Gene Murphy)	1968
4000	Live It Up – Various Artists (prod Various)	1968
4001	Once More – Various Artists (prod Various)	1968

BIG SHOT (PREFIX BILP)

101	Top Of The Ladder – Clancy Eccles/Various Artists (prod Clancy Eccles)	1973
102	Captivity – Delroy Wilson (prod Edward 'Bunny' Lee)	1973
103	Ready Or Not – Johnny Osbourne/Various Artists (prod Winston Riley)	1973
104	Turntable Reggae – Various Artists (prod Edward 'Bunny' Lee)	1973

BLUE CAT (PREFIX BCL)

| 1 | Jamaican Memories – Various Artists (prod Various) | 1968 |

HIGH NOTE (PREFIX BSLP)

5001	ABC Rocksteady – The Original Orchestra (prod Sonia Pottinger)	1968
5002	Dancing Down Orange Street – Various Artists (prod Sonia Pottinger)	1968
5005	Reggae With the Hippy Boys – The Hippy Boys (prod Sonia Pottinger)	1969

HORSE (PREFIX HRLP)

701	Images Of You – Nicky Thomas (prod Various)	1973
702	Just Tito Simon – Tito Simon (prod Clancy Eccles/Joe Sinclair)	1973
703	Blackbird Singing – Rosalyn Sweat & The Paragons (prod Arthur 'Duke' Reid)	1973

704	Hit Picks – Various Artists (prod Rupie Edwards)	1974
705	Atlantic One – Various Artists (prod Alvin Ranglin)	1974
706	Cookin' – Tommy McCook & The Aggrovators (prod Edward 'Bunny' Lee)	1975
707	The Great Junior English – Junior English (Ellis Breary)	1976
708	Still In Love With You – Alton Ellis (prod Alton Ellis/Various)	1977

TROJAN (PREFIX TTL)

1	Tighten Up – Various Artists (prod Various)	1969
2	Not issued	
3	Not issued	
4	This Is Desmond Dekker – Desmond Dekker (prod Leslie Kong)	4.69
5	Seven Letters – Derrick Morgan (prod Various)	1969
6	Not issued	
7	Tighten Up Volume 2 – Various Artists (prod Various)	1969
8	Duke Reid Golden Hits – Various Artists (prod Arthur 'Duke' Reid)	1969
9	You Left Me Standing – Various Artists (prod Various)	1969
10	Reggae Power – The Ethiopians (prod Karl 'JJ' Johnson)	. 1969
11	Red Red Wine – Various Artists (prod Various) (issued on Downtown label)	11.69
12	Blow Your Horn – Reco & The Rudies (prod Robert Thompson [Dandy])	1969
13	The Upsetter – Lee Perry/Various Artists (prod Lee Perry)	1969
14	No More Heartaches – Various Artists (prod Harry Johnson)	1969
15	Independent Jamaica – Various Artists (prod Various)	1969
16	Guns Of Navarone – Various Artists (prod Various)	1969
17	Millie & Her Boyfriends – Millie Small/Various (prod Various)	1969
18	Ride Your Donkey – Various Artists (prod Various)	1969
19	Not issued	
20	Not issued	
21	Fire Corner – Clancy Eccles/Various Artists (prod Clancy Eccles) (issued on Clandisc label)	1969
22	Freedom – Clancy Eccles/Various Artists (prod Clancy Eccles) (issued on Clandisc label)	1969
23	Memorial – Don Drummond/Various Artists (prod Arthur 'Duke' Reid)	1969
24	Reggae With Soul – Owen Gray (prod Owen Gray)	1969
25	Reggae Is Tight – Lloyd Charmers (prod Lloyd Charmers for Winston Lowe)	1969
26	Dandy Your Musical Doctor – Dandy & The Music Doctors (prod Robert Thompson [Dandy]) (issued on Downtown label)	2.70
27	Reggae Fever – Inspirations (prod Joe Gibbs) (issued on Amalgamated label)	1970
28	Scratch The Upsetter Again – Lee Perry & The Upsetters (prod Lee Perry)	1970
29	Come Back Darling – Johnny Osbourne & The Sensations (prod Winston Riley)	2.70
30	Reggae Charm – Lloyd Charmers & The Dragonaires (prod Lloyd Charmers/ Byron Lee)	1970

31	Moonlight Groover – Various Artists (prod Arthur 'Duke' Reid)	1970
32	Tighten Up Volume 3 – Various Artists (prod Various)	1970
33	Not issued	
34	What Am I To Do – Various Artists (prod Harry Johnson)	1970
35	Version Galore – U Roy (prod Arthur 'Duke' Reid) (scheduled but not issued)	
36	Hard Road To Travel – Jimmy Cliff (prod Jimmy Cliff)	1970
37	Keith & Enid Sing – Keith & Enid (prod Chris Blackwell)	1970
38	Forward March – Derrick Morgan (prod Leslie Kong)	1970
39	The Silver Stars – The Silver Stars (prod WIRL) (possibly unissued)	1970
40	The Most Of – Jackie Edwards (prod Leslie Kong) (possibly unissued)	1970
41	Dr Kitch – Various Artists (prod Various)	1970
42	Behold – The Blues Busters (prod Byron Lee/Ronnie Nasralla)	1970
43	The Best Of – Derrick Harriott (prod Derrick Harriott) (possibly unissued)	1970
44	Kiss Me Neck – Charlie Hyatt (prod Island) (possibly unissued)	1970
45	Come On Home – Jackie Edwards (prod Island) (possibly unissued)	1970
46	By Demand – Jackie Edwards (prod Island) (possibly unissued)	1970
47	Pledging My Love – Millie & Jackie Edwards (prod Island) (possibly unissued)	1970
48	Club Ska Volume 1 – Various Artists (prod Various)	1970
49	The Best Of – Millie Small (prod Various)	10.70
50	Derrick Harriott's Rock Steady Party – Various Artists (prod Derrick Harriott) (possibly unissued)	1970
51	Club Ska Volume 2 – Various Artists (prod Various) (possibly unissued)	1970
52	The Best Of – Jackie Edwards & Millie (prod Various)	1970
53	Duke Reid Rock's Steady – Various Artists (prod Arthur 'Duke' Reid) (possibly unissued)	1970
54	Club Rock Steady – Various Artists (prod Various) (possibly unissued)	1970
55	The Best Of Derrick Harriott, Volume 2 – Derrick Harriott (prod Derrick Harriott) (possibly unissued)	1970
56	Treasure Chest – The Merry Men (prod WIRL) (possibly unissued)	1970
57	Premature Golden Sands – Jackie Edwards (prod Jimmy Miller & Chris Blackwell)	1970
58	Caribbean Music Fair – Pioneers/Byron Lee & Dragonaires (prod Leslie Kong/Byron Lee)	1971
59	Not issued	
60	Not issued	
61	Not issued	
62	Not issued	
63	Not issued	
64	Not issued	
65	Soul Revolution Volume 2 – Bob Marley & The Wailers (prod Lee Perry) (scheduled but not issued)	
66	The Good, The Bad And The Upsetters – The Upsetters (prod Lee Perry) (scheduled but not issued)	

TROJAN (PREFIX TBL)

101	Let's Catch The Beat – Brother Dan All Stars (prod Robert Thompson [Dandy])	1968
102	Skinhead Moonstomp – Symarip (prod Philigree)	4.70
103	Long Shot – The Pioneers (prod Leslie Kong)	4.70
104	Liquidator – Harry J All Stars (prod Harry Johnson) (issued on Harry J label)	1969
105	Reggae Chart Busters – Various Artists (prod Various)	4.70
106	Brixton Cat – Joe's All Stars (prod Joe Mansano)	1969
107	Monkey Man – The Maytals (prod Leslie Kong)	1970
108	Time Will Tell – Millie (prod Philigree)	1970
109	Unity – Freddie Notes & The Rudies (prod Joe Sinclair/Trojan)	9.70
110	Reggae Blast Off – Byron Lee & The Dragonaires (prod Byron Lee)	1970
111	Greater Jamaica – Various Artists (prod Arthur 'Duke' Reid)	1970
112	Woman Capture Man – The Ethiopians (prod Karl 'JJ' Johnson)	1970
113	Sufferer – The Kingstonians (prod Derrick Harriott)	1970
114	The Undertaker – The Crystalites (prod Derrick Harriott)	1970
115	Reggae Flight 404 – Various Artists (prod Alvin Ranglin)	4.70
116	Red Red Wine Volume 2 – Various Artists (prod Robert Thompson [Dandy]) (issued on Downtown label)	9.70
117	Reggae In The Summertime – The Music Doctors (prod Robert Thompson [Dandy])	9.70
118	Morning Side Of The Mountain – Dandy & Audrey (prod Robert Thompson [Dandy]) (issued on Downtown label)	9.70
119	The Good The Bad & The Upsetters – The Upsetters (prod Bruce Anthony)	4.70
120	Tighten Up – Various Artists (prod Various) (reissue of TTL1)	1973
121	Reggae Happening – Boris Gardiner (prod Boris Gardiner)	9.70
122	Young Gifted & Black – Bob & Marcia (prod Harry Johnson)	1970
123	Foolish Fool – Cynthia Richards/Various Artists (prod Clancy Eccles) (issued on Clandisc label)	1970
124	Herbsman Reggae – Various Artists (prod Clancy Eccles) (issued on Clandisc label)	1970
125	Eastwood Rides Again – Lee Perry/Upsetters (prod Lee Perry) (issued on Upsetter label)	1970
126	Soul Rebels – Bob Marley & The Wailers (prod Lee Perry) (issued on Upsetter label)	1970
127	Prisoner Of Love – Dave Barker & The Upsetters (prod Lee Perry) (issued on Upsetter label)	1970
128	Hot Shots Of Reggae – Various Artists (prod Leslie Kong)	9.70
129	Man From Carolina – Various Artists (prod Alvin Ranglin) (issued on GG label)	11.70
130	Reggae Reggae Reggae – Various Artists (prod Various)	9.70
131	Who You Gonna Run To – Various Artists (prod Winston Riley) (probably unissued)	1970
132	Mudie's Mood – Rhythm Rulers/Various Artists (prod Harry Mudie)	1970
132	Tighten Up Volume 2 – Various Artists (prod Various) (reissue of TTL7) (issued on Moodisc label)	1973

133	Groovy Jo – Jo Jo Bennett & Mudie's All Stars (prod Harry Mudie) (issued on Moodisc label)	1970
134	Not issued	
135	Lochness Monster – Various Artists (prod Various)	11.70
136	Queen Of The World – Various Artists (prod Bush)	1970
137	Funky Chicken – Various Artists (prod Various)	1970
138	Stay A Little Bit Longer – Delano Stewart (prod Sonia Pottinger)	1970
139	Battle Of The Giants – The Pioneers (prod Leslie Kong)	9.70
140	King Size Reggae – Various Artists (prod Leslie Kong)	1970
141	Psychedelic Reggae – Derrick Harriott & Crystalites (prod Derrick Harriott)	1970
142	You Can't Wine – Various Artists (prod Rupie Edwards)	1970
143	Love Of The Common People – Nicky Thomas (prod Joe Gibbs)	11.70
144	Reggae Movement – Various Artists (prod Harry Johnson) (issued on Harry J label)	1970
145	That Wonderful Sound – Dobby Dobson (prod Rupie Edwards)	1970
145	Tighten Up Volume 3 – Various Artists (prod Various) (reissue of TTL32 with altered sleeve)	10.70
146	You Can Get It If You Really Want – Desmond Dekker (prod Leslie Kong)	11.70
147	Reggae Chartbusters Volume 2 – Various Artists (prod Various)	1970
148	Not issued	
149	On My Way – Gene Rondo (prod Gene Rondo)	1970
150	Not issued	
151	Reggae Steady Go – Various Artists (prod Various)	1970
152	Montego Bay – Freddie Notes & The Rudies (prod Joe Sinclair/Trojan)	1970
153	This Is Desmond Dekker – Desmond Dekker (prod Leslie Kong) (reissue of TTL4)	1973
154	Keith & Enid Sing – Keith & Enid (prod Chris Blackwell) (reissue of TTL 37)	
155	The Best Of – Jackie Edwards & Millie (prod Island) (reissue of TTL 52)	1973
156	Premature Golden Sands – Jackie Edwards (prod Island) (reissue of TTL57)	1973
157	Not issued	
158	Not issued	
159	Club Reggae – Various Artists (prod Various)	1971
160	Issued as TBL 161	
161	Version Galore – U Roy (prod Arthur 'Duke' Reid)	1971
162	Double Barrel – Dave & Ansel Collins (prod Winston Riley) (issued on Techniques label)	1971
163	Tighten Up Volume 4 – Various Artists (prod Various)	1971
164	Club Reggae Volume 2 – Various Artists (prod Various)	1971
165	Tighten Up Volume 5 – Various Artists (prod Various)	1971
166	Africa's Blood – Various Artists (prod Lee Perry)	1971
167	Battle Axe – Various Artists (prod Lee Perry)	1972
168	Not issued	
169	Reggae Chartbusters Volume 3 – Various Artists (prod Various)	1971

170	Music House – Various Artists (prod Bush)	1971
171	Caribbean Dance Festival – Various Artists (prod Various)	1971
172	Trojan Reggae Party – Various Artists (prod Robert Thompson [Dandy])	1971
173	Not issued	
174	Miss Labba Labba – Various Artists (prod Various for Bush)	1971
175	Version Galore Volume 2 – Dennis Alcapone & U Roy (prod Various)	1972
176	Reggae Reggae Volume 2 – Various Artists (prod Various)	1972
177	Music House Volume 2 – Various Artists (prod Various for Bush)	1972
178	Club Reggae Volume 3 – Various Artists (prod Various)	1972
179	Not issued	
180	Trojan's Greatest Hits – Various Artists (prod Various)	1972
181	Reggae Jamaica – Various Artists (prod Various)	1972
182	Version To Version – Various Artists (prod Various)	1972
183	The Heptones & Friends – Various Artists (prod Joe Gibbs)	1972
184	Pledging My Love – John Holt (prod Edward 'Bunny' Lee)	1972
185	Tighten Up Volume 6 – Various Artists (prod Various)	1972
186	Just A Dream – Slim Smith (prod Edward 'Bunny' Lee)	1972
187	Guns Don't Argue – Dennis Alcapone (prod Edward 'Bunny' Lee)	1972
188	Club Reggae Volume 4 – Various Artists (prod Various)	1972
189	Reggae Power Volume 2 – Various Artists (prod Various)	1972
190	Trojan's Greatest Hits Volume 2 – Various Artists (prod Various)	1972
191	16 Dynamic Hits – Various Artists (prod Various for Dynamic)	1.73
192	Music House Volume 3 – Various Artists (prod Various)	1972
193	Reggae Jamaica Volume 2 – Various Artists (prod Various)	1973
194	Not issued	
195	Rhythm Shower – The Upsetters (prod Lee Perry) (scheduled but not issued)	
196	Tighten Up Volume 7 – Various Artists (prod Various)	1973
197	You Are My Angel – Horace Andy (prod Edward 'Bunny' Lee)	1973
198	Memorial – Slim Smith (prod Edward 'Bunny' Lee)	1973
199	Cornel Campbell – Cornell Campbell (prod Edward 'Bunny' Lee)	1973
200	Version Galore Volume 3 – Various Artists (prod Various)	1973
201	Charmers In Session – Various Artists (prod Lloyd Charners)	1973
202	Not issued	
203	Pipeline – Various Artists (prod Alvin Ranglin)	1973
204	Reggae Jamaica Volume 3 – Various Artists (prod Various)	1973
205	Club Reggae Volume 5 – Various Artists (prod Various)	1973
206	Version To Version Volume 3 – Various Artists (prod Various)	1973
207	Tighten Up Volume 8 – Various Artists (prod Various)	1973
208	Trojan's Greatest Hits Volume 3 – Various Artists (prod Various)	1973
209	16 Dynamic Hits Volume 2 – Various Artists (prod Various for Dynamic)	1973

210   Early Years – Slim Smith (prod Edward 'Bunny' Lee) (scheduled but not issued)
211   Tighten Up Volume 9 – Various Artists (prod Various) (scheduled but not issued)

TROJAN (PREFIX TRL/TRLS)

1	Follow That Donkey – Brother Dan All Stars (prod Robert Thompson [Dandy])	1968
2	Dandy Returns – Dandy (prod Robert Thompson [Dandy])	1968
3	Soul Of Jamaica – Various Artists (prod Arthur 'Duke' Reid)	1968
4	Sand & Steel – Rising Sun Steel Band (prod WIRL)	1968
5	Rock Steady Explosion – Byron Lee & The Dragonaires (prod Byron Lee)	1968
6	Here Comes The Duke – Various Artists (prod Arthur 'Duke' Reid)	1968
7	Top Of The Ladder – Byron Lee & The Dragonaires (prod Byron Lee) (scheduled but not issued)	
8	Sparrow Meets Dragon – Mighty Sparrow & Byron Lee (prod Byron Lee)	1969
9	Not issued	
10	Not issued	
11	This Is Antigua – Hells Gate Steel Band (prod WIRL)	1969
12	Not issued	
13	Not issued	
14	Not issued	
15	Absolutely – The Uniques (prod Lloyd Charmers for Winston Lowe)	1969
16	Jimmy Cliff – Jimmy Cliff (prod Leslie Kong)	12.69
17	I Need You – Dandy & Audrey (prod Robert Thompson [Dandy]) (issued on Downtown label)	1969
18	Reggae – Byron Lee & The Dragonaires (prod Byron Lee)	2.70
19	Return Of Django – Lee Perry/Upsetters (prod Lee Perry) (issued on Upsetter label)	1.70
20	Not issued	
21	Not issued	
22	Not issued	
23	Rain – Bruce Ruffin (prod Herman Chin Loy/Leslie Kong/Bruce Anthony)	1971
24	Yeah! – The Pioneers (prod The Pioneers/Jimmy Cliff)	1971
25	Tell It Like It Is – Nicky Thomas (prod Nicky Thomas)	1972
26	Pied Piper – Bob & Marcia (prod Keith Anderson [Bob Andy])	1971
27	Black & White – Greyhound (prod Dave Bloxham/Greyhound/Graham Walker)	2.72
28	Reggay Splashdown – Byron Lee & The Dragonaires (prod Byron Lee)	1971
29	Not issued	
30	Not issued	
31	Not issued	
32	Not issued	
33	School Days – Scotty (prod Derrick Harriott)	1971
34	Not issued	

35	Not issued	
36	Grooving Out On Life – Hopeton Lewis (prod Neville Hinds for Dynamic)	1972
37	Still In Chains – John Holt (prod Edward 'Bunny' Lee)	1972
38	Vic Taylor Does It His Way – Vic Taylor (prod Neville Hinds for Dynamic)	1972
39	Bridge Over Troubled Water – Jimmy London (prod Vincent Chin)	1972
40	Reggay Hot Cool & Easy – Byron Lee & The Dragonaires (prod Neville Hinds for Dynamic)	1972
41	One Life To Live – Phyllis Dillon (prod Arthur 'Duke' Reid)	1972
42	Eric Donaldson – Eric Donaldson (prod Edward 'Bunny' Lee/Dynamic)	1972
43	Holt – John Holt (prod Edward 'Bunny' Lee)	1972
44	Better Must Come – Delroy Wilson (prod Edward 'Bunny' Lee)	1972
45	Dandy Livingstone – Dandy Livingstone (prod Robert Thompson [Dandy])	1972
46	Greyhound – Greyhound (prod Dave Bloxham) (scheduled but not issued)	
47	I Do Love You – Jackie Edwards (prod Jackie Edwards)	1972
48	I Believe In Love – The Pioneers (prod The Pioneers)	1972
49	Hotter Then Ever – Mighty Sparrow (prod Byron Lee)	1972
50	Slatyam Stoot – Toots & The Maytals (prod Warrick Lyn) (scheduled but not issued)	
51	From Bam Bam To Cherry Oh Baby – Various Artists (prod Various)	1972
52	Beat Down Babylon – Junior Byles (prod Lee Perry)	1972
53	Star Trek – The Vulcans (prod Joe Sinclair, Bunny Lee, Webster Shrowder & Des Bryan)	1972
54	Reggae Strings – Johnny Arthey Orchestra (prod Johnny Arthey)	1972
55	The Further You Look – John Holt (prod Tony Ashfield)	1972
56	Hit After Hit – The Chosen Few (prod Derrick Harriott)	1973
57	Super Hits – Dennis Brown (prod Derrick Harriott)	1973
58	Black Gold & Green – Ken Boothe (prod Lloyd Charmers)	1973
59	Thin Line Between Love And Hate – BB Seaton (prod Lloyd Charmers)	1973
60	Dreadmania – Judge Dread (prod Bush)	1973
61	Screaming Target – Big Youth (prod Augustus Clarke)	1973
62	African Herbsman – Bob Marley & The Wailers (prod Lee Perry/Bob Marley)	1973
63	Presenting – I Roy (prod Augustus Clarke/Various)	1973
64	Freedom Feeling – The Pioneers (prod The Pioneers)	1973
65	From The Roots – The Maytals (prod Leslie Kong)	1973
66	Soulful Reggae – Various Artists (prod Various)	1973
67	The Marvels – The Marvels (prod Robert Thompson & A Hinds for Shady Tree)	1973
68	Not issued	
69	Silver Bullets – The Silvertones (prod Lee Perry)	1973
70	Double Seven – Lee Perry/Upsetters/Various Artists (prod Lee Perry)	1973
71	Hell & Sorrow – I Roy (prod Roy Reid [I Roy])	1973
72	Double Dekker – Desmond Dekker (prod Leslie Kong) (scheduled but not issued)	
73	Not issued	

74	Soul To Soul DJ's Choice – Dennis Alcapone & Lizzy (prod Arthur 'Duke' Reid)	1973
75	1,000 Volts Of Holt – John Holt (prod Tony Ashfield)	1973
76	Build Me Up – Brent Dowe (prod Sonia Pottinger)	1974
77	Sparrow Power – Mighty Sparrow (prod Slinger Francisco)	1974
78	For The Good Times – Now Generation (prod J Franscique)	1974
79	Life Is For Living – Ernie Smith (prod Lloyd Charmers)	1974
80	Jimmy Brown – Ken Parker (prod Arthur 'Duke' Reid/Ken Parker)	1974
81	20 Explosive Reggae Hits – Various Artists (prod Various)	1974
82	Hit Me With Music – Various Artists (prod Various)	1974
83	Let's Get It On – Ken Boothe (prod Lloyd Charmers)	1974
84	The Same One – Danny Ray (prod Various for Shady Tree)	1974
85	Dusty Roads – John Holt (prod Tony Ashfield & Mike Berry)	1974
86	The Best Of Lloyd Charmers – Various Artists (prod Lloyd Charmers)	1974
87	In Time – The Cimarons (prod Webster Shrowder for Kush)	1974
88	Presenting – Winston Groovy (prod Sidney Crooks)	1974
89	Rasta Revolution – Bob Marley & The Wailers (prod Lee Perry)	1974
90	20 Tighten Ups – Various Artists (prod Various)	1974
91	Many Moods Of I Roy – I Roy (prod Roy Reid [I Roy])	1974
92	Reggae Strings Volume 2 – Johnny Arthey Orchestra (prod Johnny Arthey)	1974
93	Rock The Boat – Inner Circle (prod Tommy Cowan)	1974
94	Sweet Bitter Love – Marcia Griffiths (prod Lloyd Charmers)	1974
95	Everything I Own – Ken Boothe (prod Lloyd Charmers)	1974
96	Moody And Blue – Lloyd Charmers (prod Lloyd Charmers) (scheduled but not issued)	
97	Club Reggae – Various Artists (prod Various)	1974
98	I'm Gonna Knock On Your Door – The Pioneers (prod Sidney Crooks)	1974
99	Here I Am Baby – Al Brown (prod Geoffrey Chung)	12.74
100	Working Class 'Ero – Judge Dread (prod Bush)	1974
101	Original Reggae Hits – Various Artists (prod Various)	6.74
102	In Person – Gregory Isaacs (prod Alvin Ranglin)	1975
103	Peace And Love – Dadawah (Ras Michael) (prod Lloyd Charmers)	3.75
104	This Is Reggae Music – Various Artists (prod Various)	3.75
105	Not issued	
106	Everybody Plays The Fool – The Chosen Few (prod 'Prince' Tony Robinson)	3.75
107	Just Dennis – Dennis Brown (prod Winston 'Niney' Holness)	5.75
108	This Monday Morning Feeling – Tito Simon (prod Clancy Eccles/Joe Sinclair/Keith Foster)	3.75
109	Girl In The Morning – Lloyd Parks (prod Lloyd Parks)	1975
110	Live At The Turntable Club – Various Artists (prod Winston 'Niney' Holness)	1975
111	20 Tighten Ups Volume 2 – Various Artists (prod Various)	1975
112	Ja Gan – Leslie Butler (artist in fact Joe White) (prod Harry Johnson)	1975

113	Nyahbinghi – Ras Michael & Sons Of Negus (prod Tommy Cowan)	1975
114	Blame It On The Sun – Inner Circle (prod Tommy Cowan)	5.75
115	Ital Dub – Augustus Pablo (prod Tommy Cowan & Warrick Lyn)	5.75
116	Greatest Reggae Hits – Derrick Harriott (prod Derrick Harriott)	1975
117	Speak Softly – Barrington Spence (prod 'Prince' Tony Robinson)	1975
118	Original Reggae Hot Shots – Various Artists (prod Leslie Kong)	1975
119	Not issued	
120	Freedom Street – Ken Boothe (prod Leslie Kong)	1975
121	All I Have Is Love – Gregory Isaacs (prod Sidney Crooks)	1976
122	Susan Cadogan – Hurt So Good (prod Lee Perry)	1976
123	Natty Cultural Dread – Big Youth (prod Manley Buchanan [Big Youth])	1976
124	In The Ghetto – Dave& Ansel Collins (prod Larry Lawrence)	1976
125	Strange Thoughts – Honey Boy (prod Keith Williams [Honey Boy])	1976
126	Loving You – Lloyd Parks (prod Lloyd Parks)	1976
127	Greatest Reggae Hits – Various Artists (prod Various)	1976
128	Cool Rasta – The Heptones (prod Harry Johnson)	1976
129	My Jamaican Girl – The Fab Five (prod Harry Johnson)	1976
130	Revolution – Zap Pow (prod Harry Johnson)	1976
131	In Miami – The Chosen Few (prod King Sporty [Noel Williams])	1976
132	Tribute To The Emperor – Ras Michael & Sons Of Negus (prod Jazzbo Abubaka)	1976
133	Dreadlocks Affair – Jah Woosh (prod Neville Beckford [Jah Woosh])	1976
134	2,000 Volts Of Holt – John Holt (prod Keith Bonsoir/Tony Asfield/John Holt)	1976
135	DJ Round Up – Various Artists (prod Various)	1976
136	The Best Of – Barbara Jones (prod Alvin Ranglin)	1976
137	Hit The Road Jack – Big Youth (prod Manley Buchanan [Big Youth])	1976
138	Satta I – Lizzard (prod Clive Hunt [Lizzard])	1976
139	Fire And Bullets – Owen Gray (prod Owen Gray)	1977
140	Personal Choice – Various Artists (prod Various)	1977
141	Stars Of The Seventies – Various Artists (prod Various)	1977
142	Barry Biggs & Inner Circle – Barry Biggs & Inner Circle (prod Byron Lee/ Tommy Cowan)	1977
143	3,000 Volts Of Holt – John Holt (prod Edward 'Bunny' Lee)	1977
144	Roll On Muddy River – The Pioneers (prod Various)	1977
145	The Best Of – Matumbi (prod Dennis Bovell)	1977
146	16 Greatest Reggae Hits – Various Artists (prod Various)	1977
147	Roots Of Holt – John Holt (prod Jo Jo Hookim/Bunny Lee/John Holt)	1977
148	Blood Brothers – Ken Boothe (prod Lloyd Charmers)	1978
149	Reggae Rock – Various Artists (prod Various)	1978
150	Dreams Of Own Gray – Owen Gray (prod Owen Gray)	1978
151	I Love Marijuana – Linval Thompson (prod Linval Thompson)	1978

152	African Princess – Big Joe (prod Linval Thompson)	1978
153	Negrea Love Dub – Revolutionaries (prod Linval Thompson)	1978
154	Sweet 16 Hits – Desmond Dekker (prod Leslie Kong)	1978
155	The Groovy Collection – Winston Groovy (prod Winston Tucker [Groovy])	1978
156	Pusher Man – The Pioneers (prod Sidney Crooks)	1978
157	Religious Dread – Jah Woosh (prod Neville Beckford [Jah Woosh])	1978
158	Sincerely – Jackie Edwards (prod Jackie Edwards & Bunny Lee)	1978
159	Peace And Love – Mighty Sparrow (prod Slinger Francisco)	1978
160	Holt Goes Disco – John Holt (prod John Holt & The Now Team)	1978
161	Just A Country Boy – John Holt (prod Edward 'Bunny' Lee)	1978
162	Only A Fool – Mighty Sparrow (prod Mark Arthurworrey)	1978
163	Let It Go On – John Holt (prod John Holt)	1978
164	Who Gets Your Love – Ken Boothe (prod Phil Pratt/Bunny Lee/Lloyd Charmers)	1978
165	Never Get To Zion – Pancho Alphonso & Revolutionaries (prod Pancho Alphonso)	1978
166	The One Eyed Giant – King Sighter (prod Phil Pratt)	1978
167	Tell The Youths The Truth – Jimmy Riley (prod Jimmy Riley)	1979
168	16 Irie Reggae Rockers – Various Artists (prod Various)	1979
169	Outlaw Dub – The Revolutionaries (prod Linval Thompson)	1979
170	Rock In The Ghetto – Trinity (prod Linval Thompson)	1979
171	The Best Of – Toots & The Maytals (prod Leslie Kong/Warrick Lyn)	1979
172	Greatest Reggae Hits – The Pioneers (prod Various)	1979
173	Ghetto-Ology – Sugar Minott (prod Lincoln 'Sugar' Minott)	1979
174	Kamikazi Dub – Prince Jammy (prod Prince Jammy)	1979
175	Free From Sin – Prince Far I (prod Prince Far I)	1979
176	20 Reggae Blockbusters – Various Artists (prod Various)	1979
177	Love Affair – Marie Pierre (prod Dennis Bovell)	1979
178	Dread At The Controls – Mikey Dread (prod Mikey 'Dread' Campbell)	1979
179	Darling Ooh! – Errol Dunkley (prod Sonia Pottinger/Various)	1979
180	Creation Rockers Volume 1 – Various Artists (prod Various)	1979
181	Creation Rockers Volume 2 – Various Artists (prod Various)	1979
182	Creation Rockers Volume 3 – Various Artists (prod Various)	1979
183	Creation Rockers Volume 4 – Various Artists (prod Various)	1979
184	Creation Rockers Volume 5 – Various Artists (prod Various)	1979
185	Creation Rockers Volume 6 – Various Artists (prod Various)	1979
186	Black Ash Dub – Sly (Dunbar) & The Revolutinaries (prod Jah Thomas)	1980
187	Skinhead Moonstomp – Symarip (prod Philligree) (reissue of TBL102 with new sleeve)	1980
188	Monkey Business – Various Artists (prod Various)	1980
189	Every Day Skank (The Best Of) – Big Youth (prod Various)	1980
190	Jamaican Heroes – Prince Far I (prod Prince Far I [Michael Williams])	1980

191	Cool Pon Your Corner – Barry Brown (prod Barry Brown)	1980
192	20 Golden Love Songs – John Holt (prod Various)	1980
193	A1 Dub – The Morwells (prod Maurice Wellington)	1980
194	Dub It In A Dance – Ranking Joe (prod 'Ranking' Joe Jackson)	1980
195	The Upsetter Collection – Lee Perry/Upsetters/Various Artists (prod Lee Perry)	1981
196	The Early Years – Gregory Isaacs (prod Alvin Ranglin/Winston, 'Niney' Holness/ Sidney Crooks)	1981
197	Money In My Pocket – Dennis Brown (prod Various)	1981
198	Songs For Midnight Lovers – Derrick Harriott (prod Derrick Harriott)	1981
199	The Best Of Beverley's – Various Artists (prod Leslie Kong)	1982
200	Melodica Melodies – Various Artists (prod Various)	1981
201	Funky Kingston – Toots & The Maytals (prod Warrick Lyn)	1981
202	In The Dark – Toots & The Maytals (prod Warrick Lyn)	1981
203	Disarmament – Ras Michael & Sons Of Negus (prod Ras Michael [George Henry])	1981
204	Voice Of Thunder – Prince Far I (prod Prince Far I [Michael Williams])	1981
205	Cry Tuff – Prince Far I (prod Prince Far I [Michael Williams])	1981
206	Gems From Treasure Isle – Various Artists (prod Arthur 'Duke' Reid)	1982
207	Tighten Up Volume 2 – Various Artists (prod Various)	1982
208	We Must Unite – The Viceroys (prod Linval Thompson)	1982
209	Poor Man Style – Barrington Levy (prod Linval Thompson)	1982
210	Scientist & Jammy Fight Back – The Roots Radics Band (prod Prince Jammy)	1982
211	Ravers Party – U Brown (prod Hugh Brown)	1982
212	Revelation – Ras Michael & Sons Of Negus (prod Ras Michael [George Henry])	1982
213	Mix Up – Reggae George (prod Parince Far I [Michael Williams])	1982
214	Musical History – Prince Far I (prod Parince Far I [Michael Williams])	1983
215	Settle Down Girl – Tristan Palma (prod Linval Thompson)	1983
216	One Of A Kind – Charlie Chaplin (prod Roy Cousins)	1983
217	Not issued	
218	Not issued	
219	The Royals Collection – The Royals (prod Roy Cousins)	1983
220	Not issued	
221	In The Beginning – Bob Marley & The Wailers (prod Various)	1983
222	20 Reggae Classics – Various Artists (prod Various)	1984
223	For Lovers And Dancers – John Holt (prod John Holt & The Roots Radics Band)	1984
224	20 Reggae Classics Volume 2 – Various Artists (prod Various)	1984
225	A Love I Can Feel – John Holt (prod Clement Seymour Dodd)	1985
226	Original Reggae Hit Sound – Desmond Dekker & The Aces (prod Leslie Kong)	1985
227	Battle Of Armageddon – Lee Perry (prod Lee Perry)	1986
228	Original Reggae Hit Sound – The Ethiopians (prod Various)	1986

229	The Dynamic Duo – Audrey Hall & Don Evans (prod Edward 'Bunny' Lee & Don Evans)	1986
230	The Reggae Christmas Hits Album – John Holt (prod Edward 'Bunny' Lee)	1986
231	16 Dynamic Reggae Hits – Various Artists (prod Edward 'Bunny' Lee & Joe Richards)	1986
232	Greatest Hits Volume 1 – Frankie Jones (prod Edward 'Bunny' Lee)	1986
233	Sarge – Delroy Wilson (prod Lloyd Charmers)	1986
234	Lovers Paradise – Ken Parker (prod Lloyd Charmers) (scheduled but unissued)	
235	Sweet Memories – Lloyd Charmers (prod Lloyd Charmers) (scheduled but unissued)	
236	Sweet Memories Volume 2 – Lloyd Charmers (prod Lloyd Charmers) (scheduled but unissued)	
237	Sweet Memories Volume 3 – Lloyd Charmers (prod Lloyd Charmers) (scheduled but unissued)	
238	The Exit – Dennis Brown (prod Prince Jammy)	1986
239	Perfidia – Pam Hall (scheduled but unissued)	
240	Taxi Gang Versus Purple Man – Sly & Robbie (prod Edward 'Bunny' Lee) (scheduled but unissued)	
241	Best Of Live – Dillinger (prod Webster Shrowder & Larry Sevitt)	1988
242	Not issued	
243	This Is Augustus Pablo – Augustus Pablo (prod Clive Chin) (scheduled but unissued)	
244	Not issued	
245	Not issued	
246	Trojan Explosion – Various Artists (prod Various)	1987
247	Not issued	
248	Not issued	
249	The Ken Boothe Collection – Ken Boothe (prod Various)	1987
250	Not issued	
251	Classic – Junior Soul (prod Willie Lindo)	1987
252	Not issued	
253	Beat Down Babylon (The Upsetter Years) – Junior Byles (prod Lee Perry)	1987
254	Give Me Power – Lee Perry/Various Artists (prod Lee Perry)	1988
255	Keep On Coming Through The Door – Various Artists (prod Various)	1988
256	20 Reggae Classics Volume 3 – Various Artists (prod Various)	1988
257	Blow Mr Hornsman – Various Artists (prod Various)	1988
258	Studio Kinda Cloudy – Keith Hudson/Various Artists (prod Keith Hudson)	1988
259	Music Is My Occupation – Various Artists (prod Arthur 'Duke' Reid)	1988
260	Dance Crasher – Various Artists (prod Various)	1988
261	The Reggae Train – Joe Gibbs/Various Artists (prod Joe Gibbs)	1988
262	Fattie Fattie – Clancy Eccles/Various Artists (prod Clancy Eccles)	1988
263	Blood & Fire – Niney/Various Artists (prod Winston 'Niney' Holness)	1988
264	Unbelievable Sounds – Scotty (prod Derrick Harriott/Various)	1988

265	Ba Ba Boom – Duke Reid/Various Artists (prod Arthur 'Duke' Reid)	1988
266	Let Me Tell You Boy – Harry Mudie/Various Artists (prod Harry Mudie)	1988
267	Step Softly – Derrick Harriott/Various Artists (prod Derrick Harriott)	1988
268	With A Flick Of My Musical Wrist – U Roy/Various Artists (prod Various)	1988
269	When Will Better Come – Junior Byles (prod Lee Perry/Winston 'Niney' Holness)	1988
270	Jumping With Mr Lee – Bunnie Lee/Various Artists (prod Edward 'Bunny' Lee)	1989
271	Hold Me Strong – Various Artists (prod Various)	1989
272	My Voice Is Insured For Half A Million Dollars – Dennis Alcapone (prod Various)	1989
273	Bring The Cushie – Niney/Various Artists (prod Winston 'Niney' Holness)	1989
274	Birth Of Ska – Various Artists (prod Arthur 'Duke' Reid)	1989
275	Shuffling On Bond Street – Various Artists (prod Arthur 'Duke' Reid)	1989
276	Now This Is What I &I Call Version – Various Artists (prod Edward 'Bunny' Lee)	1989
277	They Talk About Love – Various Artist (prod Phil Pratt) (scheduled but unissued)	
278	Version Like Rain – Lee Perry/Various Artists (prod Lee Perry)	1990
279	It's Rocking Time – Various Artists (prod Arthur 'Duke' Reid)	1990
280	Ire Feelings: Chapter & Version – Rupie Edwards/Various Artists (prod Rupie Edwards)	1990
281	Let There Be Version – Rupie Edwards (prod Rupie Edwards)	1990
282	My Time Is The Right Time – Alton Ellis (prod Various) (scheduled but unissued)	
283	The Magnificent 14 – Various Artists (prod Various)	1990
284	20 Reggae Classics Volume 4 – Various Artists (prod Various)	1990
285	Celebration – Leon D (Delroy) Williams (prod Delroy Williams)	1990
286	Just My Imagination – Various Artists (prod Various)	1990
287	Dance All Night – Various Artists (prod Various)	1991
288	Doing The Moonwalk – Nicky Thomas (prod Joe Gibbs/Nicky Thomas)	1991
289	I Shall Sing – Various Artists (prod Various)	1991
290	Babylon A Fall Down – Various Artists (prod Various)	1991
291	Solid Gold – Various Artists (prod Various)	1991
292	King Of Ska – Desmond Dekker (prod Delroy Williams & Desmond Dekker)	1991
293	Solid Gold Volume 2 – Various Artists (prod Various)	1991
294	Yesterday – Various Artists (prod Various)	1991
295	Solid Gold Volume 3 – Various Artists (prod Various)	1991
296	We Chat You Rock – Jah Woosh & I Roy (prod Neville Beckford [Jah Woosh]/Roy Reid [I Roy])	1991
297	Out Of Many The Upsetter – Various Artists (prod Lee Perry)	1991
298	Tears Of A Clown – Various Artists (prod Various)	1991
299	My Best Girl Wears My Crown – The Paragons (prod Arthur 'Duke' Reid)	1992
300	I Am The Ruler – Derrick Morgan (prod Various)	1992
301	Music Like Dirt – Desmond Dekker (prod Leslie Kong)	1992
302	Solid Gold Volume 4 – Various Artists (prod Various)	1992
303	Rain From The Skies – Slim Smith (prod Edward 'Bunny' Lee)	1992

304	Tougher Than Tough – Various Artists (prod Various)	1992
305	Adults Only – Various Artists (prod Various)	1992
306	Not issued	
307	Not issued	
308	Adults Only Volume 2 – Various Artists (prod Various)	1992
309	Not issued	
310	Not issued	
311	Dock Of The Bay – Various Artists (prod Various)	1992
312	The World Goes Ska – The Ethiopians (prod Various)	1992
324	King Of Kings – Desmond Dekker & The Specials (prod Roger Lomas)	1993
328	Midnight Train To Georgia – Various Artists (prod Various)	1993

TROJAN REGGAE SUNSPLASH ALBUMS (PREFIX TRLS)

8901	Live At Reggae Sunsplash – Toots & The Maytals (only issued on cassette)	1982
8902	Not issued	
8903	Not issued	
8904	Live At Reggae Sunsplash – Day One – Various (only issued on cassette)	1982
8905	Live At Reggae Sunsplash – Big Youth	1982
8906	Live At Reggae Sunsplash – Eek A Mouse plus Michigan & Smiley	1982
8907	Since I Throw The Comb Away – Live At Reggae Sunsplash – The Twinkle Brothers	1982

LOWBITE ALBUMS (PREFIX LOW)

001	Censored – Lloydie & The Lowbites	1970
002	Censored Volume 2 – Lloydie & The Lowbites (unissued)	

TROJAN ALBUM (PREFIX TRJC)

100	Unlimited – Jimmy Cliff	1990

TROJAN ALBUMS (PREFIX TRPT)

100	Bush Doctor – Peter Tosh	
101	Mystic Man – Peter Tosh	

TROJAN ALBUM (PREFIX TMLP)

1	Tight Rock – Various Artists	1977

TROJAN ALBUM (PREFIX TRBLP)

1	The Trojan Sound – Various Artists	1974

TROJAN SAMPLER ALBUMS (PREFIX TRS)

1   Out Of Many, One – Jamaican Music, 1962 to 1975 – Various Artists

2   Out Of Many, One – Jamaican Music, Part 2 – Various Artists

TROJAN DOUBLE ALBUMS (PREFIX TRLD)

401	Double Dekker – Desmond Dekker	1973
402	The Trojan Story – Various Artists	1976
403	Rebel Music – Various Artists	1979
404	Officially, Live And Rare – Desmond Dekker	1987
405	Not issued	
406	Soul Revolution Parts 1 & 2 – Bob Marley & The Wailers	1988
407	Skinhead Classics – Various Artists	1988
408	Musical Fever, 1967–68 – Clement Dodd/Various Artists (prod Clement Seymour Dodd)	1989
409	King Tubby's Special '73/'76 – Various Artists	1989
410	Wake The Town And Tell The People – U Roy (scheduled but unissued)	
411	Reggae Phenomenon – Big Youth	1990
412	Return Of The Liquidator – Harry J/Various Artists	1991
413	Celebration – Various Artists	1992

TROJAN DOUBLE ALBUM (PREFIX BYD)

BYD 1	Reggae Phenomenon – Big Youth	1977

TROJAN TRIPLE ALBUMS (PREFIX TALL)

1	The Trojan Story – Various Artists	1972
100	The Trojan Story – Various Artists	1980
200	The Trojan Story Volume 2 – Various Artists	1982
300	The Tighten Up Box Set – Various Artists	1988
400	In Memoriam – Bob Marley & The Wailers	1991
500	Bob Marley & The Story Of Reggae – Various Artists	1992

TROJAN TRIPLE ALBUMS (PREFIX PERRY)

1	The Upsetter Box Set – Various Artists	1985
2	Open The Gates – Various Artists	1989
3	Build The Ark – Various Artists	1990

MOONCREST LP (PREFIX CREST) - REGGAE RELEASE ONLY

5	Conscious – Dandy Livingstone (prod Robert Thompson)	1973

ACTION (PREFIX ACT) - SOUL RELEASES ONLY

4500	Give Me One More Chance/Get It - Wilmer (Alexander) & The Dukes	9.68
4501	Competition Ain't Nothing/Three Way Love – Little Carl Carlton	1968
4502	Dancing Man/Later For Tomorrow – Ernie K-Doe	1968
4503	Grab Your Clothes And Get On Out/No Love At All – Minnie Epperson	1968
4504	Got To Get Myself Together/Darling Depend On Me – Buddy Ace	1968
4505	Oh Baby Mine/Working On Your Game – OV Wright	1968
4506	Earthquake/How Long – Al 'TNT' Braggs	10.68
4507	Tore Up/I Get So Tired – Harmonica Fats	1968
4508	Shine It On/Things Are Looking Better – Vernon Garrett	1968
4509	Baby I Eed Your Love/Try It Again – Bobby Williams	1968
4510	Tell Him No/Throw Away The Key – The Bell Brothers	1968
4511	I'll Forget You/Be My Aby – John Roberts	1968
4512	Gotta Pack My Bag/How Sweet You Are – Ernie K-Doe	1968
4513	Here I Am In Love Again/I'm Tired Of You – Brothers Two	1968
4514	Drums, 1 Guitar/Why Don't They Leave Us Alone – Carl Carlton	1968
4515	People Make The World Go Round/Hard To Forget – Roosevelt Grier	12.68
4516	Omar Khayyam/Tomorrow – Rubaiyats	1968
4517	Call On You/The Woodsman – Chuck Trois & The Amazing Maze	1968
4518	Young Boy Blues/You Were Meant For Me – Eddie 'Buster' Forehand	1969
4519	So Anna Just Love Me/Boogaloo No 3 – Roy Lee Johnson	1969
4520	You Got A Deal/Say You'll Never – Alice Clark	1969
4521	Not released	
4522	What Kind Of A Lady/You're Gonna Miss Me – Dee Dee Sharp	1969
4523	Slow Drag/So Glad I'm Yours – The Intruders	1969
4524	Rockin' In The Same Old Boat/Wouldn't You Rather – Bobby Bland	1969
4525	Don't Make The Good Girls Go Bad/Your Love Is All I Need – Della Humphrey	1969
4526	I'm A Good Man/I Like What You Do To Me – Al 'Tnt' Braggs	1969
4527	I Want Everyone To Know/Gonna Forget About You – OV Wright	1969
4528	Baby What You Want Me To Do (Parts 1 And 2) – Little Richard	1969
4529	You're Everything/Our Love Will Grow – Norman Johnson & The Showmen	1969
4530	Hot Tamales (Parts 1 And 2) – The Prime Mates	1969
4531	Save It/This Love Was Meant To Be – Melvin Davis	1969
4532	Make Me Yours/What Am I Living For – ZZ Hill	1969
4533	Ain't No Reason For Girls To Be Lonely (Parts 1 And 2) – Bobby Marchan	1969
4534	Stuff/You Gotta Come Through – Jeanette Williams	1969
4535	Ride Your Pony/Trouble With My Lover – Betty Harris	1969
4536	Shing-A-Ling Stroll/Don't Kick The Teenagers Around – Eddie Wilson	1969
4537	Look At Mary Wonder/Bad For Each Other – Carl Carlton	1969
4538	Got To Get To Know You/Baby I'm On My Way – Bobby Bland	1969

4539	Baby Do The Philly Dog/Mine Exclusively – The Olympics	1969
4540	Don't Hurt Me No More/Get Yourself Together – Al Greene	1969
4541	That's In The Past/I Can't Get Over You – Brenda & The Tabulations	1969
4542	Slipping Away/Half A Love – Barbara Mason	1969
4543	Is There Anything Better Than Making Love/New Love – Fantastic Johnny C	1969
4544	Hide Out/Jolly Joe – Hideaways	1969
4545	Take It Baby/In Paradise – Norman Johnson & The Showmen	1969
4546	He's Got A Blessing/Rockin' A Weary Land – The Wash Hopson Singers	1969
4547	I Love You/I Surrender – Eddie Holman	1969
4548	Share Your Love With Me/Honey Child – Bobby Bland	1969
4549	She Shot A Hole In My Soul/We're Gonna Hate Ourselves – Clifford Curry	1969
4550	Black Gal/Frog Legs – Clifton Chenier	1969
4551	I Can't Save It/I Can Take Care Of Myself – Gene Chandler	1969
4552	I Can't Stop You/LA Stomp – The Performers	1969
4553	Chains Of Love/Ask Me About Nothing But The Blues – Bobby Bland	1969
4554	Not released	
4555	Get Out In The Street/It Must Be Love – Eddie Wilson	1970
4556	I'll Do A Little Bit More/Same Old Thing – Olympics	1970
4557	Hound Dog/I Can Feel A Heartbeat – Jeanette Williams	1970

ACTION (PREFIX ACT)
SECOND SERIES

4601	You're Everything/Our Love Will Grow – Norman Johnson & The Showmen	10.71
4602	Rae – Do It/Crying Clown – Billy Sha	1971
4603	That's A Bad Thing To Know/All In Your Mind – The Bobbettes	1971
4604	I'm In Love With You/Married Lady – Bobby Patterson	1972
4605	Why Didn't You Let Me Know/What Life Is All About – The Hoagy Lands	1972
4606	Born To Make You Cry/Thunder Road – Kim Fowley	1972
4607	Sign Of The Crab/May The Best Man Win – Joe S. Maxey	1972
4608	Women's Lib/ – Buster Pearson (prod Buster Pearson)	1973
4609	Check Your Bucket (Parts 1 And 2) – Eddie Bo	1973
4610	Soul Makossa (Parts 1 And 2) – Gaytones (prod Sonia Pottinger)	1973
4611	Sticky Fingers – (Parts 1 And 2) – Jamaica Band (prod M Wesley & D Paramour)	1973
4612	Big Funk/Pretty Woman – Buster Pearson Band (prod Buster Pearson) (NB: Five Star's dad)	1973
4613	Get It While You Can/Amen – Wilbert Harrison	1973
4614	Super Sweet Girl Of Mine/Set Your Mind Free – Five Miles Out	1973
4615	I'll Go Out And Getcha Part 1/Part 2 – Stanley	1973
4616	Just Keep On Truckin'/Never Can Say Goodbye – Backyard Heavies	1973
4617	I Found Myself/Don't Forget About Me – Mill Edwards	1973

4618	My Sweet Baby/Henry Ralph – Esquires	1973
4619	Soul Of A Black Man/Reap What You Sow – Aaron McNeil	1973
4620	Black, Foxy Woman/God Bless The Children – Chuck Armstrong (prod King Sporty)	1973
4621	Rock Springs Railroad Station/Endless Confusion – Tom Green	1973
4622	I Want To Make It With You (Parts 1 And 2) – Bobbi Houston (prod King Sporty)	1974
4623	Funky Butter/Wondering – Chosen Few (prod King Sporty)	1974
4624	Get Some/Plan For The Man. – Wee Willie (Armour) & The Winners	1974

SPECIAL ISSUE
People/Action promo 45 (V/A, Action label 1 side, People the other)

B&C SINGLES (PREFIX CB) - SOUL RELEASES ONLY
101	Freedom Train/That's The Way Love Turned Out For Me – James Carr	1969
102	Dancing Everywhere/Baby It's Over – Bob & Earl	1969
104	Spinning Wheel/Like I Used To Do – Horace Faith (prod Stan Biederbeck)	1969
105	Whether It's Right Or Wrong/Baby I'm Satisfied – Jackie Lee & Dolores Hall	1969
106	Denver/Tell Me – Clyde McPhatter	1969

MIAMI (PREFIX MIA)
401	Night And Day/Funky Buttercup – The Chosen Few (prod Noel Williams aka King Sporty)	1976
402	Thinking Of You/Dancing Mood – King Sporty (prod Noel Williams aka King Sporty)	1976
403	Morning, Noon And Night/Fighting Time – Dean Lewinson (prod Ralph Adu)	1976
404	Help Yourself/Why – Jimmy James & The Vagabonds (prod Phil Wainman for Dawn Productions)	1975
405	Sweet Temptation/Sugar M,Y Love – The Love Dimension (prod Berek Nemeceb)	1976
406	Don't It Feel Good/Watcha Do To Me – City Lights (prod Mack Fleming)	1976
407	This Old Man/Always Friends – The Playgrouns (prod Rupert Holmes)	1976
408	Reggae Rock Road/Reggae Rock Road (Version) – King Sporty (prod Noel Williams aka King Sporty)	1976

PEOPLE (PREFIX PEO)
101	Forever/Baby Let Me Get Close To You – Baby Washington & Don Gardner	1973
102	Lonely Days Lonely Nights/I'm So Proud Of You – Don Downing	1973
103	Dynamite Explodes/Bring It On Home – Gentle Persuasion	1973
104	Get On Board/Get On Board (instrumental) – Wee Three	1973
105	Just Can't Get You Out Of My Mind/You're Just A Dream – Baby Washington	1973
106	Who Is She And What Is She To You/If Loving You Is Wrong – Della Reese	1974
107	I've Got To Get Away/Can't Get Over You – Baby Washington	1974

108	Dream World/The Miracle – Don Downing	1974
109	/I'll Take You There/Cisco Kid – Reuben Wilson	1974
110	Stick Up/Who Do You Think You Are – Krissie K	1974
111	Running In And Out Of My Life/Highway – Westside (Matumbi)	1974
112	Stretchin' Out/Don't Tell Your Mama – Doris Troy	1974
113	She Called Me Baby/Signed Sealed And Delivered – J Kelly & The Premiers	1974
114	NYT	
115	The Hostage/Let's Work Together Now – Donna Summer	1974
116	I Don't Know What You Got (Parts 1 And 2) – Wee Willie & The Winners	1974
117	NYT	
118	In The Pocket/Everybody Loves A Winner – Brothers	1975

ACTION LPs (PREFIX ACLP)

6001	Boogaloo Down Broadway – Fantastic Johnny C 1969	
6002	Oh How It Hurts – Barbara Mason	1969
6003	Dry Your Eyes – Brenda & The Tabulations	1969
6004	A Whole Lotta Soul – ZZ Hill	1969
6005	Various Artists – Action Packed Soul	1969
6006	A Piece Of Gold – Bobby Bland	1969
6007	Soul Perfection – Betty Harris	1969
6008	Back Up Train – Al Greene	1969
6009	Various Artists – These Kind Of Blues	1969
6010	Live On Stage – Gene Chandler	1969
6011	Down In Virginia – Jimmy Reed	1969

ACTION MID-PRICE LP (PREFIX ACMP)

100	Bottle Up And Go – Eddie 'Guitar' Burns (prod Jim Simpson for Big Bear Records)	1972

B&C BUDGET-PRICED LP (PREFIX BCB)

1	Bob & Earl – Bob & Earl	1969

PEOPLE LPS (PREFIX PLEO)

1	Cisco Kid – Reuben Wilson	1973
2	NYT	
3	Dawn Of A New Day – O'Donel Levy & Larry Willis	1974
4	You Don't Have To Be Black To Love The Blues – Junior Parker	1974
5	Sweet Sister Funk – Ramon Morris	1974
6	NYT	
7	Let Me In Your Life – Della Reese Carmen McRae	1974
8	Sundance – Chick Corea	1974

9	NYT	
10	American Pie – Groove Holmes	1974
11	Fly Dude (Advertised With This Number) – Jimmy McGriff	1974
12	Madame Foo Foo – Dakota Staton	1974
12	Stretching Out – Doris Troy (prod by Dandy)	1974
13	Lay Some Loving On Me – Baby Washington & Don Gardner	1974
14	Fly Dude – Jimmy McGriff (existence unsubstantiated)	1974
15	NYT	
16	NYT	
17	Friday 13th, Cook County Jail – Jimmy McGriff & Lucky Thompson	1974
18	Love Ain't Nothing But A Business Going On – Junior Parker	1974
19	Let's Stay Together – Jimmy McGriff	1974
20	The Sweet Life – Reuben Wilson	1974
21	NYT	
22	NYT	
23	NYT	
24	Super Sweet Soul – Various Artists	1975
25	Disco Soul – The Brothers/Various Artists	1975

PEOPLE DOUBLE LP (PREFIX PLEO)

| 501 | Black And Blues – Jimmy McGriff | 1974 |

Index